STORIED CITIES

Recent Titles in
Contributions to the Study of World Literature

STORIED CITIES

Literary Imaginings of Florence, Venice, and Rome

Michael L. Ross

Contributions to the Study of World Literature, Number 51

GREENWOOD PRESS
Westport, Connecticut • London

To the memory of my Father

Library of Congress Cataloging-in-Publication Data

Ross, Michael L.
   Storied cities : literary imaginings of Florence, Venice, and Rome /
Michael L. Ross.
      p. cm.—(Contributions to the study of world literature,
   ISSN 0738-9345 ; no. 51)
   Includes bibliographical references and index.
   ISBN 0-313-28717-1 (alk. paper)
   1. English literature—Italian influences. 2. American
literature—Italian influences. 3. City and town life in
literature. 4. Florence (Italy) in literature. 5. Venice (Italy)
in literature. 6. Rome (Italy) in literature. I. Title.
II. Series.
   PR129.I8R67   1994
   820.9'3245—dc20   93-13011

British Library Cataloguing in Publication Data is available.

Library of Congress Catalog Card Number: 93-13011
ISBN: 0-313-28717-1
ISSN: 0738-9345

First published in 1994

Greenwood Press, 88 Post Road West, Westport, CT 06881
An imprint of Greenwood Publishing Group, Inc.

Printed in the United States of America

The paper used in this book complies with the
Permanent Paper Standard issued by the National
Information Standards Organization (Z39.48-1984).

10 9 8 7 6 5 4 3 2 1

Copyright Acknowledgments

Excerpts from *This Journey* by James Wright. Copyright (c) 1982 by Anne Wright, Executrix of the Estate of James Wright. Reprinted by permission of Random House, Inc.

I would also like to thank the following for permission to reprint, in altered form, portions of my own previously published work:

Adrienne Munich, Editor of *Victorian Literature and Culture*, for my article "Henry James's 'Half-man': The Legacy of Browning in 'The Madonna of the Future,'" *Browning Institute Studies* Vol. 2   (1974), pp. 25-42.

Robert Langenfeld, Editor of *English Literature in Transition*, for my article "Forster's Arnoldian Comedy: Hebraism, Hellenism, and *A Room with a View*," *ELT* Vol. 23 No. 3 (1980), pp. 155-67.

Contents

Illustrations

Preface

The view presented here of the literature that has grown up around the three great, storied cities of Florence, Venice, and Rome is manifestly incomplete. It has not been my intention to undertake an exhaustive survey of that literature, which has by now grown so vast as to render any such aim quixotic. There exist, without a doubt, countless literary works set in one or another of the three cities that have not come to my attention. Of others I have made little or no mention owing to limitations on available space, to say nothing of the reader's patience. My discussions of a whole catalogue of relevant and fascinating examples--Henry James's "The Last of the Valerii," *Daisy Miller,* and *The Wings of the Dove*, John Cheever's Italian stories, Susan Hill's *The Bird of Night*, to name a few--have had either to be severely telescoped or simply eliminated. The conclusions I draw from the works I do discuss should, therefore, be tested and extended by a reading of these and other such additional texts.

I would like to thank the friends and colleagues from whose encouragement and counsel I have profited. Paul Fussell and Anthony Nuttall read preliminary drafts of my general introduction and made useful suggestions, some of which I have incorporated. Alwyn Berland and Ronald Granofsky read and commented on the entire manuscript; I am substantially indebted to their generous expenditure of time and their critical acumen. My daughter, Silvia Ross, contributed expert help with translations from Italian sources. Above all, I owe thanks to Lorraine York, who has cheerfully followed the emergence of this text through all its tortuous permutations, providing unfailing encouragement and criticism. Needless to say, responsibility for any inadequacies to be found in what follows remains squarely on my own shoulders.

The completion of the book was facilitated by a generous grant from the Social Sciences and Humanities Research Council of Canada. Costs for permission to quote copyright material have been defrayed by a grant from the Arts Research Board of McMaster University. My examination of the unpublished manuscripts of L. P. Hartley was made especially pleasant by the helpfulness of the staff of the John Rylands University Library of Manchester. I am indebted to the Bodleian Library and the Balliol College Library of Oxford for access to material relating to Robert Browning and Arthur Hugh Clough, and to the librarian of the Keats-Shelley House in Rome for access to material on

early English travellers in Italy. I am grateful to Egmont Lee, Director of the
Canadian Academic Centre in Italy, for his advice concerning resources in Rome.

The people at Greenwood Press who have been concerned with my book—
Marilyn Brownstein, Maureen Melino, William Neenan, and Penny Sippel—
have been consistently helpful and encouraging. Susan Badger deserves praise
for her scrupulous copy-editing of the manuscript. Finally, I must give warm
thanks to Sarah Fick and her colleagues in the McMaster University Humanities
Word Processing Centre for the expertise and patience they have shown in
preparing a lengthy and frustratingly complicated manuscript for publication.

STORIED CITIES

1

Introduction: A Tale of Three Cities

This book was not written to prove a theory, but it has a theoretical premise: that setting enters more profoundly into the life of literary works than it is fashionable to suppose. Instead of remaining a mere "backdrop" against which the "important" elements—plot, character, theme—unfold, setting may constitute the encompassing medium of a novel or poem, coloring all that it touches. According to Lawrence Durrell, "What makes 'big' books is surely as much to do with their site as their characters and incidents" (163). Eudora Welty argues in a similar vein that "fiction depends for its life on place. Location is the crossroads of circumstance, the proving ground of 'What happened? Who's here? Who's coming?'—and that is the heart's field" (118).

As writers whose own fictions thrive on particulars of scene and region, Welty and Durrell may be suspected of inflating the importance of locality. Some recent academic critics, however, concur with them. For Alexander Gelley, "It will clearly not suffice to speak of setting as a corner of the real world isolated for purposes of the story, nor as a mere backdrop akin to a stage set. The material world as it is depicted in fiction needs also to be understood as solicitations to the reader, as modifications of his perceptive capacities" (189). And Leonard Lutwack's extended study *The Role of Place in Literature* (1984) has bestowed upon the whole issue of locality a long-overdue seriousness of intellectual attention. In his book, Lutwack attempts to adumbrate "a beginning model for a rhetoric in which the many uses of place in literature are classified and exemplified" (vii).

My own focus, more restricted than Gelley's or Lutwack's, has to do with the importance of urban settings as theaters of fictive action. My subject is the way in which non-Italian imaginations have re-invented three great Italian cities. What I mean to show is that works set in any one of these places absorb, and in turn radiate, a whole spectrum of local associations. They thus substantiate Welty's bold claim that "[e]very story would be another story, and unrecognizable as art, if it took up its characters and plot and happened somewhere else" (122).

When a writer like Henry James locates a fiction in one city rather than another, the choice has a fateful impact upon the sort of narrative produced. In his preface to *The Aspern Papers* (1888), James explains that the idea for the novella came to him in Florence, when he learned that Byron's quondam mistress, Claire Clairmont, had until her recent death been living there. The story was consequently imbued for him with "the air of the old time Italy . . . , a mixture that on the faintest invitation I rejoice again to inhale" (*Art of the Novel* 159). However, for the sake of "covering one's tracks" (166), he decided to seek out a non-Florentine setting. Even "'old' New York" (165) occurred to him as an alternative. But he found that "the Italian side of the legend closely clung" (163), and he eventually hit upon another Italian city—Venice—as its destined clinging-place. This roundabout process of selection may make Venice appear an arbitrary setting for *The Aspern Papers*—a mere *pis aller*. The point, however, is that for James the locale, once established, became not a *pis aller* but the sole appointed *aller*, expressly *the* milieu that his leading lady demanded for her inner significance to emerge:

Juliana, as I saw her, was thinkable only in Byronic and more or less immediately post-Byronic Italy; but there were conditions in which she was ideally arrangeable, as happened, especially in respect to the later time and the long undetected survival; there being absolutely no refinement of the mouldy rococo, in human or whatever other form, that you may not disembark at the dislocated water-steps of almost any decayed monument of Venetian greatness in auspicious quest of. (166)

The Aspern Papers might, indeed, have been set in Florence or Rome or, for that matter, Manhattan; but then the story would hardly have evolved into the fantasia of decadence, bereavement, and voyeurism that James ended up writing. The setting claimed the story, as much as the story the setting.

A second example: Aldous Huxley, for his short story "The Rest Cure," in typical fashion "borrowed" an idea from his friend D. H. Lawrence. In appropriating Lawrence's theme, however, Huxley introduced a crucial shift of setting. Lawrence's story "Sun" (1926) traces the experiences of Juliet, the neurasthenic wife of a New York businessman, who is ordered to Sicily for her health. There she basks in the restorative rays of the Italian sun and narrowly misses an affair with a local peasant that might have been a still more restorative exposure: "a bath of warm, powerful life . . . like sun" (141). Huxley's tale, which appeared in *Brief Candles* (1930), follows Moira Tarwin, the sickly wife of an eminent English surgeon, as she seeks regeneration at the hands of a young and handsome Italian Romeo. With careful malice, Huxley moves the locale northward from Lawrence's bucolic Sicily to the supercivilized ambiance of Florence, a setting congenial to the ironies attending Moira's progress toward erotic disillusionment and death. The light that shines here is not that of the procreative Sicilian sun. It is a light that failed, the last, attenuated glimmer of the Florentine Renaissance; and Moira (whose name means "fate") stands no chance of being sexually reborn. She arrives, instead, at a dead end, the foredoomed victim of predatory Tuscan machinations. The shift of setting is essential to Huxley's satiric aim, the subjecting of Lawrence's procreation myth to corrosive scepticism.

Place and time are interlocking literary dimensions. The sense of place, as reflected in literature, has itself been shaped by historical currents. The Elizabethans were no strangers to the importance of local habitations; but it was the rise of the novel in the eighteenth century that finally established individualized setting as intrinsic to the literary imagination. According to Alexander Gelley, however, it was not until the nineteenth century that place achieved full partnership with the other properties of the novelist's fictional repertory:

But, for the nineteenth-century novelist, description of place and scenery represents an inescapable challenge. . . . The locale of the action gives rise to an ambient world charged with intention and emotion. Action does not stop so that description may take over. Settings are involved in the action from the start. They seem impregnated with the feelings and experiences of the characters of a novel and thus assume that sort of intenser reality which, in our own lives, we grant to only a few chosen places where something important has happened. . . . The recurrence of locales, the accumulation of descriptive matter, constitute on one level simply the presentation of the setting. But, more significantly, they coalesce into a system of symbolic space which defines the ethical and affective values of the action in an entirely new manner. (187)

For Lutwack, the sort of shift identified by Gelley derives instead from the burgeoning of the place-conscious romantic movement: "To romantic literature, which owes so much to the inspiration of travel, belongs the credit of changing our sensibility of geographical place from ignorant supposition and curiosity in the bizarre to sentimental valuation" (8). Lutwack's and Gelley's views are by no means irreconcilable. The new romantic apprehension of the world helped to consolidate the novel's position as the dominant literary mode; the vogue both of romanticism and of the novel encouraged the exploiting of scene for symbolic ends. It was now that Italian settings, long cherished by foreign writers as congenial to the cloak and the dagger, assumed a new, more complex importance.

Kenneth Churchill, in his study *Italy and English Literature 1764-1930* (1980), has traced the emergence of Italy from its traditional literary role as a source of melodramatic intrigue and Gothic horror. To nineteenth-century writers, the country eventually became a ground upon which to pursue less sensational and more serious effects of local color. There are a number of parallels between the development of literary images of Italy and more general intellectual trends in the English-speaking world. A land that had been the historic arena for the conflict of paganism and Christianity naturally lent itself to elaborations of the Arnoldian antithesis between "Hellenism" and "Hebraism." It lent itself equally to the Victorian concern with the workings of history itself. The legacy of Italian history was, moreover, inseparable from the country's unrivalled treasury of artistic accomplishments; and the nature and sources of the artist's creative power have been contentious riddles of nineteenth- and twentieth-century literary and philosophical debate.

Already by 1755, the year in which George Keate composed his poem *Ancient and Modern Rome*, it was a commonplace that the Latin race enjoyed gifts denied to more northerly peoples:

> OH ever-wond'rous Art, that from the Schools
> Of GREECE, cam'st hither, to this favour'd Clime,
> Yet rarely hast vouchsaf'd to pass the Cliffs
> Of the proud APENNINE, or cheer the cold,
> And Genius-chilling Regions of the NORTH! (13)

For Keate (as earlier for Joseph Addison, in his "A Letter from Italy" [1703]), the artistic superiority of the southern country was offset by the benign political climate of his own northerly one. England's air might chill genius, but its institutions warmed the spirit and freed the mind. By the end of the next century, however, the prevailing aestheticist temper had begun to scorn such reservations in its savoring of the rich Italian atmosphere. Witness the jubilant outburst of Cecily Doran to her cousin Miriam Bradshaw in George Gissing's *The Emancipated* (1890):

"Art is the grandest thing in the world; it means everything that is strong and beautiful—statues, pictures, poetry, music. How could one live without art? The artist is born a prince among men. What has he to do with the rules by which common people must direct their lives? Before long, you will feel this as deeply as I do, Miriam. We are in Italy, Italy!" (28)

For writers of the past two centuries, Italy has embodied the idea of emancipation that Cecily's rhapsody (like, of course, the title of Gissing's novel) suggests. The land has opened to them an avenue of personal freedom that transcends, while it includes, artistic licence. Ian Watt, speaking of "the human values which Italy has traditionally represented to the Northern literary imagination," points to "the unrestrained public enactment of the emotions and appetites" (Maves x-xi). For foreign refugees from Puritanism, Italy has stood as a kind of delectable anti-home: the paradise of the pliable upper lip, of the unabashed frolic of consciousness. To the Romantics and their successors, the country has come as a blessed "relax" after the damnable "brace" of the northern homeland.

But the licence that such travellers have identified with the Italian scene has also tended to polarize the responses embodied in their writings. Watt points out how sharply two writers as closely akin as Henry James and E. M. Forster diverged in their attitudes toward the "public enactment" of ungoverned impulse, and the same had been true, earlier, of Byron and Shelley. Lutwack observes that "literature always reflects ambivalent attitudes toward earth and its constituent places" (11). Among constituent places, few have been more copiously productive of ambivalence than Italy. Italian locales have elicited a bewildering diversity of responses from the numberless foreigners who have written about them. Any study of the ways in which Italian cities have been presented must of necessity be a study in idiosyncrasies of perception.

Yet not all hinges on sheer personal idiosyncrasy. The great, historic Italian towns have themselves developed personalities whose distinctiveness can come as an enlivening shock to those familiar only with more uniform cityscapes. Writers may respond to that distinctiveness in an infinite variety of ways; what they find virtually impossible is to ignore it. According to one distinguished nineteenth-century observer, Margaret Oliphant,

The great centres of old Italian life, Rome and Venice and Florence, are all as distinct as individuals, incapable on the spur of the moment . . . of being trimmed into any breadth of nationality, or made to represent more than themselves—the one strongly-marked and individual phase of character which their municipal separateness and independent history have impressed upon them. (1)

Any adequate discussion of how such places have been used as literary settings must recognize both types of individuality: that of the city and that of the artistic mind that engages with it. My aim in what follows, then, will be to trace the interaction of personal sensibility with local uniqueness.

Each of the three great cities I consider has acquired a literary "signature," as unmistakable as the city's own skyline. There is, needless to say, overlap among these signatures. Writing about any single Italian city cannot escape being, in some sense, writing about Italy in general. Works dealing with such places are bound to have features in common, such as a concern with those questions of historicity, aesthetics, and religion that have long fascinated visitors to the whole famous peninsula. If I tend to take this overlap somewhat for granted, the reason is that such shared territory has already been amply explored, while the uniqueness of the separate urban strands has received only passing attention.

But a question inevitably arises: How can the literary imagination best reflect the potent singularity of a Rome, of a Venice? Is exact fidelity of representation the *sine qua non*? The Italian novelist and poet Giorgio Bassani, in his essay *"Le parole preparate"* (1966), observes regretfully that the Venice of literature is "a city of convention, to be repopulated at will according to the exigencies and caprices of fancy" (22). He searches for soberly accurate depictions of the city but is forced to concede "the substantial impotence of a poetics founded on the myth of the Flesh, Death and the Devil to render an objectively plausible image of Venice" (29). L. P. Hartley, discussing Thomas Mann's *Death in Venice* (1911) in *The Saturday Review*, similarly deplores the submergence, in Mann's novella, of objective reality by myth:

A terrible story, lurid, morbid, painful in the last degree. But it would have been more painful, perhaps, if Herr Mann had been less anxious to harrow us. His Venice is the Venice of nightmare, filled with warning shadows, made in every respect to correspond to the dramatic appeal it makes to the eye of the new-comer. Its innocent smells are described as breathing pestilence; its gentle, patient, good-natured, prosaic inhabitants are represented as sinister to the last degree. The whole story stands in the same relation to real life as Herr Mann's impression of Venice stands to the real Venice. (621)

The first difficulty such criticisms raise is the patent dubiousness of distinctions between "objectively plausible" images of a city like Venice and unacceptably "distorted" ones. Whether, or in what sense, any observer's impression of a human settlement might be called "objective" is a hoary and still vexed philosophical question. A case in point is Hartley's staunch defence of Venice's "innocent smells"; the smells are undeniably there, but what is presumed innocent by one nose may well receive a guilty verdict from another.

Let us, however, provisionally concede that Mann's image of Venice distorts the palpable reality of the place. The further question remains: Is such distortion inadmissible in a work of the imagination? Is it, indeed, avoidable? The evidence even of Hartley's own fictional treatments of Venice suggests that it is not. In his story "The White Wand" (1954, *Complete Short Stories*), the city's meaning is as violently subjective as it is for Mann's Aschenbach. It is epitomized by a single stark image: the flickering wand that the protagonist glimpses fleetingly in the window of a palace, and that eventually turns out to be the hand of death. Here, as in so many other fictional renderings of Venice, such acts of symbolic impressionism triumph over values of fidelity to literal fact.

In his fascinating collection of parables, *Invisible Cities* (1974), Italo Calvino implies that expectations of such fidelity are inherently misplaced. When telling his auditor, Kublai Khan, of "Zaira, city of high bastions," the narrator, Marco Polo, renounces any attempt to describe such details as "how many steps make up the streets rising like stairways, and the degree of the arcades' curves"; "The city does not consist of this," he assures Kublai, "but of relationships between the measurements of its space and the events of its past" (13). Not accuracy in enumerating externals but insight into the inwardness of site and history defines one's knowledge of any such community. The city of Tamara, again, boasts "streets thick with signboards"; "Your gaze scans the streets as if they were written pages: the city says everything you must think, makes you repeat her discourse, and while you believe you are visiting Tamara you are only recording the names with which she defines herself and all her parts" (15). Such a place, like any other human collectivity, is inextricably bound up with the operation of language. It must consequently be "read" as a text for whatever meaning we may derive from it, while it is futile for us to endeavor to unearth any underlying, stable reality we may imagine it to possess.

If, however, a city is a text, it is, for Calvino, a hermetic one. As Marco says,

> With cities it is as with dreams: everything imaginable can be dreamed, but even the most unexpected dream is a rebus that conceals a desire or, its reverse, a fear. Cities, like dreams, are made of desires and fears, even if the thread of their discourse is secret, their rules are absurd, their perspectives deceitful, and everything conceals something else. (36)

The city-as-text must therefore be "decoded" as we might try to decode the symbolism of our own clandestine fantasy-life. Ultimately, for Calvino, cities function as projections of our own private inner worlds. "Arriving at each new city," he explains, "the traveller finds again a past of his that he did not know he had: the foreignness of what you no longer are or no longer possess lies in wait for you in foreign, unpossessed places" (25). It is, finally, the individual bias of the interpreter that endows the city-as-text with the defining structure to be discovered in it:

> It is the mood of the beholder which gives the city of Zemrude its form. If you go by whistling, your nose a-tilt behind the whistle, you will know it from below: window sills, flapping curtains, fountains. If you walk along hanging your head, your nails dug into the palms of your hands, your gaze will be held on the ground, in the gutters, the manhole covers, the fish scales, wastepaper. You cannot say that one aspect of the city is truer than the other. (54)

Calvino's subjectivist view of the perception of place is, of course, not unique. Recent academic critics have tended to voice comparable ideas, though in more soberly prosaic terms. According to Lutwack,

> Places lend themselves readily to symbolical extension because there is so little that is inherently affective in their physical properties. Spatial dimensions and climatic conditions. . . do not in themselves stimulate a constant emotional response; rather the qualities of places are determined by the subjective responses of people according to their cultural heritage, sex, occupation and personal predicament. Gibraltar is impregnable not because it is a rock but because people *think* a rock is impregnable. . . . Places are neither good nor bad in themselves but in the values attached to them, and literature is one of the agencies involved in attaching values to places. (35)

Such an analysis is a sophisticated, and therefore welcome, corrective to more
literal-minded thinking about the value of place. It is, however, one-sided
enough to stand itself in need of correction. A more balanced account is
provided by Susan Hill, a contemporary English novelist whose own work has
been extensively involved with place. Hill stresses the importance of subjective
response from the standpoint of the creative writer herself. Describing the
composition of her novel *I'm the King of the Castle* (1970), she records:

I'd got my setting, and settings are always very, very important to me, every bit as much
as characters or themes. I have a strong sense of place, and this one [the English West
Country] gave off all the right vibrations, which struck answering chords deep in my
imagination. Whenever I go to a place and this starts happening, it is as though I develop
another sense, or else all my other senses become more acute—I see, hear, smell things
more vividly and strongly, and there is an atmosphere which is partly real, partly made-
up, so that I can't precisely tell which is the real place and which is the place within me,
the one I am creating.   I think this is often true, and why it is sometimes a
disappointment to visit "the real setting" of a novel. (*The Lighting of the Lamps* 59-60)

The places Hill perceives are "partly made-up"—already well on their way
to fictiveness before the author writes a word. Yet, Hill grants, they are also
"partly real," a concession a thoroughgoing subjectivist would be unwilling to
make. To exclude the "partly real" as a component of the literary representation
of cities is to oversimplify a complicated state of affairs. Verbal configurations
and physical ones are not, after all, mutually irrelevant. The Venice of *Death
in Venice* may strike readers like Hartley as warped by Mann's fevered fancy,
but it can hardly be categorized as simply an inspired personal hallucination. To
put an extreme case, Gustave Aschenbach's eerie drift towards death would
surely have been more difficult to evoke in a Venice bereft of canals. It is one
thing to claim, like Lutwack, that descriptive exactitude is not the central issue
in one's response to fictional place, quite another thing to suppose that an
acquaintance with Venice's unique physiognomy has no bearing whatever on
one's understanding of Mann's novella. In fact, an awareness of what Mann's
imagination has actually done to observable features of the locale can only
enhance one's apprehension of Aschenbach's inward collapse.

Having said that, however, one must immediately add that a knowledge of
other writing about Venice is as relevant to an appreciation of Mann's story as
an eyewitness familiarity with Venice and its canals. Typically, the use of Italian
cities as settings involves the recollection of literary precedent as much as it does
the reduplication of observed thoroughfares and buildings. Literary Rome, like
the literal one, was not built in a day; it is a grand intellectual monument that
generations of writers have collaborated to fashion. In his *Roman Holidays*
(1908), William Dean Howells proudly lays claim to "that Rome of the
imagination which is greater than any material Rome, and which it needs no

archaeologist to discover in its indestructible integrity" (227). Tales of Italy have been penned by writers who never actually set foot there but whose imaginations had been fired by travellers' accounts or simply by other writers' imaginings of the country. Susan Hill recognises that even the "made-up" component of the places she depicts in her fiction may depend not purely on her personal invention but on pre-existing messages implanted in her consciousness: "[Y]ou can't altogether discount or escape the literary associations of a place if they're at all significant" (*The Lighting of the Lamps* 192).

This last point has received considerable attention from academic theorists. Lutwack argues "that in the final analysis all places in literature are used for symbolical purposes even though in their descriptiveness they may be rooted in fact" (31). He goes on, however, to note that such symbolism often derives from sources beyond the inventions of individual authors. "Repeated association of some generic places with certain experiences and values has resulted in what amounts almost to a system of archetypal place symbolism. Thus, mountains have come to represent aspiration and trial; forests and swamps, peril and entrapment" and so on (31). What is true of mountains and forests is equally true of churches, palaces, and canals, a fact of much moment for our discussion of Italian cities. Indeed, as will appear, each of the three famous cities functions as a *transmitted* literary paradigm with a resonance all its own.

Consequently, I will not, in what follows, be primarily concerned with local verisimilitude, though I do not discount its relevance. What will matter for my purposes is less the *vraisemblance* of the picture one author or another projects than that picture's position within the gallery of literary portraits a city has accumulated over time. The "world" of a Venetian work like Mann's operates according to a special fictive code, which may differ from the rules governing the world in which we (and flesh-and-blood Venetians) actually live. According to Alexander Gelley, "Between [the fictive] world . . . and the phenomenal, 'real' world, there exists only a link of analogy, not of continuity" (190). "Only in . . . acknowledging an essential discontinuity between fiction and experience," Gelley elaborates, "does the reader achieve appropriate modes of access to the structure of a work" (193).

> So if I wished to describe Aglaura to you, sticking to what I personally saw and experienced, I should have to tell you that it is a colourless city, without character, planted there at random. But this would not be true, either: at certain hours, in certain places along the street, you see opening before you the hint of something unmistakable, rare, perhaps magnificent; you would like to say what it is, but everything previously said of Aglaura imprisons your words and obliges you to repeat rather than say. (Calvino 55)

Marco Polo's caution to Kublai Khan is pertinent: Storied cities are in some ways more treacherous to write about than those that are unstoried. The long shadow of literary precedent may thrust itself between place and pen, allowing small room for vivid originality. Convention, with such places, has a habit of hardening into cliché. Henry James, from the time of his earliest visits to the fabled city, was uneasily aware of "the risk of stamping poor Venice beyond repair as the supreme bugbear of literature" (*Italian Hours* 54). A contemporary American poet, James Wright, warns in "Fresh Wind in Venice": "And it is no use to try to gather / Anything new out of Venice, even the sea, / Even the dark eyes of the faces" (349). As early as the 1850's, Nathaniel Hawthorne confided to his Roman notebook his dismay at Lord Byron's preemptive strikes on local literary targets: "Wherever he has to deal with a statue, a ruin, a battlefield, he pounces upon the topic like a vulture, and tears out its heart in a twinkling; so that there is nothing more to be said" (*French and Italian Notebooks* 267). By the 1980's, the anxiety of influence had supplanted Roman fever as the most menacing local literary disease. As William Weaver observes,

It is hard to sit in the Colosseum without thinking of Henry James and Daisy Miller. For that matter it is hard to look at any monument, ruin, square, without recalling what previous articulate visitors—from Stendhal and Augustus Hare to Eleanor Clark and Anthony Burgess—have observed and described. At times the weight of the past becomes almost unbearable, and a few years ago, when a brilliant American painter of my acquaintance fled Rome after his first twenty-four hours, I understood him. (Rosenthal and Gelb 349-50)

Among modern writers, it is perhaps Siegfried Sassoon who has most wryly lamented this Laocoön-grip of literary indebtedness. Sassoon describes an evening spent in the Villa d'Este Gardens "imbibing sunset; / Wrapped in my verse vocation":

My language favoured Landor, chaste and formal.
My intellect (though slightly in abeyance)
Functioned against a Byronistic background.
Then Browning jogged my elbow; bade me hob-nob
With some forgotten painter of dim frescoes
That haunt the Villa's intramural twilight.
While roaming in the Villa d'Este Gardens
I felt like that . . . and fumbled for my note-book. (143-4)

The pressures of Roman, Florentine, or Venetian precedent may well prompt the latter-day writer to nervous fumbling rather than to confident inspiration. Conversely, however, all the rich deposit of prior literary example may also create a topsoil of allusion, a wealth of tradition that writers can valuably exploit if they do not allow themselves to be entombed by it. The very depth of the literary ground upon which they walk may interact productively with the strata of history underlying each of the cities. While the risk of derivativeness dogs those who attempt to write about such localities, the achievements of the past can be enabling, as well, for the aspirants of the present. Hawthorne in Rome felt "scooped" by the prior brilliance of Byron; but in composing *The Marble Faun* (1860) he used as a point of departure another of the most popular romantic treatments of the Eternal City, Madame de Staël's *Corinne* (1807). James, in turn, used Hawthorne's novel for his own largely parodic purposes in his early story "The Last of the Valerii" (1874) and reworked it more searchingly in his first full-length novel, *Roderick Hudson* (1875). L.P. Hartley in "The White Wand" and Susan Hill in the Venetian section of her novel *The Bird of Night* (1972) both, for diverse purposes, recall elements of James's evocation of Venice in *The Aspern Papers*. Supreme bugbears sometimes turn out to be literary gift-horses. Even Sassoon himself benefits from the whole preposterous weight of precedent; it inspires him to execute a deft and funny piece of poetic handwringing. Storied cities have a knack of propagating still more stories; the art of evoking place is typically an art of allusion.

Accordingly, conventions of writing about each city get handed down from writer to writer, until they turn into virtual *topoi*. In the chapters to follow, we will repeatedly encounter female characters who personify the cities they inhabit. George Eliot's Romola in Florence, Henry James's old Miss Bordereau in Venice, and Hawthorne's Miriam in Rome are but three conspicuous instances. Such a symbiosis between character and city involves the merging of setting with theme, so that the two become in effect one. The motif of the "fall"—a fall that is at once physical and moral in *The Marble Faun* and James's *Roderick Hudson*—is a more peculiarly "Roman" one, for reasons arising from that city's history and topography. Because of the persistence of such conventions, transmitted from writer to writer, the grouping together of works in a city-by-city format provides a useful springboard for analysis. The fashion in which each writer continues, varies, or (like the American novelist Bernard Malamud) subverts the established norms highlights literary effects that, abstracted from the local context, might pass unglimpsed.

Owing to the rich literary overlay that each city has amassed, all three cities have by now become impossible to perceive innocently, with an eye uncontaminated by textual reminiscence. Each place, as Calvino would insist, has been indelibly inscribed by the ink that has been spilled over it. "Everybody dies in Venice," Jan Morris has observed. "The Venetians die in the normal course of events, and the visitors die as a matter of convention" (152). Morris's joke is a serious one. Time-honored literary stereotypes potently mold the observer's experience of the objects to which they adhere. I have accordingly

chosen to introduce each of the three major sections of this study with a survey
chapter that attempts to trace the unique literary profile of the city in question.
These introductory surveys are designed to provide an enveloping ground for the
extended analyses of specific works that follow them.

Because of the futility of trying to isolate the "real" Florence, Venice, or
Rome—what a German metaphysician might call the *Stadt an sich*—I have made
few attempts, in my general introductory surveys, to segregate the casual
impressions of literati from more "objective" or documentary accounts of the
cities. Jan Morris on Venice, Mary McCarthy on Venice and Florence, Eleanor
Clark on Rome—such testaments of travel are intensely personal, and all the
more compelling for being so. Although such writing does not provide my
central focus, it establishes a surrounding climate for the poems and narratives
that do. It suggests, as it were, the fund of shared informal fictions belonging
to these storied cities, out of which the more formally composed fictions grow.

Within the scope of this study, I have been unable to give as much attention
to historical dimensions of the subject as they ideally deserve. Not only have the
three storied cities themselves changed over the past two centuries; the sorts of
stories that tend to get told about them have also changed. The fascination with
the past, with artifice, and with social convention common in Victorian
treatments of Italian places has yielded, in our own century, to an emphasis on
spontaneous "natural" impulse, on the passionate immediacy of living. The more
modern preoccupation is with the quality that Aldous Huxley, in *On the Margin*
(1923), calls Italian "Presentism":

They are all Futurists in that burningly living Italy where we from the North seek only
an escape into the past. Or rather, they are not Futurists. . . . They are Presentists. The
early Christians preoccupied with nothing but the welfare of their souls in the life to come
were Futurists, if you like. (10)

Overlapping this historical divide is a geographical one that I have likewise
been obliged to scant: the far from negligible differences between the premises
North American and British writers have brought to their treatment of
Continental cities. Fortunately, a valuable survey of American responses to one
of my three cities has lately appeared: William L. Vance's *America's Rome*
(1989). Drawing on numerous examples from both literature and the visual arts,
Vance convincingly demonstrates how, as he says, "[b]oth the uniqueness of [the
American visitors'] political identity and the deprivations of their cultural
circumstances intensified their experience of Italy" (xix). My principal concern,
however, unlike Vance's, is the wealth of preconceptions *shared* by foreign
visitors to Italy, and the way literary configurations have of cheerfully ignoring
national boundaries.   I have therefore indulged at times in a promiscuous
cosmopolitanism, drawing on testimony from well-known French and German

literary travellers when it seemed illuminating. In one instance—*Death in Venice*—I have yielded to the temptation of treating *in extenso* a text not written in English. Mann's novella is so formidably central to the evolution of "Venetian" writing that it refused to be excluded.

Here, as elsewhere, when I speak of "Venetian" works or of "Florentine" or "Roman," I am wrenching those terms somewhat willfully from their standard sense, applying them to the use of the cities as locales in fictions by non-Italian writers. I have judged it best to avoid the huge question of how these places have been treated by native Italians, who necessarily approach them from a different angle. Nevertheless, I have drawn occasionally on the impressions of respected Italian commentators, such as Guido Piovene and Giorgio Bassani, when their observations about one or another of the cities amplify or help explain the experience of foreign visitors.

Foreignness itself, however, is in every instance an intrinsic part of that experience, and a part in which native writers can hardly be expected to share. In all three cities, what our non-Italian Marco Polos are exploring is, among other things, their own undiscovered interior terrain. As Calvino says, "[T]he foreignness of what you no longer are or no longer possess lies in wait for you in foreign, unpossessed places"; but so does the foreignness of what you still are, what you still possess.

View of Florence from Piazzale Michelangelo. From *All Florence: Monuments, Buildings, Churches, Museums, Art Galleries, Outskirts,* page 120. New York: Charles Scribner's Sons, 1971. Photograph reproduced courtesy of Bonechi Edizioni "Il Turismo," August 20, 1992.

PART I

FLORENCE

Of all the fairest Cities of the Earth
None is so fair as FLORENCE. 'Tis a gem
Of purest ray; and what a light broke forth,
When it emerged from darkness! Search within,
Without; all is enchantment; 'Tis the Past
Contending with the Present; and in turn
Each has the mastery.

Samuel Rogers, *Italy*

2

The Etrurian Athens

The Florence of the literary imagination, like the Florence of historical chronicle, is steeped in controversy. The motif of "contention" finds its way even into Samuel Rogers's bland encomium. As Margaret Oliphant long ago observed, the city's physiognomy itself sets it at odds with stock notions of the blithely "Italian":

[I]t is scarcely possible to conceive a combination of circumstances which could have detached Florence from her grandiose and austere personality and made of her a national centre. So long as her dark palaces cut their stern outline against the sky, and her warlike tower lifts itself high over the housetops, and the hills stand round her in embattled lines, must the great city remain herself . . . a grave, serious, almost solemn presence, full of passion too profound and thought too vast to be capable of light utterance, amid all the sunshine and the songs, the gaiety and levity of the south. (1-2)

The Florentine hallmarks, noted by observer after observer, are clarity of outline, severity, and elegance. Arthur Symons sets Florence pointedly apart from her two renowned sister-cities:

In Florence there is nothing of the majesty of Rome nor of the sea-magic of Venice. Rome is made out of the eternal hills, on which the ends of the world have come, age by age; it is the city made glorious by Michelangelo and Michelangelo typifies its glories. Venice is born out of the marriage of land and sea, and it was Titian who took up the Doge's ring out of the water, and perpetuated the new ecstasy of colour. But Florence, marvellously built, every stone set decorously on stone, a conscious work of craftsmen upon material naturally adaptable, is represented rather by sculpture than by painting, and in painting, by precise and sensitive design, an almost sculptured outline. Florence, the city of all the arts, the corridor through which all the arts have passed and in which they still linger, is the city made to be a shrine to Donatello. (135-6)

One leading quality of the city's life has been universally acknowledged: its intellectual bent. As Guido Piovene puts it, "Florence is the cultural city *par excellence*. . . . In Florence, culture is a constitutional fact, and anyone who neglected to speak of it would be omitting the essential feature of its physiognomy. Everything that arises there takes on a mien of culture; it is dictated by the very temper of a city tending toward an extreme limit of clarity and self-consciousness" (287). Along with self-consciousness there goes what

Mary McCarthy calls "an undertone of irony, typically Florentine" (*Stones of Florence* 19). "The defects [of the Florentine character]," says Piovene, "were the reverse of its virtues: a certain tendency towards disdain and rejection, an unbridled conviction of intellectual aristocracy, an excess of criticism, a reserve, at once timid and haughty, in the face of a too emphatic expression or the risk of a *faux pas*" (288).

That such a shrine to Renaissance severity should have fascinated writers of our own troubled and ironic era is perhaps not surprising. To begin with, any community boasting so coherent a cultural impress has a natural appeal to an age in which the dominant urban experience has been one of social "noise" and fragmentation. The cerebral bias of the Florentine civic spirit makes the city all the more congenial to the often baffled modern quest for rationality. Yet along with the intellectual enterprise for which it is renowned, Florence's legacy includes, paradoxically, an endemic violence and self-division, tendencies with which non-Florentine moderns also find it all too easy to identify.

"Florentine history is the typical history of a city in which intelligence predominates," Piovene observes. "In its most vital centuries, more than any other Italian city, Florence has displayed the logical unfolding of all the possible experiments in the social and political sphere; we see them following one after the other exactly like the experiments in a great laboratory" (283). No city, however, is "exactly like" a laboratory; indeed, vigorous social experimentation can result in something more closely resembling an abattoir. Inseparable from its proud past of collective accomplishment is Florence's inheritance of seething factional strife. "In no other city of Italy," observes Jacob Burckhardt, "were the struggles of political parties so bitter, of such early origin, and so permanent" (49). Nor have the factions been solely political; Norman Douglas refers waspishly to the "fifty squabbling art-coteries of that City of Misunderstandings" (217). Oliphant traces, from before Dante's time up to its "climax" in Savonarola's, "the perennial struggle which raged between one citizen and another, one family and another, one side of a street against the dwellers opposite, without rhyme or reason, or thought of any loftier meaning" (xviii).

"Such divisions, such extremism, such contrasts" are what Mary McCarthy, too, discerns in the past of Florence—"a terrible city, in many ways, uncomfortable and dangerous to live in, a city of drama, argument, and struggle" (*Stones of Florence* 25). Viewed in this light, the personal plea that opens Robert Browning's "Andrea del Sarto"—"But do not let us quarrel any more, / No, my Lucrezia" (*The Poems* Vol. 1)—touches the very quick of the local spirit. External antagonisms have a way here of sinking inward into the psyche, generating what McCarthy terms "an interior struggle . . . typically Florentine" (*Stones of Florence* 174). The hectic metaphor that Elizabeth Barrett Browning applies to the city's river in *Casa Guidi Windows* (1851)—"golden Arno as it shoots away / Through Florence' heart beneath her bridges four: / Bent bridges, seeming to strain off like bows, / And tremble while the arrowy undertide / Shoots on and cleaves the marble as it goes" (53-57)—perfectly expresses the dominant motifs of warfare and division. So do the still more violent metaphors of a poem composed a century later, Robert Lowell's "Florence" (1964):

> Oh Florence, Florence, patroness
> of the lovely tyrannicides!
> Where the tower of the Old Palace
> pierces the sky
> like a hypodermic needle,
> Perseus, David and Judith,
> lords and ladies of the Blood,
> Greek demi-gods of the Cross,
> rise sword in hand
> above the unshaven,
> formless decapitation
> of the monsters, tubs of guts,
> mortifying chunks for the pack.
> (*For the Union Dead* 14)

As Lowell's lines attest, even the architecture lends itself readily to symbolic use, intimating the persistence of rancor and division. This city of antagonisms is a city of antinomies; and the sense of duality is integral to the richness and troubling complexity of its cultural heritage. Lowell is not unique in finding contradictory sermons in the stones of Florentine towers. For E. V. Lucas, the two tallest of them become emblems of the city's divided soul: "The tower rising from this square fortress [the Palazzo Vecchio] has at once grace and strength and presents a complete contrast to Giotto's campanile; for Giotto's campanile is so light and delicate and reasonable and this tower of the Signoria so stern and noble" (97). The black-against-white color scheme of the city's church facades itself recalls ancient feuding factions, the "Neri" against the "Bianchi."

But what most forcibly struck nineteenth-century visitors was the age-old antithesis between the Christian and the Pagan. The city's architecture, indeed, can seem the virtual embodiment in stone of Matthew Arnold's celebrated pair of contraries: Hebraism and Hellenism. Literary travellers of both Arnold's century and our own have responded vividly, yet diversely, to these scenic dualisms. That diversity is a measure of the sharply conflicting assumptions they have imported into the city in their own cultural baggage.

One of the most august among them, John Ruskin, found the confluence of the two competing Florentine currents, the Christian and the classical, reason to rejoice. In his rhapsodic vein, Ruskin explains why, before the intrusion of modern urban life, few spots of ground were so worthy of "joyful reverence" as the square before Giotto's bell-tower:

For there the traditions of faith and hope, of both the Gentile and Jewish races, met for their beautiful labour: the Baptistery of Florence is the last building raised on the earth by the descendants of the workmen taught by Daedalus; and the Tower of Giotto is the loveliest of those raised on earth under the inspiration of the men who lifted up the tabernacle in the wilderness. Of living Greek work there is none after the Florentine Baptistery; of living Christian work, none so perfect as the Tower of Giotto; and, under the gleam and shadow of their marbles, the morning light was haunted by the ghosts of the Father of Natural Science, Galileo; of Sacred Art, Angelico, and of the Master of Sacred Song. (*Mornings* 413)

But where Ruskin celebrates the peaceful coexistence of opposed traditions, others have dwelled on the shifting historic currents of warfare between them. The American visitor William Dean Howells places the blame for this instability on the burly shoulders of Lorenzo the Magnificent. "One effect of that study of antiquity which was among the means Lorenzo used to corrupt the souls of men" is that "the Florentines are half repaganized" (*Tuscan Cities* 55). Harold Acton, by contrast, sees Lorenzo's archrival, Savonarola, as the agent of a grim backsliding into Christian piety, "a brief and bloodthirsty return to the Middle Ages" (35). The force mainly responsible for thawing the despotic Hebraism of the Florentine Middle Ages was, as Lucas calls it, "the Greek invasion of Florence" (25), an invasion that had its literal Hellenist vanguard in the advent of educated Greeks—like George Eliot's fictional Hellene, Tito Melema—during the early Renaissance.

One outcome of the Hellenizing of Florence has been the inevitable comparison, drawn grandiloquently by Byron in *Childe Harold's Pilgrimage* (1818, *Poetical Works*):

> But Arno wins us to the fair white walls,
> Where the Etrurian Athens claims and keeps
> A softer feeling for her fairy halls.
> Girt by her theatre of hills, she reaps
> Her corn, and wine, and oil, and Plenty leaps
> To laughing life, with her redundant horn.
> Along the banks where smiling Arno sweeps
> Was modern Luxury of Commerce born,
> And buried Learning rose, redeem'd to a new morn. (4.48)

Byron's paean to Florence as the reincarnation of the glory that was Athens only reaffirms what was already by his time a grand-touristic commonplace. And the well-worn analogy has evidently not lost its appeal for later commentators. Mary McCarthy speculates: "The affinity with fifth-century Athens may be due partly to geography, partly to political structure—to the clear outlines of landscape and to a tradition of sharp, clear thought" (42).

But if a shared intellectual clarity explains one side of this Attic connection, there is another side, succinctly defined by Acton: "Boundless curiosity was combined with a talent for exact observation, and the visual arts flowered from a passionate awareness of the tangible, visible world. Like the Greeks, the Florentines were guided by some peculiar instinct toward temperance and beauty" (12). The keynote of Hellenism in this sense, as Acton goes on to imply, is really less temperance than an unblushing embrace of the physical: "The artist went straight to flesh and blood essentials; the human body cast off its cloistral cocoon and leapt into the Arcadian sunlight" (13). "Leaping into the sunlight" is, not coincidentally, a movement executed by a whole troupe of fictional Florentine performers, from Barrett Browning's Aurora Leigh to E. M. Forster's Lucy Honeychurch.

As Forster, among others, emphasizes, the two sides of reawakening Hellenism, the cerebral and the physical, are by their nature twinned. "The miracle of Florence," according to Emilio Cecchi in his essay "*Fiorentinità*" (1950), "lies in this coexistence of forces, of feelings, of homely energy, of the lust for life and the capacity for abstraction" (32). Walter Pater extols the wholeness of the Florentine revival, "that reassertion of [man's] self, that rehabilitation of human nature, the body, the senses, the heart, the intelligence, which the Renaissance fulfils" (43). The promise of such an integration is always latent in Florentine settings, though it may (as in Huxley's "The Rest Cure") be ironically defeated.

The example of Florence thus helps to focus, if not to resolve, the mind-body dualism that bedevilled the century before our own. It involves, as well, another dualism that continues to perplex the present century: the Carlylean alternatives of past and present. To those shaken by the volcanic changes of modern life, the problem of Florentine historical continuity (or discontinuity) is charged with a special, and controversial, significance. For Ruskin, the rage for the new threatened to obliterate the city's ancient greatness. The scourge of the sacred past was the living, thriving populace, at best grossly indifferent to their city's priceless heritage, at worst bent on defiling that heritage through oafish attempts at restoration. The restorers—"the devil-begotten brood of modern Florence" (*Mornings* 383)—draw Ruskin's fiercest fire; but the civic "conveniences" of the nineteenth century are scarcely less damnable. Hackney coaches, omnibuses, and other obstructions, he complains, have eliminated any proper vantage point for viewing Giotto's immortal tower, "not a soul in Florence ever caring now for sight of any piece of its old artists' work" (414).

Few have savored the mellow aftertaste of the Florentine past more keenly than Henry James; yet in *Italian Hours* (1909) even James demurs at Ruskin's outrage over the ill-placed cab-stands of the present:

[T]he sensitive stranger who has been walking about for a week with his mind full of the sweetness and suggestiveness of a hundred Florentine places may feel at last in looking into Mr. Ruskin's little tracts [*Mornings in Florence*] that, discord for discord, there isn't much to choose between the importunity of the author's personal ill-humour and the incongruity of horse-pails and bundles of hay. (126)

For James's more forward-looking countryman, Howells, the appeal of the ancient city lay precisely in its up-to-dateness, pails, bundles, and all. Florence's superiority over a rival such as Venice derived from the Tuscan city's modern spirit of egalitarian bustle. Of the Piazza della Signoria, Howells writes: "There is nothing superfine, nothing of the *salon* about the place, nothing of the beauty of Piazza San Marco at Venice, which expresses the elegance of an oligarchy and suggests the dapper perfection of an aristocracy in decay; [Florence] is loud with wheels and hoofs, and busy with commerce, and it has a certain ineffaceable rudeness and unfinish like the structure of a democratic state" (*Tuscan Cities* 88). In his valediction to the city, as viewed from the tower of the Palazzo Vecchio, Howells benignly flatters it with transatlantic comparisons: "And my heart still warms to the famous town, not because of that past which, however heroic and aspiring, was so wrong-headed and bloody and pitiless, but because of the present, safe, free, kindly, full of possibilities of prosperity and fraternity, like that of Boston or Denver" (137).

Nearly a century later another American visitor, Mary McCarthy, goes her distinguished predecessor one better. For McCarthy, the Florentine past amounts essentially to a granite roadblock on the superhighway to Denver:

Historic Florence is an incubus on its present population. It is like a vast piece of family property whose upkeep is too much for the heirs, who nevertheless find themselves criticized by strangers for letting the old place go to rack and ruin. . . . History, for Florence, is neither a legend nor eternity, but a massive weight of rough building stone demanding continual repairs, pressing on the modern city like a debt, blocking progress. (22-23)

The complete gamut from Ruskin has been run. To those whose enthusiasm for progress is more guarded, however, it is precisely the continuity of past and present—the sustained immediacy of history—that provides the key to the Florentine experience. According to Arthur Symons, "Time scarcely changes her, and she suffices to the American tourist as easily as she sufficed to Cosimo. Hers are all tangible beauties and all forms of life in which the rhythm is never broken" (135). "Here the past does not need to be excavated," Acton concurs; "by sunlight or moonshine it is alive and omnipresent" (6).

No one was more sensitive to the sometimes stifling weight of the Florentine past than James; yet no one has evoked more touchingly the persistence, in the city's atmosphere, of an afterglow of the Renaissance, which has left "a heritage of beauty that these three enjoying centuries since haven't yet exhausted":

This forms a clear intellectual atmosphere into which you may turn aside from the modern world and fill your lungs as with the breath of a forgotten creed. The memorials of the past here address us moreover with a friendliness, win us by we scarcely know what sociability, what equal amenity, that we scarce find matched in other great aesthetically endowed communities and periods. Venice, with her old palaces cracking under the weight of their treasures, is, in her influence, insupportably sad; Athens, with her maimed marbles and dishonoured memories, transmutes the consciousness of sensitive observers, I am told, into a chronic heartache; but in one's impression of old Florence the abiding felicity, the sense of saving sanity, of something sound and human, predominates, offering you a medium still conceivable for life. (*Italian Hours* 274)

It is the "sense of saving sanity" that fictional visitors like Margaret Johnson, the protagonist of Elizabeth Spencer's novella *The Light in the Piazza* (1960), regularly find in Florence. Sitting in the Piazza della Signoria, Margaret "looked at the splendid old palace and forgot that her feet hurt. More than that: here she could almost lose the sorrow that for so many years had been a constant of her life" (4).

James's "medium still conceivable for life" is precisely what an earlier Florentine heroine, Barrett Browning's Aurora Leigh, discovers on returning to her native terrain. Aurora, whose very name conjures up Florentine associations (compare Byron's "And buried Learning rose, redeem'd to a new morn"), must, to achieve emotional rebirth, end her prolonged English exile and resume life in her actual birthplace. The continuity of existence is gravely endangered for Aurora; she begins her narrative by likening her motive for writing to a lover's purpose in contemplating the portrait of the one he no longer loves, "just / To hold together what he was and is" (*Aurora Leigh* 1.7-8). "Just holding together" the disjointed chapters of her life poses the grand challenge for Aurora.

Late in Aurora's account, however, after her return to Florence, the pieces begin to meld in a way that fulfills the tenuous hopefulness of the opening lines. Now the metaphor Aurora applies to the recapturing of the past is more nostalgically communal: "I took up the old days, / With all their Tuscan pleasures worn and spoiled, / Like some lost book we dropped in the long grass / On such a happy summer-afternoon / When last we read it with a loving friend" (7.1040-5). Figuratively as well as literally, Aurora is at long last "finding her place." For a time, she is overwhelmed by the blended "incubus" of the city's long history and of her personal past—the local precincts hold the graves not only of her mother and father but of her beloved old nurse: "My old Assunta, too, was dead, was dead— / O land of all men's past! for me alone, / It would not mix its tenses. I was past, / It seemed, like others" (7.1156-9). What eventually allows Florence to mix its tenses for Aurora is the appearance in her mother city of a figure from her more recent English past, Romney Leigh. Amid the restorative Tuscan atmosphere, Romney becomes capable of repenting his besetting male arrogance and dogmatism, so that the grievous breach between Aurora's past and her present can at last be healed with love.

Such a gift for healing, though it may seem paradoxical in the proverbial city of divisions, is celebrated in a number of the works to be discussed hereafter. It has its source in a widespread sense of the city's inherent vitality, a dynamism pointed up by historical contrasts. As Piovene observes, whereas in Florence the Middle Ages were superseded by the lavish building projects of the Renaissance, a city like nearby Siena "remains medieval and almost immobilized in time" (297). Nevertheless, Florence itself has not always been exempt from stasis. Here, once again, the city's history helps to account for the dichotomies inescapably associated with it.

According to Piovene, the Tuscan spirit, though at bottom practical and realistic, is capable of breeding a quixotic "idealism of the highest type." However, "in weary times and in weary men, Tuscan realism can decline instead into a limitedness of views and intents, a taste for the mediocre, an inert sterility, a predilection for the petty and mean" (281). For McCarthy, too, Florence is "a city of extremes, hot in the summer, cold in the winter, traditionally committed to advance, to modernism, yet containing backward elements narrow as its streets, cramped, stony, recalcitrant" (24). Still, the town remains for her essentially "a city of progress" (23). Other commentators agree. Burckhardt applauds the way in which "that wondrous Florentine spirit, at once keenly critical and artistically creative, was incessantly transforming the social and political conditions of the State, and as incessantly describing and judging the change" (48). During the several centuries between the Renaissance and modern times, however, creative change was conspicuously absent. Under a series of despotic grand dukes, the city's chronic turmoil and progressive dynamism alike subsided into a lull: "the years of deadly quiet," as Oliphant calls them, "in which she has languished under native and foreign masters, fighting no longer" (xv). For the Florentine imagination, therefore, stasis is not a remote possibility but a readily recollected fact of life.

For all that, foreign writers have persistently read the aspiration to go onward in the city's flinty physiognomy. Elizabeth Barrett Browning, writing near the end of the Grand-Ducal doldrums, asks in *Casa Guidi Windows*: "What word will men say,—here where Giotto planted / His campanile like an unperplexed / Fine question Heavenward, touching the things granted / A noble people who, being greatly vexed / In act, in inspiration keep undaunted?" (1.68-72). (Her husband Robert, in "Old Pictures in Florence" (1855; *The Poems* Vol. 1), finds in Giotto's great bell-tower a similar upward point of interrogation.) Aurora Leigh, at the end of her story, is instructed by her blinded but undaunted lover "'how by mounting ever we attain, / And so climb on'" (9.938-9).

"By mounting ever" one is apt to broaden one's view. The emphasis on visual experience, prominent too in the literature of Rome and Venice, takes on a uniquely positive value within the Florentine framework. What Burckhardt calls the Italian "universal education of the eye" (208) finds its major seat in the Tuscan capital. "The Florentines have a twin predilection for astronomy and the science of optics," McCarthy notes (*Stones of Florence* 54); and Piovene observes that the stone architecture of the city "has the magic of a precision optical instrument" (284). Symons complains of an actual overdose of visual instruction: "If we could endure so continual a pressure and solicitation of beauty, no city would be so good to live in as Florence; but the eyes cannot take rest in it: they are preoccupied, indoors and out of doors; this prevalence of rare things becomes almost an oppression" (134). Yet most visitors, like Elizabeth Spencer's heroine Margaret value the clarity of vision to be obtained in the city: "In Florence . . . everything seemed to take a step nearer, more distinctly, more totally to be seen" (56).

"'Tis a gem / Of purest ray; and what a light broke forth, / When it emerged from darkness!" In many literary treatments of Florence, as in that of Samuel Rogers, light itself assumes a special symbolic valence, closely bound up with the city's intellectual heritage. Dickens, calling the honor roll of native artists, poets, and philosophers, exclaims: "What light is shed upon the world, at this day, from amidst these rugged Palaces of Florence!" (*Pictures* 241). Aurora Leigh, freshly displaced from her beloved Tuscany, finds herself in a dark, Satanic England bereft of the element encoded in her name: "Did Shakespeare and his mates / Absorb the light here?—not a hill or stone / With heart to strike a radiant colour up / Or active outline on the indifferent air" (1.266-9). In recompense, when she at last returns, she finds "a house at Florence on the hill / Of Bello-sguardo," where her commanding view allows her to gaze her fill at dawns and sunsets: "No sun could die nor yet be born unseen / By dwellers at my villa: morn and eve / Were magnified before us in the pure / Illimitable space and pause of sky" (7.524-7). It is such a radiant vista that will again symbolize passional fulfillment in E. M. Forster's novel with that most Florentine of titles, *A Room with a View* (1908).

But if Florence is the city of lucid seeing, its literary image continually projects that most familiar of visual dualisms, the contrast between light and its opposite. Dickens begins his "picture" of the city with a sun-drenched panorama viewed from the summit of a hill:

See where it lies before us in a sun-lighted valley, bright with the winding Arno, and shut in by swelling hills; its domes, and towers, and palaces, rising from the rich country in a glittering heap, and shining in the sun like gold! (*Pictures* 238)

Against this long shot he quickly juxtaposes a close-up of massed shadows:

Magnificently stern and sombre are the streets of beautiful Florence; and the strong old piles of building make such heaps of shadow, on the ground and in the river, that there is another and a different city of rich forms and fancies, always lying at our feet. (238-9)

Another walker in the city, Howells, is struck by similar contrasts:

As you stroll along one of these light-yellow avenues you say to yourself "Ah, *this* is Florence!" And then suddenly you plunge into the gray-brown gloom of such a street as the Borgo degli Albizzi, with lofty palaces climbing in vain toward the sun, and frowning upon the street below with fronts of stone, rude or sculptured, but always stern and cold; and then that, too, seems the only Florence. They are in fact equally Florentine. (*Tuscan Cities* 34)

Again and again, writers have capitalized on this ubiquitous *chiaroscuro*. In George Eliot's *Romola* (1863), a symbolic interplay of light and shadow is sustained throughout the entire tumultuous narrative, reinforcing its artistic cohesiveness.

"Views" of the sort enjoyed by Aurora Leigh, by Forster's Lucy Honeychurch, or by Romola herself are often closely associated with one final, characteristic Florentine *leitmotif*: that of personal rebirth. "Florence is called the City of Flowers," Lucas notes at the beginning of *A Wanderer in Florence* (1927); but he suggests that a more appropriate name "would be the City of the Miracle, the miracle being the Renaissance" (1). By a process of metaphorical extension, narratives set in the city repeatedly enact such miracles within the lives of individual characters. The pattern crops up even in personal reminiscences, such as those of Osbert Sitwell. The young Sitwell, fresh from the dull rigors of military service in England, experiences a "youthful ecstasy" that is in effect a resuscitation: "That Florence and Aldershot could be situated in the same globe was scarcely to be believed. Never had people looked so beautiful, or appeared so interesting as in this city" (185).

The sudden reawakening of a character to vibrant life becomes a regular motif of Florentine narratives, though never a foregone conclusion. Aurora Leigh, only a few lines after lamenting that she is "past," suddenly finds within herself the happy power

> To be, as if you had not been till then,
> And were then, simply that you chose to be:
> To spring up, not be brought forth from the ground . . .
>   possess, yourself,
> A new world all alive with creatures new,
> New sun, new moon, new flowers, new people—ah,
> And be possessed by none of them!   (7.1195-1203)

Aurora concludes her story in a triumphant moment of Florentine apotheosis, contemplating, over her native hills, the "new, near Day" of which her name has been a prophecy. For her, the harrowing clash of opposed principles leads to personal resurgence, as it will for George Eliot's heroine Romola. Such, too, is the path followed by Robert Browning's embattled Fra Lippo Lippi, who discovers through his art "[A] new world all alive with creatures new" (*The Poems* Vol. 1). Meanwhile, for Browning's other Florentine protagonists, the eagerly awaited morning refuses to dawn. Conflict, within this most chronically divided of settings, has the power to generate rebirth; but it can also, at worst, crush the tremulous stirrings of new life.

3

Robert Browning's Dialectical City

Robert Browning's "dialectical temper," as W. David Shaw has called it, ensured that poet's fascination with the most dialectical of cities. Past and future, immanence and transcendence, stasis and progress—such polarities haunted Browning's imagination, and a city bristling with contraries inevitably became not only his dwelling place but a companion piece for his mind. The works he set there culminate in the masterly dramatic monologues "Fra Lippo Lippi" and "Andrea del Sarto," which themselves stand in an illuminating dialectical relation to each other.

In general, Browning's treatment of Florence wavers between opposing poles; the city may foster the momentum required for the achieving of personal fulfillment, but its influence is also capable of bringing that momentum to a standstill. A relatively obscure work, the play *Luria* (1846), shows Browning's approach to Florentine dualisms at its most negative. The prospectus the poet drew up for Elizabeth Barrett suggests that the play's action, though it takes place in the late Middle Ages, corresponds to serious divisions within his own psyche:

Luria is a Moor, of Othello's country, and devotes himself to something he thinks Florence, and the old fortune follows—all in my brain, yet, but the bright weather helps and I will soon loosen my Braccio and Puccio (a pale discontented man), and Tiburzio (the Pisan, good true fellow, this one), and Domizia the Lady—loosen all these on dear foolish (ravishing must his folly be), golden-hearted Luria, all these with their worldly-wisdom and Tuscan shrewd ways; and, for me, the misfortune is, I sympathise just as much with these as with him—so there can no good come of keeping this wild company any longer. (*Letters* 1: 26)

The major antithesis in *Luria* between Moor and Florentine matches a deep cleavage in the poet's own allegiances. The Florentine characters he mentions act as a collective antagonist opposing the golden-hearted folly of the alien protagonist. Florence is presented as a chill "North," the polar opposite to the sultry "East" embodied by Luria.

Seldom, indeed, has an Italian city been pictured in so unpromisingly boreal a light. Here, the fabled venturesomeness of Florentine intellect is reduced to a prying, cynical, and essentially destructive ingenuity. The "sagacity" with which the natives are credited (and which "golden-hearted" Luria himself sadly lacks) amounts to little more than a scheming penchant for expediency. It is Braccio, the commissary, "Braccio, the cold acute instructed mind," as Luria calls him (3.273), who most bluntly personifies the unattractive turn that Florentine alertness has taken. The official, whose name itself means "arm," stands for the civil government's outreach to the theater of military action. His characteristic, equivocating weapon, the pen, turns out unluckily to be mightier than Luria's bold Moorish sword. In Braccio's eyes, Luria represents exactly the wrong "type" to command his polished city: "Brute-force shall not rule Florence! Intellect / May rule her, bad or good as chance supplies" (1.190-1). The Florentine's belief in the divine sway of mind does not, however, open his own mind to inventiveness or originality; instead, it pinions him to tradition and precedent. Such intellect supplies no momentum to release his Florence from its besetting, rearward-looking collective stasis.

It is Braccio who most pointedly spells out the alternatives encompassed in Browning's plot:

> Florence took up, turned all one way the soul
> Of Luria with its fires, and here he glows!
> She takes me out of all the world as him,
> Fixing my coldness till like ice it checks
> The fire! So, Braccio, Luria, which is best?   (3.225-9)

Braccio's question answers itself. The fiery Moor represents a force that has at least a chance to thaw the icy grip of precedent and sceptical intellect on the city he has undertaken to defend, and to which he remains unswervingly devoted. Here it is not Florence that is identified with the sun's light and warmth but Luria himself, rising out of his remote East.

Still, bound by his belief in Florence as the prototype of civilization, Luria makes his relationship with the city the keystone of his being. Disregarding his aide Husain's warning that a "wall" separates the two peoples, Luria yearns for a bond between them. The most tangible evidence of this naive hope is his projected facade for the unfinished cathedral: "his fancy how a Moorish front / Might join to, and complete, the body,—a sketch" (1.124-5). Unfortunately, such a synthesis is likelier to remain an artist's conception than to become a reality. In the event, the greybeard wisdom that rules Florence decides to rid itself of the splendid but violent Luria, without waiting to see whether his Moorish front might harmonize with its own architecture—whether the exotic captain might be naturalized to the uses of peace.

Although Luria dies, the example of his devotion goes far toward justifying the optimism at which the Florentine lady Domizia somewhat surprisingly arrives: "How inexhaustibly the spirit grows! . . . / Already are new undreamed energies / Outgrowing under, and extending farther / To a new object; there's another world!" (5.187-93). According to Domizia, the passage of many civilized generations had deprived her fellow townspeople of any vibrant, immediate contact with heroic virtue; all that remained was "truth copied falteringly from copies faint." Now, fired by the Moor's living display of instinctual passion, "trace by trace / Old memories reappear, old truth returns, / Our slow thought does its work, and all's re-known" (5.276-8).

So the instinctual warmth Luria stands for receives a local consecration, and the Renaissance is at last free to erupt through the glacial surface of Florentine decorum. According to Clyde de L. Ryals, "[T]he play is unequivocal in pronouncing that though the 'completeness' for which Luria . . . was seeking may not be attainable, the best form of 'incompleteness' lies in the recognition of the superiority of feeling to reason, of the individual to society, of love to power" (240). Nevertheless, "unequivocal" seems too hopeful a word to apply to Browning's treatment of Florentine contraries in this play; one still senses, as a subtext, what he termed the "misfortune" of his own divided loyalties. The joining of antagonistic cultural values requires a stronger intellectual cement than is available here. Luria's own lament—"Incompleteness, incompleteness!" (1.238)—reverberates into the concluding pages of the drama.

The polarities played off against each other in *Luria* reappear in Browning's more successful Florentine poems; but there they are treated in a fashion at once more economical and more complex. A case in point is "The Statue and the Bust" (1855, *The Poems* Vol. 1), which takes as its setting a Florence already beginning to lapse into post-Renaissance lethargy. Ian Jack, speaking of "the fatal . . . procrastination which is the theme of the poem" (176), sums up the critical consensus. In fact, however, it would be nearer the mark to define the poem's subject as the Florentine opposition (already treated in *Luria*) between acting and watching. This idea is immediately suggested in the opening lines: "There's a palace in Florence, the world knows well, / And a statue watches it from the square" (lines 1-2). The description of the lady who fascinates the Medici duke—

> Hair in heaps lay heavily
> Over a pale brow spirit-pure—
> Carved like the heart of the coal-black tree,
>
> Crisped like a war-steed's encolure—
> And [she] vainly sought to dissemble her eyes
> Of the blackest black our eyes endure (19-24)—

hints at her kinship with the sun-burnt Moor, Luria. Luria comes to Florence from his sultry East; the lady has arrived from the sunny Italian South. In the later work, the northern city again displays its chilling influence; but that influence is now counterbalanced by a potentially enlivening spirit.

Where the Moor confronts Florence as a wide-eyed innocent, the southern lady is a Sleeping Beauty; it is in the Tuscan capital that her dark eyes first open to the possibilities of life. A single glance suffices to kindle passion: "He looked at her, as a lover can; / She looked at him, as one who awakes: / The past was a sleep, and her life began" (28-30). But her unlawful ardor at length cools in the temperate Tuscan atmosphere that inspired it. Instead of enjoying the sunrise of a new birth, she finds herself "In a bedchamber by a taper's blink" (54) with a superfluous husband, her private renaissance blocked by the prospect of a living burial: "the door she had passed was shut on her / Till the final catafalk repassed" (56-57).

Henceforth she exchanges action for spectatorship. She puts off to some other lifetime her passional dawn; until then, as a feeble recompense, she can observe the sun rising day after day on the bustle of life from which she is cloistered. "The world meanwhile, its noise and stir, / Through a certain window facing the East, / She could watch like a convent's chronicler" (58-60).

The poem's peculiar rhythmic briskness makes a wry comment on her stationary posture, evoking the Florentine "noise and stir" from which she has been excluded. Its *terza rima* invites association with Dante's *Divine Comedy*; but an anapestic tetrameter vehicle for such verse is bound to smack of travesty.[1] The lady herself regards her imprisoning bed chamber as her living "inferno": "'If I spend the night with that devil twice, / May his window serve as my loop of hell / Whence a damned soul looks on paradise!'" (67-69). Yet even while she so broods, her eye, inuring itself to spectatorship, "grows dim"; she finds pretexts for delay and joins the ranks of Dante's neutral souls loitering amid the outskirts of hell.

For the Duke, too, glancing and gazing become a mimicry of "action" that is mere paralysis on horseback: "'For I ride—what should I do but ride? / And passing her palace, if I list, / May glance at its window—well betide!'" (118-20). "Woe betide" would be more apt. For both lovers, observation establishes its own seditious diurnal rhythm, feeding their starved passion with the shadow of nourishment:

> Meantime, worse fates than a lover's fate,
> Who daily may ride and pass and look
> Where his lady watches behind the grate!
>
> And she—she watched the square like a book
> Holding one picture and only one,
> Which daily to find she undertook:
>
> When the picture was reached the book was done,
> And she turned from the picture at night to scheme
> Of tearing it out for herself next sun. (142-50)

Instead of producing real movement, the interminable series of "stills" merely protracts stasis. The page turns, but the picture never changes.

In the witty denouement, the lady, stirred to panic by the first symptoms of age, finds watching no longer enough. She compulsively resorts to Florentine artifice as a stay against time's drift:

> "Let Robbia's craft so apt and strange
> Arrest the remains of young and fair,
> And rivet them while the seasons range.
>
> "Make me a face on the window there,
> Waiting as ever, mute the while,
> My love to pass below in the square!" (169-74)

Such an attempt to leapfrog from temporal impotence to an artistic "eternity" amounts to what Lee Erickson terms a "reduction of love to symbol at the cost of experience" (173). All that Florentine craft can really accomplish is to "arrest" and "rivet" the fair subject's "remains"; and it is only too fitting that what does remain of her is a bust—a bodiless head. What that head is doing is likewise appropriate: "Eyeing ever, with earnest eye / And quick-turned neck at its breathless stretch, / Some one who ever is passing by" (193-5). The pun on "breathless" deftly focuses the art object's ironic ambiguousness; the bust captures at once the ardent eagerness of the lady's first passion, and the lifelessness of the mere unbreathing clay image into which she has dwindled. Transformation into a monument of perpetual ogling is the perfect fate for her; it might have won the approval of Dante himself.

Apt, too, is the bronze equestrian statue that the Duke commissions:

> "John of Douay shall effect my plan,
> Set me on horseback here aloft,
> Alive, as the crafty sculptor can,
>
> "In the very square I have crossed so oft:
> That men may admire, when future suns
> Shall touch the eyes to a purpose soft,
>
> "While the mouth and the brow stay brave in bronze—
> Admire and say, 'When he was alive
> How he would take his pleasure once!'" (202-10)

The reality is far different from what the Duke sentimentally imagines. It is in fact he and his might-have-been mistress whose eyes, from sun to sun, have been "touched to a purpose soft." In the poem's much-debated postscript, the "sin" that the poet "imputes to each frustrate ghost" is not the viciousness of "the end

in sight," adultery. Instead, fittingly, it is "the unlit lamp": the inadequacy of
their seeing itself. The crepuscular light of the fading Florentine Renaissance
dims the pair's vision, leading them to eke out pretend-lives by fixing their eyes
on mere picture-book images:

> Only they see not God, I know,
> Nor all that chivalry of his,
> The soldier-saints who, row on row,
>
> Burn upward each to his point of bliss—
> Since, the end of life being manifest,
> He had burned his way thro' the world to this.   (220-5)

It is the golden in heart, like that chivalrous soldier-saint, Luria, who see God.
As elsewhere in Browning, only those who pursue ardently the things of this
world have a hope of transcending it; the others, so to speak, "miss fire." Those
who, like the Duke and his lady, allow contemplation and artifice to replace
experience may have their effigies admired, but they themselves are doomed to
lie inanely through the centuries in their separate Florentine tombs. The "palace
the world knows well" turns out to be the palace, not of art but of death. Life,
above all life in Florence, means risk.

> I could have painted pictures like that youth's
> Ye praise so. How my soul springs up! No bar
> Stayed me—ah, thought which saddens while it soothes!
> —Never did fate forbid me, star by star,
> To outburst on your night with all my gift
> Of fires from God . . . .   (lines 1-6)

"Pictor Ignotus" (1845, *The Poems* Vol. 1), the earliest of Browning's three
Florentine painter monologues, comments ironically on risk-taking and
achievement.   The unknown painter begins by dreaming of a personal
renaissance. His "soul springs up" at the thought that he might have "outburst"
on his fellow townsmen's night with his "gift / Of fires from God," a sunrise that
could have transformed his life.   But he has refused the vitalizing leap, and the
ensuing monologue amounts to an *apologia pro morte sua.*
       Unlike the Florence of *Luria*, the city that surrounds Pictor is not altogether
gripped by paralysis; Raphael—"that youth ye praise so"—is, after all,
flourishing there. Pictor's retreat into artistic uniformity, though it has the
institutional blessing of the Church, is thus an individual choice, the consequence
of his suppression of the fire within. As one critic tersely puts it, "In fearing the
unknown he has ironically predetermined that he become the unknown" (Slinn
45). Like the obsessively gazing lovers of "The Statue and the Bust," the painter

is afflicted by a life-narrowing type of tunnel vision. He might have turned his gaze in a number of directions,

> . . . with eyes uplift
> And wide to heaven, or, straight like thunder, sunk
> To the centre, of an instant; or around
> Turned calmly and inquisitive, to scan
> The license and the limit, space and bound,
> Allowed to truth made visible in man. (7-12)

He has been free, that is, either to reproduce and share his personal vision of transcendent truth or to emulate the early masters who achieved growth through the inwardness of self-acquaintance or to record scrupulously the Florence visible around him, counting it crime, like Fra Lippo Lippi, to let a truth slip. Instead, he has accustomed his fearful eyes to "the sanctuary's gloom," filling the walls of "endless cloisters and eternal aisles" with dreary rows of holy stereotypes. As justly as the Duke and the lady in "The Statue and the Bust," he can be charged with the sin of "the unlit lamp."

Faced with a Florentine choice between a kinetic and a static view of art, the painter has yearned for the first but clung to the second. He has dreamed

> Of going—I, in each new picture,—forth,
> As, making new hearts beat and bosoms swell,
> To Pope or Kaiser, East, West, South, or North,
> Bound for the calmly-satisfied great State,
> Or glad aspiring little burgh, it went,
> Flowers cast upon the car which bore the freight,
> Through old streets named afresh from the event. (26-32)

Such works "go" far beyond the walls of Florence itself; they reach the greater, circumambient world and modify it. They transform feelings—hearts beat and bosoms swell—and even geography; streets are renamed. In the process, they enlarge the ego of the artist himself, who is inseparably "linked" with them. In place of this expansive but risky option, Pictor has chosen to assume a posture of resigned detachment from his unadventurous frescoes:

> Only prayer breaks the silence of the shrine
> While, blackening in the daily candle-smoke,
> They moulder on the damp wall's travertine,
> 'Mid echoes the light footstep never woke.
> So, die my pictures! surely, gently die! (65-69)

Such work "goes" nowhere and modifies nothing. Unlike the ghosts of the ancient masters Browning evokes in "Old Pictures in Florence," its creator cannot be fancied hovering protectively near his flaking painted surfaces. A true poet of his Romantic century, Browning always identifies artistic greatness with assertive individualism. For him, to embrace cloistered anonymity is to betray the finest spirit of a city whose name "the world knows well."

That spirit at last springs to vibrant life in "Fra Lippo Lippi" (1855, *The Poems* Vol. 1). Here again, Browning's protagonist is beset by the tension between the two major Florentine opposites: stasis and motion. Where the unknown painter is a pathetic victim, however, Lippi is a seriocomic hero. The religious establishment naggingly tries to impose on Lippi a static, hieratic conception of art and its aims, leaving the painter to murmur, like a later harassed Florentine genius, Galileo, "*Eppur si muove!*" Unlike the stationary, shut-in Pictor Ignotus, Lippi is himself a monk in motion. The picaresque misadventure that occasions his speech—his *arrest* in full career by the city guard—amusingly epitomizes his larger problem: his entire life, both artistic and personal, has been a series of halted dashes out of the "bounds" set by the powers that order his Florentine world. The very subject from which he is now playing truant, Saint Jerome "knocking at his poor old breast / With his great round stone to subdue the flesh" (lines 73-74), comments mockingly on the constraint under which he is doomed to labor: the command to conquer the wanton impulses he harbors in his own unmonkish breast.

By contrast with the unknown painter, Lippi is anything but "ignotus"; he can rely even on the leader of the guard to nod at his name. He is not one to rest content with confinement to the treadmill of piety. Exasperated at being "shut within my mew, / A-painting for the great man, saints and saints / And saints again" (47-49), he risks his neck to savor the freedom and diversity of the Florence streets. Such an "outbursting on the night" makes him a prime mover of the Florentine Renaissance on the verge of flowering. The season in which his discourse is set—"Here's spring come, and the nights one makes up bands / To roam the town and sing out carnival" (45-46)—recalls "the season of Art's spring-birth so dim and dewy" that Browning celebrates in "Old Pictures in Florence." Time of day is as seasonable as time of year; while Lippi speaks, the "small hours" of the night inch forward toward the great Florentine hour of sunrise.

If Pictor Ignotus is a quietistic speaker, Lippi is from the start an explosive one. There could be no more apt exemplar of the most verbal of cities. His discourse begins with a minor explosion—"I am poor brother Lippo, by your leave! / You need not clap your torches to my face. / Zooks, what's to blame? you think you see a monk!" (1-3)—and builds to a major one: "Hang the fools!" (335) Throughout, his stream of language follows an impetuous course, interspersing rapid consecutive expositions with abrupt questions, expostulations, asides, and scraps of Florentine *stornelli*, swerving from the truculent to the companionable, from the earnest to the sarcastic, from the heatedly outraged to the stoically resigned. The sense of movement is unremitting. Lippi's agility in climbing down "all the bed-furniture" to chase "sportive ladies" is but the more coarsely erotic side of the kinetic energy that thrusts him ever forward in his art. If the bronze Medici Duke's eternal riding of a motionless bronze horse exemplifies one pole of the Florentine spectrum of mobility, Lippi's hot pursuit of "the skipping of rabbits by moon-light" (59) represents the other.

Lippi the forward-moving is also Lippi the forward-looking. "But see, now—why, I see as certainly / As that the morning-star's about to shine, / What will hap some day" (271-3). Lippi plumes himself on his gift of foreseeing a new birth of artistic glory in his painter's crystal ball. His penetration into the future depends on his bent for taking long views back to ultimate origins: "For me, I think I speak as I was taught; / I always see the garden and God there / A-making man's wife" (265-7). Above all, however, his wide-open eye focuses indefatigably on the present. To the task of deflowering "*le vierge, le vivace et le bel aujourd' hui*" he brings a matchless visual gusto. Latin, a hallowed tongue for Florentine humanists, signifies for him the mere sour aftertaste of his early Carmelite training: "Lord, they'd have taught me Latin in pure waste!" (109). Master as he is of living languages, both visual and verbal, he takes no stock in dead ones. While such a dismissive attitude may seem to place him as a philistine at odds with the intellectual vanguard of his own city, for him the "rebirth of learning" must remain a stillbirth until he can connect it with the quick of immediate experience. Even as a Florentine street urchin, he is driven by such an impulse to flesh out the skeletal abstractions his masters make him con, transmuting colorless signs into miniatures of the visible world's opulence:

> I drew men's faces on my copy-books,
> Scrawled them within the antiphonary's marge,
> Joined legs and arms to the long music-notes,
> Found eyes and nose and chin for A's and B's,
> And made a string of pictures of the world
> Betwixt the ins and outs of verb and noun. (129-34)

Lippi can be excused for scorning Latin; his incorrigibly concrete personal idiom belongs as thoroughly to the Florentine vernacular as the untutored Giotto's great campanile.

Like his fellow townsman's great tower, however, Lippi's own aspirations are doomed to remain disappointingly incomplete. For all his agility in clambering down (and into) bedsheets, Lippi never gains entire release from the imprisoning "mew" of the past. His genius, bold as it is, suffers from its subjection to the thrall of precedent. So often have his precursors been held up to him as models that he has internalized, to paralyzing effect, the admonitions he has received: "And yet the old schooling sticks, the old grave eyes / Are peeping o'er my shoulder as I work, / The heads shake still—"'It's art's decline, my son! / You're not of the true painters, great and old'" (231-4).

A consummate Florentine ironist, Lippi suffers the humiliation of being himself the constant butt of ironies. Vaunting himself as the spearhead of the new, he must perpetually fight a tiresome rearguard action against the clutch of the old. His fellow Florentines, "taught what to see and not to see," are barred by stolid orthodoxy from giving his work an unblinkered viewing. The good people of neighboring Prato are transported by misplaced sacred enthusiasm:

> I painted a Saint Laurence six months since
> At Prato, splashed the fresco in fine style:
> "How looks my painting, now the scaffold's down?"
> I ask a brother: "Hugely," he returns—
> "Already not one phiz of your three slaves
> Who turn the Deacon off his toasted side,
> But's scratched and prodded to our heart's content." (323-9)

The pious, in an insensate rage, apply to Lippi's masterwork savage hands instead of understanding eyes; the Church, meanwhile, looks on smugly, "'For pity and religion grow i' the crowd— / Your painting serves its purpose!'" (334-5). Not surprisingly, this vandalising notion of art's "purpose" drives even the street-smart Lippi to an outburst ("'Hang the fools!'"[335]) that perilously forgets his auditors' official commission.

"'Make them forget there's such a thing as flesh,'" the Prior exhorts Lippi (182). Such instructions might have encouraged the painters of Giotto's generation, for whom (as Browning observes in "Old Pictures") it was still a pioneering achievement to "[m]ake new hopes shine through the flesh they fray"; but they do not encourage Lippi. In admonishing the young Lippi to "stop" with Giotto—"'Here's Giotto, with his Saint a-praising God, / That sets us praising, why not stop with him?'"(334-5)—the Prior is merely acting as another captain of the Florence local guard. He is proposing to "arrest" that very march of art's development that Giotto, in his time, had thrust forward. Lippi's own sense of the Florentine "movement" to which he belongs is boldly evolutionary rather than conventional and static. His endeavor to mimic on panel or masonry the fluid, kaleidoscopic dance of visible forms qualifies him as a true Renaissance futurist.

The poem that Browning himself has produced compellingly mirrors, in its form, its subject's Florentine sensibility. One's discovery of Lippi's personality comes as an evolutionary unfolding, a continuous series of "changes" and "surprises." As David Shaw observes, "His dialectical advance beyond the 'beast' and 'flesh' that he celebrates at the beginning is reenacted in the very structure of his monologue" (156). Only at the end does the apparently simple-hearted, blustering, companionable, lecherous, impudent scapegrace-friar of the opening stand painted in his full colors. He is not only an acute observer of surfaces but also a discerning moral seer, not only the performer of carnal peccadillos but the victim of a harsh conflict with the prohibitions of his time and town, beset by a rage that he can but imperfectly repress.

Lippi has always trained an avid eye on the degrading sordidness of the life around him, as well as on its beauty; while still a novice, he has observed

> [t]he breathless fellow at the altar-foot,
> Fresh from his murder, safe and sitting there
> With the little children round him in a row
> Of admiration, half for his beard and half
> For that white anger of his victim's son
> Shaking a fist at him with one fierce arm,
> Signing himself with the other because of Christ
> (Whose sad face on the cross sees only this
> After the passion of a thousand years). (149-57)

In Lippi's contradictory Florence, profane violence lurks amid the most sacred places; while the right hand traces the rote gestures of pious submission, the left quiveringly betrays the pressure of unChristian fury. The spectacle travesties Christ's admonition, "But when thou doest alms, let not thy left hand know what thy right hand doeth" (Matthew 6:3); and Lippi's vision here coincides with that of Christ, the crucified captive audience of man's unceasing show of unkindness toward his neighbor.

The painter's vision is nowhere more pungently captured than in the tableau with which he concludes his monologue. According to David DeLaura, "Modern editors correctly assume that the rollicking scene at the end is meant for Lippo's *Incoronazione di Maria. . .* , but this solemn, almost static painting . . . is quite different from what Browning suggests" (381). The claimed discrepancy indeed exists; but it does not, as DeLaura argues in his well-known article, betray Browning's inaccuracy in treating Florentine art—instead, it is of a piece with his entire portrait of the artist. Nothing could be more typical than the gusto with which this speaker transforms a "still" painting, "unfreezing" the frame to turn the scene into a humorous synopsis of his own life predicament. Lippi himself bursts "[o]ut of a corner when you least expect" (361) into the "bowery flowery" paradise of his imagined panel.

It is the crowning misstep of "a poor monk out of bounds"; the Christian heaven, the upper sanctum of the Florentine establishment, is flagrantly off-limits for a creative reprobate. Once again he is "arrested," literally stopped in his tracks, at a loss to justify his presence: "Mazed, motionless and moonstruck —I'm the man!". (364) Even in his own fancied painting he is plagued by his lifelong Florentine nightmare: being immobilized in the midst of movement.

The poem's concluding lines, which shift the scene back from the celestial heights to the streets of Florence, allow Lippi a release from embarrassment and from stasis: "The street's hushed, and I know my own way back, / Don't fear me! There's the gray beginning. Zooks!" (391-2). It is altogether appropriate that Lippi's nocturnal discourse should end with a beginning. While light begins to encroach on darkness, Lippi goes scuttling off once more to safety. As always, he must pick his way gingerly between two Florences: the static Florence of the Prior's medieval past and the dynamic, dawning Florence of his own choice. His final word is a hearteningly explosive verbal outburst.

In "Fra Lippo Lippi," Browning allows his protagonist to burst the bounds of the sterile and precedent-choked Florence he had evoked in *Luria*. In "Andrea del Sarto" (1855, *The Poems* Vol. 1) the city's influence becomes once again life defeating, but that negative image is now placed within a richly complex ironic perspective. The Florences of the two monologues act as foils to each other, as do the two protagonists. Where Lippi is explosive, Andrea del Sarto is implosive. If Lippi draws the first lusty breath of the Renaissance, Andrea utters its expiring sigh; if the Florence of the one is a universe on the verge of a mighty expansion, that of the other has begun wearily to shrivel. Like his fellow Florentine, Andrea is incorrigibly verbal. But the two protagonists' speeches obey different clocks; while Lippi talks through the Florentine night and finishes with the auspicious first glimmer of dawn, Andrea haunts a silvery twilight zone, a "gray remainder of the evening" that shades imperceptibly into dusk.

Although the breathless Lippi proposes to the guard-captain to "sit hip to haunch," his characteristic mode is motion. Andrea, by contrast, is sedentary. He begins by cajoling his wife Lucrezia to be seated—"Sit down and all shall happen as you wish" (3)—and not long after pleads with her to "let me sit / Here by the window with your hand in mine / And look a half-hour forth on Fiesole" (13-15). The "faultless painter's" gloomy verdict on what he has accomplished, as compared with his less skilled rivals, is simply, "My works are nearer heaven, but I sit here" (87). Near the end of his speech he is still coaxing Lucrezia: "Only let me sit / The gray remainder of the evening out, / Idle, you call it, and muse perfectly / How I could paint were I but back in France" (226-9). Sitting and musing are the anodynes Andrea substitutes for moving and doing. The action of "Andrea del Sarto," as Roma King points out, "moves from present to past, from past to present, and, finally, to an imaginary future in the New Jerusalem" (11). The past, however, is the time with which the painter is most potently engaged. Such an orientation cleanly reverses Lippi's impatient auguries of future glory, just as Andrea's dejected acceptance of the role of has-been reverses Lippi's zest for the yet-to-be.

True, Andrea has his own way of talking about "tomorrow":

Oh, I'll content him,—but to-morrow, Love! (10)

I might get up to-morrow to my work

> Cheerful and fresh as ever . . . .
> To-morrow, how you shall be glad for this! (18-20)

Tomorrow and tomorrow creeps in a petty pace for Andrea, without ever getting him a step forward. His work, unlike that of the Florentine "primitives" Browning celebrates in "Old Pictures in Florence," hardly "seethes with the morrow"; it is rather a throwback to the stony perfection of ancient sculpture ("They are perfect — how else? they shall never change" ["Old Pictures" 123]) or to the monotony of the endless aisles of Pictor Ignotus. As for the prospect of any creative change in Andrea's life or art, never shall sun that morrow see. All the painter's talk about "to-morrow" boils down to a procrastinating evasion of today; while the place where his mind prefers to dwell is yesterday.

> I am grown peaceful as old age to-night.
> I regret little, I would change still less.
> Since there my past life lies, why alter it? (244-6)

A disabling trait of Andrea's is his insistence on taking an "artistic" view of his own past life, on seeing it as a judiciously ordered "composition" that any added brush stroke might spoil: "Eh? the whole seems to fall into a shape / As if I saw alike my work and self / And all that I was born to be and do, / A twilight-piece" (46-49). As one critic notes, "The object of Andrea's detached, aesthetic contemplation . . . is his own life . . . , a masterpiece of willed defeat" (Tucker 194). A true child of his latter-day aestheticist Florence, Andrea will go to any lengths to find harmonious proportions in the glacier of the past—"All that's behind us"—which looms chillingly over him. The act of admiring his own sad life-history from an aesthetic arm's-length remove has become for him an automatic defence against regret.

By summoning up a spurious calm, Andrea bolsters the remnants of his self-esteem against his knowledge of his fellow artists' more passionate sensitivity. "I, painting from myself and to myself, / Know what I do, am unmoved by men's blame / Or their praise either," he meditates (90-92), and he goes on complacently to identify his own "unmovedness" with Monte Morello, a mountain visible from Florence. His readiness to project himself into a motionless feature of the Tuscan horizon betrays his fatal abstraction from the bustling Florence streets, where the companionable Lippi is cheerfully at home.

Andrea's essential condition is indeed homelessness, a fact underscored by the disarray of his home life. His "moon," Lucrezia, far from orbiting as she presumably should Andrea's settled, mountainlike massiveness, simply adds her giddiness to his petrifaction: "My face, my moon, my everybody's moon, / Which everybody looks on and calls his, / And, I suppose, is looked on by in turn, / While she looks—no one's" (29-32). Such "looking," by contrast to the eager reverent attentiveness espoused by Lippi, reduces itself to mere "turns" in a frivolous parlor game. The artist's fond whim of standing hand-in-hand with Lucrezia while they look "a half-hour forth on Fiesole, / Both of one mind, as married people use" (15-16), is ironically self-deluding. Lucrezia, by Andrea's own testimony, has no mind with which to look, an especially damning flaw in the wife of a Florentine master.

In one respect, however, husband and wife are indeed "both of one mind"; Lucrezia's sense of time seems as stunted as Andrea's. Her gaze forward into the future appears to stop short at her imminent rendezvous with her lover. Lucrezia might fittingly be called, to adapt Henry James's title, a "Madonna of the Past." Her influence has helped to keep her husband's ensnared eyes turned backward; she has certainly failed to instill in him visions of a more glorious, less materialistic future:

> Had the mouth there urged
> "God and the glory! never care for gain.
> The present by the future, what is that?
> Live for fame, side by side with Agnolo!
> Rafael is waiting: up to God, all three!"
> I might have done it for you. So it seems:
> Perhaps not. (127-33)

Such dreaming of might-have-beens is especially futile, not only because it disregards Lucrezia's all-too-glaring limitations— she barely recognizes the name of Michelangelo—but also because her beauty itself simply mirrors Andrea's own hollowness. As Park Honan says, she is "one of his paintings, come to life" (157). By extension, she is also her city come to life, or to half-life; in this latter-day Florence, beauty persists, but the vital creative impulse of a Lippi has faded to listlessness.

"Do you feel thankful, ay or no," Lippi asks rhetorically, "For this fair town's face, yonder river's line, / The mountain round it and the sky above, / Much more the figures of man, woman, child, / These are the frame to?" (286-90). Where Lippi could descant compellingly about his city and its people as a work of art, complete with "frame," by Andrea's time Florence itself has begun to harden into an unliving artifact. His "frames" enclose only vacuity—the specious union of his and his wife's figures in the window, his offer to "frame" her face in the fool's gold of her hair (175). The only glimpse he obtains of a possible "renaissance" in his own career comes not in Florence but in another country:

> That Francis, that first time,
> And that long festal year at Fontainebleau!
> I surely then could sometimes leave the ground,
> Put on the glory, Rafael's daily wear,
> In that humane great monarch's golden look. (149-53)

But Andrea's "golden age," of course, does not last. As he himself admits, "[I]ncentives come from the soul's self; / The rest avail not" (134-5). Something more than the external stimulus of Francis's "golden look" and "the jingle of his gold chain" is needed to keep Andrea aloft in artistic realms of gold.

As is his habit, Andrea locks the memory of unfulfilled possibilities within the strongbox of ancient history: "'Tis done and past" (167). His sometime glimpses of golden achievement fade, leaving him only with the bleary glow of ill-gotten ingots, the cruelly exact image of his failure:

> King Francis may forgive me: oft at nights
> When I look up from painting, eyes tired out,
> The walls become illumined, brick from brick
> Distinct, instead of mortar, fierce bright gold,
> That gold of his I did cement them with! (214-8)

He concludes by looking wanly back to a vanished foreign yesterday—"How I could paint, were I but back in France" (229)—and ahead to a mortifying Florentine tomorrow: "To-morrow, satisfy your friend" (234).

In the end, Andrea turns to survey yet again the waste land of his past, then escapes to a final dream of a less sullied future. His verdict on the past has a strong flavor of inauthenticity:

> Since there my past life lies, why alter it? (246)
>
>   ... Yes,
> You loved me quite enough, it seems tonight. (257-8)

Seldom has so much thinly veiled bitterness infused one simple past tense. Indeed, the painter's Florence itself, like Aurora Leigh's, will not "mix its tenses." He remains a prisoner of the bygone, but without Aurora's prospect of release. All that remains to Andrea is to imagine a substitute city—one that might lend itself more readily to self-fulfillment. Yet even the heavenly New Jerusalem, like the earthly Florence, defeats his dreams of a redemptive competition:

>   What would one have?
> In heaven, perhaps, new chances, one more chance—
> Four great walls in the New Jerusalem,
> Meted on each side by the angel's reed,
> For Leonard, Rafael, Agnolo and me
> To cover—the three first without a wife,
> While I have mine! So—still they overcome
> Because there's still Lucrezia,—as I choose. (259-66)

On the surface, Andrea's imagined "festal year" in heaven resembles the painterly extravaganza that concludes Lippi's monologue. In fact, however, the two fantasies could not be more revealingly unlike. Where Lippi's, despite his farcical embarrassment, is an expansive act of self-assertion, Andrea's is an escape mechanism that cannot "leave the ground." In the fabled "City of Gold" Andrea's destiny remains what it has been in the great Italian City of Art: dross. Unwilling or unable to embark on the task of renovating his own nature, he settles for a life history of sterile repetition and a destiny of stifling closure. The "choice" he claims to have made is a chimaera that allows him to accept paralyzing fetters as God's fiat: "So free we seem, so fettered fast we are! / I feel he laid the fetter: let it lie!" (51-52). The sputtering alliteration betrays the self-deceiving, self-defeating glibness of the sentiment.

Lippi, scuttling off into the Florentine dawn, though headed back to confinement remains still on the loose; Andrea, issuing his final imperative—"Go, my Love"—only caps the self-portrait of his bondage. The impression of Florentine paralysis earlier projected in *Luria* thus persists in "Andrea del Sarto"; but here it is keyed to one specific historical phase of the city's evolution. As "Fra Lippo Lippi" vividly testifies, between inert strata of development the Florentine Renaissance gorgeously explodes. Robert Browning's great admirer, George Eliot, was to examine the complex nature of that explosion in the most strenuously historical of her novels.

4

A Blind Worship of Clashing Deities: Romola Agonistes

"It is indubitably the work of a very gifted mind, but of a mind misusing itself" (63). F. R. Leavis's well-known verdict sums up the modern consensus on George Eliot's Florentine novel. By applying to *Romola* evaluative criteria appropriate to her more celebrated studies of English provincial life, such as *The Mill on the Floss* (1860) or *Middlemarch* (1871-72), critical opinion has scanted Eliot's achievement in creating a far different fictional milieu, one that is temporally and geographically remote. Eliot's use of Florence as a setting has, indeed, itself been a target for criticism. According to K. M. Newton, "[T]he Florentine dimension fails to come to life" (14), while for Avrom Fleishman "[t]here is nothing in the main movement of the plot . . . that could not be situated in another time and place" (159-60). One welcomes Lawrence Poston's wry witticism: "On the assumption that [Eliot's] choice of setting was quite purposeful, I shall offer . . . the admittedly unorthodox suggestion that *Romola* is a novel in which the Italian Renaissance has some intrinsic importance" (356).

Only lately, indeed, have critics become willing to defy orthodox wisdom on the subject. Felicia Bonaparte, in her study *The Triptych and the Cross* (1979), has argued that the Florentine locale represents "that still point in Western history around which the millennia turned": "It was in the Renaissance that the two cultures that shaped Western civilization collided, and they collided most fruitfully in Florence" (28). Bonaparte's analysis dispels any idea that Eliot's choice of locale was capricious. She shows how the clashing elements of Florentine life provide a tension that animates Eliot's presentment of characters and scenes. Eliot's earlier novels had given abundant play to the struggle of irreconcilable opposites, but in *Romola* personal antagonisms are transfigured by the unique historical stage on which they are enacted.

Like Browning's, Eliot's imagination thrived on antithesis, and it was therefore similarly attuned to the turbulence of Florentine history. In *Romola*, antithesis appears, above all, in a thematic opposition that gives the whole narrative its structure: "the fundamental conflict," as Sally Shuttleworth puts it, "between hebraism and hellenism" (98). The setting provides an ideal ground for Eliot to develop in narrative form the sort of dialectic that Matthew Arnold was soon to make current in *Culture and Anarchy* (1869). Bonaparte notes that Florentine topography itself becomes, in Eliot's hands, a map of the fierce intellectual and ethical conflict that tormented the capital of the Renaissance. The shop of the Hellenistic barber, Nello, and the Cathedral, closely associated with the Hebraist Savonarola, "face one another as though on opposite sides of the line of battle" (132). But local topography can embody, as well, the will to harmonise dialectical opposites. Eliot identified this reconciling tendency chiefly with Giotto's great bell-tower, spotlighted early in *Romola*: "[A]s the campanile in all its harmonious variety of colour and form led the eyes upward, high into the clear air of the April morning, it seemed a prophetic symbol, telling that human life must somehow and some time shape itself into accord with that pure aspiring beauty" (76).

Other objects on the Florence horizon share this skyward impetus. The eyes of the ancient revenant conjured up in the Proem

are drawn irresistibly to the unique tower springing, like a tall flower-stem drawn towards the sun, from the square turreted mass of the Old Palace in the very heart of the city—the tower that looks none the worse for the four centuries that have passed since he used to walk under it. The great dome, too, greatest in the world, which, in his early boyhood, had been only a daring thought in the mind of a small, quick-eyed man—there it raises its large curves still, eclipsing the hills. (45)

The Florence thus evoked through its monuments is a place where human enterprise and ingenuity can mimic nature's most delicate forms and "eclipse" her mightiest masses. It is a place where culture—"the study of perfection," as Arnold would define it—has been encoded in the very skyline.

Within an ambiance so vexed by the clashes between contrary forces, truth becomes, in Nello's words, "a riddle for eyes and wit to discover" (82). Throughout Eliot's novel, eyes and wits are closely linked, as they are for Browning's vigilant Fra Lippo. Her evocation of setting, by appealing insistently to the reader's visual sense, makes constant demands on his or her powers of intellectual discernment.

For the Lippi-like Piero di Cosimo, "'the only passionate life is in form and colour'" (137). In *Romola*, the interplay of light and shadow consistently reflects the passionate life inherent in human speaking and doing. Patterns of light counterpointed against shadow continually recur, until the unruly city becomes one vast emblem of life's checkered but enduring order. "Only look at the sunlight and shadows on the grand walls that were built solidly, and have endured in their grandeur," the narrator urges in the Proem,

look at the faces of the little children, making another sunlight amid the shadows of age; look, if you will, into the churches, and hear the same chants, see the same images as of old—the images of willing anguish for a great end, of beneficent love and ascending glory; see upturned living faces, and lips moving to the old prayers for help. These things have not changed. The sunlight and shadows bring their old beauty and waken the old heart-strains at morning, noon, and even-tide. (50)

What Eliot's Florence stands for is, above all, the City of Man as transmitter of humane values from generation to generation, a hallowed "old bridge" between past and future. For all its cruelty and disarray, the town holds within its walls the promise of a slow but steady Comtean advance from barbarism to civility. It displays "a mixed condition of things which is the sign, not of hopeless confusion, but of struggling order" (560). The constancy of its essential character points, like its enduring skyline, not to lifeless stasis but to growth-nurturing stability.

Yet despite that stability Eliot's city, like her human agents, remains radically imperfect. The *dramatis personae* of *Romola* are a kaleidoscopic mixture of lights and shadows, an aggregation of fragments in search of some healing force of cohesion. The city itself becomes, therefore, a leading definer of character in the novel; the life of each individual actor attains to moral meaning only in relation to the unique historic collectivity within which he or she moves.

Amid the *chiaroscuro* of Florence, good eyesight becomes a *sine qua non*. Romola's father, Bardo, is, as he laments, "'totally blind: a calamity to which we Florentines are held especially liable'" (106). Such an affliction is especially ironic because Bardo, as an apostle of Florentine illuminism, abhors the "dim mysticism" that his son Dino has embraced, abandoning "the clear lights of reason and philosophy" (180). "One of the few frank pagans of his time" (209), Bardo has evinced a candor of belief, matched with a consistency of behavior, that should entitle him to a place in the vanguard of his city's intellectuals. And yet, as his friend Bernardo del Nero sadly admits, this Renaissance luminary has paradoxically chosen to "'hang over the books and live with shadows all his life'" (347). What Poston calls "Florence's blindness to her own interests" (359) is manifested symbolically in Bardo. His fixation upon antiquity has blocked him off from the wholesome daylight of present reality, just as his physical blindness shuts him away from the dearest of his human ties. "'Our old Bardo de' Bardi,'" as Nello says, "'is so blind that he can see no more of his daughter than . . . a glimmer of something bright when she comes near him'" (85).

If Bardo's antiquarianism puts him in harmony with the best Florentine minds of his time, it also condemns him to live in a fragment-strewn past that his blindness places at a double remove; he "sat among his books and his marble fragments of the past, and saw them only by the light of those far-off younger days which still shone in his memory" (92). The old scholar does possess a certain Renaissance grandeur in his allegiance to ideals that allow him to scorn the physical handicap of his blindness. "'[W]hat is that grosser, narrower light,'" he asks, "'by which men behold merely the petty scene around them, compared with that far-stretching, lasting light which spreads over centuries of thought . . . and makes clear to us the minds of the immortals who have reaped the great harvest and left us to glean in their furrows?'" (96). Yet such a lofty perspective involves a deadly entrapment by stasis. It provides scant nourishment for the burgeoning vitality of a daughter of Florence such as Romola, who is compelled to look "with a sad dreariness in her young face at the lifeless objects around her—the parchment backs, the unchanging mutilated marble, the bits of obsolete bronze and clay" (98). As Eliot says in an essay, "Nothing is more pitiable than that want of noble self-reliance in a people which neglects the treasures of their own hearts and minds, in order to recur to a lifeless imitation of extinct form and spirit, and calling incessantly on the heroic Past, is obstinately blind to the heroic Present" (*Notebook* 239). Noble though he is, Bardo, undervaluing his own time, his own city, and his own daughter, stands convicted of neglecting the treasure of his own heart and mind.

Bardo's repudiation of his son, Dino, involves a disavowal of Christian beliefs that, despite Bardo's contempt for them, are inextricably interwoven with the fabric of his native city. In a review, Eliot refers to "the spiritualism of the fourteenth century" according to which "the body was but the transient and unworthy dwelling of the immortal soul" (*Notebook* 281). With Dino de' Bardi, this *trecento* asceticism persists into the century following. Dino's contempt for the immediate, sensible world of his day matches his father's, but it reflects the dim radiance of the Life to Come, rather than the last glimmer of a life that has fled. His eyes, in contrast to those of the blind Bardo, see far into the distance, but the result is curiously similar: a failure to perceive distinctly the form of the person closest to him. "He looked at the little sister returned to him in her full womanly beauty, with the far-off gaze of a revisiting spirit" (210). Shunning, like his estranged father, "that grosser, narrower light in which men behold merely the petty scene around them," Dino, too, becomes the inmate of a Florentine Hades, "the shadowy region," as Eliot calls it, "where human souls seek wisdom apart from the human sympathies which are the very life and substance of our wisdom" (218).

The native father and son, then, embody opposite yet equally reclusive extremes of Florentine character. By contrast, the Greco-Italian newcomer, Tito Melema, would seem to possess the traits—good humor, sociability, quick-wittedness, a winning appearance—likely to suit him for survival amid the actual, hectic currents of life in late fifteenth-century Florence. The narrative, however, defeats this expectation. The organism of Florence, after an initial acceptance, rejects the Hellenic transplant. Here, the city's refusal to assimilate an exotic alien does not, as it does in Browning's *Luria*, betoken an underlying malaise. On the contrary, it is a symptom of vigor.

Until near the end of his sojourn in Florence, Tito's prospects appear excellent. In this novel, eyesight serves as a gauge of character, and Tito possesses a pair of eyes exempt from the distortions of sight that confine Bardo and Dino to the dim fringes of Florentine affairs. "The slow absent glance he cast around at the upper windows of the house had neither more dissimulation in it, nor more ingenuousness, than belongs to a youthful well-opened eyelid with its unwearied breadth of gaze; to perfectly pellucid lenses . . . " (153). The "perfectly pellucid lenses," Bardo is relieved to find, free Tito from any taint of Dino's mysticism ("'You see no visions, I trust, my young friend?'" [119]). Yet Tito, though a scholar, is no mere slave of antiquity like Bardo himself. It is not on the past that Tito's eyes focus but on the here and now and on the foreseeable future. Tito's pragmatic turn of mind leads a son of Florence like Lorenzo Tornabuoni to envision golden honors lying on the young stranger's path: "'[Y]ou have only to play your game well, Melema, and the future belongs to you. . . . There's a cardinal's hat at the end of that road, and you would not be the first Greek who has worn that ornament'" (418).

The young Greek is admirably equipped to play the game that will decide the ownership of the future. His artistic taste, as befits the prospective wearer of a Renaissance cardinal's hat, is up-to-date. He shrinks fastidiously from the "'Christian barbarism'" (77) of the Duomo's architecture. He gazes up that grand Florentine emblem of aspiration, Giotto's campanile, with "a slight touch of scorn on his lip, and when his eyes fell again they glanced round with a scanning coolness" (76). On the other hand, his blithe spirit of Greek rationalism allies him with the most eminent Florentine Hellenists. "'You are of the same mind as Michele Marullo,'" Nello tells him, "'ay, and as Angelo Poliziano himself, in spite of his canonicate, when he relaxes himself a little in my shop after his lectures, and talks of the gods awaking from their long sleep and making the woods and streams vital once more'" (77-78). Such crypto-pantheist heresies find a hospitable soil in Tito's mind, if only because they fit in handily with his self-serving hedonist agenda.

As Bonaparte demonstrates, Tito's hedonism associates him with the Bacchic abandon of Lorenzo the Magnificent's carnival song and the chorus from Poliziano's *Orfeo* and, still more insistently, with the god of sunlight and song, Apollo. No Florentine shadow-dweller like Bardo or Dino, he is regularly pictured as both absorbing and emitting rays of light. Two months after his arrival in Florence, he sits watching the procession of San Giovanni characteristically "bright, in the midst of brightness" (134). Since his first appearance in the city, he has acquired "that added radiance of good fortune, which is like the just perceptible perfecting of a flower after it has drunk a morning's sun-beams" (135). Yet Tito, who is at first identified (by Bratti) with "Messer San Michele" (54) and (by Nello) with "the Angel Gabriel" (76), comes eventually to resemble more closely another, tarnished angel whose name in fact signifies "light-bearer." Nello's remark to the newly arrived young man that his faded garments give him "the air of a fallen prince" (81) has sinister overtones that escape the worthy barber. For the rationalist temper that Tito brings with him into the receptive city constitutes not a perfection of mind but a perversion of it. The newcomer's mentality easily accommodates accepted Florentine notions of what the well-polished ego will wear; Tornabuoni assures Tito that he, like Tornabuoni himself, possesses "'that power of concealment and finesse, without which a rational cultivated man, instead of having any prerogative, is really at a disadvantage compared with a wild bull or a savage'" (417). But Eliot's own conception of the rational cultivated man extends beyond that of a Tornabuoni, whose finesse does not keep him from dying the victim of a savage Florentine imbroglio.

In common with most of the Florentine intelligentsia, Tito is all too ready to equate philosophy with peering expediency. To Romola's indignation over his sale of her late father's precious library, he replies coolly, "'It is useless . . . to answer the words of madness, Romola. Your peculiar feeling about your father has made you mad at this moment. Any rational person looking at the case from a due distance will see that I have taken the wisest course'" (357). To Tito, personal feeling is merely steam clouding the lenses of cool perception. At the great crux of his life, he disclaims guilt and involvement by turning the knife-edge of "rationality" against his father, Baldassarre. "'This is another escaped prisoner,' said Lorenzo Tornabuoni. 'Who is he, I wonder?' '*Some madman, surely,*' said Tito" (283). Baldassarre's "peculiar feeling" for his son, like Romola's for her father, becomes in Tito's troubled eyes the touchstone of insanity.

The cutting blade of Tito's reason makes it a potent tool in dealing with the tangle of Florentine affairs, but it severs the ties between him and those who should be closest to him, while it simultaneously slices away vast tracts of his pre-Florentine past. "The backward vista of his remembered life" (150) is worth no more to him than a ball and chain impeding his sprint toward the promised cardinal's hat; he snaps such connections as readily as he parts with Baldassarre's talismanic ring. He does not hesitate to liquidate the historical and family past, both embodied in Bardo's library. It is not so simple a matter, however, to expunge his own personal past. He must steel his lucid gaze to the prospect of recurrent encounters with it, in the shape of his father: "[H]e should be prepared to see this face rise up continually like the intermittent blotch that comes in diseased vision" (331). He trusts that even if once, on the Duomo steps, "the Past had grasped him with living quivering hands" (376), his native agility will hereafter allow him to elude the clutching fingers of memory: "as Tito galloped with a loose rein towards Siena, he saw a future before him in which he would no longer be haunted by those mistakes. . . . Could he not strip himself of the past, as of rehearsal clothing, and throw away the old bundle, to robe himself for the real scene?" (464).

Tito's loose-reined gallop, undertaken ostensibly to serve Florentine interests, aims at the betrayal both of those interests and of the grander cause of Florentine humanism. The currency he embezzles from the city's coffers matters less than his debasement of its intellectual coinage. A community whose meaning depends as much on tradition as on innovation is wasted on one who regards it merely as a stage upon which to rehearse "the real scene." A classic quick-change artist, Tito is forever donning and doffing clothing. One of his first actions, significantly, is to exchange the soiled garments in which he has been travelling for bright new ones, but his assumed Florentine dress never really becomes more than a "costume." To the dyed-in-the-wool Florentine Bernardo del Nero he seems "'one of the demoni, who are of no particular country'" (252).

When Savonarola, in Piazza San Marco, makes an impassioned, eleventh-hour appeal to divine judgment, Tito, "watching the scene attentively from an upper loggia," is typically stationed above and beyond the excitement, where he can pass impartial judgments on the "striking moment" that the Frate has managed to arrange (595). Tito belongs among those whom Eliot had called in an essay "your philosophers whose elevation above their fellow-beings consists in their ability to laugh at the ties which bind women and children" (*Essays* 20). Such an "elevation" helps him to scoff at the attachment to Florence itself that his own wife comes increasingly to feel. "'This rivalry of Italian cities is very petty and illiberal,'" he tells her loftily. "'The loss of Constantinople was the gain of the whole civilized world'" (353). Where Bardo, however blindly, had made the city the focus of his dearest aspirations, Tito makes of it a mere convenience; he cherishes "the project of leaving Florence as soon as his life there had become a high enough stepping-stone to a life elsewhere" (494). His adoptive city, like his adoptive father, provides him with a ladder rung upon which to thrust his insolent, climbing foot. Such an attitude travesties the aspiration of which the Florence skyline is an enduring symbol.

Tito reveals his nature, above all, in his antipathy to the city's essential spirit of arduous, impersonal striving, a resentment that surfaces unexpectedly during his courtship of Romola:

"There is something grim and grave to me always about Florence," said Tito . . . "and even in its merriment there is something shrill and hard—biting rather than gay. I wish we lived in Southern Italy, where thought is broken, not by weariness, but by delicious languors such as never seem to come over the 'ingenia acerrima Florentina.' I should like to see you under that southern sun, lying among the flowers, subdued into mere enjoyment, while I bent over you and touched the lute and sang to you some little unconscious strain that seemed all one with the light and the warmth." (240)

Like the hapless lady in Browning's "The Statue and the Bust," Tito "leaves the South." In Eliot's novel, however, a nostalgic yearning to return there from Florence represents not an escape from life-denying stasis but a flight back to it. Despite Tito's objections, it is precisely the "shrillness" and "hardness" of the more northerly city that lend it its distinctive dynamism, and in dreaming of his bride-to-be "'lying among the flowers, subdued into mere enjoyment,'" Tito is seducing both himself and her into an uncreative, sensual thralldom.

Ultimately, Tito is responsive not to the finer values that Florence embodies but only to the hard-handed code of expediency that has come to dominate the city's public life. As a consequence, his stay there does not modify his basic nature but only reinforces his native opportunism. Romola's vigorous intelligence, nurtured by Florentine influences, signifies to him nothing better than a threat; he can feel only "a certain repulsion towards a woman from whose mind he was in danger" (314). The marriage between Tito and Romola thus becomes a mirror image of Florentine political cut-and-thrust. At moments of crisis, Tito counters Romola's bids for intellectual and moral autonomy by using his "masculine force" to impose his mastery, a type of conduct endorsed by the aggressive spirit of the presiding Florence patriarchy. His unquestioning conviction of male supremacy makes it natural for him to suggest to his misty-eyed wife that she would do well to accept the loan of his own clear lenses: "'I am obliged to take care of you in opposition to your own will: if those dear eyes, that look so tender, see falsely, I must see for them, and save my wife from wasting her life in disappointing herself by impracticable dreams'" (352). Such an offer is a patronizing attempt to lure Romola away from the personal attachments ("'those superstitions,'" as Tito predictably calls them, "'which hang about your mind like bedimming clouds'") that are her birthright as a Florentine.

Finally, for all his vaunted rationality, Tito's isolation in Florence leaves him a prey to irrational terror. Scorning local traditions, he is left at last only with the tradition of his fear itself: "He no longer wore his armour, he was no longer afraid of Baldassarre; but from the corpse of that dead fear a spirit had risen—the undying *habit* of fear. He felt he should not be safe till he was out of this fierce, turbid Florence; and now he was ready to go" (635). At this very point, the alien subscriber to all the Florentine factions and to none becomes the ironic victim of the multitude's blundering rage: "'Piagnone! Medicean! Piagnone! Throw him over the bridge!'" (636). It is fitting that this despiser of human connections should, in the end, be driven to jump from a bridge into the turbid waters of the Arno. It is likewise fitting that his repressed past should return, in the waiting form of Baldassarre, to foil his getaway. "Death," the fugitive reflects at a prophetic moment, "might mean this chill gloom with the face of the hideous past hanging over him for ever" (638). The Florence dawn brings no happy re-awakening for Tito. Instead, it discloses a grisly tableau: the "hideous face of the past" conjoined in death with the would-be "man of the hour." It is an anarchic spectacle toward which the young Greek's entire Florentine career, in its flouting of humane values, has tended.

Tito's victim, Baldassarre, suffers from an involuntary amnesia that complements his enemy's calculated, destructive forgetfulness. Both his memory failure and his savage lust for revenge exclude him from the historic center of Renaissance enlightenment to which he tracks his adopted son. Appropriately, his alien condition within Florence is persistently linked with images of blindness and darkness. Producing "a blank confusion in his face, as of a man suddenly smitten with blindness," his mental handicap leaves him cut off, more drastically even than the physically blind Bardo, from the citadel of the new learning. His inner darkness is aggravated by compulsive, sporadic recollection that blots out the daylight of the Florentine present: "Images from the past kept urging themselves upon him like delirious visions strangely blended with thirst and anguish" (290). His smoldering bitterness blocks his access to the accumulated scholarship that Tito has at his unimpassioned fingertips. As a consequence, he perceives the luminous city around him only as an "unknown labyrinth" (360). He scrutinizes Greek characters by the light of a small window, "but no inward light arose on them"; the fall of dusk matters little to him, for "[h]is strained eyes seemed still to see the white pages with the unintelligible black marks upon them" (342). The "black marks" compose for Baldassarre the key to the city of letters and thus to his self-vindication. Unfortunately, he does not know how to turn that key in the Florentine lock.

A man who, by contrast, has no trouble in "reading" Florence to his own satisfaction is Savonarola, the one major male character whose objectives by and large transcend the personal. Although the Ferarra-born monk is, like Tito and Baldassarre, by birth an outsider, his commitment to the idea of Florence causes him to make the place absolutely his own. His conviction is adamant that it is God's "'chosen city in the chosen land'" (292). His importance in the novel derives, in fact, from his burning sense of "'the mighty purpose that God has for Florence'" (432). It is his zeal on behalf of that purpose that prompts him to rebuke Romola for assuming toward the town's affairs a stance of elevated disengagement: "'Your life has been spent in blindness, my daughter. You have lived with those who sit on a hill aloof, and look down on the life of their fellow-men'" (431).

Savonarola himself, though elevated, is the reverse of aloof. His preaching, like his city, is of a "highly mixed character," and its mixedness constitutes "one secret" of his "massive influence" (299) over the citizens. Even though he looks beyond personal goals, he is well enough acquainted with them to appeal to his Florentine flock's "partial and narrow sympathies" (300), of which Baldassarre's crazed vengefulness represents "only an extreme case." He commands a prophetic power that is "like a mighty beacon," beside which the gifts of others look like a mere "farthing candle" (270). His radiance, however, emanates from a purely Hebraist source, intolerant of the lamps of classical learning that his more profane fellow Florentines have attempted to relume. The earth, and Florence above all, he perceives as an arena wherein "'the light is still struggling with a mighty darkness'" (433). Tragically, however, he knows all too well whereof he speaks, for his own mixed nature is the site of a contest that duplicates the larger strife tormenting his city. He never succeeds entirely in separating his more enlightened aims from the "darkness" of personal ambition, or in keeping his lofty principles unstained by compromise with shady expediency. Ardently though he strives to be a spiritual beacon for the town he has made his own, he can never be more than one flickering light among the many that guide Florence's grand, gradually unfolding destiny.

The part he plays in shaping Romola's destiny is, however, crucial. If, as Bonaparte argues, Tito and Savonarola "are not only the ordinary characters of a realistic novel but also embodiments of Bacchus and Christ" (19), then Romola's shift of allegiance from the one to the other must amount to a momentous experience of conversion. But ultimately the key to Romola's development lies in her relationship with the city that encompasses Tito and Savonarola alike. The entire narrative could be summed up as the "Florentinizing" of the heroine. It is the story of one woman's success in recognising and salvaging, on her own terms, her city's heritage.

Even before her first appearance, Romola is vaunted by the barber Nello to be "'as fair as the Florentine lily before it got quarrelsome and turned red'" (84). Repeated later references cement her identification with her birthplace. Nevertheless, when she first arrives on the scene, Romola is described in a way that makes her actual identity fluid and doubtful. Her face belongs to a type "of which one could not venture to say whether it would inspire love or only that unwilling admiration which is mixed with dread; the question must be decided by the eyes" (46-47).

In *Romola*, the most important questions are decided by that most Florentine of means. The heroine's eyes, on her first appearance, are bent on the pages of her erudite fellow townsman Poliziano's Latin work, *Miscellanea*. Her vision will gradually broaden to include the vernacular of the Florentine present and future. Up to now, however, her life has "inherited nothing but memories . . . memories of far-off light, love and beauty, that lay embedded in dark mines of books, and could hardly give out their brightness again until they were kindled for her by the torch of some known joy" (105-6). Only years later, from the lips of Savonarola, will she learn of the fuller inheritance into which she has been born: "'My daughter, you are a child of Florence; fulfill the duties of that great inheritance. Live for Florence—for your own people, whom God is preparing to bless the earth'" (436).

But obeying this stirring directive embroils Romola in painful contradictions. These have already begun some chapters earlier. Loving the unabashed pagan Tito, she has prepared to make her bed with Apollo and his sunlight; but the death of her estranged brother Dino, and his somber last words to her, give her pause. "It seemed to her as if this first vision of death must alter the daylight for her for ever more" (217). Her engagement thus forces her to decide between two antithetical bands of the Florentine spectrum: the candlelight of Christian devotion and the sunlight of Hellenist hedonism. This jarring clash between two contrary but compelling Florentine ways of seeing creates a dilemma that Romola's inward vision cannot yet resolve:

Strange, bewildering transition from those pale images of sorrow and death to this bright youthfulness, as of a sun-god who knew nothing of night! What thought could reconcile that worn anguish in her brother's face—that straining after something invisible—with this satisfied strength and beauty, and make it intelligible that they belonged to the same world? Or was there never any reconciling of them, but only a blind worship of clashing deities, first in mad joy and then in wailing? (238)

Marriage to the sun-god fails to reconcile the deities; Romola's personal renaissance still lies hidden in the mists of the future. She gropes toward it through a series of cruel shocks. First, Tito's sale of her father's library, which symbolically obliterates her familial past, traumatically darkens her perception of the city in which she has been dwelling. Characteristically, however, even in her anguish she keeps her powers of observation undimmed; "instead of shutting her eyes and ears" she "had watched the process" of packing and removal (386):

Arno ran dark and shivering; the hills were mournful; and Florence with its girdling stone towers had that silent, tomb-like look, which unbroken shadow gives to a city seen from above. Santa Croce, where her father lay, was dark amidst that darkness, and slowly crawling over the bridge, and slowly vanishing up the narrow street, was the white load, like a cruel, deliberate Fate carrying away her father's life-long hope to bury it in an unmarked grave. (386)

The city's pealing bells only toll her alienation from her community: "[S]he stood aloof from that common life—that Florence which was flinging out its loud exultation to stun the ears of sorrow and loneliness" (386). Her spiritual rebirth cannot occur until she finds some way of brightening, within herself, her image of the city that has become for her dark, dead, and hostile.

The first step in this process is her turn from joy to lamentation in the deities she worships, her abandonment of her husband's callow hedonism in favor of her brother's code of asceticism. This change she signals visually by putting aside her gay wedding-dress and taking up the somber nun's habit she will wear on her way out of Florence. Her action has ambiguous overtones, for it signals a disavowal of the past that bears a disquieting resemblance to Tito's rapid changes of costume. For Romola, however, the Florentine past cannot be so nonchalantly doffed. Ultimately, her city holds for her a destiny, an identity, that she cannot evade. Even as she walks out of its walls, the scene around her sends a subtle message:

The bare wintry morning, the chill air, were welcome in their severity: the leafless trees, the sombre hills, were not haunted by the gods of beauty and joy, whose worship she had forsaken for ever.

But presently the light burst forth with sudden strength, and shadows were thrown across the road. (400)

The sun's brusque emergence throws before Romola's fleeing steps the familiar local checkerboard of light and shadow, which she can no more elude than she can "the long shadow of herself that was not to be escaped" (400). On the point of grasping a new, uncharted freedom, she hears a peremptory voice reminding her of her public Florentine identity: "'You are Romola de' Bardi, the wife of Tito Melema'" (428).

The voice is Savonarola's. Coming forward to champion the collective cause of Florence as against wayward individual impulse, he speaks with an authority, at once civic and religious, that Romola must perforce recognise. Only now, when she has put her younger illusions behind her, is Romola sufficiently mature to judge actual separation from Florence a worse fate even than the internal exile of her father's house. Only now is she ready to embrace as her own the "'great work'" in which the monk offers her a share: "'Here in Florence it is beginning, and the eyes of faith behold it'" (436). As Savonarola testifies, the power of vision, like the "'waters at which men drank and found strength in the desert,'" can spring only from a self-devoting solidarity with God's chosen city. Such a promise gives Romola the courage to turn her eyes back toward home, with a renewed conviction that it *is* in fact home. When we next see her, she is, as the chapter heading proclaims, "in her place," ensconced in a Florence menaced by the attentions of the French king and his followers.

The ample walls of her native city have now supplanted in her affections the narrow, imprisoning walls in which she has spent her cloistered maidenhood. "The idea of home had come to be identified for her less with the house in the Via de' Bardi, where she sat in frequent loneliness, than with the towered circuit of Florence, where there was hardly a turn of the streets at which she was not greeted with looks of appeal or of friendliness" (452). Yet even now her existence has not been altogether broadened. Romola's emotional life, its other avenues darkened, is at this point wholly diverted to "the one narrow pathway on which the light fell clear": "All that ardour of her nature which could no longer spend itself in the woman's tenderness for father and husband, had transformed itself into an enthusiasm of sympathy with the general life" (463).

So thoroughgoing an embrace of an ideal of self-renouncing service shows that the ex-pagan's shift of loyalties from Tito to Savonarola has been complete. Her acquiescence to the monk's most arbitrary dogmas and prophecies goes hand in hand with a profound change in her perception of "the well-known figure" of her husband, "once painted in her heart by young love, and now branded there by eating pain" (487). The metaphors are precisely chosen; the unstable course of Romola's life has taken her from the Hellenistic extreme of the Florentine spectrum to the Hebraistic one, from "painting" to "branding." Such moral pendulum-swings guarantee that she will, through a type of personal dialectic, progress rather than stagnate, but they also involve a serious risk of imbalance. Her revulsion from "painting" of any sort renders her unwisely tolerant of the

Bonfire of Vanities organized by Savonarola's party, on which articles of feminine adornment and works by distinguished artists are indiscriminately destroyed. At length, however, she must acknowledge that "the enthusiasm which had come to her as the only energy strong enough to make life worthy" is "bound up with vain dreams and wilful eye-shutting" (526). In reaction she reverts not to any hedonist "lust of the eyes" but to the sensible Florentine clear-sightedness of Bernardo del Nero.

Trapped thus painfully in the conflicts tormenting her cleft city, Romola finds herself again obliged to confront the unwelcome prospect of exile. Up to now, she has been under the intellectual or moral tutelage of one male figure or another, a sequence culminating in her submission to Savonarola. The time has finally arrived for her, as a woman, to assert her personal "warrant" for action. Only after she has found her own secure individual basis for ethical choice will she feel prepared to rejoin the community of Florence on her own terms.

Her climactic, unhappy interview with Savonarola to plead for the life of her godfather completes her disengagement from the factionalism countenanced by Florentine male authority. Her very identity, which she had returned to Florence to reclaim, now seems worthless, because rooted in a community that has so bitterly rewarded her dedication: "Why should she care about wearing one badge more than another, or about being called by her own name?" (586). Nevertheless, in planning her escape from the bedevilled and bedevilling city, she intuitively seizes upon a Florentine cultural monument for her model: Boccaccio's tale of the lovelorn Gostanza, who commits her unwanted life to a boat in which she drifts off to sea. Significantly, at a time when so many other connections have been severed for her, Romola turns to vernacular literature to pick up the threads of her Florentine patrimony. They will lead her, circuitously but unerringly, over the waters and back to her native ground, to the awaiting "text" of a city become once more readable for her.

Her directionless voyage and its hectic aftermath subject Romola to a type of transformative test. She finds herself in an idyllic "green land," soothing yet still eerily reminiscent of familiar Florentine image-contrasts: "The rays of the newly-risen sun fell obliquely on the westward horn of this crescent-shaped nook: all else lay in shadow" (640). Even in this pastoral retreat she cannot escape the famous skyline, harshly and indelibly inscribed on her brain: "*Could* she not rest here? No sound from Florence would reach her. Already oblivion was troubled; from behind the golden haze were piercing domes and towers and walls, parted by a river and enclosed by the green hills" (641). Far though Romola may flee, Florence, like some stony-profiled Fury, implacably pursues.

The episode in the village, however, is crucial in reconciling the heroine to the home from which she has been so violently alienated. Here, at last, she unreservedly embraces the role that will define her stable, Florentine identity. Already, in the paired chapters "The Unseen Madonna" and "The Visible

Madonna," her efforts to aid her suffering fellow townspeople have established her as the living counterpart of the "mysterious hidden image" that is carried in procession at times of civic crisis, the holy "Pitying Mother" (455). After her return to Florence, it will be Romola's mission to make the Madonna again visible and active, correcting the male divisiveness of the local power games with her large, maternal tolerance and compassion.

Before that can happen, however, her own "rebirth" must be ritually confirmed by her ordeal in the green valley of exile. Risking herself unstintingly to care for the plague victims, she figuratively "walks through fire" as Savonarola, not long before, has declined to do in fact; and her exposure is an act of consecration. Her success in getting a Jewish orphan accepted into the Christian fold betokens the moderating influence her feminine nature exerts over Hebraist rigidity. By the time she departs, "the Hebrew baby was a tottering tumbling Christian, Benedetto by name, having been baptized in the church on the mountainside" (649).

For Romola, too, her experience in the village is "like a new baptism" (650), one that puts an end to her own tottering and tumbling. It is an enabling rite of passage, ensuring her reintegration into the city she has fled. It grants her "that rare possibility of self-contemplation which comes in any complete severance from our wonted life" (650-1), endowing her with the perspective to see the turbid course of her career steadily and whole, to knit her future together with her rejected Florentine past. As she lies with "her mind travelling back over the past and gazing across the undefined distance of the future," she sees "all objects from a new position" (650). The result of her expanded vision is that "the past arose with a fresh appeal for her" (650). Soon she finds herself irresistibly drawn back to the city she must finally acknowledge as her destined home: "Florence, and all her life there, had come back to her like hunger; her feelings could not go wandering after the possible and the vague: their living fibre was fed with the memory of familiar things" (651-2).

Reversing Tito's posture, Romola at last recognises in Florence the stage of her adult life. It is her experiences elsewhere that have been a mere rehearsal. If she has earlier been thrust from her city "by the sense of confusion in human things which made all effort a mere draggling at tangled threads," she has by this point been led to accept the "web of inconsistencies" (652) woven from "the many-twisted conditions of life" as the "living fibre" of her personal reality.

In the Epilogue, Romola presides as the matriarch of an unusual household, where her wise influence fosters the lives of Lillo and Ninna, Tito's children by Tessa, his peasant mistress, as well as the life of the infantile Tessa herself. Romola sits "in a handsome upper room opening on to a loggia" that looks over Andrea del Sarto's familiar prospect: "all along the Borgo Pinti, and over the city gate towards Fiesole, and the solemn heights beyond it" (672). Her eyes are "fixed absently on the distant mountains" (673). By this point the farthest-seeing character in the novel, Romola takes the storied city spread before her within her nurturing purview. Soon she turns her gaze to the small citizen whose character it is her special responsibility to mold: Lillo, who as the bastard child of a Hellene and a superstitious Tuscan peasant has a rich, complex Florentine heritage to grow into. In the closing tableau, the two magi, Piero di Cosimo and Nello, the avatars of Florentine art and learning, are advancing through the streets of the City of Flowers with a reverential bouquet for the Florentine Madonna and her adopted child.

Romola's career, then, culminates in her embrace of "the ties which bind women and children," the very ties scorned by "superior" philosophers. Savage though its public life may be, Eliot's Florence finally sustains the ties for which Romola stands. There is, in fact, every reason to suppose that Romola's concluding matriarchal ascendancy augurs well for the Florence she has made her home. Unlike Andrea del Sarto's Lucrezia, that ironic Madonna of the Past, Romola has become in an unironic sense a Madonna of the Future, whose magnificent head of blond hair is not fool's gold but an incipient halo. In her single self she has managed to still the clashing deities troubling the life of Renaissance Florence. Yet one must add that by enthroning a Madonna—even a Madonna of the Future—as the city's queen, Eliot has left little room for Apollo and Bacchus. The gods of profane mirth and joy have exited Florence along with Lorenzo the Magnificent and Tito the Treacherous. It will be the task of later novelists to recall those ebullient Florentine deities from their exile.

5

Madonnas of the Past and Future: Howells and James

A twentieth part of the erudition would have sufficed, would have given us the feeling and colour of the time, if there had been more of the breath of the Florentine streets, more of the faculty of optical evocation, a greater saturation of the senses with the elements of the adorable little city. (Henry James, *Partial Portraits* 55-56)

Henry James's verdict on *Romola*, with its call for sensuous immediacy of presentation, signals a turning away from historical revival as the preferred mode of treating the capital of the Renaissance. In their use of Florence as a fictional setting, both James and his friend and compatriot William Dean Howells shift the focus from the past to the present, from memory to "the breath of the Florentine streets." If Florentine history is not laboriously explored by the two Americans, however, the shadow of the past continues to haunt their protagonists. Theodore Colville, the aging hero of Howells's novel *Indian Summer* (1886), and Theobald, the languishing expatriate artist of James's story "The Madonna of the Future" (1873), must each contend with the convulsive grip of Florentine bygones. As Americans and contemporaries confronting a storied Italian city, Howells and James share common ground. But in treating the American protagonist's relation to the past, the two writers reveal the essential unlikeness of their own sensibilities. In *Indian Summer* and "The Madonna of the Future," one encounters two radically divergent impressions of the weight that Florentine yesterdays impose on the individual life of today.

OLD AND NEW FORTUNES AND THEIR HAZARDS

A character in *Indian Summer* remarks of that noted American novelist William Dean Howells, "'[H]e's very particular when he's on Italian ground'" (173). What made Howells himself "very particular" in his feelings toward his Florentine novel was no doubt its closeness to his own effort, in middle age, to recapture his youthful enthusiasm for Italy. The story, as he described it, "is that of a man whose youth was broken sharp off in Florence twenty years ago, and who after a busy newspaper life in our West, fancies that he can resume his youth by going back to Italy. There he falls in love with a girl young enough to be his daughter. It is largely a study of the feelings of middle-life in contrast with those of earlier years" (Qtd. *Indian Summer* xii). Even so barely outlined, Howells's plot already raises familiar Florentine questions of continuity and renewal. The main problem for the protagonist, Theodore Colville, is to bridge gaps. There is, first of all, the gap between his eager youth and his disillusioned maturity; years earlier, he had been jilted in Florence by the girl he was courting. Along with this goes the gap between his idealistic early aspirations (he had dreamed of becoming an architect) and his later prosaic career as an editor in Des Vaches, Indiana—inferentially a "cow-town." The novel's opening shows him, appropriately, "midway of the Ponte Vecchio at Florence" (3), stationed on a bridge and staring at the turbulently swirling Arno. The sordidness of political infighting back at Des Vaches has left him disenchanted with his involvement in local public affairs. It has prompted him to take "the prodigious risk of breaking his life off sharp from the course in which it had been set for many years, and of attempting to renew it in a direction from which it had long been diverted" (4). Florence, the city he has chosen for this venture, is a likely place to risk attempting renewal but an unlikely refuge from contention. The very violence of the river implies that, here above all, the turbid current of life cannot be easily redirected. Colville walks for hours in Florence, hoping to savor the sights, sounds, and smells he had once enjoyed; but he finds that now "he could not warm over the old mood in which he once treasured them all away as of equal preciousness" (9).

A confirmed ironist, Colville shares in the temper of the city he aims to re-adopt. His intellectuality suits him well to the storied capital of the life of the mind, though it evidently did him little good with the girl he pursued there during his first, youthful visit. "'I think if he hadn't talked Ruskin so much, Jenny Milbury might have treated him better,'" remarks his old friend, Lina Bowen (47). Now, on his return, he faces a life dilemma that cannot be resolved by mind alone: the choice between Imogene Graham, a charming American ingenue, and Lina, his long time acquaintance. Imogene "reincarnates" Colville's lost first love, and his vanished youth; Lina embodies a *recollected* tie to that same long-past epoch of his life.

When he begins to lavish attentions on Imogene, Colville stumbles into misadventures. His unwise bid to join in the youthful gaiety of a dancing party only recalls the bitterness of his past disappointment and casts doubt on his entire Florentine project. "A whole world of faded associations flushed again in Colville's heart. This was Italy; this was Florence; and he execrated the hour in which he had dreamed of returning" (61). Having lost the suppleness of youth, he feels a fool amid the Florentine dance of life.

The painfulness of absorbing the Florentine yesterday into a belated today deflects Colville back, for solace, to intellectual pursuits. These, however, are themselves backward looking, for they involve an attempt to resuscitate the city's buried past.

> He . . . could not only supply that brief historical sketch of Florence which Mrs. Bowen had lamented the want of, but he could make her history speak an intelligible, an unmistakable tongue in every monument of the past. . . . With this object in his mind, making and keeping him young, he could laugh with any one who liked at the vanity of the middle-aged Hoosier who had spoiled a set in the Lancers at Madame Uccelli's party. . . . Henceforth his life would be wholly intellectual. (62-63)

Colville sets himself to embark on a scholarly mission as daunting, in its documentary fashion, as Eliot's *tour de force* of historical resuscitation in *Romola*.

Predictably, however, the subject that continues to absorb him is not Tuscan annals but the unhistoric American, Imogene Graham. The girl herself possesses certain affinities with the foreign city in which she is sojourning. Her freshness and charm recall the fleeting beauty of youth that Lorenzo the Magnificent sang in one of the most famous of Renaissance poems. "She was an expression of youth, of health, of beauty, and of the moral loveliness that comes from a fortunate combination of these; but beyond this she was elusive in a way that seemed to characterize her even materially" (68). Colville cajoles her into admitting a belief in "pre-existence" (107), as if she were the reincarnation of the Jenny Milbury who had jilted him two decades earlier; but such maneuvering hardly suffices to close the gulf of age that yawns between them.

It is the *raisonneur* of Howells's novel, an eccentric retired New England clergyman named Waters, who opens a channel along which Colville can move back toward contact with the vigor of the Florentine past, without sacrificing his own hard-won maturity. Holding up, Diogenes-like, a lamp to assist Colville in descending his stairs, Mr. Waters becomes himself the image of the ancient Florentine *illuminatus*, a latter-day Bardo de' Bardi: "The light fell upon the white locks thinly straggling from beneath his velvet skull-cap, and he looked like some mediaeval scholar of those who lived and died for learning in Florence when letters were a passion there almost as strong as love" (130). In answer to Colville's sceptical query, "'And is the past such good company always?'", Waters replies: "'Yes; in a sense it is. The past is humanity set free from circumstance, and history studied where it was once life is the past rehumanized'" (158). All this may have a sententious ring, but it gives Colville an inkling of how to go about connecting bygones with actualities. That, in fact, is precisely what he needs to do in his personal life. There is more to be gained from simply accepting the past, Waters intimates, than from a misdirected effort, like Colville's with Imogene, to disinter the past and relive it by proxy. Not coincidentally, it is Waters who suggests to Colville the notion of his old friend Lina Bowen's possible romantic interest in him. The elderly cleric is not above a bit of matchmaking; while he reveres the past, he knows that fantasies of a "wholly intellectual" life are futile.

On the morning of Colville's visit to Waters, the Florence weather takes a surprising turn. "The sunshine had looked cold from his window . . . but when he got out into the weather he found the breeze mild and the sun warm" (156). From its opening in January, Howells's narrative moves steadily not—despite its title—toward autumn, but toward spring and warmth. It is a Botticellian movement befitting a Florentine drama of renewal. Colville himself has a stubborn tendency to remain frozen in the winter of his youthful discontent. Walking in the Boboli Garden, near the spot where Jenny had rejected him, he reflects: "'Yes, it's spring'"; but "then, with the selfishness of the troubled soul, he wished that it might be winter still and indefinitely" (165-6). Winter has kept Colville minimally warm, though numb. Reluctantly, he must yield, at length, to the seductive vernal thaw of the "City of Flowers." As a consequence, his own past becomes—to apply Waters's term—"rehumanized." But the road to such a rehumanizing is crooked; it leads for Colville through the palace of error and the circus tent of farce.

Farcical, above all, is Colville's involvement in domestic warfare, complete with shifting "factional" alliances: a scenario that sorts well with the chronic Florentine habit of contention. As the relations among the principals grow more tangled, the language of combat is more persistently applied to their meetings. After Imogene has sent Colville a naively compromising letter, he and Mrs. Bowen engage in a nervous skirmish. "'You have no right to laugh!' [Mrs. Bowen] cried, losing herself a little, and so making her first gain upon him" (139). His old friend presses him to undertake a strategic retreat from Florence; but while walking about the city he determines, in defiance of her wishes, to don the well-worn mantle of Florentine masculine assertiveness:

And now was he running away from Florence because his will was weak? He could look back to that squalid tragedy of his youth and see that a more violent, a more determined man could have possessed himself of the girl whom he had lost. And now would it not be more manly, if more brutal, to stay here, where a hope, however fleeting, however fitful, of what might have been, had revisited him in the love of this young girl? (162)

He stays on, and hostilities mount. Imogene's avowal to Colville of her feelings breeds animosity between her and her friend and hostess, Mrs. Bowen: "'It must be that I've done her some deadly wrong, without knowing it,'" the girl bursts out, "'or I couldn't hate her as I know I do'" (178). The encounters between Colville and Lina Bowen, too, grow more bellicose. "Now they were enemies; he did not know how or why, but he said to himself, in the bitterness of his heart, that it was better so; and when Imogene appeared, and Mrs. Bowen vanished . . . he folded the girl in a vindictive embrace" (196). The concluding phrase is telling. So vexed has the complex of hostilities become that even a gesture of love is conscripted into a Florentine wargame.

Imogene's own "campaign" causes her to assume vaingloriously the role of the avenger of Colville's ancient wrong, of "'the anguish he had suffered'" at the hands of the heartless Miss Milbury:

"She had killed his youth; she had spoiled his life: if I could revive them, restore them! It came upon me like a great flash of light at last, and as soon as this thought took possession of me, I felt my whole being elevated and purified by it, and I was enabled to put aside with contempt the selfish considerations that had occurred to me at first." (186-7)

Imogene's project of bestowing a personal "renaissance" on Colville by *fiat* is manifestly a generous but hopeless piece of quixotry. When she confides it to the appalled Colville—"'It's been this idea, this hope with me always . . . that you might go back in my life and take up yours where it was broken off; that I might make your life what it would have been—complete your destiny'" (198)—he recognises it at once for the mere romantic whim that it is. Despite his uneasy agreement to become engaged to the girl, his real feelings reflect his advancing age and his dawning spirit of sober Florentine common sense: "'I am very comfortable. I don't need any compensation for the past. I need—sleep'" (215).

By this point, indeed, the aspiring historian of Florence has become less engrossed by the past. During an excursion to Fiesole, he remarks to Imogene that "'[y]ou can do nothing with'" the local landscape:

"It's too full of every possible interest. What a history is written all over it, public and private! If you don't take it simply, like any other landscape, it becomes an oppression. It's well that tourists come to Italy so ignorant, and keep so. Otherwise they couldn't live to get home again: the past would crush them." (242)

The personal bearing of Colville's words is patent. He has himself failed to "take simply" his own private history—his ancient defeat in Florence—and it has become an oppression for him. His entanglement with Imogene, far from redeeming the defeat, has only aggravated the past's oppressiveness. Imogene herself, whose attachment to Colville has depended solely on a morbid exhuming of bygones, grows understandably impatient with her fiancé's historical fetishism; she interrupts his humorous discourse on the Etruscans by exclaiming, "'How you always like to burrow into the past!'" (246). The girl's entrapment within a contrived, history-haunted love affair is by now bringing her to the edge of desperation. It is not long before she has "a narrow escape" from that most Florentine of fictional diseases: "brain fever" (258).

Colville, for his part, makes a complete recovery from his perverse bout of youth-seeking. Ironically, he now at last finds an authentic way of mending the great gap in his life, by turning with new eyes to an "old bridge": his friend of years past, Lina Bowen, whom he tardily realizes that he loves. Instead of being the test-tube brain-child of an abstract, idealistic theory, this alliance is rooted deep in Colville's past, and in Lina's; it dates from his first, miserable but memorable Italian visit. Consequently, it can issue in a true renewal, a healing of the gulf between past and present.

Before going to propose to his old friend, Colville dons new, flamboyant clothing: "the coat was of the lightest serge, the trousers of a pearly gray tending to lavender, the waistcoat of cool white duck. . . . [H]e had stopped in Via Tornabuoni and bought some silk gauze neckties, of a tasteful gayety of tint" (270). To Lina's polite inquiry as to how he is feeling, he replies pointedly, "'Like a new man'" (271). In his quizzical fashion he tells Lina's young daughter, Effie, "'how comfortable and home-like'" he has found Florence during his walk around the town in the summer heat: "'all the statues loafing about in their shirt sleeves, and the objects of interest stretching and yawning around, and having a good rest after their winter's work'" (272). His fancy neatly expresses his own novel feeling of at-homeness and relaxation in his long-familiar adopted city. The crux of his difficult negotiation with the high-minded, exacting Lina comes when he declares his intention to leave Florence for good. The infatuated Effie collapses into childish sobs, and the beleaguered Lina finally capitulates: "'Oh, you must stay!' said Lina, in the self-contemptuous voice of a woman who falls below her ideal of herself" (278).

So Florence revisited becomes for Colville, after all, Florence recaptured. It restores to him his lost youth, but in an amusingly unexpected fashion. His final word on his union with Lina—"'*I* have married a young person'" (280)—contains a complete emotional, if not literal, truth. After a course of nearly fatal missteps (foreshadowed by his clownish stumbling at the dancing party), he has found in Florence a path that will effectually connect his past with his present, and so restore him to a new, whole life. The devisers of the Florentine Renaissance, who grasped the key to the future by turning back to the forgotten knowledge of the ancients, did no more.

THE PSYCHOSIS OF INFLUENCE: "THE MADONNA OF THE FUTURE"

Although Theodore Colville finally awakens to a new morning through his exposure to Florence, he is aware of the city's potentially hostile influence. "'If you don't take it simply, like any other landscape,'" as he tells Imogene, "'it becomes an oppression.'" George Eliot, on her first visit, found Florence difficult to "take simply":

As for me, I am thrown into a state of humiliating passivity by the sight of the great things done in the far past—it seems as if life were not long enough to learn, and as if my own activity were so completely dwarfed by comparison that I should never have courage for more creation of my own. (*Letters* 3: 294)

Such a "humiliating passivity" provides the theme of Henry James's early Florentine story, "The Madonna of the Future." Less cheered than Howells by signs that the "go-ahead" spirit of Boston and Denver was taking root in Florence, James was far more preoccupied by the cultural abyss separating the great age of the city from its mediocre present. His artist-protagonist, accordingly, faces obstacles in his quest for fulfillment that Colville does not encounter. James himself detected in the Florentine atmosphere an oppressive tinge of sadness and dissatisfaction, as he notes in an early travel sketch. "'Lovely, lovely, but it makes me "blue,"' the sensitive stranger couldn't but murmur to himself" (*Hours* 125). He blames the blueness on "a sense of the perfect separateness of all the great productions of the Renaissance from the present and the future of the place, from the actual life and manners, the native ideal" (125). He concludes regretfully,

It is this spiritual solitude, this conscious disconnection of the great works of architecture and sculpture that deposits a certain weight upon the heart; when we see a great tradition broken we feel something of the pain with which we hear a stifled cry. (125)

For James, the paramount symptom of this "conscious disconnection" is the startling decline of Italian taste and creativity.

That the people who but three hundred years ago had the best taste in the world should now have the worst; that having produced the noblest, loveliest, costliest works, they should now be given up to the manufacture of objects at once ugly and paltry; that the race of which Michael Angelo and Raphael, Leonardo and Titian were characteristic should have no other title to distinction than third-rate *genre* pictures and catch-penny statues—all this is a frequent perplexity to the observer of actual Italian life. (110)

At the same time, James maintains a balancing awareness that modern Italy cannot reasonably be expected to stay bound within the straitjacket of her magnificent past. His recognition of the necessity of change makes him impatient with the facile criticisms of foreign visitors:

After thinking of Italy as historical and artistic it will do . . . no great harm to think of her for a while as panting both for a future and for a balance at the bank; aspirations supposedly much at variance with the Byronic, the Ruskinian, the artistic, poetic, aesthetic manner of considering our eternally attaching peninsula. (111)

The Hebraist severity of Ruskin's *Mornings in Florence* (1875-77) prompts him to a brusque rejoinder: "For many persons, [Ruskin] will never bear the test of being read in this rich old Italy, where art, so long as it really lived at all, was spontaneous, joyous, irresponsible" (129). He deplores Ruskin's applying of "Draconic legislation" to matters of aesthetic taste: "Differences here are not iniquity and righteousness; they are simply variations of temperament, kinds of curiosity. We are not under theological government" (130).

As his name perhaps hints, Theobald, the protagonist of "The Madonna of the Future," shares Ruskin's theological solemnity in his reverence for the great art of the Florentine past. There is truth in what his rival, the bumptiously "modern" Florentine sculptor of cats and monkeys, says of him: "'[H]e wouldn't admire me. . . . He's a purist!'" (226). Yet Theobald is more than the cranky offshoot of Ruskinian fastidiousness. The ardor of his engagement with Florence and its great, broken tradition of artistic excellence is a measure of his folly, but it is also a measure of his humanity.

The narrator's first glimpse of Theobald coincides fatefully with his first impressions of Florence. On the evening of his arrival, he strays into

a great piazza, filled only with the mild autumn moonlight. Opposite rose the Palazzo Vecchio like some huge civic fortress, with the great bell-tower springing from its embattled verge like a mountain-pine from the edge of a cliff. At its base, in its projected shadow, gleamed certain dim sculptures which I wonderingly approached. One of the images . . . was a magnificent colossus shining through the dusky air like some young god of Defiance. In a moment I recognised him as Michael Angelo's David. I turned with a certain relief from his sinister strength to a slender figure in bronze (203).

James's evocation of the Piazza della Signoria recalls familiar motifs. In particular, the "mild autumn moonlight" conjures up the atmosphere of Browning's "Andrea del Sarto".[1] Florentine antitheses of light against shadow, reach against grasp, are implied by descriptive detail. The bell-tower of the Palazzo Vecchio thrusts aspiringly into the moonlight out of the shadows below. The godlike form of Michelangelo's David, gleaming amidst the dusk, betokens the triumphant union of reach and grasp, both in the daring Old Testament hero represented and in the artist who dared so to represent him. Still, the observer turns "with a certain relief" from David's "sinister strength" to Cellini's slender bronze Perseus. The ensuing narrative clarifies why the David's strength should be sinister.

A stranger emerges from the shadows, revealing "a mass of auburn hair, which gleamed in the moonlight, escaping from a little mediaeval *berretta*" (203). The particulars at once associate this figure with the city's "illumination" and with its brilliant past. His opening words comment on both:

"I've known Florence long, sir, but I've never known her so lovely as tonight. It's as if the ghosts of her past were abroad in the empty streets. The present is sleeping; the past hovers about us like a dream made visible. . . . That was the prime of art, sir. The sun stood high in heaven, and his broad and equal blaze made the darkest places bright and the dullest eyes clear. We live in the evening of time! We grope in the grey dusk, carrying each our poor little taper of selfish and painful wisdom, holding it up to the great models and to the dim idea, and seeing nothing but overwhelming greatness and dimness. The days of illumination are gone!" (203-4)

Theobald, the speaker, has indeed "known Florence long"; his mind is wholly bound up with the place and its history.

He seemed deeply versed in local history and tradition, and he expatiated *con amore* on the charms of Florence. I gathered that he was an old resident, and that he had taken the lovely city into his heart. "I owe her everything," he declared. "It's only since I came here that I have really lived, intellectually." (206)

"So imbued with the local genius" is he that he can serve as a walking Baedeker; so ardent is his passion that, for all its intellectual purity, it takes on a warmly erotic tinge.

He talked of Florence like a lover, and admitted that it was a very old affair; he had lost his heart to her at first sight. "It's the fashion to talk of all cities as feminine," he said, "but, as a rule, it's a monstrous mistake. Is Florence of the same sex as New York, as Chicago? She's the sole true woman of them all; one feels towards her as a lad in his teens feels to some beautiful older woman with a 'history.'" (211)

His nocturnal patrolling of the city's streets and squares is his courtship of his aging beauty, his rapturous litany of her charms his lover's serenade.

Florence, with its garland of immortals, plays Laura to Theobald's Petrarch; it inspires his own artistic flights. Raphael, above all, gives him a miraculous vision of how far an artist's "reach" may extend. He rhapsodizes on the "Madonna of the Chair":

"Think of his seeing that spotless image, not for a moment, for a day, in a happy dream, or a restless fever-fit, not as a poet in a five minutes' frenzy, time to snatch his phrase and scribble his immortal stanza, but for days together, while the slow labour of the brush went on, while the foul vapours of life interposed, and the fancy ached with tension, fixed, radiant, distinct, as we see it now! What a master, certainly! But ah, what a seer!" (209)

It is Raphael's power to "leave the ground," as Browning's Andrea would say, to soar splendidly above the mere literal image imprinted on his retina, that enraptures the American idealist.

At the base of Theobald's idealism there lies the fact of his transatlantic birth. As the narrator shrewdly observes, "The very heat of his devotion was a sign of conversion; those born to European opportunity manage better to reconcile enthusiasm with comfort" (209). Nonetheless, the poor artist's homage to the city's treasures makes him worthier of a place there than his compatriot, Mrs. Coventry, who is "famously 'artistic,'" and whose efforts to duplicate the legacy of Florence within her own busy walls succeed only in reducing artistic grandeur to the triviality of a "collector's" knick-knacks.

Her apartment was a sort of Pitti Palace *au petit pied.* She possessed "early masters" by the dozen. . . . Backed by these treasures, and by innumerable bronzes, mosaics, majolica dishes, and little worm-eaten diptychs showing angular saints on gilded panels, our hostess enjoyed the dignity of a sort of high-priestess of the arts. She always wore on her bosom a huge miniature copy of the Madonna della Seggiola. (213)

The size of the oxymoronic "huge miniature" captures the essence of Mrs. Coventry's connoisseurship: it is a swollen pettiness. By comparison, Theobald's amorous endeavor to "possess" Florence is honorable; he is at least the priest of a heartfelt cult.

But while Theobald escapes his fellow expatriate's acquisitive preciosity and can claim to be a truer heir of the city's cultural tradition, he considers himself spiritually orphaned. "He confessed with a melancholy but all-respectful head-shake to his American origin. 'We are the disinherited of Art!' he cried. 'We are condemned to be superficial! We are excluded from the magic circle. The soil of American perception is a poor little barren, artificial deposit'" (205). Although James, as a fledgling writer, may himself have entertained such thoughts, Theobald's emphatic way of formulating the plight of the American artist merely caricatures it. Despite his orotund assurances—"'Don't take me, in Heaven's name, for one of your barren complainers,—querulous cynics who have neither talent nor faith. I'm at work! . . . I've undertaken a *creation!*'" (205)—Theobald is doomed to barrenness because of his underlying defeatism. In this respect he resembles Andrea del Sarto; but where Andrea's defeatism stems essentially from personal self-doubt, Theobald's derives from a sense of dislocation at once temporal ("We live in the evening of time") and geographical ("We [Americans] are the disinherited of Art"). Andrea, a native son of Florence, still has the crest of a Renaissance to ride, though he is riding it downward.

Theobald's unlucky remedy for his double estrangement is to "commune" with the Florentine master-spirits of the great age. Such communion is best effected, he thinks, by gazing raptly at the visible evidences of their genius. Instead of spurring him to duplicate their marvelous achievements, however, all his habit achieves is the paralyzing of his own talent. In his peculiar fashion, he reenacts the fate of the Florentine would-be lovers in Browning's "The Statue and the Bust," whose indefatigable "looking" finally freezes them in a lifeless stasis. His viewing and reviewing of masterpieces displayed in the Florence galleries becomes both a cause of procrastination and its pretext. He extracts a killingly plausible "moral" from the "superb triptych of Andrea Mantegna" in the Uffizi: "But before we left the Mantegna, he pressed my arm and gave it a loving look. '*He* was not in a hurry,' he murmured. 'He knew nothing of "raw haste, half-sister to Delay"!'" (207). Such a view of supreme art as the product of infinite, painstaking leisure contains much truth. By embracing that truth unwarily, however, Theobald aggravates his own worst vice: his tendency to warp leisure into its blood-brother, inertia, and thus to sabotage his own talent.

For Theobald does possess, if not the "magnificent genius" his model Serafina fondly claims for him, at least a talent worth cultivating. Mrs. Coventry alleges that "'the man didn't know the very alphabet of drawing'" (214); but her own claims to aesthetic literacy, founded on her "trumpery Peruginos" (215), are hardly robust. Offsetting her bias, the narrator vouches credibly for the excellence of Theobald's "*bambino*"—the chalk drawing he once did of Serafina's infant: "It was executed with singular freedom and power, and yet seemed vivid with the sacred bloom of infancy. A sort of dimpled elegance and grace, in the midst of its boldness, recalled the touch of Correggio" (219). Yet the artist half-apologizes for the rushed quality of the workmanship: "'You saw a feverish haste in it, I suppose; I wanted to spare the poor little mortal the pain of his position'" (220). Ironically, it is only when prodded by a kindly impulse into "raw Haste" that Theobald shows himself capable of producing something first-rate—or of producing anything. He may thus be violating the precedent of Mantegna; but he is being more deeply true to the spirit of "this rich old Italy, where art, so long as it really lived at all, was spontaneous, joyous, irresponsible."

Ultimately, Theobald's tragedy stems from his neurotic, mesmerized backward gaze at the Florentine past. The artistic milestones he worships turn out to be millstones; they repay his monomaniac passion by sinking his creative impulse. The strength of Michelangelo's David, in view of what it has meant for the susceptible expatriate, might well be called "sinister." The correlative in personal terms of Theobald's artistic fixation is his fascination with his aging "Madonna," Serafina. Like Andrea del Sarto's beautiful, hollow Lucrezia, Theobald's *femme fatale* is less the cause of her admirer's artistic failure than its symbolic projection, objectifying his deadly embrace of the past at the expense of present and future. Though she poses for Theobald's grandiosely conceived "Madonna of the Future," she is, like Lucrezia, a Madonna of the Past, a contradiction that supplies a central irony of the tale. Ironically, too, Serafina personifies Theobald's idolatrous image of Florence itself ("He talked of Florence like a lover . . . it was a very old affair; he had lost his heart to her at first sight. . . . 'some beautiful older woman with a "history" . . . aspiring gallantry'"); the terms he applies to the city he labels "the sole true woman of them all" fit with signal exactitude his sole true Madonna. Unfortunately, however, the woman Theobald has taken for a walking Renaissance masterpiece ("'You would have said . . . that Raphael had found his match in common chance'" ([220]) really exemplifies what James terms in his travel sketch "the perfect separateness of all the great productions of the Renaissance from the present and the future of the place, from the actual life and manners, the native ideal."

Serafina falls painfully short of Renaissance dynamism in her inner life. According to the narrator, "A certain mild intellectual apathy belonged properly to her type of beauty, and had always seemed to round and enrich it; but this *bourgeoise* Egeria, if I viewed her right, betrayed a rather vulgar stagnation of mind" (218). Such a woman is all too likely to compound paralysis in the artist who adores her. The idea of decline from antique excellence is accentuated by the lapsing of such faculties as Serafina does possess: "There might have been once a dim, spiritual light in her face; but it had long since begun to wane" (218). Her whole personality sardonically confirms her friend's conviction that "'the days of illumination are gone.'" By bringing up candles to provide "brighter illumination" for his Madonna, Theobald simply exposes more cruelly her age and her ingrained coarseness. The location of her dwelling—the Mercato Vecchio (Old Market)—revealingly connects her with her town's mercantile tradition, not its artistic one.

To prepare himself for executing the supreme masterpiece he has conceived, Theobald has for years "studied" his chosen model with the adoring attention he has lavished on his beloved Florence itself. His endless poring over Serafina's features has, finally, the same result as his poring over the city's: it abstracts him from the fluid reality of the present and curtails his chances of achieving anything substantial in the future. Appropriately, it is his youthful new acquaintance who thrusts him back into reality by informing him that the woman he worships belongs (like the city she lives in) irretrievably to the past; for his artistic purposes, she is simply "obsolete." "'She's an old, old woman—for a Madonna!'" (221). The narrator's assurance that Serafina has, again like her city, "beaux restes" hardly mends the situation. Sadly, Theobald must confront the truth: by dwelling for years in the still shadow of immortal greatness, he has numbed his perception of the movement of time. "Then at last I understood the immensity of his illusion; how, one by one, the noiseless years had ebbed away, and left him brooding in charmed inaction, forever preparing for a work forever deferred" (221). The artist's repeated moan, "'Old—old! Old—old!'", mourns not merely the faded beauty of the townswoman he has worshipped but the charm of the ancient town that has been his shrine and his undoing.

As a foil to the unworldly Theobald, James introduces a local "artist": the little sculptor of obscenely coupled cats and monkeys. According to Giorgio

Melchiori, the contrast between the two men externalizes a conflict in James's mind corresponding to the opposition between American and European sensibilities:

James . . . in "The Madonna of the Future," represents in the characters of the American painter and the Florentine sculptor the dilemma which he felt deeply: the morally sound, idealizing artist's purity of intentions issues in creative sterility, while the unquestionable skill and creative fecundity of the artist who belongs to the great European tradition is execrable on ethical grounds. (2.177)

Melchiori's analysis leads him to diagnose James as still psychologically bound, at this early stage of his career, by the puritan heritage he brought with him to Europe from the New World. Yet it is unlikely that the creator of amorous cats and monkeys can belong to any "great European tradition," or that his "skill and creative fecundity," whatever their moral status, imply true *aesthetic* merit. The late-nineteenth-century Florence that the sculptor inhabits is precisely the Florence from which James received a painful sense of "a great tradition broken"; the man's very presence there attests to the breakage. Even his dress suffices to place him in relation to tradition and the past: "On the side of his head he wore jauntily a little crimson velvet smoking-cap" (223). Such an accessory is "artistic" in a chic, affected fashion; it is the negation of the "little mediaeval *berretta*" that Theobald habitually wears.

Not surprisingly, the little Florentine differs equally from Theobald in his attitude toward his city's artistic heritage. Defending his productions, he protests: "'It is not classic art, signore, of course; but, between ourselves, isn't classic art sometimes rather a bore?'" (226). He plumes himself on the statuettes he calls "'these modest products of my own ingenuity'" not only because they are ingenious but because they are new, unsullied by the passing of time and men's eyes—"'They are brand-new, fresh from my *atelier*, and have never been exhibited in public'" (226). The novelty of his subject matter pointedly sets off the antiquity of Theobald's idols. No wonder the narrator, pocketing the sculptor's card, asks himself if Serafina "had an eye for contrasts" (227); this is Florentine antithesis with a vengeance.

But the sculptor's chief motive for pride is the "mystery" whereby he has invented an ideal medium in which to model his piquant caricatures:

"For this purpose I have invented a peculiar plastic compound which you will permit me not to divulge. That's my secret, signore! It's as light, you perceive, as cork, and yet as firm as alabaster! I frankly confess that I really pride myself as much on this little stroke of chemical ingenuity as upon the other element of novelty in my creations,—my types" (226).

If the American painter has undergone a conversion to the hallowed mode of Tuscan painting, the little Florentine has undergone his own passionate conversion to the cult of Yankee ingenuity. Where the one has his eye fixed adoringly on the splendid walls of the Uffizi and the Pitti, the other longs for the splendors of the U.S. Patent Office.

The single accomplishment that the sculptor shares with a Renaissance master like Browning's Lippi, the accuracy with which he observes and copies objects from nature, hardly redeems him. The narrator says of his figures, "[T]heir imitative felicity was revolting"; the artist himself, with his gift for mimicry, seems "little more than an exceptionally intelligent ape" (227). The loving attention Theobald bestows on the beauties of Florence ("'If you but knew the rapture of observation! I gather with every glance some hint for light, for colour or relief!'" [213]) the sculptor lavishes on his monkeys and cats ("'Since I have begun to examine these expressive little brutes, I have made many profound observations!'" [227]). The sculptor goes so far as to claim for his work not only the variety that belongs to great art ("'I think that you will admit that my combinations are really infinite'" [227]) but also its immortality: "'My statuettes are as durable as bronze,—*aere perennius*, signore,—and, between ourselves, I think they are more amusing'" (227). His impudence in quoting Horace perfectly sums up his whole vandalising relation to the heritage of the past.

Such a figure manifestly springs from James's perplexed awareness, as a visitor to Florence, "that the people who but three hundred years ago had the best taste in the world should now have the worst; that having produced the noblest, loveliest, costliest works, they should now be given up to the manufacture of objects at once ugly and paltry." The little sculptor is a producer of just those "catch-penny statues" whose currency in modern Italy James deplored. Yet his significance transcends national bounds; his abject artistic aims raise doubts whether less abject ones, in our "twilight of time," are still within the reach of artists on either side of the Atlantic.

The narrator himself voices such doubts by questioning Theobald's hope of emulating Raphael's Madonnas. In earlier times, he argues, "'people's religious and aesthetic needs went hand in hand, and there was . . . a demand for the Blessed Virgin, visible and adorable, which must have given firmness to the artist's hand. I'm afraid there is no demand now'" (210). To this analysis according to the best modern principles of the marketplace, Theobald replies magniloquently:

"There is always a demand!" he cried; "that ineffable type is one of the eternal needs of man's heart; but pious souls long for it in silence, almost in shame; let it appear, and this faith grows brave. How *should* it appear in this corrupt generation? . . . But it can spring now only from the soil of passionate labour and culture. Do you really fancy that while, from time to time, a man of complete artistic vision is born into the world, that image can perish?" (210)

Unhappily, lacking moral support from "this corrupt generation," which prefers lewdly coupled cats and monkeys to masterly Madonnas, Theobald is thrown, with his grandiose aims, back on his own limited resources. Predictably, he ends by wasting his opportunities through self-deluding, self-defeating maneuvers of delay and avoidance. Chief among these has been his adoration of the divine Serafina; and when this prop is toppled by the narrator's tactless words, the whole fabric of evasion falls into ruins. Although the narrator hopes his *gaffe* will have startled his friend "into the vulgar effort and hazard of production" (222), Theobald is in no position to pick up, like Howells's more resilient Colville, the shattered pieces of his life. The actual result is simply crushing: "The poor fellow's sense of wasted time, of vanished opportunity, seemed to roll in upon his soul in waves of darkness" (222). When after some days the narrator tracks Theobald down to his "grim ghost of a studio," the "immortal work" he finds on the easel is no Madonna, but an image that mirrors with pitiless precision the emptiness of Theobald's time-warped Florentine years: "a canvas that was a mere dead blank, cracked and discoloured by time" (228).

Throughout, Theobald has repeatedly been connected with the ambiguous gesture of tapping the forehead with the finger; now, dying, he taps his head one final time and speaks of having been "taking stock of [his] intellects" (229). The huge treasure-house of artistic greatness in which he has languished has stocked his brain to overflowing, while stultifying his power to execute what his brain has conceived. It is fitting that the protagonist of James's story should die of a Florentine "brain fever," raving about "the phantasmal pictures with which his brain seemed to swarm" (230). His death leaves the city itself such a "phantasmal picture." For the young newcomer who narrates it, the whole episode tinges the city with an unlovely coloring: "I was excessively impatient to leave Florence; my friend's dark spirit seemed diffused through all things" (231).

Theobald himself, even in his final, despairing delirium, does not draw so dark a conclusion from his own failure. But while he does not disavow his idealism, he recognises his tragic lack of the facility possessed by practitioners like the cats-and-monkeys man: "'I'm the half of a genius! Where in the wide world is my other half? Lodged perhaps in the vulgar soul, the cunning, ready fingers of some dull copyist or some trivial artisan who turns out by the dozen his easy prodigies of touch'" (229).

In fact, the complement Theobald wistfully imagines dwells among the pages of a poet he himself admires, Robert Browning. Andrea del Sarto, as Browning portrays him, is more than a "trivial artisan." Yet Andrea, too, longs to combine with an alter ego suited to complete his own fatal halfness:

> In this world, who can do a thing, will not;
> And who would do it, cannot, I perceive:
> Yet the will's somewhat—somewhat, too, the power—
> And thus we half-men struggle. (137-40)

Each character envisions the synthesis between desire and potency that has been achieved by the Florentine spirit at its most triumphant; both remain in their own lives doomed, in contrary ways, to incompleteness. Only through an oblique form of transmission do Andrea and Theobald unite to produce an untoward offspring: T. S. Eliot's J. Alfred Prufrock. Eliot plainly found hints in both Browning's poem and James's tale for his paralyzed anti-hero. Although Prufrock is no Florentine, his account of himself is introduced by lines from Dante's *Inferno*, and his impotence, like Theobald's, is placed in relief by ironic reference to the colossal counter-example of Michelangelo. All three characters—Andrea, Theobald, and Prufrock—have heard the mermaids singing, but only to drown the more surely within the engulfing human medium.

The resemblances among Andrea, Theobald, and Prufrock belong to a well-thumbed chapter in the story of modern culture: the progressive dissolution of the aspiring individual ego exposed to the corrosive force of self-consciousness. In James's tale, however, what dooms the protagonist is not simply the morbidness of his own psyche, or the haplessness of his response to his social milieu. It is, rather, the swamping of his individual talent by an overpowering tradition: the example of Florence. Of his final visit to the Pitti with Theobald, the narrator says:

I shall never forget our melancholy stroll through those gorgeous halls, every picture on whose walls seemed, even to my own sympathetic vision, to glow with a sort of insolent renewal of strength and lustre. The eyes and lips of the great portraits seemed to smile in ineffable scorn of the dejected pretender who had dreamed of competing with their glorious authors; the celestial candour, even, of the Madonna in the Chair, as we paused in perfect silence before her, was tinged with the sinister irony of the women of Leonardo. (229-30)

The monuments of the Florentine past have proved unkind familiars for the American whose too ardent devotion has sapped his creative daring, and who therefore remains a "dejected pretender." For James's fictional inheritor, E. M. Forster, the encounter between the modern imagination and the legacy of Florence is a subject not for tragedy but for brisk comedy. In Forster's turn-of-the-century Florentine novel, *A Room with a View*, another dejected pretender is transformed by her exposure to the magic city into a buoyant truth-teller.

Florence: Piazza della Signoria with Palazzo Vecchio. From *All Florence: Monuments, Buildings, Churches, Museums, Art Galleries, Outskirts*, page 43. New York: Charles Scribner's Sons, 1971. Photograph reproduced courtesy of Bonechi Edizioni "Il Turismo," August 20, 1992.

6

A Room with a View:
A Sense of Deities Reconciled

After a dispiriting evening arrival at the Pensione Bertolini, with its cockney *padrona* and its "portraits of the late Queen and the late Poet Laureate" (*Room* 2), Lucy Honeychurch awakes the next morning to a more satisfying impression:

It was pleasant to wake up in Florence, to open the eyes upon a bright bare room, with a floor of red tiles which look clean though they are not; with a painted ceiling whereon pink griffins and blue amorini sport in a forest of yellow violins and bassoons. It was pleasant, too, to fling wide the windows, pinching the fingers in unfamiliar fastenings, to lean out into sunshine with beautiful hills and trees and marble churches opposite, and, close below, the Arno, gurgling against the embankment of the road. (14)

The description engagingly conveys the synthesis of contrary qualities that E.M. Forster's post-Victorian Florence embodies: simplicity blended with opulence, fact with fancy, nature with artifice. As against the "clashing deities" that dominate the hectic Renaissance Florence of *Romola*, deities here are already on their way to becoming reconciled. The painted mythological figures sport in a "forest" of instruments, and all this interior contrivance mingles harmoniously with an outer prospect—"beautiful hills and trees and marble churches"—which itself genially combines the natural and the man-made. Amid the scene, the gurgling Arno suggests the life-renewing magic that in this novel water invariably contains. This "view" has a potentially subversive impact on the young English girl's puritan, Victorian literal-mindedness. She is exposed to the southern nonchalance that accepts appearances as realities—the floor tiles, for example, "which look clean though they are not." Her dawning susceptibility is intimated by her act of flinging the windows apart; pinching her fingers, she suffers only the enlivening discomfort that attends exposure to a vibrant otherness.

In Forster's Florentine novel, literal views shade subtly into moral discoveries. Lucy's duenna, Charlotte Bartlett, though offended by the *padrona*'s failure to provide the promised south view, plays a part metaphorically obstructive to vision. Spreading, as Lucy perceives, "a haze of disapproval in the air" (9), Charlotte seems to have brought the English climate along in her

luggage. Her beclouding influence makes her a foil for Mr. Emerson, who is
intent on securing views for the two ladies:

Miss Bartlett only sighed, and enveloped [Lucy] in a protecting embrace as she wished
her goodnight. It gave Lucy the sensation of a fog, and when she reached her own room
she opened the window and breathed the clean night air, thinking of the kind old man
who had enabled her to see the lights dancing in the Arno, and the cypresses of San
Miniato, and the foothills of the Apennines, black against the rising moon. (12)

Charlotte's life-shunning hermeticism reverses the welcome Lucy gives to
foreignness when she flings her windows wide apart: "Miss Bartlett, in her room,
fastened the window-shutters and locked the door, and then made a tour of the
apartment to see where the cupboards led, and whether there were any oubliettes
or secret entrances" (12-13).
     It is crucial to Lucy's Florentine "education" that she resist her cousin's
efforts to seal her vision—that she see Florence plain. Through her resistance,
local landmarks become impregnated with symbolic value, acting on the young
woman with an admonitory force. Just before witnessing a murder in the Piazza
della Signoria, Lucy has an epiphanic "view" of the tower of the Palazzo
Vecchio emerging from the Florentine shadows:

She fixed her eyes wistfully on the tower of the palace, which rose out of the lower
darkness like a pillar of roughened gold. It seemed no longer a tower, no longer
supported by earth, but some unattainable treasure throbbing in the tranquil sky. Its
brightness mesmerized her, still dancing before her eyes when she bent them to the
ground and started towards home. (41)

The famous tower has here acquired phallic overtones, relevant both to the
masculine aggressiveness Lucy is about to behold and to the male companionship
and protection she will afterward receive from George Emerson. But its
associations are not jarringly violent, as they are in an earlier draft of the scene:
"She saw the tower of the Palazzo, red in the sunset like a bleeding spear" (*Lucy
Novels* 98). In the final version, the tower is no longer a lurid phallic omen of
imminent bloodshed but a beacon revealing to the inhibited English girl an image
of life at once full-blooded and exalting.
     Italy, according to Philip Herriton in *Where Angels Fear to Tread* (1905),
is "'a country . . . that's upset people from the beginning of the world'" (73).
The town of Florence has a notably upsetting effect on Lucy's efforts to maintain
a maidenly composure. "The well-known world had broken up, and there
emerged Florence, a magic city where people thought and did the most
extraordinary things. . . . Was there more in her frank beauty than met the
eye—the power, perhaps, to evoke passions, good and bad, and to bring them
speedily to a fulfillment?" (55). In Lucy herself, the city will evoke a

passion—a good one—though her unreasoning flight from passion will provide the mainspring of the plot. In reality, even what does "meet the eye" suffices to give Florence its magical power to foster intense feeling, to conduct a neophyte like Lucy into emotional adulthood without exposing her to the tragic dislocations a Romola must face. The rugged visual potency of a place like the Piazza della Signoria works on Lucy with a quasi-occult persuasiveness:

The Piazza Signoria is too stony to be brilliant. It has no grass, no flowers, no frescoes, no glittering walls of marble or comforting patches of ruddy brick. By an odd chance—unless we believe in a presiding genius of place—the statues that relieve its severity suggest, not the innocence of childhood nor the glorious bewilderment of youth, but the conscious achievements of maturity. . . . Here, not only in the solitude of Nature, might a hero meet a goddess, or a heroine a god. (57)

"Unless we believe in a presiding genius of place"—but of course Forster's novel presupposes such a belief. Nor is it only Florentine piazzas that harbor genii; Lucy's home, Windy Corner, has one of its own, one that grips her as compellingly as the Italian city's. There exists, moreover, a covert kinship between the genius of the one place and that of the other. When Lucy, back in England, confuses the painter Francesco Francia with Piero della Francesca, her priggish fiancé Cecil accuses her of "forgetting her Italy" (149). But Lucy's Italy is not, in the vicinity of Windy Corner, so easily forgotten:

Ah, how beautiful the Weald looked! The hills stood out above its radiance, as Fiesole stands above the Tuscan plain, and the South Downs, if one chose, were the mountains of Carrara. She might be forgetting her Italy, but she was noticing more things in her England. One could play a new game with the view, and try to find in its innumerable folds some town or village that would do for Florence. (156)

For Cecil, Lucy's new game would be unplayable. To confuse an indifferent Sussex landscape with the supreme Italian art center is as shameful as to confuse Francia with della Francesca. However, in Forster remembering one's Florence means more than keeping one's artists pigeonholed; it means, above all, keeping one's visual perception constantly alert, as Browning's Lippi counsels. Although details of art history may elude her, Lucy "sees" more truly than Cecil, because her vision is less cluttered by convention; she has come back from Italy "with new eyes" (110). Where the affected Cecil excludes Windy Corner from his slim catalogue of liveable habitats—"'Italy and London are the only places where I don't feel to exist on sufferance'"(91)—the newly-awakened Lucy senses the affinity between Tuscany and her own unassuming home. London—the effete, snobbish London of the Vyses—is at the antipodes from both Windy Corner and Florence:

The food was poor, but the talk had a witty weariness that impressed the girl. One was tired of everything, it seemed. One launched into enthusiasms only to collapse gracefully, and pick oneself up amid sympathetic laughter. In this atmosphere the Pension Bertolini and Windy Corner appeared equally crude, and Lucy saw that her London career would estrange her a little from all that she had loved in the past. (121)

Crude or not, Florence and Lucy's Sussex home share one saving grace: they are vital, not vapid. But Mrs. Vyse, "thinking of the museum that represented Italy to her" (122), is blind to that vitality, and her son's perceptions mesh with hers.

Forster's modern Florence is less apt even than James's to allow a museum to represent it. Where "The Madonna of the Future" exposes the perils of a Ruskinian adoration of the Florentine past, Forster's novel celebrates the robust vigor of the Florentine present, which gives no cause for "blueness." Consequently, Forster's stance is more cheerfully anti-Ruskinian even than James's. In A Room with a View, any pompous intolerance for the Florentine present becomes fair game for satire. Lucy yearns to tour the city, alone, on the most up-to-date conveyance, defying Victorian propriety: "Conversation was tedious; she wanted something big, and she believed that it would have come to her on the wind-swept platform of an electric tram" (39). Her impulse is later implicitly rebuked by the Reverend Cuthbert Eager's comments on an English expatriate couple:

"Doubtless you know her monographs in the series of 'Mediaeval Byways'? He is working at 'Gemisthus Pletho.' Sometimes as I take tea in their beautiful grounds I hear, over the wall, the electric tram squealing up the new road with its loads of hot, dusty, unintelligent tourists who are going to 'do' Fiesole in an hour in order that they may say they have been there, and I think—I think—I think how little they think what lies so near them." (60-61)

For Mr. Eager, the best refuge against such mechanized horror belongs to Lady Helen Laverstock, "'at present busy over Fra Angelico,'" who has turned her villa into a fortress, screening out (as Charlotte Bartlett would have Lucy do) both vulgarity and life: "'She is very proud of that thick hedge. Inside, perfect seclusion. One might have gone back six hundred years'" (60). Eager regards with fastidious horror the violence Lucy has inadvertently observed: "'This very square—so I am told—witnessed yesterday the most sordid of tragedies. To one who loves the Florence of Dante and Savonarola there is something portentous in such desecration—portentous and humiliating'" (50). What he forgets is that Dante and Savonarola witnessed acts of violence just as sordid; the great Dominican friar was, indeed, portentously and humiliatingly hanged and burned in "this very square."

The Reverend Cuthbert's anachronistic pastoralism—his precious, Ruskinian disdain for the present—is shared by characters who in other ways differ from him. Charlotte Bartlett is scandalized to discover George Emerson's occupation:

"Miss Bartlett had asked Mr. George Emerson what his profession was, and he had answered 'the railway.' She was very sorry that she had asked him. She had no idea that it would be such a dreadful answer, or she would not have asked him" (64). George's involvement with a rapid, modern means of transport associates him with the Florentine tram from which Lucy has expected "something big"; but by the same token it condemns him to a social limbo in the eyes of Edwardian gentility, which shrinks from too close a contact with dynamism of any sort. The urbane, sprightly Mr. Beebe, another guest at the Bertolini, has traveled beyond such jejune prejudices, yet even Beebe is oriented more towards the past than the present—"It was one of Mr. Beebe's chief pleasures to provide people with happy memories" (37). Only the Emersons, in the spirit of their forward-looking American namesake, direct their sight eagerly towards the present and future.

Like Lippi, the elder Emerson "always see[s] the Garden and God there / A-making man's wife" ("Fra Lippo Lippi" 266-7), but his version of sacred history reverses orthodox chronology: "'The Garden of Eden . . . which you place in the past, is really yet to come. We shall enter it when we no longer despise our bodies'" (126). The course of the narrative obeys Mr. Emerson's program: by the end, Lucy has emerged from a bodiless yesterday and entered into the Edenic tomorrow of sexual fulfillment. This shift from past to future is confirmed by the appeal of the Florentine cabman, which runs as a refrain through the novel's closing pages: "'Signorino, domani faremo un giro'" ("'Young sir, tomorrow we'll go for a ride'"). And the symbolic agent of the shift has been the cabman's city, which has taught Lucy to look forward instead of back and has prompted her "no longer to despise her body." Her Florentine days begin in sightseeing and end in vision; they lead her out of the "Middle Ages" and into her own personal renaissance. Her progress thus resembles that of Romola, who must break with Savonarola's ascetic ideal before she can locate herself in her own city; but the two heroines' personal destinies could not be more unlike.

The art of Florence assumes an unusual role in Forster's novel. Instead of stifling Lucy, as it does James's Theobald, it contributes its share to her liberation. Yet its tendency is not automatically liberating; its effect depends on the viewer's perspective. As Jeffrey Meyers argues, "Forster contrasts two distinct approaches to art: the expert and sterile, sanctified by the German's [Baedeker's] guidebooks, and the emotional and intuitive, employed by those liberated English who have abandoned themselves to the experience of the exquisite peninsula" (31). To be "busy over Fra Angelico," for Mr. Eager a commendable trait, is, by other lights, to be dismally idle. The masterworks of the Florentine past serve life valuably as long as they do not usurp the primacy of life itself: as long as painted surfaces are not allowed to obscure "the blue sky and the men and women who live under it" (14-15), as long as Giotto's "tactile values" are not preferred to the value of touch. Meyers's dual categories—"two distinct approaches"—recall Matthew Arnold's more general distinction between Hebraism and Hellenism, which I have applied to the conflicting forces at work in Eliot's *Romola*. Forster's interest in Arnold, though tinged with ambivalence, ran deep; and it is not surprising that Arnold's famous dualism illuminates the major conflicts in *A Room with a View*, as well.

Miss Charlotte Bartlett is the purest exemplar among Forster's cast of those qualities to which Arnold applied the term "Hebraism." Throughout her stay in the Etrurian Athens, she strives to abide by the puritan "strictness of conscience" that Arnold opposes to the Hellenist "spontaneity of consciousness" (*Culture and Anarchy* 132); as Alan Wilde says, "[Charlotte's] reactions lack all spontaneity, following from her allegiance to this or that code of formalized behavior" (52). Her life is devoted to the Hebraist values of "conduct and obedience," rather than to the Greek ideal of "seeing things as they really are" (*Culture* 131). To cite Rickie Elliot's Arnoldian observation in *The Longest Journey* (1907), "'[T]he Greeks looked very straight at things'" (174); Miss Bartlett is no Greek, and she looks askance. Like her more assertive spiritual sister, Harriet Herriton of *Where Angels Fear to Tread*, Miss Bartlett is apt to get symbolic smuts in her eye. Not only is Charlotte's view of Florence consequently impaired; she insists on blinkering her young cousin's field of vision as well. For Charlotte, naked reality—above all, human nudity—is something to be shrouded. She impresses on Lucy that a painted nude figure, like Botticelli's Venus, is a "pity" (40). Even her insistence on "concealing the sex" of the man who has rescued Lucy in Piazza Signoria (51) betrays her squinting, figleaf mentality.

"Charlotte's energy! And her unselfishness!" (12). In imbuing Lucy with her own cloistered notions of propriety, Miss Bartlett displays what Arnold calls "the intense and convinced energy with which the Hebrew . . . threw himself upon his ideal of righteousness" (*Culture and Anarchy* 38). Her mind rigidly categorizes behavior according to fixed and polarized absolutes, "delicacies," for example, as against "brutality" (*Room* 4); naively, she assumes that "delicacy" and "beauty" are synonyms (10). To her, Florence, with its rare synthesis of apparently discordant values—vigor and grace, nature and art—is a closed book. Like a latter-day *Piagnone*, she walks through the city by the best light she has but does not take sufficient care that her light be not darkness; her squeamishness keeps her from seeing things "in their beauty . . . with a kind of aerial ease, clearness, and radiancy" (*Culture* 134). If Charlotte, as the narrator says, "works like a great artist," she does so only by evolving a life-defeating Hebraist grand design, "a shame-faced world of precautions and barriers which may avert evil, but which do not seem to bring good" (78-79).

In the Reverend Cuthbert Eager, a basically Hebraist cast of mind coexists with a lofty claim to aesthetic connoisseurship. When he first appears, in the church of Santa Croce, expounding Giotto to his respectful followers, he is rendering double service as both a spiritual and cultural Baedeker: "The lecturer was a clergyman, and his audience must also be his flock, for they held prayerbooks as well as guidebooks in their hands" (23). Even though his primary function is ecclesiastical, Mr. Eager has established himself as an authority on matters artistic among the Florentine colony of expatriate English. His discourse on the Bardi Chapel exemplifies his expertise:

"Remember," he was saying, "the facts about this church of Santa Croce; how it was built by faith in the full fervour of medievalism, before any taint of the Renaissance had appeared. Observe how Giotto in these frescoes . . . is untroubled by the snares of anatomy and perspective. Could anything be more majestic, more pathetic, beautiful, true? How little, we feel, avails knowledge and technical cleverness against a man who truly feels!" (22)

Mr. Eager is the spiritual heir of Lippi's censorious Prior, who was scandalized by the growing Renaissance hunger for artistic naturalism. His traditionalist bias, like the Prior's, arouses in the reader no doubts about the greatness of Giotto; it simply reveals the narrowness of his own aesthetic creed.

Although Lucy's "fiasco," Cecil Vyse, appears to be the most culturally adept Hellenist in the novel, he, too, weighed in the Florentine balance, is found wanting. What is original in Forster's treatment of Cecil is his disclosure of a hidden affinity between the aestheticist temper and the ascetic one. Their kinship is grounded on the common detachment of both tempers from the unblushing, sensuous experience for which Forster's Florence stands: from "the snares of anatomy." Cecil's absorption in Italian Renaissance art is painfully literary and factitious. Far from reflecting any "pagan" impulses within him, it merely provides fashionable drapery for a medieval torso:

He was medieval. Like a Gothic statue. Tall and refined, with shoulders that seemed braced square by an effort of the will, and a head that was tilted a little higher than the usual level of vision, he resembled those fastidious saints who guard the portals of a French cathedral. Well educated, well endowed, and not deficient physically, he remained in the grip of a certain devil whom the modern world knows as self-consciousness, and whom the medieval, with dimmer vision, worshipped as asceticism. A Gothic statue implies celibacy, just as a Greek statue implies fruition. (86-87)

As the description hints, Cecil's moral angle of vision is as "tilted" as his physical one; he lacks the Hellenist's capacity to "see things as they really are" (*Culture* 131), and there is little that is fruitful in his nature. Later in the novel, when he gives Lucy a circumspect kiss, his gold pince-nez becomes dislodged and gets "flattened between them" (108), a perfect image of the way the tilted lenses of snobbish affectation screen him from reality, above all the reality of Lucy's body.

When she at length dismisses Cecil, Lucy painfully explains to him that he is conventional: "'Cecil, you're that, for you may understand beautiful things, but you don't know how to use them; and you wrap yourself up in art and books and music, and would try to wrap up me'" (172). In order to arrive at this difficult but needed distinction between "understanding" beauty and "using" it, Lucy herself has had to undergo a process of schooling in how to see, a process begun in the sun-filled schoolroom of Florence. Her tutors have been "'those Florentine Emersons,'" as Mr. Beebe insists on calling them (114).

"Seeing things as they really are," for Arnold a hallmark of the Hellenist temper, is a virtue that Forster identifies with the Etrurian Athens. It is a virtue to which the medieval Cecil attains only once, when Lucy is already on the point of vanishing from his sight: "He looked at her, instead of through her, for the first time since they were engaged. From a Leonardo she had become a living woman, with mysteries and forces of her own, with qualities that even eluded art" (171).   As Meyers observes, "In the course of the novel . . . Lucy Honeychurch moves from a separation to an integration of art and life, and her development is measured by her change from a purely aesthetic object to a mature woman awakened through art to self-knowledge" (38). Nevertheless, it is in Cecil's eyes alone that Lucy has ever been "a purely aesthetic object," and her awakening to self-knowledge comes not only through art but also through "qualities that even eluded art." Art may help to awaken her, but her movement toward maturity is gauged by the broader Florentine-Hellenist criterion of clear-sightedness.   It is a sudden clairvoyance that moves her to break her engagement—"The scales fell from Lucy's eyes" (168). "'There are days when one sees clearly, and this is one of them,'" she tells the perplexed Cecil (170).

Lucy's journey toward such Florentine clarity is a Hellenist pilgrim's progress, one that takes her beyond the dampening ethical conventions upon which she has been raised. In *Culture and Anarchy* Arnold repeatedly draws on Swift's metaphor of "sweetness and light" to express "the central and happy idea of the essential character of human perfection," an idea whose discovery he attributes to the ancient Greeks (54). The name Forster chose for his heroine, Lucy Honeychurch, incorporates Arnold's pair of watchwords, along with the idea of religious consecration. While Lucy's actual day-to-day behavior hardly achieves an "essential character of human perfection," her name adumbrates an ideal toward which she moves by traversing a lengthy, circuitous route away from "darkness" and into the "light." Here, again, she is a literary fellow-traveler of Romola.

Lucy's mentor, Mr. Emerson, resembles Savonarola in wielding the personal authority that accompanies absolute conviction. In all else, however, he is the Frate's opposite. "'Hateful bishop!'" he fumes over a monument in Santa Croce, "'Hard in life, hard in death'" (20). His address to the child who has tripped over the bishop's tomb is truculently anticlaustral: "'Go out into the sunshine, little boy, and kiss your hand to the sun, for that is where you ought to be'" (20). Unlike Romola, who in order to attain clarity must learn to live with Florentine shadows, Lucy's main mission is to go out into the sun and kiss her hand to it. Only by performing that unchurchly obeisance will she earn the right to utter for herself Mr. Emerson's famous first words: "'I have a view, I have a view'" (3).

Old Emerson's advice to Lucy is strenuously anti-Hebraist: "'Let yourself go. Pull out from the depths those thoughts that you do not understand, and spread them out in the sunlight and know the meaning of them'" (26). The art of Florence helps Lucy to spread her thoughts in the sunlight, but not by subjecting her to the studiousness that blocks off the sun for the sake of being "busy over Fra Angelico." The masterpiece that starts her on her way is emphatically secular in tendency, and she comes upon it in a setting that is spacious and open to the sunlight:

For one ravishing moment Italy appeared. She stood in the Square of the Annunziata and saw in the living terracotta those divine babies whom no cheap reproduction can ever stale. There they stood, with their shining limbs bursting from the garments of charity, and their strong white arms extended against circlets of heaven. Lucy thought she had never seen anything more beautiful. (18)

"Della Robbia's craft," which in Browning's "The Statue and the Bust" had icily confirmed emotional stasis, here does the precise opposite. Luca's frieze for the portico of the Spedale degli Innocenti embodies values that Forster associates with the Florentine Renaissance and that persist into the Florentine present: youth, vigor, and joyous vitality. The clay of which the divine babies have been modelled is "living." The babies themselves resist with Blakean unruliness the swaddling bands meant to confine them ("their shining limbs bursting from the garments of charity"), and they rise triumphantly in relief against their own material medium ("their strong white arms extended against circlets of heaven"). Tellingly, Lucy finds that she prefers this quintessence of Renaissance *joie de vivre* to Giotto's more sober and revered medieval frescoes; and the always pragmatic Mr. Emerson gives his profane blessing to her preference: "'A baby is worth a dozen saints'" (25).

But if it takes an artwork to stir Lucy out of her Hebraist slumber towards an uninhibited embrace of life, it takes different Florentine experiences to lend momentum to her change. The stabbing she witnesses in the Piazza della Signoria is one such experience: "[The wounded man] frowned; he bent towards Lucy with a look of interest, as if he had an important message for her. He opened his lips to deliver it, and a stream of red came out between them and trickled down his unshaven chin" (41). The red stream, a shocking counterpart to the river that Lucy had heard gurgling under her window that morning, affects the girl all the more powerfully because of the contrast it makes with the bloodless respectability of her Victorian upbringing. Lucy is so frightened of her own repressed impulses—"those thoughts that you do not understand"—that only so sensational a message can jolt them into the sunlight. The brutal display of passion compels her to "let herself go," and as a result she obtains a momentously altered image of George Emerson: "Even as she caught sight of him he grew dim; the palace [the Palazzo Vecchio] itself grew dim, swayed above her, fell on to her softly, slowly, noiselessly, and the sky fell with it" (49). When Lucy swoons, Florence itself falls erotically on top of her. George's subsequent action of tossing her blood-stained art photos into the Arno has symbolic as well as dramatic value: it affirms the primacy of immediate experience over artistic representation.

Both through its art and its life, Forster's Florence possesses the power to open Lucy's eyes with tableaus that are sometimes passionate, sometimes terrible, but always arousing. The handsome young couple who drive Lucy and her friends to Fiesole are at once believable Florentine scapegraces and figures from a mythological Renaissance pageant: Phaethon and Persephone. Leaping back beyond both the modern and the medieval, they evoke a primal, Etrurian-Hellenic spirit of place:

It was Phaethon who drove them to Fiesole that memorable day, a youth all irresponsibility and fire, recklessly urging his master's horses up the stony hill. Neither the Ages of Faith nor the Age of Doubt had touched him; he was Phaethon in Tuscany driving a cab. And it was Persephone whom he asked leave to pick up on the way, saying that she was his sister—Persephone, tall and slender and pale, returning with the spring to her mother's cottage, and still shading her eyes from the unaccustomed light. (58)

The Florentine Phaethon and Persephone make an apt pair to conduct Lucy into the sunlight and to provide her with one of her climactic "views," a prospect upon which she stumbles while searching for the two clergymen, Eager and Beebe:

The view was forming at last; she could discern the river, the golden plain, other hills . . .
      At the same moment the ground gave way, and with a cry she fell out of the wood. Light and beauty enveloped her. She had fallen onto a little open terrace, which was covered with violets from end to end. (67)

Her fall takes her, against her conscious will, into a secular baptism, immersing her in the creative element of the flowering Tuscan countryside:

From her feet the ground sloped sharply into view, and violets ran down in rivulets and streams and cataracts, irrigating the hillside with blue, eddying round the tree stems, collecting into pools in the hollows, covering the grass with spots of azure foam. But never again were they in such profusion; this terrace was the well-head, the primal source whence beauty gushed out to water the earth. Standing at its brink, like a swimmer who prepares, was the good man. (67-68)

The "good man" is of course George, and Lucy finds herself, to her thrilled consternation, plunging along with him. The impulse prompting them to kiss originates in the profusion of nature, but its roots extend down to the flowerless, waterless square in the town below. If "the Piazza Signoria is too stony to be brilliant," still, "[h]ere, not only in the solitude of Nature, might a hero meet a goddess, or a heroine a god." It is crucial to Lucy's process of self-discovery that she meet George in both places; crucial that she *see* the young man in such a way that his physical being comes home to her. Later, after the Emersons have turned up in the neighborhood of Windy Corner, she begins more consciously to "[entertain] . . . an image [of George] that had physical beauty" (143), and the conclusion of her story is sealed.

By now Lucy has encountered George again, not as a figurative swimmer but as a real and quite naked one. The effect has been disarming. "Who could foretell that she and George would meet in the rout of a civilization, amidst an army of coats and collars and boots that lay wounded over the sunlit earth?" (134). Lucy nevertheless continues to fight a last-ditch Hebraist battle against the Hellenist-Florentine menace of ungarbed perception, against Mr. Eager's "snares of anatomy." She refuses to admit to herself her love for George: "Life is easy to chronicle, but bewildering to practise, and we welcome 'nerves' or any other shibboleth that will cloak our personal desire" (142). The Hebraic word nicely captures Lucy's frame of mind. In these late chapters, as Lucy's internal conflict nears its crisis, the language of warfare becomes (as it does in Howells's *Indian Summer*) increasingly frequent. Still shunning Hellenist nudity (that "pity"), Lucy dons a suit of dour Hebraist armor: "The armour of falsehood is subtly wrought out of darkness, and hides a man not only from others, but from his own soul. In a few moments Lucy was equipped for battle" (161).

In essence, Lucy is waging war against herself and her own real desires. Retreating in panic from the lucidity her name betokens, she has joined the Arnoldian ignorant armies that clash by night, "the vast armies of the benighted, who follow neither the heart nor the brain, and march to their destiny by catchwords" (174). Heart and brain, in this novel, are not antagonistic but married, and their bridal place is the Arno valley. For the Victorian Arnold, the supreme principle of the Hellenist spirit was intellect, a principle with which "the *alma Venus*, the life-giving and joy-giving power of nature" (*Culture* 137) could maintain only a shaky alliance. In *Romola*, Arnold's contemporary, Eliot, shows how Tito's Hellenist creed of "natural" self-gratification fails to harmonise with his aspiration to intellectual eminence. But for Forster, the child of a later literary generation, "passion and truth"—"Eros" and "Pallas Athene"—are "allied deities" (174). Arnold's "central fault," as Forster wrote to Malcolm Darling in 1910, "is prudishness—I don't use the word in its narrow sense, but as implying a general dislike to all warmth" (*Letters* 1:111). According to Forster's updated understanding of the concept, Arnold himself is a Hellenist *manqué*; and the same could be said of Lucy, who has failed to make the Forsterian connection between passion and truth. It is Mr. Emerson who connects them for her, giving her at last "a sense of deities reconciled" (204), and thus completing her "view": "It was as if he had made her see the whole of everything at once" (204).

It has not been easy for him to stop Lucy's panicky retreat from "that king of terrors—light" (191-2). Only his determined verbal assault on her, for the cause of those Florentine allies, Pallas and Eros, brings her to her final illumination: "'Passion does not blind. No. Passion is sanity.'" (196). Amusingly, in her anxiety to block Hellenist projectiles she is driven to screen her view with a slab of Hebrew law: "Lucy selected a book—a volume of Old Testament commentaries. Holding it up to her eyes, she said: 'I have no wish to discuss Italy or any subject connected with your son'" (196). But her kindly adversary's words succeed in purging her obstinate Hebraist blindness: "As he spoke the darkness was withdrawn, veil after veil, and she saw to the bottom of her soul" (202). Mr. Emerson intuitively hits on the radiant images that have the power to release Lucy from the fetishes that have held her: "'Now it is all dark. Now Beauty and Passion seem never to have existed. I know. But remember the mountains over Florence and the view'" (204). The title of the novel's last chapter—"The End of the Middle Ages"—eloquently sums up the outcome of Lucy's "remembering."

Having come to terms with her passion for an "unsuitable" man, and having thereby alienated her world of Windy Corner, Lucy celebrates her renaissance, inevitably, in Florence. The Hellenist pilgrim at last reaches the Celestial City, which turns out—as one has foreseen all along—to be a solidly earthly one. In the book's closing sentence, the two lovers hear "the river, bearing down the snows of winter into the Mediterranean" (209). The northern winter of Hebraism has yielded to a southern, Hellenistic thaw. Lucy has taken possession of that "sweetness and light" that her name has always pledged, and on terms that do not exclude her body.   The city that, in *Luria* and *Romola*, was the locus of chill intellection and factional strife has suddenly become a haven of concord and erotic warmth, a transformation which demonstrates that the literary history of a city can be as wayward as human history itself. Little more than a decade after the appearance of *A Room with a View*, under the impress of D. H. Lawrence's heterodox imagination, Florence was to undergo a metamorphosis into a storied city arrestingly different from any of the versions so far encountered.

7

The Extreme South of the
Lily's Flowering: *Aaron's Rod*

"Over *Romola* he shook his head," reports Jessie Chambers of her girlhood friend D. H. Lawrence (98). In *Aaron's Rod* (1922), Lawrence was to produce a portrait of Florence that would have made George Eliot's head shake. The Florentine chapters of *Aaron's Rod* reverse the premises of *Romola*. Eliot, seeking a model of community that could reconcile continuity with vital change, locates that community in the historic Florence of Savonarola and Lorenzo the Magnificent. Lawrence plunges the reader into discontinuity and bewildering flux, a contemporary earthquake-zone of which Florence is the epicenter. His narrative proceeds by disconcerting leaps; its favored mode is the non-sequitur.

For this reason, the form of *Aaron's Rod* has been widely condemned. H. M. Daleski, to cite one well-known example, speaks of "the flabby flesh of its structure" (190). Nevertheless, there is method in the madness of Lawrence's narrative, above all in the destination at which it ultimately arrives. The protagonist, Aaron Sisson, has thrown over his domestic routine in his bleak Midlands town, dismissing it as a "little home stunt." With his treasured flute, "Aaron's Rod," symbol both of his sexual and his artistic prowess, he stays in a number of other localities in England and Italy. These serve only to convince him of the absence of stable values in his post-war world. Florence, his *terminus ad quem*, stands at the end of the dusty trail leading from his *terminus a quo*; the English "little home" and the great Italian city balance each other symmetrically. In the cradle of the Renaissance Aaron finds the answer to the stillborn Midlands, a place that seems to afford him an outlet for his blocked creative impulses. What the city does in fact offer Aaron Sisson turns out, however, to be not what he expects, and to be quite unlike what it has offered the protagonists of earlier Florentine fictions.

Aaron has a view. Since Lawrence gives the fictional hotel at which Aaron first stays—the Bertolini—the same name as Lucy Honeychurch's, his view presumably resembles hers; and his awakening in Florence brings a similar sense of transformative magic:

Then morning found him out early, before his friends had arisen. It was sunny again. The magic of Florence at once overcame him, and he forgot the bore of limited means and hotel costs. He went straight out of the hotel door, across the road, and leaned on the river parapet. There ran the Arno: not such a flood after all, but a green stream with shoals of pebbles in its course. . . . There was a noise and clatter of traffic: boys pushing handbarrows over the cobble stones, slow bullocks stepping side by side, and shouldering one another affectionately, drawing a load of country produce, then horses in great brilliant scarlet cloths, like vivid palls, slowly pulling the long narrow carts of the district: and men hu-huing!—and people calling: all the sharp, clattering morning noise of Florence. (206)

Like Forster's picture of Lucy's Florentine awakening, the description highlights the scene's variety and color, while it suggests an easy, companionable mating of the human and the natural. More emphatically than Forster's, however, it evokes the town's "go," the dynamism of its daily life. Aaron's positive first impressions are soon reinforced. Scanning the Piazza della Signoria, where "passionate, fearless Florence had spoken herself out," he feels an unaccustomed satisfaction: "Here men had been at their intensest, most naked pitch, here, at the end of the old world and the beginning of the new. Since then, always rather puling and apologetic" (212). In him, as in Lucy, exposure to the town promises to inspire a personal renaissance: "Aaron felt a new self, a new life-urge rising inside himself. Florence seemed to start a new man in him" (212). Ultimately, however, Aaron's Florentine renaissance proves abortive; and the reasons lie in Lawrence's peculiar feelings about the town and its position in the modern world.

   "Obviously northerners must love Florence," Lawrence argues in his essay "David," which dates from the period of *Aaron's Rod*. "Here is their last point, their most southerly. The extreme south of the Lily's flowering" (*Phoenix* 61). Lawrence's perception of Florence as a place where diverse gods may be reconciled resembles Forster's, but only up to a point. His exclamatory prose in the essay conjures up an image of the city as a great theater of anticlimax:

But Florence, the Lily-town among her hills! Her hills, her hovering waters. She can be hot, brilliant, burnt dry. But look at David! What's the matter with him? Not sun but cold rain. Children of the South, exposing themselves to the rain. Savonarola, like a hot coal quenched. The South, the North: the fire, the wet downfall. Once there was a pure equilibrium, and the Lily blossomed. But the Lily now—livid! David, livid, almost quenched, yet still strained and waiting, tense for that orgasm. (61)

(The last detail refers to a local legend according to which Michelangelo's David attains "an anticipatory orgasm . . . at midnight of the New Year" [60].)
   Like earlier portraits of the city, Lawrence's "David" is a study in polarities. Here, however, these have become so harshly opposed as to be mutually annihilating. The Renaissance witnessed a miraculous union: "The South to the North. Married!" (62). But the moment of synthesis was soon followed by the wet downfall: "Cinque-Cento, a fleeting moment of adolescence. In that one

moment the two eternal elements were held in consummation, forming the perfect embodiment of the human soul. And then gone" (62).

What prompted Lawrence's picture of a post-coital Florence was his visit there soon after the war. As he describes the place in his epilogue to *Movements in European History* (1921), its charmed adolescence has vanished: "In the summer of 1920 I went north, and Florence was in a state of continual socialistic riot: sudden shots, sudden stones smashing into the restaurants where one was drinking coffee, all the shops suddenly barred and closed" (316). His impressions becloud the view of the modern city he presents in *Aaron's Rod*. There, civil disruption is a sign (to reverse Eliot's positivist formula) not of struggling order but of encroaching chaos.

For Lawrence, the influence of Savonarola himself, that "hot coal quenched," helped to account for the city's decline from its glorious moment of consummation. In *Movements in European History* he portrays "the fanatic friar" (182) as "the last, almost degenerate representative of the Dark Age of Faith" (186), whose reforming zeal dimmed the luster of Lorenzo de' Medici's "gay and beautiful court in Florence" (182). "The city looked suddenly grey, for none wore bright clothes any more," while on the Bonfire of Vanities "the followers of Savonarola, called the Weepers or Snivellers," managed to destroy "many exquisite things, that could never be replaced" (183). The anarchy that will waste Aaron's flute was first kindled by the snivelling Dominican's bonfire.

However, the gravest menace to "exquisite things" in the modern Florence of *Aaron's Rod* is not, as in *A Room with a View*, the puritanism of the medieval cloister but rather the minefield of the modern boudoir. James Argyle, a self-styled "'great reformer, a Zwingli and Savonarola in one'" (277), states the case categorically: "'And Women. Oh, they are the very hottest hell once they get the start of you. There's *nothing* they won't do to you, once they've got you. . . . Especially if they love you. Then you may as well give up the ghost: or smash the cart behind you, and her in it'" (244). Aaron has already smashed up the domestic cart containing his hellishly loving wife, Lottie. In Florence, his aspiring spirit will be seared one final, infernal time by woman's love.

What captivated Lawrence in the Italian island of Sardinia was the absence of "the grovelling Madonna-worship" (*Sea and Sardinia* 66). It is therefore logical that his treatment of Florence in *Aaron's Rod* should reverse the pattern of *Romola*, where the savage power-struggles of the city's male-dominated public life are eventually tempered by the ascendancy of the Madonna-like heroine. It is precisely the tonic atmosphere of male potency that impresses Aaron in Florence. In the Piazza della Signoria he finds the principle of male predominance enshrined in stone:

There he stood still and looked round him in real surprise, and real joy. The flat, empty square with its stone paving was all wet. The great buildings rose dark. The dark, sheer front of the Palazzo Vecchio went up like a cliff, to the battlements, and the slim tower soared dark and hawk-like, crested, high above. And at the foot of the cliff stood the great naked David, white and stripped in the wet, white against the dark, warm-dark cliff of the building—and near, the heavy naked men of Bandinelli. (211)

The "naked David" epitomizes the ancient, soaring masculine strength erected in the palace's proud tower. The famous tower itself has become, in Lawrencean terms, David's Rod.

Having deserted in revulsion his literal home, Aaron now feels that he is "coming home" to his authentic self. Although Keith Sagar claims that "[t]he whole structure of [*Aaron's Rod*] is centrifugal" (107), the narrative also includes a contrary, centripetal movement, with Florence at its hub:

And [Aaron] felt that here he was in one of the world's living centres, here, in the Piazza della Signoria. The sense of having arrived—of having reached a perfect centre of the human world: this he had.

And so, satisfied, he turned round to look at the bronze Perseus which rose just above him. Benvenuto Cellini's dark hero looked female, with his plump hips and his waist, female and rather insignificant: graceful, and rather vulgar. The clownish Bandinellis were somehow more to the point. (212)

The narrator of Henry James's "The Madonna of the Future" turns "with a certain relief" from the "sinister strength" of the David "to a slender figure in bronze," the Perseus. In *Aaron's Rod* it is the Perseus, suddenly robbed of slenderness and masculinity, that seems repellent. Following immediately after "female," the phrase "rather insignificant" is no accident. Throughout the novel, it is manly sinew, not feminine grace, that is "to the point."

The charisma of maleness irradiates, as well, the crowd of Tuscan farmers Aaron finds bargaining in the Piazza on Friday morning:

And then, when he went out, he found the Piazza della Signoria packed with men: but all, all men. And all farmers, land-owners and land-workers. The curious, fine-nosed Tuscan farmers, with their half-sardonic, amber-coloured eyes. Their curious individuality, their clothes worn so easy and reckless, their hats with the personal twist . . . The dangerous, subtle, never-dying fearlessness, and the acrid unbelief. But men! Men! A town of men, in spite of everything. . . . Just men. The rarest thing left in our sweet Christendom. (212-3)

Evidently, the city that James's Theobald called "the sole true woman of them all" has undergone a sex change.[1] A character like Aaron's effeminate fellow-tourist Francis Dekker stands out as an interloper in such masculine precincts. Coming just after the narrator's incantation "But men! Men! A town of men," Francis's rhapsody over the Florence social whirl—"'People! People! People! Isn't it amazing how many there are, and how many one knows, and gets to know!'" (213)—brands him as alien to the *genius loci*. His insistence on the genderless noun "people" subtly suggests that he has himself been neutered.

What has more serious consequences for Aaron, however, is the presence in the "town of men" of a disturbingly attractive woman, the Marchesa del Torre. Although she is American by birth, the Marchesa's name associates her and her Italian husband with the proud towers symbolizing Florence's ancient heritage. Unfortunately, the couple are only spurious heirs of that tradition. The neurotic Marchesa has a phobia against musical harmonies: "'A number of sounds all sounding together. It just makes me ill'" (225). This atomism *à l'outrance* is a far cry from the individuality of the farmers Aaron admires in the square; it implicitly denies any sort of vitalizing human interchange. The Marchesa's husband is unlike the farmers in a different way. His army uniform, which confers on the wearer a sterile anonymity, represents the contrary of the farmers' hats, each worn with its own "personal twist." In this latter-day Florence, it turns out to be the uniform, not the hats, that sets the fashion.

More urgently than earlier fictional treatments of the city, *Aaron's Rod* prompts the question: Is modern Florence a mere fossilized relic? Does anything remain of its proverbial power to foster rebirth? Lawrence's mouthpiece in the novel, Rawdon Lilly, proffers an optimistic answer:

"I love it," said Lilly. "I love this place. I love the cathedral and the tower. I love its pinkness and its paleness. The gothic souls find fault with it, and say it is gimcrack and tawdry and cheap. But I love it, it is delicate and rosy, and the dark stripes are as they should be, like the tiger marks on a pink lily. It's a lily, not a rose; a pinky white lily with dark tigery marks. And heavy too, in its own substance: earth-substance, risen from earth into the air: and never forgetting the dark, black-fierce earth—I reckon here men for a moment were themselves, as a plant in flower is for the moment completely itself. Then it goes off. As Florence has gone off. No flowers now. But it *has* flowered. And I don't see why a race should be like an aloe tree, flower once and die. Why should it? Why not flower again? Why not?" (332-3)

As Lilly evokes it, Florence remains a stirring image of life at the full, a testimony that human inventiveness can arise directly out of vital, earth-born impulse. Yet it is no more than an image, an emblem of a once and (arguably) future grandeur. For Lilly, Florence is no longer what it was for George Eliot, a monument to the unbrokenness of human effort, or what it had more recently been for Forster, a magic stage where art and nature could still conspire to kindle passion.

Aaron's major Florentine experience, his affair with the neurotic Marchesa, leaves little hope that Florentine greatness is anything more than a memory. True, Aaron at first believes himself to be on the road to his personal renaissance by virtue of sexual conquest. "Aaron's black rod of power, blossoming again with red Florentine lilies and fierce thorns. He moved about in the splendour of his own male lightning, invested in the thunder of the male passion-power. He had got it back, the male godliness, the male god-head. . . . The phoenix had risen in fire again, out of the ashes" (258). But he is a premature phoenix, and sexual consummation leaves him a scorched one. "He felt curiously blazed, as if some flame or electric power had gone through him and withered his vital tissue . . . , his mind had only one of its many-sighted eyes left open and unscorched" (263). He has "violent dreams of strange, black strife" (258) that warn him of what he will find to be true: in the Florence of this late date, there is no way of shielding personal virility from the virus of public anarchy. Contact with an anarchic personality like the Marchesa's only renders Aaron more vulnerable.

It is Rawdon Lilly who, by contrast, affirms in his very being the once-vital spirit of the city. Lilly's name itself clinches his kinship with Florence, the lily-city. Like that other Florentine lily, Romola, he comes to personify the place where he dwells and which he loves. But the gender of Lawrence's Florentine lily bespeaks the distance between his vision and George Eliot's. Aaron's revulsion from his Florentine love-entanglement has a providential outcome precisely because it allows him to recognise in a man—Lilly—his potential refuge from the city of women that Florence is perversely becoming.

It is the climactic bomb-explosion in the cafe that puts paid to Aaron's two vexed, complementary love affairs: his affair with the lily-town and his affair with his fascinating Florentine hostess. Revealingly, the blast that shatters his libido leaves the field clear for his allegiance to Lilly. A philosophical conversation has been in progress among Aaron, Lilly, Argyle, and a man named Levison. Lilly begins to defend the sacredness of the individual life:

"Why, I'll tell you the real truth," said Lilly. "I think every man is a sacred and holy individual, *never* to be violated. I think there is only one thing I hate to the verge of madness, and that is *bullying*. To see any living creature *bullied*, in *any* way, almost makes a murderer of me. That is true. Do you believe it—?"

"Yes," said Levison unwillingly. "That may be true as well. You have no doubt, like most of us, got a complex nature which—"

C R A S H !

There intervened one awful minute of pure shock, when the soul was in darkness. Out of this shock Aaron felt himself issuing amid a mass of terrible sensations: the fearful blow of the explosion, the noise of glass, the hoarse howl of people, the rushing of men, the sudden gulf, the awful gulfing whirlpool of horror in the social life.

He stood in agony and semi-blindness amid a chaos. (282-3)

Florence, chronically quarrelsome, has become apocalyptic. In the latter days of the Etrurian Athens, fine sentiments are demolished by insensate violence. Aaron's posture following the blast—"He stood in agony and semi-blindness amid a chaos"— sums up wordlessly his whole spiritual predicament. The "chaos"—the lurid tableau in the cafe—speaks for itself:

And now Aaron saw that a man was lying there—and horror, blood was running across the floor of the cafe. Men began now hastily to return to the place. Some seized their hats and departed again at once. But many began to crowd in—a black eager crowd of men pressing to where the bomb had burst—where the man was lying . . . Men surged in with that eager, excited zest of people, when there has been an accident. Grey carabinieri, and carabinieri in the cocked hat and fine Sunday uniform pressed forward officiously. (283)

In *A Room with a View* the murder in Piazza Signoria was a shocking but arousing act of red blooded Florentine impulsiveness. Here, the spilled blood arouses nothing except prurient curiosity. It blurs individuality of person and of place alike. The police uniforms, both the gray and the fine Sunday ones, testify to the unlocalized modernity of the outrage and its consequences. The cadences of the paragraph—"a man was lying there . . . men began now hastily to return . . . a black eager crowd of men . . . where the man was lying . . . Men surged in"—deflatingly echo the narrator's earlier hymn to Florentine masculinity: "But men! Men! A town of men, in spite of everything." The point is plain. In this new Florence, "maleness" displays itself as a riot of sensation-addicts surging around a pool of blood on a cafe floor. The fact of what Henry James had called "a great tradition broken" emerges in a poignant image: "On the other side of the crowd excited angry men were wrestling over overcoats that were mixed up with a broken marble table-top" (283). The birth place of the Renaissance has dwindled to a mad scramble for personal effects amid fragmented stone.

What Aaron takes most to heart in the whole episode is the loss of his flute. That talisman of his artistic, erotic powers, which had seemed to be blossoming in the historic center of culture and masculinity, has been wasted by the emasculating violence that infects the modern city. The disaster brings Aaron to the end of his tether—"He just didn't care any more about anything in life or death" (284)—and causes him to hand the tether over to his friend. Lilly, for his part, is not unwilling to take it. The first action he instructs Aaron to perform, when the two are standing on a bridge over the Arno, is to throw the broken flute into the water.

"Throw it in the river, Aaron," said Lilly.
Aaron turned and looked at him.
"Throw it in the river," repeated Lilly. "It's an end."
Aaron nervelessly dropped the flute into the stream.
The two men stood leaning on the bridge-parapet, as if unable to move. (284)

When Forster's George Emerson tosses Lucy Honeychurch's blood stained art photographs into the Arno, his action symbolically exalts life at the expense of artistic representation. Aaron's gesture points, by contrast, not to dawning promise but to closure and stasis. It is a forced relinquishment of the values of male passion and artistry that this etiolated Florence can no longer sustain. Aaron is no Prospero. He drowns his rod not because it has fulfilled its magic purpose but because it no longer has a purpose to fulfill.

The dream that Aaron has afterwards recapitulates his whole Florentine experience.[2] The eerie city of the buried-alive through which he drifts is a nightmarish transformation of Florence itself. The flowers worn by the children Aaron sees putting themselves to bed—"And each child went to bed with a wreath of flowers on its head, white flowers and pink, so it seemed" (286)—recall Lilly's tribute to the City of Flowers as "a pinky white lily." But this positive image is followed by "many grey domestic apartments, where were all women, all greyish in their clothes and appearance" (286). According to Lawrence's history text, after Savonarola's rise "the city looked suddenly grey, for none wore bright clothes any more." Here, however, it is not ascetic medievalism that has blighted the Florentine bloom; it is the grey, smothering spirit of the feminine-domestic. The danger is confirmed by an ominous idol that soon comes into view: "An Astarte he knew it as, seated by the road, and in her open lap were some eggs: smallish hen's eggs, and one or two bigger eggs, like swans'" (288). The imagery directly recalls the Marchesa, who, when enthralled by Aaron's flute playing, resembled a swan ("She was as a swan which never before would get its wings quite open" [257]). More generally, however, the Astarte, with its egg horde, is the novel's culminating image of "sacred motherhood." Such a dream vision is only what one might expect of a man in panic flight from woman and from the modern society that empowers her.

Aaron's dream is definitive because it helps him make a life-and-death choice "between the world and the uncertain, assertive Lilly" (336). The other man arrives in the morning to issue Aaron an expressively worded invitation: "'I wondered . . . if you'd like to walk into the country with me: it is such a nice day. I thought you might have gone out already. But here you are in bed like a woman who's had a baby'" (290). Lilly himself is not one to lie ignominiously in a child bed. The lavish praiser of Florentine greatness now discloses his plans to travel, first to Naples, eventually to a different continent altogether. "'Anyhow, I know I must oscillate between north and south, so oscillate I do,'" he says. "'It's just my nature'" (290). Since Florence no longer creatively mediates between north and south, Lilly adapts his life plans to include the best of both half-worlds. Tito Melema's vagrant fickleness was a fatal sign of his foreignness to human community; but for Lilly vagrancy, in such a world, is the sole remaining *modus vivendi*. Fixity, above all fixity among the ruins of a once-perfect civilization, has become a suicidal anachronism.

The most futile anachronism of all is fixity in the pursuit of love. To replace it, Lilly proposes a different life-motive: "'that great dark power-urge which kept Egypt so intensely living for so many centuries'" (297). In the closing chapters of *Aaron's Rod* an exchange of idols is managed. The glistening David gets lowered from its pedestal, to have its orgasm elsewhere; a statue of dark Pharaoh gets erected in its place. The old Florentine ideals—intellectual grasp, wisdom, the force embodied by Botticelli's Venus—are written off. It is a conclusion spelled out in *Movements in European History*: "There are two great passions that rule mankind—the passion of pride and power and conquest, and the passion of peace and production. The Renaissance was the time when the desire for peace and production triumphed over the desire for war and conquest" (293). By now, however, "[w]e none of us believe in our ideals any more. Our ideal, our leading ideas, our growing tip were shot away in the Great War" (311). Only one alternative remains: to welcome the remorseless historical counterforce now slouching toward Lilly's Egypt to be born.

Lawrence's Florentine history thus stands George Eliot's on its head. In *Romola*, the love impulse, embodied by the Madonna-heroine, supersedes the power-lust personified by her cutthroat, limelight-seeking husband. Lawrence's narrative shows how feminine allure has infiltrated the male citadel of Florence, a catastrophe confirming his belief that our civilization has reached a dead end. At its close, the novel gropes toward a struggling new renaissance of male power and charisma. Attention is shifted away from the city and toward the character— Lilly— who has draped his own, single person in its mighty mantle. The result is curiously paradoxical: Lilly takes personal possession of the Florentine heritage and, after lavishly praising it, absconds with it. Devoid of Lilly's animating presence, Florence has nothing to offer Aaron but obsolete promises and shockingly violent actualities.

Much has been said about Lawrence's responsiveness to the "spirit of place." *Aaron's Rod* reveals not only how acute were Lawrence's perceptions of place but also how sensitive he was to the literary nuances connected with it. In *Aaron's Rod* Lawrence's goal was to unmask the bankruptcy of traditional values in a time of crisis and instability. Sexual love, above all, could no longer serve as an avenue to personal renewal. Of all imaginable settings, Florence was the one whose historical and literary significance enabled Lawrence to make such a statement most resonantly.

In a sense, Lawrence was only extending the pattern that Forster had established, before the war, in *A Room with a View*. Forster's novel, too, uses the Florence setting for revisionist ends, questioning the values of self-abnegation and self-transcendence that Eliot had made paramount in *Romola*. And yet, even years before the writing of *Aaron's Rod*, Lawrence had made clear to Forster himself his dissatisfaction with the timidity of the Forsterian vision. "It is time for us now to look all round, round the whole ring of the horizon—not just out of a room with a view; it is time to gather again a conception of the Whole," he had urged the other man in a letter of early 1915 (*Letters* 2: 265-6).

In those early months of the war, Lawrence's quarrel was not yet with the ideal of erotic renewal advanced by Forster's Florentine novel but rather with that ideal's incompleteness. In the fragmented Florence of the 1920's, however, any "conception of the Whole" had become for Lawrence himself futile to pursue. *A Room with a View* had made use of Florentine surroundings to enact the still imaginable synthesis of art with life, of cultural transmission with erotic impulse. Aaron Sisson makes one final attempt to achieve such wholeness, but awakens to find his life and his art disastrously splintered. In a Europe torn and tormented by modern warfare and its aftermath, Florence itself needs a rebirth too desperately to foster one more belated British expatriate's personal renaissance. As Lawrence said of *Aaron's Rod* in a letter to Thomas Seltzer, his American publisher, "It had to be written—and had to come to such an end" (*Letters* 4: 92-93).

8

A Great Tradition Travestied:
Fidelman in Florence

In more recent twentieth-century writing, the Florentine tragedy of thwarted rebirth tends to repeat itself as burlesque. One notable exponent of this mode is the American writer Bernard Malamud, whose novel *Pictures of Fidelman* (1969) plays self-consciously, in its interconnected episodes, on the literary associations of one Italian city after another. "A Pimp's Revenge," the Florence section, uses for parodic purposes the well-worn subject of the expatriate artist's hope to be creatively born again in the cradle of the Renaissance. Malamud's protagonist, the painter Arthur Fidelman, aspires to keep faith (as his name suggests) with the loftiest ideals of art. He has selected Florence as the logical place in which to make his bid for immortality.

One has (and one is meant to have) an instant sense of *déjà vu*. As Christof Wegelin has pointed out, *Pictures of Fidelman* is "a portrait of the American specifically as artist, and the treatment of a similar theme in 'The Madonna of the Future' . . . seems to have haunted Malamud" (146). "A Pimp's Revenge" is not, however, simply James at second hand; it is James turned inside out through ironic reversals of tone and situation.

In James's story the fact of "a great tradition broken" lends pathos to the hero's effort to find creative fulfillment amid the splendid reminders of the Renaissance. But in Malamud's Florence, the artist's attempt to locate his individual talent within tradition becomes *ipso facto* comic. Sample though he may the special appeal of one famous Italian city after another, Fidelman has no hope of finding his true artistic home in any of them. The discoveries he does make have to do with his own problematic identity; the cities themselves act as way stations on the lengthy pilgrimage of self-location. What Fidelman must learn is to assimilate models of past greatness, while resisting the claims to final authority of any of them. Malamud's story itself constitutes an example of how this might be done. By burlesquing Jamesian paradigms, he invokes masterly precedents only to question their relevance to the problems facing American writers and artists a century later.

The Fidelman of "A Pimp's Revenge" shares with his precursor Theobald an emotional bond with Florence and a maddening frustration in pursuing his artistic aims. The convulsive opening of the story proclaims both sentiments: "F, ravaged Florentine, grieving, kicked apart a trial canvas, copy of one he had been working on for years, his foot through the poor mother's mouth, destroyed the son's insipid puss, age about ten. It deserved death for not coming to life" (93). The initial "F," which stands for Fidelman's name throughout this section, stresses the kinship between the artist and the city where he, like Theobald, hopes to create a supreme masterpiece. However, as his self-destructive first action foretells, the path to such accomplishment is likely to be rugged.

Fidelman, naturally, has a view. Gazing from his window at the Tuscan hills a century later than Theobald, he reflects that he, too, lives in "the evening of time": "That's my trouble, everything's been done or is otherwise out of style—cubism, surrealism, action painting. If I could only guess what's next" (94). Unlike James's precedent-plagued aspirer, Fidelman is as much concerned with art "futures" as with past milestones. Nevertheless, he has been toiling for five years on his version of a crowning Madonna and child: the picture of his own mother (who died when he was small) and himself, on a trial copy of which he vents his punishing wrath as the section opens.

For Theobald "the noiseless years had ebbed away, and left him brooding in charmed inaction, forever preparing for a work forever deferred" (221). Fidelman's years in Florence have been comparably barren. He has not been inactive—most days he works on his Mother and Son—but his labors have had a troubling resemblance to those of Sisyphus:

The faces were changed almost every day he painted, his as a young boy, hers as herself (long since departed); but now though for a year he had let the boy be, his face and all, he was still never satisfied with hers—something always missing—for very long after he had put it down; and he daily or nightly scraped it off (another lost face) with his rusty palette knife, and tried once again the next day; then scraped that face the same night or the day after; or let it harden in hope for two days and then frantically, before the paint stiffened, scraped that face off, too. All in all he had destroyed more than a thousand faces and conceived another thousand for a woman who could barely afford one; yet couldn't settle on her true face—at least true for art. (111)

Little wonder if he moans, in a speech closely recalling Theobald's dying lament, "'I'm a time-ravaged man, horrible curse on an artist'" (100). He, too, has grown so obsessed with the perfect image lodged in his brain that he cannot leave off the discouraging fight to externalize it: "'If I could complete it the way I sometimes see it in my mind's eye, I bet it could be something extraordinary. If a man does only one such painting in his lifetime, he can call himself a success'" (118). He also has faith that, if he could succeed, "'much that was wrong in [his] life would rearrange itself and add up to more'" (118).

In trusting to art to provide the magic formula that will set his own life into satisfying order, Fidelman is harboring risky illusions about the *rapport* between life and art. It is precisely their relation that his Florentine experience will clarify. "'With my paintings I try to stop the flow of time'" (122), he pontificates in an interpolated interview; but time overtakes him in his King Canute posture, dissolving stasis in surprising ways. When a young prostitute from Fiesole, Esmeralda, offers to share his studio, he is "momentarily panicked": "'I wouldn't want it to interfere with my painting. I mean I'm devoted to that. Besides, this is a small place'" (102-3). ("'I'm a small girl,'" Esmeralda winningly replies, "'I'll take care of your needs and won't interfere with your work'" [103]). Fidelman gives in, but soon discovers a new source of interference, Esmeralda's "cousin" Ludovico, secretly a pimp with whom she has quarrelled and who hopes to reclaim her services.

Like James's little sculptor of cats and monkeys, Ludovico has the gift of ready repartee. He quotes the Gospels in his own defence with an aplomb that recalls the sculptor's in quoting Horace. When Fidelman self-righteously condemns his pimping—"'All in all, it isn't much of a moral thing to do'" (107)—he replies blandly: "'Considering the circumstances, how can this be an evil thing? The basis of morality is recognizing one another's needs and cooperating. Mutual generosity is nothing to criticize other people for. After all, what did Jesus teach?'" (107). A versatile as well as glib-tongued son of Florence, Ludovico reveals himself, on seeing Fidelman's unfinished painting, to have qualifications as an art dealer that rival his credentials as a pimp. Where he has earlier spoken of managing Esmeralda's business in return for a "'modest but necessary commission'" (107), he now offers to get Fidelman "'an excellent price'" for his work, "'of course for the usual commission'" (109).

Esmeralda herself, though obliging, does not bestow on Fidelman the pitying indulgence that Serafina accords Theobald. She at length becomes anxious to know "'if all artists had it so hard'"—"'So that it takes them years to paint a picture'" (126). She observes caustically that, in her life as a whore, she was possibly "'working up to be an artist's mistress'" (116); by serving Fidelman's needs, she has in effect prostituted herself to the cause of art. Shrewdly, she guesses that his obsession with his supreme "Mother and Son" has roots in a buried yearning for emotional compensation—"'To me it's as though you were trying to paint yourself into your mother's arms'" (117). To blunt this thrust, the artist invokes the dogma of aesthetic autonomy ("'It's first and foremost a painting'" [118]), but over time Esmeralda's theory is confirmed. Just as Theobald's unstarted masterpiece enables him to rationalize his fondness for poring over the features of his idolized Serafina, so Fidelman's endlessly retouched double-portrait is his covert attempt to fix in pigment his own mother's lost affection and give utterance to his troublesomely unuttered grief.

Fidelman's insistence on the autonomy of the artistic object does not prevent him from voicing an exalted belief, like Theobald's, in art's mission for mankind. A painting, he argues, "'sort of gives value to a human being as he responds to it. You might say it enlarges his consciousness. If he feels beauty it makes him more than he was, it adds, you might say, to his humanity'" (123). To this sentiment, which the arch-Florentine Lippi would have applauded, he adds another concerning the enlarging effect of the painter's work on the artist himself: "'I feel most moral when I'm painting, like being engaged with truth'" (124).

Such a lofty conception of art as truth-centered and consciousness-expanding accords with the extract from Nietzsche blazoned on Fidelman's wall: "Art is not an imitation of nature but its metaphysical supplement, raised up beside it in order to overcome it" (94). But it glibly ignores the wisdom contained in two of Fidelman's other mottoes, the first from Jackson Pollock—"What is it that escapes me? The human? That humanity is greater than art?" (94)—and the second (crushingly applicable to Fidelman) from Picasso: "People seize on painting in order to cover up their nakedness" (94). In effect, while spending years on his painting of himself and his mother, Fidelman has accumulated a "history"—"layer on layer giving it history, another word for thick past in the paint itself"—that cloaks the naked truth of his actual past and his feeling for his mother, arresting them as "eternally mother and son" (110). (In fact, he hardly remembers his mother and must paint from an old snapshot in order to re-create her perished image.)

Fidelman comes crazily to see his entire future as bound up with his success in "remodelling" his past in paint: "I might as well scrap what's left of my life if I have to start over again" (112). Yet he senses a hidden connection between his lack of progress and his dread that the picture, once completed, might make bruising revelations: "The truth is I am afraid to paint, like I might find out something about myself" (112). Meanwhile, however, his dedication to the precedence of art over life creates tension between him and Esmeralda. "'Art isn't life,'" he tells her. She replies with Florentine downrightness:

"Then the hell with it. If I have my choice I'll take life. If there's not that there's no art."
    "Without art there's no life to speak of, at least for me. If I'm not an artist, then I'm nothing."
    "My God, aren't you a man?"
    "Not really, without art."
    "Personally, I think you have a lot to learn."
    "I'm learning it," F sighed. (119)

As Fidelman crisply proclaims in his interview, "'I make art, it makes me'" (123); but just what it is that Fidelman's art "makes" him belongs to the lot he has to learn. His experience in Florence, that mercantile as well as artistic city, sardonically recalls a line from Browning's "Pictor Ignotus" quoted proudly by James's Theobald: "At least no merchant traffics in my heart" (*Tales* 2.206). A moral detour now re-routes the traffic in Fidelman's heart, a change signalled by a geographical shift in the focus of his activities. His studio is located in Piazza

Santo Spirito ("Holy Ghost Square"), and the opening of the story finds him stolidly ignoring Brunelleschi's fine Renaissance church of that name: "Across the broad piazza Santo Spirito, nobly proportioned, stared him in the bushy-mustached face, but he would not look back" (94). Towards the end, to finance his artistic obsession, he persuades the desperate, devoted Esmeralda to resume her old calling, Fidelman himself acting as her procurer. Their center of operations is Piazza della Repubblica, in Theobald's time the market square and by Fidelman's a nondescript urban space cluttered with cars and scarred by neon signs. "They went together to the Piazza della Repubblica, almost merrily. 'For art,' she said, then after a moment, bitterly, 'art, my ass'" (131).

The girl's disgruntled coupling of the abstract and the concrete has its own peculiar aptness. The equivalence of sexual and artistic "performances" has been suggested earlier, when Fidelman obtains Esmeralda's services (otherwise unaffordable) by offering her a sketch of a nude in payment. Ludovico's mention of the "usual commission" as applied to the marketing both of Fidelman's painting and Esmeralda's body makes the same point. Later, "bowled over" by a portrait Fidelman has done of the girl, the Florentine pimp promises the threadbare artist that he can get a million lire for the work; he is as happy to peddle Esmeralda's painted charms as her flesh and blood. "F agreed, so the pimp, crossing himself, left with the painting" (130). By this point Esmeralda has become understandably perplexed by the confusion, endemic in her local surroundings, between the sacred and the profane, the aesthetic and the commercial. "'Even Ludovico, when he's not adding up his accounts, he's talking about art,'" she muses (130).

Art answers to life. Irresistibly, the subject of Fidelman's masterpiece-in-progress undergoes an uncanonical change:

It was then that it occurred to F to use the girl as a model for his mother. Though she was only eighteen, it might help to have a living model for Momma as a young woman though she was touching middle age when Bessie [his sister] took the photo, and was of course another sort of person; still, such were the paradoxes of art. (125)

The outburst of Fidelman's rent-starved landlord—"'You're no Florentine,' Fabio shouted. 'You're not even an Italian'" (130) —contains more truth than he knows. Although local painters such as Lippi did not scruple to use their mistresses as models for Madonnas, Fidelman's substitution of a whore for his own mother sets a new and dubious precedent. Like Theobald, though for different reasons, Fidelman is mocked by the looming monuments of past achievement. His cajoling of Esmeralda to go back to whoring looks all the odder in the neighborhood where Dostoevsky finished the history of his self-forgetful hero, Prince Myshkin:

He went out for a long walk and for a while hung around the palazzo where Dostoevsky had written the last pages of *The Idiot*. It did no good. When he returned he said nothing to Esmeralda. In fact he did not feel too bad though he knew he ought to. In fact he had been thinking of asking her to go to work, whatever she might do. It's circumstances, he thought. (131)

By this point, Fidelman's true source of inspiration is no monument of the Florentine past but that past-master of the Florentine present, Ludovico. The pimp's very idiom infiltrates Fidelman's self-justifying rhetoric (compare Fidelman's "It's circumstances" with the pimp's "'considering the circumstances, how can this be an evil thing?'"). Eventually, it is the native's dingy identity that the American assumes (he has even exchanged his beret for a hat more like Ludovico's).

Thus, Fidelman's integration into the squalid contemporary Florentine scene has drastic effects on his own moral threshold. As he slides into pimpdom, the tones of his work darken sympathetically: "He painted out of anguish, a dark color" (125). Standing guard near the room where Esmeralda takes her customers, he "waits outside the door, sketching little pictures in the dim electric glow, as Esmeralda performs" (132-3). Theobald's "evening of time" has thickened. And although Fidelman deposits their take, not noticing the irony, in the "Banco di Santo Spirito," the unholy darkening of his vision continues. Absentmindedly, he begins to wear for his artistic work the shady regalia in which he goes pimping. "One morning F paints with his dark glasses on, until [Esmeralda] wakes up and screams at him" (134)—yet another disturbing confusion between his aesthetic calling and his commercial one. Anxiety for the future drives the girl to burn the snapshot of Fidelman and his mother, thereby cutting the artist's "only visible link to Ma, Bessie, the past" (135). But he easily reconciles himself to the loss, and actually seems spurred on by it: "He painted with new confidence, amusement, wonder. The subject had changed from 'Mother and Son' to 'Brother and Sister' (Esmeralda as Bessie) to let's face it, 'Prostitute and Procurer'" (135).

Such are the paradoxes of art. Unlike Theobald, who idealizes the humdrum Serafina by investing her with the majesty of the Madonna, the later painter comes into his own when he espouses a realism that trumpets his abasement. He congratulates himself on his own stubborn, heroic veracity: "And though he considered sandpapering his own face off and substituting Ludovico as pimp, the magnificent thing was that in the end he kept himself in. This is my most honest piece of work" (135). What this "magnificent" view of himself misses is one more piquant piece of irony. By obliging his lover to become a tart for art's sake, he has transformed himself into a double of the scorned Ludovico. Even by the late Renaissance standards of Andrea del Sarto, this represents no mean feat of moral sinking.

By a culminating paradox, Fidelman's picture becomes a perfected artistic whole only when it mirrors its maker's utter moral collapse, incurred through his monomania for "art":

But the picture was, one day, done. It assumed a completion: This woman and man together, prostitute and procurer. She was a girl with fear in both black eyes, a vulnerable if stately neck, and a steely small mouth; he was a boy with tight insides, on the verge of crying. The presence of each protected the other. A Holy Sacrament. The form leaped to the eye. He had tormented, ecstatic, yet confused feelings, but at last felt triumphant—it was done! Though deeply drained, moved, he was satisfied, completed—ah, art! (136)

Esmeralda's "'Art, my ass'" springs inevitably to mind. What the painter's mimetic skill makes all too plain is the inner stuntedness of both parties to this "Holy Sacrament," a title that in its outrageousness rivals Ludovico's question, "'After all, what did Jesus teach?'".

Ludovico himself, appropriately, is impressed by the completed "masterpiece." His judgment is couched in the approved Florentine imagery: "'[M]y only criticism is that maybe the painting suffers from an excess of darkness. It needs more light'" (138). That same night Fidelman "wonder[s] what to paint next. Maybe sort of a portrait of Ludovico, his face reflected in a mirror, with two sets of aqueous sneaky eyes" (139). The "sort of" portrait of the pimp he contemplates is in reality a double self-portrait. The "two sets of aqueous sneaky eyes" bespeak the corrupted vision of Florentine and non-Florentine alike. By contrast, the innocent prostitute Esmeralda can still justly claim "'I have my eyes'" (138) when warning Fidelman not to meddle further with his finished painting.

Unwisely heedless of her caution, Fidelman during the night adds "a touch of light" to rectify his picture's darkness of tone and then yields to the temptation to strive for a still more unflinching reflection of reality: "And then he thought he would work a bit on the girl's face, no more than a stroke or two around the eyes and mouth, to make her expression truer to life. More the prostitute, himself a little older" (139). With dawn comes a terrible realization, like Theobald's, of waste: "Five long years down the drain." The narrative now staggers to its slapstick conclusion. Fidelman smears his unlucky canvas with black paint; Esmeralda, calling him a murderer, attacks him with a bread knife; he seizes the knife and "in anguish lift[s] the blade into his gut." Ludovico, arriving on the scene with an expectant art-dealer in tow, speaks the acerbic Florentine last word: "'A moral act'" (139).

Reenacting through parody "The Madonna of the Future," "A Pimp's Revenge" provides a wry post-Jamesian perspective on the morality of art, the self-destructiveness of the artist, and the nature of "seeing." One of the most

revealing bits of dialogue bears on this latter theme. Fidelman is speaking to
Esmeralda:

"The mystery of art is that more is there than you put down and every stroke adds to it.
You look at your painting and see this bull's eye staring at you though all you've painted
is an old tree. It's also a mystery to me why I haven't been able to finish my best
painting though I am dying to."

"If you ask me," Esmeralda said, "my idea of a mystery is why I am in love with
you, though it's clear to me you don't see me for dirt."

She burst into tears. (119)

As Fidelman's motto from Pollock asks, "What is it that escapes me? That
humanity is greater than art?" Where James's Theobald, as idealizing "seer," has
visions too exalted for his powers of execution, Fidelman suffers from a more
mundane, more modern handicap. Gifted with imaginative insight, however
warped, and with technical facility, however limited, he remains unable to see
human beings, himself included, for dirt—or for paint. To enable himself to
apply pigment to canvas, he is capable of reducing a woman to dirt, while in the
process filthying himself. Browning's Luria, in his earlier century, laments the
"incompleteness" to which his hopes have been condemned by Florence, cold
city of his warm heart. Arthur Fidelman, a latter-day aspiring interloper, fares
still worse. Luria does at least complete not his facade for the cathedral but an
object lesson for Florentine sceptics on the importance of feeling. Fidelman
completes only the "project" of his self-destruction as an artist, thereby
confirming the cynicism of the local onlookers.

Malamud, however, is not using parody for bleakly nihilistic ends. As
critics have pointed out, the repeated collapse of Fidelman's ideals and illusions
throughout *Pictures of Fidelman* marks the protagonist's comic yet steady growth
as man and artist. The Florence of "A Pimp's Revenge" is a city whose great
tradition has been broken; but in an age inured to brokenness, the fracturing of
Arthur Fidelman's illusions can generate an amusing, ribald buoyancy.
Malamud's story proves that, even reduced to the level of travesty, Florence has
not lost its old resonance as a metaphor. As a setting for fiction, the city can
still comment powerfully on human aspiration, even if only to reveal its
underlying absurdity.

PART II

VENICE

Venice: The Bridge of Sighs. Photograph reproduced courtesy of Fratelli Alinari.

There is a glorious City in the Sea.
The Sea is in the broad, the narrow streets,
Ebbing and flowing; and the salt sea-weed
Clings to the marble of her palaces.
No track of men, no footsteps to and fro,
Lead to her gates. The path lies o'er the Sea,
Invisible; and from the land we went,
As to a floating City—steering in,
And gliding up her streets as in a dream,
So smoothly, silently—by many a dome
Mosque-like, and many a stately portico,
The statues ranged along an azure sky;
By many a pile in more than Eastern pride,
Of old the residence of merchant-kings;
The fronts of some, tho' Time had shattered them,
Still glowing with the richest hues of art,
As tho' the wealth within them had run o'er.

Samuel Rogers, *Italy*

Canal smell. City that lies on the sea like a cork
Of stone & gold, manifold throng your ghosts
Of murdered & distraught.

John Berryman, *Henry's Fate*

9

This Most Improbable of Cities

Venice has long been, in the words of an eminent Italian writer, "a city of convention, to be repopulated at will according to the exigencies and caprices of fancy" (Bassani 22). From the age of Shakespeare to the present, the city has been reinvented time and again by the literary imagination. According to A. D. Nuttall,

Venice, to the Elizabethans, was in some ways what Hollywood was to the rest of the world in the 1930s, or perhaps it would be better to say a mixture of Hollywood and Paris: *the* glamorous, daring, brilliant, wicked city. Even today as the senile, jewel-encrusted Bride of the Adriatic sinks malodorously beneath the waters of the Lagoon, one can glimpse, in the real city, what the effect must once have been. The rest of the world is black, white and grey and here alone, among the gilded lions, rosy brick and white marble stained with green, is the Coloured City. The most neutral description of Venice begins to sound like overwriting. (120)

As Nuttall's comments suggest, Venice's literary image is not a product of convention pure and simple. The uniqueness of the actual place and its surroundings naturally invites aesthetic embellishment. In the Venice region, says a native son, Guido Piovene, "even poverty—its sadness, its discomforts—becomes aestheticized. Just as Venetian sunsets are sometimes a bit more red and blue than is natural, so the Venetian beggar, exaggerating for the sake of artistic pleasure, is a bit more beggarly than he really needs to be" (23).

The young Henry James, coming to Venice as to a shrine, was wary from the first of the place's power to stereotype the literary visitor's perceptions. Nevertheless, even James maintains "that to a fine healthy romantic appetite the subject can't be too diffusely treated" (*Hours* 54). The finest, though perhaps not the healthiest, romantic appetite for the subject belonged to Lord Byron; and James, like other nineteenth-century travellers, could have called readily to mind the endlessly quoted lines opening Canto Four of *Childe Harold*:

I stood in Venice, on the Bridge of Sighs;
A palace and a prison on each hand:
I saw from out the wave her structures rise
As from the stroke of the enchanter's wand:

A thousand years their cloudy wings expand
Around me, and a dying Glory smiles
O'er the far times, when many a subject land
Look'd to the winged Lion's marble piles,
Where Venice sate in state, throned on her hundred isles! (4.1-9, *Poetical Works*)

The famous stanza is a veritable compendium of those features that the passing of years has stamped as Venetian. There is the paradox of a place where palaces and prisons, splendor and misery, unabashedly rub shoulders. There is the dreamlike enchantment of human dwellings that seem to have sprung, like ponderous amphibians, from the water. There is the aura of antiquity belonging to a locale whose fame reaches back time out of mind, and there is the cloud of melancholy shrouding a grandeur whose fadedness turns it into a *memento mori*. Finally, there is the sheer anomalousness of a city that holds all these elements magically in suspension.

Byron, in his time, did much to popularize the picture of Venice as "the most singular government, city and people of modern history" (*Poetical Works* 407). His hyperbole has still not lost its point. For the author of one of the best-known modern books on the city, Jan Morris, "Venice was always alone in the world, always unique in manners as in status" (210). Thomas Mann's brooding wanderer, Gustave Aschenbach, asks himself, "When one wanted to arrive overnight at the incomparable, the fabulous, the like-nothing-else-in-the-world, where was it one went?" (*Death in Venice* 16) and answers inevitably: "this most improbable of cities" (20).

From the improbable to the fictional there is but a modest leap. It is only natural that a place whose truth is so outlandish should have inspired a horde of outlandish imaginings. Francis Croft, the poet-protagonist of Susan Hill's novel *The Bird of Night*, has learned from a childhood visit of the city's dangerous power to unleash his volatile imagination:

"I never forgot what it had been like to sail between those looming, decaying houses. It was like a magic city. But black magic. When I got home I drew pictures of it. I made them all brown and depressed-looking. I had nightmares about Venice. About being chased down alley ways by black cats and gargoyles with grinning faces. It's like Grimm's fairy tales—they terrify you and inspire you forever, they are part of the landscape of your imagination until you die." (97)

As Childe Harold testifies, Venice can become an integral part of one's mental landscape before one even sets foot there:

I loved her from my boyhood; she to me
Was as a fairy city of the heart,
Rising like water-columns from the sea,
Of joy the sojourn, and of wealth the mart;

And Otway, Radcliffe, Schiller, Shakspeare's art,
Had stamp'd her image in me. (4.18)

In Canto Four of Byron's poem, the poetic imagination provides the one possible stay against time's universal deluge. Venice becomes there the imagination's symbolic capital, a magic breakwater against the relentless, cosmic down-drift.

Such a willed coalescence of the two Venices, the literal and the literary, has become standard in writing about the city. Myth asserts itself most tenaciously in those very writers who observe the city with the most scrupulous minuteness. At times, indeed, the mythic image is so jealously cherished that it requires protection against the literal reality. Confronting the prospect of an actual visit to Venice, Proust's Marcel becomes so anxious for "the atmosphere of dreams, which my imagination had secreted in the name of Venice" (1: 427) that he falls ill and is mercifully spared the trip.

Marcel's reaction is of course paradoxical, a fact that only makes it the more Venetian. As Morris says, "Venice is a complicated place, physically and spiritually . . . . Nothing is ever quite certain. Life is enmeshed in contradictions and exceptions" (51). The dog Alidoro tells the hero of Robert Coover's recent novel *Pinocchio in Venice* (1991), "'In Venice, Pinocchio my friend, in case you hadn't noticed, there is *always* a double standard. It goes with the scenery'" (105). Arthur Symons, pondering the occult complexities of the Church of San Marco, recognises the double standard. He comments that "here, as everywhere in Venice, all contradictions seem able to exist side by side, in some fantastic, not quite explicable, unity of their own" (80-81).

Even less renowned Venetian prospects are liable to play conjurors' tricks on the beholder. Eustace Cherrington, the young protagonist of L. P. Hartley's novel *Eustace and Hilda* (1952), receives a shock when he looks out his window just after his arrival in the city:

Everything Eustace saw clamoured for attention. The scene was like an orchestra without a conductor; and to add to the confusion the sights, unlike the sounds, did not come from any one place: they attacked him from all sides, and even the back of his head felt bombarded by impressions. There was no refuge from the criss-cross flights of the Venetian visual missiles, no calculating the pace at which they came. That huge square palace opposite, with its deep windows like eye-sockets in a skull, was on you in a moment with its frontal attack. The building next to it, red, shabby and almost unadorned, was withholding its fire, but the onslaught would come—Eustace could see it collecting its charm, marshalling its simplicity, winging its pensive arrow. Nor, looking at the water, did the eye get any rest. Always broken, it was for ever busy with the light, taking it on one side of a ripple, sending it back from the other; and the boats, instead of going straight up and down, crossed each other's path at innumerable angles that were like a geometrician's nightmare, and at varying degrees of slowness that were like a challenge to a quadratic equation. (25)

"'Good-bye to the sense of squareness!'" Eustace reflects uneasily. Venetian visual intricacies have moral consequences.

Most striking among Venetian paradoxes is the confusion of a tangible fabric of stone, brick and water with an overpowering aura of unreality. For Shelley in *Julian and Maddalo* (1819, *Complete Poetical Works*), the city's aspect, viewed poetically, cannot help breeding enchantment: "from that funereal bark [his gondola] / I leaned, and saw the city, and could mark / How from their many isles, in evening's gleam, / Its temples and its palaces did seem / Like fabrics of enchantment piled to Heaven" (lines 88-92). Even that unfailing source of traveller's commonplaces, Samuel Rogers, transcends the commonplace in his charmed tableau of Venetian evanescence-in-concreteness: "I went alone beneath the silent moon; / Thy square, ST. MARK, thy churches, palaces, / Glittering and frost-like, and, as day drew on, / Melting away, an emblem of themselves" (p. 66).

Prose writers have proved no less susceptible to the air of dream and enchantment. According to the early nineteenth-century traveller Lady Morgan, "As a city, even when seen, [Venice] still appears rather a phantasm than a fact; and the reality of a spectacle is doubted, which, coming not within the prospect of belief, just verges on the precincts of impossibility!" (366). Dickens entitles the Venetian chapter of *Pictures from Italy* "An Italian Dream" (118); it is in the guise of an assumed dream that his entire sketch of the city unfolds. Howells opens a chapter of his *Venetian Life* (1866) with the conceit that "Venice seems a fantastic vision, from which the world must at last awake some morning, and find that after all it has only been dreaming, and that there never was any such city" (113). "Well might it seem," says the doyen of commentators on Venice, John Ruskin, describing an arrival by gondola, "that such a city had owed her existence rather to the rod of the enchanter, than the fear of the fugitive" (*Stones* 2: 6).

As for Proust's Marcel, when after hundreds of pages he does at last arrive in Venice, he finds that the city uncannily fulfills the presagings of his dreams. "After dinner, I went out alone, into the heart of the enchanted city where I found myself in the middle of strange purlieus like a character in the *Arabian Nights*." He is delighted to stumble upon a "vast and splendid *campo*" that "seemed to be deliberately concealed in a labyrinth of alleys, like those palaces in oriental tales whither mysterious agents convey by night a person who, brought back home before daybreak, can never find his way back to the magic dwelling which he ends by believing that he visited only in a dream" (3: 665). Arthur Symons tersely sums up the universal consensus: "Yes, it is difficult to believe in Venice, most of all when one is in Venice" (76).

In narrative, Venice's dreamlike implausibility often endows it with an occult power to unhinge a character's sense of "normal" reality. In Penelope Lively's novel *Perfect Happiness* (1983), Frances Brooklyn, revisiting Venice after her husband's death, finds bereavement yielding to bewilderment:

She went out into the piazza. She passed from the shadow of an arcade into the sun and the heat stunned her. She stood looking around and for an instant, a worrying instant, could not think where she was, why she was there. She could have been dreaming; the buildings, the colonnades, the dome of a church, were like the fantasy landscape of a dream. (48)

In writing about the city, this presumed Venetian narcolepsy becomes an obsessive motif. "Analyze the feeling as you may," says a turn-of-the-century American artist, "despise its sentiment or decry it altogether, the fact remains, that once get this drug of Venice into your veins, and you never recover" (Smith 200). Marco Bolcato, the Venetian protagonist of *The Lion's Mouth* (1982), by the Canadian novelist Caterina Edwards, has got the drug fatally into his veins. For Marco, the border between city and mainland has become a line of demarcation between reality and dream: "The stink of the real world. Strange how often he found himself thinking that; each time he crossed the wooden bridge to Piazzale Roma [opposite the train station] he saw himself crossing into the real world, crossing ill-equipped, 'a fish out of water'" (136).

Firsthand, as well as fictional, accounts of Venice conform to the pattern. In *Venice Observed* (1963), Mary McCarthy expatiates on "the unreal character of Venetian life, which appears as a shimmering surface, like Venetian music" (144). She ends her book by describing how her Venetian landlord's incursions into her living space have menaced her sense of her own individual reality:

And I shall have to go soon, I dreamily realize, or I shall come back one day to the apartment and find that *I* have vanished, following my soap and perfume. I shall no longer exist, and the signor and the signora, having swallowed me, will be back, yawning, in the *letto matrimoniale*, beneath the gold cupids, the signora's mermaid-tail tucked under her embroidered wedding sheets. (157)

In prose or verse, Venice itself habitually assumes such a mermaid-guise, luring the unwary traveller into faery-lands forlorn. A melodramatic treatment of this "spell" occurs in George Sand's early novel *Leone Leoni* (1834). From her solid, staid home in bourgeois Brussels, the heroine, Juliette Ruyter, is abducted by a Venetian dream personified: the dashing nobleman, Leone Leoni, whose double-barrelled lion of a name affirms his identification with the Lion of Saint Mark. Her adventures with the mercurial Count take Juliette through hell and high water until they lead her to the highest, most hellish water of all: the Venetian lagoon. Juliette as narrator dwells on the dreamlikeness of the whole escapade: "I walked through the vast galleries [of Leoni's Venetian home] as through an enchanted palace; all the objects about me were of strange shapes, of unfamiliar aspect; I wondered if I were dreaming, of if I were really the mistress and queen of all those marvellous things" (237-8); "It is still like a dream to me. A mist passed before my eyes" (332).

Venetian narratives are apt to hinge on misty confusions of identity. A sensational example occurs in Wilkie Collins's novella *The Haunted Hotel: A Mystery of Modern Venice* (1879). The mysterious Countess Narona disposes of her unwanted husband, Lord Montbarry, by exchanging him, in their Venetian palace, with a dying courier. "'Make the two men change names and places—and the deed is done!'" (170). When she at length "composes" a play, the "plot" turns out to be a faithful account of her fiendish murder-scheme: she "suppose[s] herself to be exercising her invention when she [is] only exercising her memory" (164). The story's hideous denouement, in which Montbarry's severed, decaying head dangles in a room of the palace before his ex-fiancée Agnes, takes such ambiguities to their macabre extreme. "Dream or reality, how had Agnes survived the sight of it?" (151).

Many observers have remarked Venice's affinity with the illusion-producing media, theater and film. There could be no more logical home for an international film festival. For Howells, Venice "is to other cities like the pleasant improbability of the theatre to every-day, commonplace life" (*Venetian Life* 2). Theatricality has also been attributed to various other Italian cities, but the Venetian variety is *sui generis*.

The emphasis on spectacle, in its more mercenary and vulgar forms, sometimes troubles visitors. Already in the past century, Henry James found cause to deplore the exploiting of the scenic for commercial profit. He protests "that Venice scarcely exists any more as a city at all; that she exists only as a battered peep-show and bazaar" (*Hours* 7). Still, James himself cherished the city's adeptness in the arts of illusion and theatrical display as integral to its uncanny allure.

Venice's deceptiveness, its knack of hoodwinking the eye and the mind, has long fascinated such literary admirers. "This grossly advertised wonder, this gold idol with clay feet, this *trompe-l'oeil*, this painted deception, this cliché" (*Venice Observed* 3)—such are the epithets that, in mock outrage, McCarthy heaps upon the place. For the writer, such protean elusiveness does not merely offer obstacles to overcome; it offers opportunities to pursue. The challenge thrown down by the Countess Narona in *The Haunted Hotel* might be the very voice of the strange city she personifies: "'I am a living enigma—and you want to know the right reading of me'" (115). Such a setting offers obvious possibilities for intrigue, which can be as lurid as it is in Collins's tale, and as delicately refined as it is in the Venetian chapters of James's *The Wings of the Dove* (1902).

The image of the mask or vizard recurs over and over in such fictions to evoke the hermetic nature of Venetian reality. Another image, the labyrinth, occurs still oftener as a trope for Venetian intricacy, a quality that can be both exhilarating and tormenting. As Symons says, "[I]n Venice one is as if caught in an immense network, or spider's web, which, as one walks in its midst, seems to tighten the closer about one" (99-100). On Frances Brooklyn, in Lively's *Perfect Happiness*, the Venetian labyrinth has just the effect Symons describes:

The city ensnared her like a web, a maze. When she tried to match her position to the lines and names on the map there seemed to be no possible relationship. What was, and what was said to be, were not the same. The crumbling fading landscape of arches and pillars and snatches of water and curving bridges and ever-shifting skylines was a stage-set, a tricksy deceptive palimpsest. (48)

Within such a maze of mirages, the power to tell the illusory from the real becomes a key to survival. It is only natural that the citizens of Venice, unreal city, have gained the reputation of being tough-minded or "realistic." McCarthy detects a spirit of "show-me" empiricism in the Venetians' conduct of life: "[T]here is a continuous testing of reality, to see how far it will yield and when it will resist—Venetian experimentation" (*Venice Observed* 155). It is this epistemological dare-deviltry that visitors like Lively's Frances Brooklyn must try to learn. Ensnared by the baffling "web," Frances resists her panic and strikes out on her own: "Alleys furtively opened in walls that appeared blank; streets swung round corners into concealed squares; canals blocked her passage. She abandoned the map and simply wandered, digested by the city" (48). In order to emerge whole from her confusion, Frances must discard her map and throw herself recklessly upon the hazards of her unmediated Venetian experience. Only after being "swallowed" by the city can she be fully assimilated, and restored to a trust in herself and in life.

Their reputed relish for the empirical is a trait the Venetians share with the citizens of Florence; but the parallel can be deceptive. In Venice, the trait goes along with a markedly unFlorentine hedonism. Guido Piovene detects a crucial difference between regional styles:

The antithesis between the Veneto and Tuscany is an easy one, but it is not for that reason mistaken. The Tuscan spirit is dialectical and clear; relations with the self and with others are devoid of complacency. There is an acknowledgment of unhappiness, and that harsh judgment upon reality, upon human nature itself, which can be so mean in the mean-minded, but which is the basic premise of the mystics and revolutionaries. The thrust of ideas and the acceptance of the real can be pushed to the point of cruelty, of fanaticism, of deformity. The culture of the Veneto is, instead, sentimental, which implies contentment and delight in oneself, a voluptuous sinking into the depths of one's own being, the refusal to accept and recognize unhappiness; and consequently a scant inclination to change. It is no accident that Venetian culture is above all colorist, architectural and idyllic, while lacking in literary and philosophical contributions of the same worth. (23)

By foreign visitors, the Venetian bent for hedonism and elegant idleness has often been treated with indulgence. "It is a city in which," Henry James tolerantly observes, ". . . there is very little strenuous thinking, and yet it is a city in which there must be almost as much happiness as misery" (*Hours* 3).

But if Venice has been perceived as a pleasure-house in which the chief pleasure is to do nothing, it has also been pictured as an arena that fosters significant action. Here is a place where the heart's desires can be pursued with decorum, yet with blessedly few inhibitions. "Every one takes what he wants; but he takes it gently, gracefully, as a matter of course," remarks Symons (110-1). It is paradoxical that so seductive a lotos land can act as a challenging stimulant to self-realization. "Exquisite hours, enveloped in light and silence, to have known them once is to have always a terrible standard of enjoyment," observes James (*Hours* 20). Such a "terrible standard" is laid upon James's young hero, Hyacinth Robinson, whose exposure to the extraordinary city crowns the change of outlook begun by his friendship with the extraordinary Princess Casamassima. "'I discover that I've been cold all my life even when I thought I was warm,'" Hyacinth marvels (*Princess* 333). The Italian city serves him as a magic casement, disclosing realms of enjoyment contained within an ancient and beautiful, albeit undemocratic, culture. Although Hyacinth afterward feels poorer because he has, for once, spent lavishly, "[h]e never for an instant regretted his squandered wealth, for he said to himself that he had made a good bargain and become master of a precious equivalent. The equivalent was a rich experience" (338).

Venice has a way of becoming one great Rialto of sensibility, on which the merchandise of "life" or "experience" may be purchased for a material or spiritual price. This city, where, as Browning says, "the merchants were the kings," has never been a stranger to transactions of any sort. According to Jan Morris, "The Venetians always had an eager eye for a monopoly or a quick return, and enjoyed the reputation of being willing to sell anything they possessed, if offered enough for it" (36).

What gives special point to the metaphor of Venice as marketplace is the local eagerness to "sell" the famed attractions, a project that has over the years reached alarming proportions. James notes acutely how the marketing of the city's uniqueness in the interest of mass tourism has aggravated the distance between Venice and the life of the present: "The Venice of to-day is a vast museum where the little wicket that admits you is perpetually turning and creaking, and you march through the institution with a herd of fellow-gazers" (*Hours* 5). The educated visitor is dogged by "the vexatious sense of the city of the Doges reduced to earning its living as a curiosity shop" (11). (James might not have been surprised by the proposal of a recent mayor actually to charge an admission fee to all visitors.) D. H. Lawrence, in *Lady Chatterley's Lover*

(1928), is provoked by the city's commercialism to a stammering outrage. "Connie looked at Venice far off, low and rose-coloured upon the water. Built of money, blossomed of money, and dead with money. The money deadness! Money, money, money, prostitution and deadness" (272).

The bargains afforded by such a marketplace are, naturally enough, not always to the northern buyer's advantage. "One thing, surely, can be said of all who have come to this island," remarks the narrator of Coover's *Pinocchio in Venice*: "[W]hether they left wiser, wearier, happier, sadder, enchanted or enlightened, exasperated or exalted, impregnated with beauty or disease or rabid hedonism, they all left poorer" (102). Edith Wharton's newlyweds in *The Glimpses of the Moon* (1922), Nick and Susy Lansing, see their parasitic stay in a friend's Venetian palace as "their golden opportunity" (66), but their bargain embroils them in an intrigue that blights their marriage with a Midas touch. "*Caveat emptor*" is a common moral of Venetian stories.

On this score, too, Venice assails the visitor with paradoxes. "A commercial people who lived solely for gain—how could they create a city of fantasy, lovely as a dream or fairy-tale?" asks Mary McCarthy (*Venice Observed* 34). She theorizes that wealth itself comes to partake of the fabulous when it is present in sufficient abundance. What adds complexity to Venetian life is the way material wealth, as McCarthy suggests, shades subtly into aesthetic or spiritual opulence. Standing before Tintoretto's immense "Paradise" in the Ducal Palace, Henry James confesses "that the spectator gets from it at first chiefly an impression of quantity. Then he sees that this quantity is really wealth; that the dim confusion of faces is a magnificent composition" (*Hours* 24-25). In *The Wings of the Dove*, the sheer magnitude and profusion of Venice make it a fitting "frame" for Milly Theale, because of the generous dimensions of Milly's bank account and spirit alike.

The Venetian trade in "rich experience" can, however, all too easily entail an expense of spirit in a waste of shame. The fatal plunge into abject sensuality is a pattern of which Mann's *Death in Venice* is only the most famous among numerous examples. Howells's prim New England heroine in *The Lady of the Aroostook* (1879), Lydia Blood, shocked by a spate of irregularities unthinkable in Massachusetts, labels Venice "'this wicked place'" (282). Lydia's real-life fellow puritan, John Ruskin, finds in the Festa di Lido only "Hopeless sensuality—not a single fine face nor kindly look nor appearance of wholesome enjoyment" (*Ruskin in Italy* 211). Even a more dispassionate modern observer like Jan Morris notes reminiscently that "[d]uring her last century of independence [Venice] was the gayest and worldliest of all cities, a perpetual masque and revelry, where nothing was too daring, too shameful or licentious. . . . No other nation ever died in such feverish hedonism" (26). The city's allure, she claims, has still "something curiously sensual to it, if not actually sexual" (309). Mary McCarthy is struck by the Venetians' "sexual vice and their delicate, voluptuous luxury, which makes one think, often, of Pompeii" (*Venice Observed* 50).

Such a comparison is not altogether farfetched. Venice, though menaced rather by gradual submersion than by instant burial, has struck numerous observers as being, like the unlucky Roman town, tinged with melancholy. To some, the city's sadness seems the reflex of its imputed decadence—"the sad-eyed old witch of Venice," James dubs her (*Hours* 72). Morris, whose book about the city includes a whole chapter on "Melancholia," sees in the townspeople a "quality of melancholy, a lagoon-like sadness" (105). She claims, "Melancholia contributes strongly to the Venetian atmosphere, whether it is expressed in overgrown gardens or nostalgic verse." Pleasure here has an uncanny habit of dissolving into its contrary.

The town's spectacular historic decline from empire to impotence is one obvious reason for this tendency. But Symons argues that "a certain sadness is inherent in the very sound and colour of still water, and a little of the melancholy which we now feel must always have been a background of shadow, even at the most splendid moment of the masque" (77). Simon Raikes, the protagonist of Barry Unsworth's recent novel *Stone Virgin* (1985), is by temperament peculiarly vulnerable to such Venetian shadows. "Like many ardent, lonely people Raikes possessed a strong vein of melancholy, and now he thought how sad it was, how very sad, this endless celebration of its own beauty the city indulged in, so long after the glory and energy had departed. It was something that could not be translated into human terms without heart-sickness—love diminishing in the midst of protestation" (55).

"Venice," Goethe moralizes, "like everything else which has a phenomenal existence, is subject to Time" (63); and the unsparing fashion in which Time has tamed the Queen of the Adriatic has provided later writers with boundless matter for threnody. Like Pompeii, the place seems to be shadowed by cataclysm. Dickens, recognising that "the greatness of the city was no more," perceives it as "a very wreck found drifting on the sea; a strange flag hoisted in its honourable stations, and strangers [the Austrian rulers] standing at its helm" (*Pictures* 124). He concludes his description with a portentous image of the water encircling the city: "Noiseless and watchful: coiled round and round it, in its many folds, like an old serpent: waiting for the time . . . when people should look down into its depths for any stone of the old city that had claimed to be its mistress" (127).

Venice, according to James, is a "place supremely . . . the refuge of endless strange secrets, broken fortunes and wounded hearts" (*Hours* 69). What helps to make it that is the "great Venetian clue—the explanation of everything by the historic idea" (67). "The beauty of the matter," James says of an arrival by gondola, "has been in the absence of all momentum—elsewhere so scientifically applied to us, from behind, by the terrible life of our day" (66-67).

To less conservative observers, it is the characteristic *absence* of momentum that seems terrible. Stasis, in Florence an option opposed to the dominant forward march of life, is in Venice an omnipresent temptation. According to Piovene, "This region nurtures a self-love, a narcissism . . . a perpetual bliss in gazing at oneself in the mirror, a contentment with its own picturesqueness, a delight in making theater out of oneself and one's own lot, which distract it from the push for change and endear to it its own *status quo*" (22-23).

By American observers, in particular, the overwhelming pressure of the past has been assigned the blame for the local sense of stagnation. e. e. cummings believes that "[t]o take refuge in the past—be your refugee a nation or an individual—means to commit a neurotic deed; the past . . . being a substitute for living" (196). Accordingly, in his dissident piece "How I Do Not Love Italy," cummings engagingly confesses "that we love Venice much but that we love Coney Island more" (167). Howells makes a comparable avowal. During his Venetian stay, he awakens to the stealthy way in which history has been sapping his personal initiative: "I had forsaken wholesome struggle in the currents where I felt the motion of the age, and had drifted into a lifeless eddy of the world, remote from incentive and sensation" (*Venetian Life* 29). For Howells, Venice is "a phantom of the past, haunting our modern world,—serene, inexpressibly beautiful, yet inscrutably and unspeakably sad" (29).

But if to such observers the city's saturation by history has left it lagging behind the great march of "progress," to others Venice becomes by that very token magically exempt from debasement at the hands of time. In *The Stones of Venice* (1851-53), Ruskin extols, in a striking metaphor, "that beauty which seemed to have fixed for its throne the sands of the hour-glass as well as of the sea" (2: 7). For Mary McCarthy, too, "Venice is an eternal present" (*Venice Observed* 88). "In the eternal carnival Venice," she explains, "nothing ever happens, except 'adventures,' that is, short-lived, dream-like episodes" (154). This impression of timeless permanence makes those spearheads of modernity that have managed to penetrate the charmed scene look all the more out of place.

Jan Morris flatly declares that "the idea of Venice [is] unreconcilable with the modern world" (10). James, a century earlier, presciently notes that modern technology, multiplying a millionfold the available images of Venice, has succeeded only in vulgarizing them. "That is only a reason the more," he argues, for first-hand observation of the place itself, "for catching at any freshness that may be left in the world of photography" (*Hours* 33).

But freshness is not easily caught in a place so haunted by the idea of mortality. James's epithet for Venice, "the most beautiful of tombs" (*Hours* 32), sums up the universal impression. The dour eye of John Eustace sees something tomblike even in the resplendent church of San Marco: "[A]dorned with clumsy mosaics, it is dark, heavy and sepulchral" (1: 191). "'Should you positively like to live here?'" Lord Mark, in *The Wings of the Dove*, tactlessly asks the terminally ill Milly Theale, who has taken up residence in a sumptuous Venetian palace. The girl's reply establishes beyond doubt her connoisseurship of place: "'I think I should like,' said poor Milly after an instant, 'to die here'" (2: 151).

Even though many characters die in Florentine narratives, no famous work is entitled "Death in Florence." Mann's resonant title draws on a distinctive, time-honored literary tradition. For the romantics and decadents of the nineteenth century, as Giorgio Bassani observes, Venice was to become "*par excellence* the city of the dead, a spectre slowly subsiding into the same sea from which it emerged a thousand years ago. The living who still linger there among its stupendous marbles, ever more tightly besieged by the stealthy waters of the lagoon, are not men but rather ghosts, shades" (27). To the literary mind even the gondola, that harmless local conveyance, becomes shrouded with funereal drapery. Byron's witty, well-known simile in *Beppo* (1818, *Poetical Works*) helped to cement the association: "It glides along the water looking blackly, / Just like a coffin clapt in a canoe" (xix). The Byron-adoring American tourist of Howells's *A Foregone Conclusion* (1875), Mrs. Vervain, insists on applying the conceit to her own gondola: "'I always feel as if I were going to my own funeral when I get into it'" (23).

Browning exploits such macabre associations in his dialogue-poem "In a Gondola" (*The Poems*, Vol. 1), in which the male speaker, who is at length "surprised, and stabbed," does indeed end up going to his own funeral. Here, passion triumphs over death—"I / Have lived indeed, and so—(yet one more kiss)—can die!" (230-1). The same poet's "A Toccata of Galuppi's" (*The Poems*, Vol. 1), however, presents a more chilling interruption of Venetian revelry and dalliance by Venetian mortality. The sybaritic revelers leave their favorite musician "for their pleasure till in due time, one by one, / Some with lives that came to nothing, some with deeds as well undone, / Death stepped tacitly and took them where they never see the sun" (28-30).

To judge from many Venetian fictions, this cheerless variety of peace is the only sort to be found in the city. From Mann's Aschenbach on down, Venetian protagonists are pathologically subject to mental fixation and breakdown. Giorgio Bassani detects in the literature that has grown up around Venice since the time of Shakespeare and Jonson "something sick, obsessive, neurotic" (25); and examples of what he means flock to mind. Shelley's *Julian and Maddalo* centers on the figure of the madman who has been deserted by his beloved and now languishes in the Venice asylum. The poem comments poignantly on the man's monomania: "it were a grief indeed / If he had changed one unsustaining reed / For all that such a man might else adorn" (537-9, *Complete Poetical Works*). In Sand's *Leone Leoni*, the title character's craze for gambling has a similar monomaniacal tinge, as does the heroine's fascination for the dissolute

Leoni himself.

In more recent fiction, Venetian obsessions continue to abound. Simon Raikes, the art-restorer in Unsworth's *Stone Virgin*, devotes himself so fanatically to his sleuthing into the mystery surrounding a Renaissance statue of the Madonna that he loses touch with day-to-day reality. The widowed Frances Brooklyn, in Lively's *Perfect Happiness*, becomes absorbed in another sort of sleuthing: the task of tracking down and "restoring" the details of her honeymoon in Venice with her late husband. Her project quickly turns into another obsessive chase after a Venetian will-o'-the-wisp. Like Mann's Aschenbach, she begins to scour the city to gain sight of the desired image—here, not a living boy but a no-longer-living man. She becomes a voyeur of her own elusive past:

She walked the rough streets and squares and saw nothing: the houses and churches and canals rolled by like stage-sets. She was obsessed, isolated, locked within herself, in feverish pursuit. She knew that something disastrous was happening to her, that possibly she was going mad. (54)

That "something disastrous" represents a chronic danger for Venetian characters. Susan Hill's Francis Croft is prompted by the sight of the island of San Clemente, where the madhouse is located, to ask disturbing questions:

"Well, I wonder how full it is and whether they've room for another. How many people go mad in Venice, do you suppose? Hundreds and hundreds, I think, it's a place where all the people are mad. It doesn't exist, you see, except in a lot of fevered brains, it's a mirage, it's a peep-show, didn't you realize?" (*Bird* 40)

Francis's intuition is sound. The fixations that grip Venetian characters (including Francis himself) have a habit of being overwhelmingly visual in nature. The connection between this literary convention and features of the Venice "surround" is self-evident. If Venice boasts a long mercantile tradition, the city's rarest form of wealth lies in its astonishing appearance. The splendor of the local panorama has, it is often claimed, bred a special acuteness in the native "eye." In Florentine fictions, too, visual motifs proliferate; but the implications of the "Venetian eye" for Venetian narratives point in other directions. Where Florentine works typically explore the metaphorical link between two sorts of "seeing," vision and intellection, Venetian stories dwell upon the act of visual perception at a more sensuous level, for its own sweet sake. Here, however, the consequences of visual indulgence are often not liberating but dire.

Howells, in *Venetian Life*, notes the characteristic local preoccupation: "Venetian neighbors have the amiable custom of studying one another's features through opera-glasses" (57). Yet the "Venetian eye" can be less than amiable. In Collins's *The Haunted Hotel* the Countess Narona's "overpowering black eyes" (19) signal trouble from the very first. The whole story hinges on the gothic nuances of eye-play. When Agnes, the girl jilted by the late Count, arrives at the ghastly Venice "hotel" where the Count has been murdered, the Countess eyes her in the best (or worst) Venetian fashion through an opera glass. During a night when Agnes beholds hideous visions, the Countess secretly infiltrates her bedroom in order "'to see what you saw'" (141). The climax occurs when the Countess and the apparition of her husband's severed head engage in a bizarre *tête-à-tête*:

The closed eyelids opened slowly. The eyes revealed themselves, bright with the glassy film of death—and fixed their dreadful look on the woman in the chair.

Agnes saw that look; saw the eyelids of the living woman open slowly like the eyelids of the dead. (139)

The girl, of course, faints. Some sights are for Venetian eyes only.

"It is all for the ear and eye, this city, but primarily for the eye," Mary McCarthy says; and she goes on to note the odd doubling or "mirroring" effect so typical of the place: "Built on water, it is an endless succession of reflections and echoes, a mirroring" (*Venice Observed* 11). A visit to Venice is a trip not through but to the looking glass, a fact that helps to explain the peculiar air of self-consciousness often adhering to Venetian characters, and sometimes to whole texts. The self-dissociation experienced in Venice by Susan Hill's fictional poet Francis Croft is at once extreme and typical. "Once I caught him staring at himself in a mirror, his face very close to the glass," reports Francis's friend Harvey. "He looked puzzled. 'I'm afraid we have not been introduced,' he said to his own reflection. 'I do not know your face. Should I know your face? Is this a good party?'" (*Bird* 110).

Henry James speaks of "that universal privilege of Venetian objects which consists of being both the picture and the point of view" (*Hours* 34). Observers sometimes find the Venetians themselves as scenic as the city they inhabit; Symons claims that "[t]he gondolier in Venice is as fine to look at as his gondola" (96). Yet looking, elsewhere normally an innocent activity, here often conduces to a risky voyeurism. In Unsworth's *Stone Virgin*, distortions of the English protagonist's vision serve to measure the gravity of his entanglement with Chiara Litsov, an ambiguous Venetian *femme fatale*. By the end of the story, his sight has been altered by a drug prescribed by a local psychiatrist, and his moral vision has undergone still more troubling distortions. He continues obsessively keeping his eye on Chiara despite his suspicion that she has (like her literary ancestor, Collins's Countess Narona) been a party to her husband's murder.

"Venetian windows and balconies are a dreadful lure," warns James, "and while you rest your elbows on these cushioned ledges the precious hours fly away" (*Hours* 13). Arthur Symons finds the city's streets as visually seductive as its windows: "This movement, the tangles of the way, the continual arresting of one's attention by some window, doorway, or balcony, put a strain upon one's eyes, and begin after a time to tire and stupefy the brain" (100). In "this city that is all eyes," as McCarthy calls it (*Venice Observed* 147), it seems natural to attribute a mesmerizing narcissism to the place itself. "The perennial wonder of Venice," McCarthy says, "is to peer at herself in her canals and find that she exists—incredible as it seems. It is the same reassurance that a looking-glass offers us: the guarantee that we are real" (150). She sums up Venetian life as a dazzling promenade among a wilderness of mirrors. "Venice is a kind of pun on itself, which is another way of saying that it is a mirror held up to its own shimmering image—the central conceit on which it has evolved" (13).

Venetian narratives, like Francis Croft's colloquy with his mirrored image, often turn on effects of "doubling." Unsworth's *Stone Virgin* goes beyond mere doubling into rampant echolalia, interweaving parallel narratives from three separate historical eras. A central symbolic motif is the occult "mirroring" between Chiara Litsov, the woman Simon Raikes is pursuing, and the Madonna he is feverishly engaged in restoring. As the narrative proceeds, the confusions between flesh and stone become more and more baffling. Such confusions provide the very stuff of Venetian tales: enigmas of appearance and reality, or (as in L. P. Hartley's "The White Wand") conundrums of identity. The librettists of Jacques Offenbach's *The Tales of Hoffmann* were brilliantly right to shift from Florence to Venice E.T.A. Hoffmann's "Story of the Lost Reflection," which tells how a luckless German traveller loses his reflection—his "guarantee that he is real."

Within such a setting, one is hardly surprised that a reflection should get lost, or that ardent love should be kindled by a face glimpsed in a window, as in Browning's "In a Gondola." "'Ah, the autumn day / I passing, saw you overhead!'" the lover in Browning murmurs. "'First, out a cloud of curtain blew, / Then a sweet cry, and last came you'" (137-40). Ultimately, there is no way of separating the "natural" Venice from the Venice of artifice. As James argues, the city's artistic heritage merges seamlessly with its workaday life:

Nowhere . . . do art and life seem so interfused and, as it were, so consanguineous. All the splendour of light and colour, all the Venetian air and the Venetian history are on the walls and ceilings of the palaces; and all the genius of the masters, all the images and visions they have left upon canvas, seem to tremble in the sunbeams and dance upon the waves. That is the perpetual interest of the place—that you live in a certain sort of knowledge as in a rosy cloud. (*Hours* 19)

The idea of living in a cloud, rosy or not, implies abstraction from the warmth of human contact. One final Venetian motif remains to be mentioned: the imprisoning pall of isolation. The idea may appear to sort oddly with a place where spectacle and gregariousness have long prevailed: "Whether for good or ill, they are always up to something together," as Goethe notes (71). Nevertheless, the accidents of topography cause overtones of separateness and solitude to link themselves irresistibly with the city's inhabitants. "[I]slanders they remain, still a people apart, still tinged with the sadness of refugees," Morris observes (23). "This grand insularity," she adds quaintly, "this isolation, this sense of queerness and crookedness has preserved the Venetian character uncannily, as though it were pickled like a rare intestine, or mummified in lotions" (28).

As an emblem of Venice, the ancient, grim prisons of the Republic remain psychologically potent. Dickens's account of a visit to them vividly illustrates the point:

[My heart] was smitten harder though, when, torch in hand, I descended from the cheerful day into two ranges, one below another, of dismal, awful, horrible stone cells. They were quite dark. Each had a loop-hole in its massive wall, where, in the old time, every day, a torch was placed . . . to light the prisoner within, for half an hour. The captives, by the glimmering of these brief rays, had scratched and cut inscriptions in the blackened vaults. I saw them. For their labour with a rusty nail's point, had outlived their agony and them, through many generations. (*Pictures* 123)

"I saw them"—Dickens's appalled eyewitness testimony sums up the Venetian sense of the tenuousness, and yet the preciousness, of human communication. In the Venice of poetry and fiction, such communication often seems what it is here: the frantic scratchings of those condemned to solitary confinement. The label that Mann bestows on his protagonist in *Death in Venice*—"our solitary"—could be extended to most of Gustave Aschenbach's literary fellow travellers. The chapters to follow will trace some of the footsteps of this troupe of solitudes.

10

"The Fair Frailty":
Prison and Abyss

Venetian dreams breed Venetian nightmares. Two of the most celebrated
treatments of the locale, the Venetian scenes of Charles Dickens's *Little Dorrit*
(1857) and Thomas Mann's novella *Death in Venice*, dissolve the city's
enchanted aura to lay bare a sinister menace underneath. But the novelists'
approaches to the setting resemble each other only in the penetrating attention
that they bestow on it. Otherwise, the two works are as unlike as the two unique
sensibilities that produced them, and as the two troubled centuries to which they
belong.

THE PRISON: *LITTLE DORRIT*

In *Little Dorrit*, the image of Venice harmonises with Dickens's "dream"
of the city in *Pictures from Italy*. Here, however, it is fed by its context, the
whole vast symbolic and moral panorama of the novel, darkened throughout by
the shadow of the Marshalsea Prison. The Dorrit family's journey to Italy
becomes an analogue of their fairy-tale turn of fortune, which has transformed
them with crazy abruptness from paupers to princes. Like that stunning
transfiguration of status, the trip itself has a numbing effect on Amy Dorrit's
perceptions:

Sitting opposite her father in the travelling-carriage, and recalling the old Marshalsea
room, her present existence was a dream. All that she saw was new and wonderful, but
it was not real; it seemed to her as if those visions of mountains and picturesque countries
might melt away at any moment, and the carriage, turning some abrupt corner, bring up
with a jolt at the old Marshalsea gate. (433)

The scenes through which she passes all confirm "the unreality of her own inner
life," which can grasp "only the old mean Marshalsea" as a reality (434).
Amy's impressions of Venice itself are rooted in long-established literary
precedent. Yet because they arise from the ground of the girl's unique individual
experience, their authenticity is beyond doubt:

In this crowning unreality, where all the streets were paved with water, and where the
deathlike stillness of the days and nights was broken by no sound but the softened ringing
of church-bells, the rippling of the current, and the cry of the gondoliers turning the

corners of the flowing streets, Little Dorrit, quite lost by her task being done, sat down to muse. The family began a gay life, went here and there, and turned night into day; but she was timid of joining in their gaieties, and only asked leave to be left alone. (436)

The expected Venetian ingredients—unreality, deathlikeness, gaiety hiding solitude in its deceitful bosom—are there, yet there is no feeling of cliché. The family's disorienting inversion of the normal rhythms of life ("turned night into day") seems but a reflex of the whole weirdly fluid cityscape. Instability, the keynote of *Little Dorrit*, finds here its metaphorical home.

The sense of unreality that dogs Amy *en route* to the city stems in part from the endlessly repeated spectacle of poverty engaged in hand-to-hand combat with wealth: "misery and magnificence wrestling with each other upon every rood of ground in the prospect, no matter how widely diversified, and misery throwing magnificence with the strength of fate" (434). In Venice itself such contrasts gain an added visual force, even in the prospects to be had from the Dorrits' labyrinthine palace:

It was quite a walk, by mysterious staircases and corridors, from Mrs. General's apartment—hoodwinked by a narrow side street with a low gloomy bridge in it, and dungeon-like opposite tenements, their walls besmeared with a thousand downward stains and streaks, as if every crazy aperture in them had been weeping tears of rust into the Adriatic for centuries—to Mr. Dorrit's apartment: with a whole English house-front of window, a prospect of beautiful church-domes rising into the blue sky sheer out of the water which reflected them, and a hushed murmur of the Grand Canal laving the doorways below, where his gondolas and gondoliers attended his pleasure, drowsily swinging in a little forest of piles. (442-3)

Within the bounds of one spacious Dickensian sentence, Venetian misery throws Venetian magnificence. The discord between social sinking and social climbing is adroitly implied by details, like the "thousand downward stains and streaks" set against the "church-domes rising into the blue sky." The visual contrast between brightness and gloom coincides with the clash in Amy's mind between the reality of the Marshalsea past and the unreality of this present:

This is why it was that, even as he [her father] sat before her on his sofa, in the brilliant light of a bright Italian day, the wonderful city without and the splendours of an old palace within, she saw him at the moment in the long-familiar gloom of his Marshalsea lodging, and wished to take her seat beside him, and comfort him, and be again full of confidence with him, and of usefulness to him. (448)

Between past and present, prisons and palaces, however, not all is contrast. The sunlit Italian city is tinged with its own special gloom, which itself soon begins to grow familiar. The room in which the family breakfasts, "a faded hall which had once been sumptuous but was now the prey of watery vapours and a settled melancholy" (442), recalls at once Dorrit's earlier collapse of fortune and the protracted decline of the "wonderful city" lying without.

The same descriptive virtuosity Dickens has already bestowed on the tottering desolation of London he now trains on the age-old dilapidation of the Italian city. An instance is the house taken by the recently married Gowans:

The house, on a little desert island, looked as if it had broken away from somewhere else, and had floated by chance into its present anchorage, in company with a vine almost as much in want of training as the poor wretches who were lying under its leaves. The features of the surrounding picture were, a church with a hoarding and scaffolding about it, which had been under supposititious repair so long that the means of repair looked a hundred years old, and had themselves fallen into decay; a quantity of washed linen, spread to dry in the sun; a number of houses at odds with one another and grotesquely out of the perpendicular, like rotten pre-Adamite cheeses cut into fantastic shapes and full of mites; and a feverish bewilderment of windows, with their lattice-blinds all hanging askew, and something draggled and dirty dangling out of most of them. . . . Below the bank, was a suite of three or four rooms with barred windows, which had the appearance of a jail for criminal rats. Above the bank was Mrs. Gowan's residence. (459)

"People like the houses they Inhabit," Dickens had written in his working notes for one of the monthly instalments of *Little Dorrit* (*Dickens' Working Notes* 281). The entry might be extended to read: "Houses like the cities that harbor them." Here, again, a traveller's commonplace, the decay so evident in Venice, has been given a personal bearing. The sketch of the house captures a moral dimension of the "floating," askew life in which marriage to the cavalier Gowan has imprisoned Minnie.

The startling final detail in the quoted passage, the "jail for criminal rats," illustrates how tightly the Venetian episode is welded to the larger symbolic structure of the novel. "All the literal and figurative rotten houses of the novel," observes F. S. Schwarzbach, are "objective correlative[s] of the diseased will of society" (162). "Look to the rats young and old, all ye Barnacles," warns Dickens early in *Little Dorrit*, "for before God they are eating away our foundations, and will bring the roofs on our heads!" (153). Venice, which begins as an apparent antitype of London, turns into its watery suburb: the Marshalsea writ large, with gondoliers for turnkeys. "It appeared on the whole, to Little Dorrit herself, that this same society in which they lived greatly resembled a superior sort of Marshalsea" (478). Poor Frederick Dorrit, when he goes "out of the palace hall, just as he might have gone out of the Marshalsea room" (455), displays perceptions apparently muddled, but at bottom correct.

For Amy, Venice becomes more cruelly imprisoning than the Marshalsea, for it isolates her more absolutely. As she gazes down from her balcony, passersby say of her, "There was the little figure of the English girl who was always alone" (436). But the saddest consequence of Amy's Venetian isolation (and of the wealth that makes it possible) is that it leaves her stranded across an emotional lagoon from her beloved father. "'I struggle with the feeling that I have come to be at a distance from him,'" she reports sadly to Arthur Clennam, "'and that even in the midst of all the servants and attendants, he is deserted, and in want of me'" (440). Mrs. General, that formidable Dogess, stands on guard against any sign of an insurgent league between blood relatives.

A distinctively Venetian function of Mrs. General's is to assist the hapless Amy in "the formation of a surface" (447). Here again, it is Venice's role to distill tendencies that recur throughout the novel. Amid a city that seems merely an assemblage of surfaces, the society for which Mrs. General is preparing her charge permits only decorous facades to be offered to the viewer. Indeed, it amounts to a breach of aesthetic etiquette to view anything else—"'Nothing disagreeable should ever be looked at'" (447). With this bland milieu the superficiality of Gowan, Sparkler, and Fanny Dorrit comfortably accords. Gowan's patronizing insensitivity to his wife comes across in terms wittily borrowed from the local topography:

He seemed so unsuspicious of the depths of feeling which [Amy] knew must lie below that surface, that she doubted if there could be any such depths in himself. She wondered whether his want of earnestness might be the natural result of his want of such qualities, and whether it was with people as with ships, that, in too shallow and rocky waters, their anchors had no hold, and they drifted anywhere. (463)

Not only does the house that Gowan has let seem shipwrecked already; his disposition itself appears to be perilously unmoored.

The brilliant Mr. Sparkler, for his part, is entirely at home with the Venetian spirit of *dolce far niente*: "As he was going to do nothing that day (his usual occupation, and one for which he was particularly qualified), he was secured [as the Dorrits' dinner guest] without postponements" (468). Arriving in his gondola, ready to shower his attentions upon Fanny, he is a figure out of a preposterously overblown Renaissance allegory: "At dinner-time Mr. Sparkler rose out of the sea, like Venus's son taking after his mother, and made a splendid appearance ascending the great staircase" (468). Fanny herself, mermaid-wise, plunges with alacrity into the Venetian social maelstrom: "[S]he had become the victim of an insatiate mania for what she called 'going into society'; and would have gone into it head-foremost fifty times between sunset and sunrise, if so many opportunities had been at her disposal" (450). Her "insatiate mania" is Venetian obsessiveness at its silliest.

Nevertheless, there are moments that offset the inanity of Dickens's Venetian *mise-en-scène*. Mr. Frederick Dorrit

had insensibly acquired a new habit of shuffling into the picture-galleries . . . and of passing hours and hours before the portraits of renowned Venetians. It was never made out what his dazed eyes saw in them: whether he had an interest in them merely as pictures, or whether he confusedly identified them with a glory that was departed, like the strength of his own mind. But he paid his court to them with great exactness, and clearly derived pleasure from the pursuit. (450-1)

Frederick's obscure pleasure is far removed from vulgar Venetian hedonism; he, at least, does not suffer from Gowan's "want of earnestness." Some study of the physiognomies of the Venetian past might have endowed the lofty Fanny with a broader perspective within which to view the spurious glory of a Merdle. Whatever its defects, Venice can still reward patient attention, a faculty the decrepit Frederick shares with the younger but more mature of his two nieces. Such attention, aesthetic or historical, has a value that transcends the aqueous bounds of this "city that is all eyes." On Dickens's whole vast mid-Victorian canvas, dream and wakefulness tend terrifyingly to merge. In such a world, Affery Flintwich's habitual expedient of hiding her eyes with her apron to screen out her unfathomable "dreams" sets a dubious example. The dreams, as Monroe Engel observes, "turn out to be not dreams at all but glimpses of a reality too dreadful to admit" (130). Within the broad fictional boundaries of *Little Dorrit*, that reality is nowhere more tempting to evade, and nowhere more inescapable, than in Venice.

THE ABYSS: DEATH IN VENICE

Yes, this was Venice, this the fair frailty that fawned and that betrayed, half fairy-tale, half snare; the city in whose stagnating air the art of painting once put forth so lusty a growth, and where musicians were moved to accords so weirdly lulling and lascivious. (*Death in Venice* 55-56)

In Thomas Mann's *Death in Venice,* too, Venetian dreams hint at a reality too dreadful to admit. Here, however, that reality is of a different sort. Unlike the Venice of *Little Dorrit*, which epitomizes the whole surrounding, imprisoning Europe of that novel, Mann's Venice is pointedly *sui generis*, and all the more disturbing for being so. The German writer's own feelings for the city were special and yet divided, as his 1932 letter to his children Erika and Klaus, who were vacationing there, suggests:

In spirit I am with you leading that unique life between the warm sea in the morning and the "ambiguous" city in the afternoon. Ambiguous is really the humblest adjective that can be applied . . . , but it is wonderfully relevant in all its meanings, and for all the city's modern silliness and corruptness, which you two also object to, this musical magic of ambiguity still lives, or at least has hours in which it is victorious. . . . For certain people, there is a special melancholia associated with the name of Venice. It is full of the home atmosphere—nowadays a spiritually rather corrupt and staled atmosphere, I grant . . . ; but still my heart would be pounding were I there again. (*Letters* 160-1)

The heart of Mann's fictional alter ego, Gustave Aschenbach, pounds so furiously in "the home atmosphere" that it pounds itself to a stop.

As critics have pointed out, the ideas of Venice and death are already conjoined in the "mortuary chapel, a structure in Byzantine style . . . silent in the gleam of the ebbing day" (4) that Aschenbach beholds before setting out for Italy. The physical death to which his Venetian pilgrimage will lead him is but the symptom of an inward, spiritual disintegration.

As he approaches Venice, the celebrated writer thinks, not unnaturally,

of the melancholy and susceptible poet who had once seen the towers and turrets of his dreams rise out of these waves; repeated the rhythms born of his awe, his mingled emotions of joy and suffering—and easily susceptible to a prescience already shaped within him, he asked his own sober, weary heart if a new enthusiasm, a new preoccupation, some late adventure of the feelings could still be in store for the idle traveller. (19)

"Venice," Henry Hatfield observes, "is suffused, for the German public, with a special richness of reminiscence: it is associated with the poet Platen, with Nietzsche, and with Wagner, who died there" (62). It is presumably Platen whom Aschenbach recalls in the quoted passage; but Mann identified Venice equally with that other "melancholy and susceptible poet," Lord Byron. In his 1932 letter to his children, he names the famous English Romantic as one who "passionately loved [Venice] the way it was," along with Platen, Nietzsche, and "your insignificant honorable sire" (*Letters* 161). Yet despite its vibrant literary associations, Venice, unlike Florence, is a locale inhospitable to personal renaissance. As Mann's novella demonstrates, a passionate love for the place can all too readily become a last attachment to the abyss.

In the event, far from giving him a new lease on life, Venice violently evicts Aschenbach from his long-accustomed peace of mind. Yet why should a city in which "the art of painting once put forth so lusty a growth," and whose history and appearance alike enshrine the urge to impose form on the formless, prove so deadly to a mature artistic sensibility, whetting to madness its latent appetite for chaos? The answer lies in Mann's ambivalence about form, which in turn lies at the root of his ambivalence about Venice. To apply Nietzschean terms, Mann tends to conceive of the classic, Apollonian mode as harboring the Dionysian virus of its own undoing.   "'But detachment, Phaedrus, and preoccupation with form lead to intoxication and desire,'" Aschenbach reminds himself in a feverish mock-Platonic inner dialogue; "'they may lead the noblest among us to frightful emotional excesses, which his own stern cult of the beautiful would make him the first to condemn. So they too, they too, lead to the bottomless pit'" (73). Venice, paragon of form, is the bottomless pit concealed under an elegant mask.

Such musings conduct Aschenbach at last to a radical scepticism as regards the value of artistic control:

"Our magisterial style is all folly and pretence, our honourable repute a farce, the crowd's belief in us is merely laughable. And to teach youth, or the populace, by means of art is a dangerous practice and ought to be forbidden. For what good can an artist be as a teacher, when from his birth up he is headed direct for the pit?" (72)

And so, to cap a career that "had been one conscious and overweening ascent to honour" (12), Aschenbach finds himself plunging into the shameful, sea-girt pit called Venice. His self-discovery proceeds by slippery stages. At first, he congratulates himself for having turned his back on his symbolically elevated "mountain home, the theatre of his summer labours" (42); he feels "transported to Elysium . . . to a spot most carefree for the sons of men." "This spot and this alone," he reflects, "had power to beguile him, to relax his resolution, to make him glad" (41).

He is overdue for relaxation; his lifelong demeanor has been all too effectively stiffened by the Goethean qualities of order and discipline. "Bearing the burden of his genius . . . upon such slender shoulders and resolved to go so far, he had the more need of discipline—and discipline, fortunately, was his native inheritance from the father's side" (10). In this last regard, Aschenbach is only too true a son, not only of his paternal parent but of the fatherland; as Hatfield observes, "Too great a devotion to the Prussian ideals of duty and discipline brings him to the point of collapse; the 'death wish' rebels against the categorical imperative of his conscious mind" (61). Venice is a mistimed antidote to Prussia, fatally nurturing the writer's unwisely postponed and hence disastrous revolt against his formative ideals.

For the soldierly Prussian genius, Venice becomes the most disheveled of battlefields, the maze, both physical and moral, in which he finds himself going irremediably astray. The main agent of his confusion, the boy Tadzio, is not literally Venetian but rather of Eastern European origin. By association, however, the boy becomes emphatically one with the city's dazzling visual allure and exotic remoteness. As Dominick LaCapra argues, "[T]here is a bewildering affinity between the erotic desire that arises in Aschenbach and the art form cultivated in a context of 'decadent' civilization. Aschenbach's desire for the boy Tadzio is itself highly aestheticized. . . . The boy's form is stylized; he is an *objet d'art*, an aestheticized fetish" (120). In the German visitor's eyes, Tadzio is identified with the Venetian hallmarks—"Mirror and image!" [literally translated, "statue and mirror"] (44). The setting for the obsessive love-quest is thus profoundly right.

One afternoon [Aschenbach] pursued his charmer deep into the stricken [with cholera] city's huddled heart. The labyrinthine little streets, squares, canals, and bridges, each one so like the next, at length quite made him lose his bearings. He did not even know the points of the compass; all his care was not to lose sight of the figure after which his eyes thirsted. (70-71)

The chase brilliantly externalizes the infatuated Aschenbach's inner state; the points of his *moral* compass, too, have become indistinguishable.

According to the glib-tongued official from whom the writer buys his boat ticket, his choice of destinations is "excellent": "'Ah, Venice! What a glorious city! Irresistibly attractive to the cultured man for her past history as well as her present charm'" (16). Nevertheless, from the moment he sets out on the sea, past and present also grow indistinguishable for him: "[I]mmeasurable unarticulated space weakens our power to measure time as well: the time-sense falters and grows dim" (18). Once in Venice, he finds long-repressed past impulses thronging back to mingle with his astonishing present: "Forgotten feelings, precious pangs of his youth, quenched long since by the stern service that had been his life and now returned so strangely metamorphosed—he recognized them with a puzzled, wondering smile" (49). In his charmed, erotic languor, he contemplates time's flow without mustering the strength of will either to halt or overtake it.

Time passed, the night went on. Long ago, in his parental home, he had watched the sand filter through an hourglass—he could still see, as though it stood before him, the fragile, pregnant little toy. Soundless and fine the rust-red streamlet ran through the narrow neck, and made, as it declined in the upper cavity, an exquisite little vortex. (63)

Aschenbach's languorous, passive contemplation of time represents a return to childhood that is more than regressive; it is deadly. Venice, whatever he may suppose, is not an exquisite little vortex—it is an enormous, devouring one.

What helps make it that is the solitude that clings to Aschenbach by nature and by vocation. Dickens's Amy Dorrit, though dreamily isolated amid the Venetian labyrinth, has a disposition that is far from unsocial; she has merely been placed in an unresponsive society. With Aschenbach, it is different. Educated at home, "he had grown up solitary, without comradeship" (9); and his life as a literary artist has redoubled his aloneness. "Solitude," the narrator philosophizes, "gives birth to the original in us, to beauty unfamiliar and perilous—to poetry. But also, it gives birth to the opposite: to the perverse, the illicit, the absurd" (24). Venice, populous home of solitude, is by this logic the natural birthplace of poetry but also of the perverse, the illicit, and the absurd. It is a place where a lurid public cover-up can transmit to a self-absorbed wanderer a prurient sense of collusion: "These things that were going on in the unclean alleys of Venice, under cover of an official hushing-up policy—they gave Aschenbach a dark satisfaction. The city's evil secret mingled with the one in the depths of his heart" (54).

The Venetian evil secret infects the solitary above all through its stealthy demoting of the spiritual to the level of the grossly carnal. Venice deconsecrates a fine sensibility. Yearning sensuality is externalized in hectic close-ups of the local scene: "There was a hateful sultriness in the narrow streets. The air was so heavy that all the manifold smells wafted out of houses, shops, and cook-shops—smells of oil, perfumery, and so forth—hung low, like exhalations, not dissipating" (35). Upon this background of rank stagnation, Mann traces a caricature of Venice's commercial profile: "Thus the charm of this bizarre passage through the heart of Venice, even while it played upon [Aschenbach's] spirit, yet was sensibly cooled by the predatory commercial spirit of the fallen queen of the seas" (36). The familiar idea of Venetian "relaxation" is similarly exaggerated so as to make it gruesomely sardonic. When Aschenbach sinks into the seat of his Lido-bound gondola, it is, inevitably, "black as nothing else on earth except a coffin" and is propelled by death personified. "And has anyone remarked that the seat in such a bark, the arm-chair lacquered in coffin-black and dully black upholstered, is the softest, most luxurious, most relaxing seat in the world?" (21). Appropriately, Aschenbach's misunderstanding of Tadzio's name—he thinks of him as "the exquisite Adgio" (32)—sounds precisely like *agio*, Italian for "ease."

It is in fact a deathly ease that ultimately liquidates the Prussian high-commander of disciplined language. To such an ease the aptly named "Adgio" invites Aschenbach; and it is mordantly ironic that a man famed "on account of his unerring gift of words" (34) should become intoxicated by the boy's unintelligible foreign chatter:

Aschenbach understood not a word he said; it might be the sheerest commonplace, in his ear it became mingled harmonies. Thus the lad's foreign birth raised his speech to music; a wanton sun showered splendour on him, and the noble distances of the sea formed the background which set off his figure. (43)

With violent abandon, Aschenbach has begun to read his own feelings about Tadzio into the Venetian cityscape. The boy's uncomprehended speech offers the writer a ductile medium with which his imagination can sport, unimpeded by fixed meaning; but then so does the whole Venetian ambiance, from which Aschenbach is distanced by ineluctable barriers of language and upbringing. A phrase from Mann's letter to his children, "this musical magic of ambiguity," is entirely to the point.

"Has it not been written," asks the narrator, "that the sun beguiles our attention from things of the intellect to fix it on things of the sense?" (44). The scene that, in *Death in Venice*, the Venetian sun irradiates appeals not to the protagonist's intellect but to his senses, and chiefly to his eyes. It is, indeed, a consuming Venetian lust of the eye that causes Aschenbach's collapse. This obsession is proleptically announced by the stray detail of the writer's smarting eyes at the time of his departure:

Aschenbach put his hand to his brow, he covered his eyes, for he had slept little, and they smarted. He felt not quite canny, as though the world were suffering a dreamlike distortion of perspective which he might arrest by shutting it all out for a few minutes and then looking at it afresh. (17-18)

The "dreamlike distortion of perspective" will pervade his whole Venetian experience. It is on the entrancing Tadzio that his visual thirst most directly fastens, but it fastens just as fiercely on the fabulous city whose seductive allure the boy personifies. When the German writer journeys, as he intends, out of Venice on the morning of his abortive departure, his susceptibility to the place erupts:

They passed the Public Gardens, once more the princely charm of the Piazzetta rose up before him and then dropped behind, next came the great row of palaces, the canal curved, and the splendid marble arches of the Rialto came in sight. The traveller gazed—and his bosom was torn. The atmosphere of the city, the faintly rotten scent of swamp and sea, which had driven him to leave—in what deep, tender, almost painful draughts he breathed it in! How was it he had not known, had not thought, how much his heart was set upon it all! (37-38)

"The hardest part," the narrator adds, "the part that more than once it seemed he could not bear, was the thought that he should never . . . see Venice again" (38). The ideas of "seeing" Venice and "seeing" Tadzio have become synonymous. In this city that is "all for the eye," the figure of the boy concentrates all the risky joy of simply looking. "Soon the observer knew every line and pose of this form that limned itself so freely against sea and sky; its every loveliness, though conned by heart, yet thrilled him each day afresh; his admiration knew no bounds, the delight of his eye was unending" (43).

Such undisciplined delight is what Aschenbach has, in his early life, sternly schooled himself to hamper. He now, succumbing to the local influence, resorts to quasi-Platonic apologetics to justify indulgence in visual hedonism:

The sun, they say, dazzles; so bewitching reason and memory that the soul for very pleasure forgets its actual state, to cling with doting on the loveliest of all the objects she shines on. Yes, and then it is only through the medium of some corporeal being that it can raise itself again to contemplation of higher things. Amor, in sooth, is like the mathematician who in order to give children a knowledge of pure form must do so in the language of pictures; so, too, the god, in order to make visible the spirit, avails himself of the forms and colours of human youth, gilding it with all imaginable beauty that it may serve memory as a tool, the very sight of which then sets us afire with pain and longing. (44-45)

The reasoning, in its fashion, is impeccable. Nevertheless, it simply confirms Byron's charge in *Don Juan* (1819-24, *Poetical Works*) that Plato is "at best, no better than a go-between" (I, cxvi).[1] For Byron, the action on "our helpless clay" of the "baking, broiling, burning" and "indecent" sun (I, lxiii) was apt to lead not to "contemplation of higher things" but to something decidedly un-platonic. To Aschenbach, too, the "language of pictures" delivers a "knowledge" that is far other than one simply of "pure form." The rapport between him and Tadzio, a bond "between two beings who know each other only with their eyes" (50), becomes for him a Venetian obsession, one whose basis he is compelled to admit is frankly carnal. He owns to himself, "not without horror, that he could not exist were the lad to pass from his sight" (54).

In Mann's notes for the novella there is an arresting phrase: "The surface is the abyss" (qtd. Reed 168). It is Aschenbach's paradoxical Venetian fate to plunge morally owing to an enthrallment by visible surfaces. Giorgio Bassani has spoken of "the touristic, and hence necessarily visual, or, so to speak, 'voyeuristic' quality of nearly all the literature about Venice" (20). In his all-absorbing pursuit of the view that has become life to him, Mann's protagonist turns into Venetian voyeurism incarnate:

Leaning back among soft, black cushions he swayed gently in the wake of the other black-snouted bark, to which the strength of his passion chained him. Sometimes it passed from his view, and then he was assailed by an anguish of unrest. But his guide appeared to have long practice in affairs like these; always, by dint of short cuts or deft manoeuvres, he contrived to overtake the coveted sight. The air was heavy and foul, the sun burnt down through a slate-coloured haze. Water slapped gurgling against wood and stone. (55)

Mann is relentless in driving home the connection between Aschenbach's libidinous peering and the genius of the milieu: "Our adventurer felt his senses wooed by this voluptuousness of sight and sound, tasted his secret knowledge that the city sickened and hid its sickness for love of gain, and bent an ever more unbridled leer on the gondola that glided on before him" (56).

Aschenbach's culminating Venetian nightmare projects symbolically the moral drift of his experience of the city, which leaves "the whole cultural structure of a lifetime trampled on, ravaged, and destroyed" (67). Conjuring up tormenting "flute notes of the cruellest sweetness" (67) and a goatish "reeling dance," the dream recapitulates in a surrealist mode the "voluptuousness of sight and sound" that has been the traveller's undoing. The "mountain scene like that about his country home" is defiled by the grotesque feast, the Dionysian "orgy of promiscuous embraces" that overruns it. The dream signals the unconditional surrender, intoxicating and lethal, of visual restraint. Hereafter, Aschenbach utterly forgets his scruples about resting his "fixed and reckless stare" (69) upon Tadzio.

In order to exploit his "Venetian privilege," as Henry James puts it, of being not only an observer but an object of vision, Aschenbach attempts to embellish his own aesthetic surface. Earlier, on his way to Venice, he had been repelled by the sight of a "young-old" man: "Aschenbach's eye dwelt on him, and he was shocked to see that the apparent youth was no youth at all. He was an old man, beyond a doubt, with wrinkles and crow's-feet round eyes and mouth; the dull carmine of the cheeks was rouge, the brown hair a wig" (17). The figure, one of the personifications of death that haunt the story, makes an apt usher at the gates of Venice, another decrepit organism desperately keeping up a facade of "carnival" color and gaiety. Now, at the end of his stay, Aschenbach himself unwisely tries to bridge the heartbreaking gap between "his own aging body" and the "youthful beauty" (69) he adores. He watches complacently while the hotel barber skims off years:

Aschenbach sat there comfortably; he was incapable of objecting to the process—rather as it went forward it roused his hopes. He watched it in the mirror and saw his eyebrows grow more even and arching, the eyes gain in size and brilliance, by dint of a little application below the lids. A delicate carmine glowed on his cheeks where the skin had been so brown and leathery. The dry, anaemic lips grew full, they turned the colour of ripe strawberries, the lines round eyes and mouth were treated with a facial cream and gave place to youthful bloom. It was a young man who looked back at him from the glass—Aschenbach's heart leaped at the sight. The artist in cosmetic at last professed himself satisfied. (70)

The closest thing to a Titian Venice now can boast is this cosmetic Mephistopheles, who, restoring his client's youthful bloom at the cost of his integrity, grotesquely travesties the Faustian compact.

Nothing could be more Venetian. Aschenbach's corrupted heart, once committed to the disseminating of higher truth, now "leaps at the sight" of his retouched visage, an image placed at one further remove from reality than the shadows in Plato's cave. The brief remnant of Aschenbach's life is wholly given over to "his care . . . not to lose sight of the figure after which his eyes thirsted" (71). His telltale posture is sketched with ungentle irony:

There he sat, the master; this was he who had found a way to reconcile art and honours; who had written *The Abject*, and in a style of classic purity renounced bohemianism and all its works, all sympathy with the abyss and the troubled depths of the outcast human soul. This was he who had put knowledge underfoot to climb so high; who had outgrown the ironic pose and adjusted himself to the burdens and obligations of fame; whose renown had been officially recognized and his name ennobled, whose style was set for a model in the schools. There he sat. His eyelids were closed, there was only a swift, sidelong glint of the eyeballs now and again, something between a question and a leer; while the rouged and flabby mouth uttered single words of the sentences shaped in his disordered brain by the fantastic logic that governs our dreams. (72)

The true Abject is to be found on the Venice Lido. Dying in his deck chair, the renowned author turns into an emblem of supine, peering prurience: "He rested his head against the chair-back and followed the movements of the figure out there, then lifted it, as it were in answer to Tadzio's gaze. It sank on his breast, the eyes looked out beneath their lids, while his whole face took on the relaxed and brooding expression of deep slumber" (75). His pose makes of him a *memento mori* in the classic Venetian mode. What takes Aschenbach's life is the local pestilence—a malignant affection of the retina.

Both *Little Dorrit* and *Death in Venice* illustrate the ease with which Venetian settings lend themselves to a presentment of the macabre, the delusive, and the decadent, but they do so in contrary ways. Where Dickens's Venice is home to a society in which spontaneous feeling becomes frozen into imprisoning conventional masks, Mann's works its black magic on a solitary alien, thawing his constraint only to lure him toward an unconventional, annihilating plunge into a private abyss. In general terms, Dickens's public focus is characteristically Victorian, where Mann's probing of the depths of the self is modern. Turning to Henry James's Venetian novella *The Aspern Papers*, one encounters a more complex balance between the social and the private, between the present century and the past one, and between negative and positive views of Venice as a scene of human endeavor.

11

Henry James's Venetian
Curiosity-Shop

Decay, dislocation, and wilted refinement were the attributes of Venice which led James to decide that his reclusive survivor, Juliana Bordereau, would be ideally arrangeable there. Nevertheless, the portentousness of the Venetian milieu in *The Aspern Papers* can be exaggerated. According to Carl Maves, the Venice of James's novella "is the medium through which the . . . characters move, the thick, immobile atmosphere of sensuous decay and neurasthenic languor that deadens their responses to reality and preserves the dreams they cherish" (89). Such a view overstates James's indebtedness to well-worn convention; one might be gliding with the doomed Aschenbach down a mephitic, cholera-infested canal. For James, Venice was not quite the consciousness-altering urban substance that it has represented for so many other writers. What Claire Clairmont's "long undetected survival" most "testified for," in James's view, was not the unreality that has often been read into the setting. It was, rather, a special type of reality that fascinated him, "the reality and the closeness of our relation to the past" (*Art of the Novel* 162). Claire's privacy had been violated by searchers for the papers of Shelley, her half-sister's husband; and the "essential charm" of the story for James was the thought of "the rich dim Shelley drama played out in the very theatre of our own 'modernity'" (163). The "beauty" lay in the "forward continuity, from the actual man, the divine poet, on" (163).

Like James himself, the narrator-protagonist of *The Aspern Papers* cherishes "forward continuity." He finds it in the circumstance that the ancient Juliana has once seen the divine American poet, Jeffrey Aspern, plain—plain enough, indeed, to have been Aspern's lover. The poet's "sacred relics," the narrator confides, "made my life continuous . . . with the illustrious life they had touched at the other end" (306). Juliana herself can be counted among these relics, and she is the putative custodian of other, more collectable, written ones.

The narrator's endeavors to gain access to these have long polarized critical opinion. Many critics, following Leon Edel, have seen the narrator as an "unfeeling cad" (*Complete Tales* 6: 9). A vigorous statement of the opposing view has recently been made by Dorothea Krook, for whom the narrator is "another paradigm of the Jamesian civilized man. He is morally sensitive, compassionate, full of scruples and misgivings about what he is doing, and passionately self-critical" (Bakker 223). According to Krook, the narrator "is, at once and inseparably, a Jamesian artist dedicated to the pursuit of perfection in his art and a superior breed of human being, a man of developed moral sensibility" (227).

Krook's major premise, that the narrator is a Jamesian artist-prototype, seems slenderly supported by the evidence of the novella itself. In his hunt for the precious papers the narrator displays considerable craft, but of artistic imagination he shows little trace. In his role of critic he considers himself "an historian, in a small way"; he conceives of his function as that of spokesman for "the great philosophers and poets of the past; those who are dead and gone and can't speak for themselves" (341). But such a function, while irreproachably academic, participates only at second hand in the achievements of actual genius.

The whole Venetian context of the action is a feature Krook largely ignores. Her neglect of it weakens her case, because the setting provides a valuable touchstone for the narrator's attitudes and behavior. Another recent analysis, by Tony Tanner, taking the use of setting as its starting point, arrives at conclusions opposed to Krook's and more plausible than hers. According to Tanner, the narrator's "blindness to Venice tells us almost all we need to know about him" (18). In the narrator, Tanner claims, Jeffrey Aspern (who must have been "an atrocious poet"!) has found "his ideal follower and devotee—as crude and provincial and . . . naked of manners, as it is possible to be; utterly devoid of art and form, and necessarily lonely since manifestly incapable of human relationships" (19-20). It is crucial that the narrator "should be so shatteringly unaware of [the values identified with Venice], insensitive to all that Venice is and means and implies," for "that, surely, is why James chose Venice as the place the narrator should be so glaringly blind to" (20).

Tanner's emphasis on the importance of the setting is welcome, but his view of the narrator is, in its own fashion, almost as one-sided as Krook's. The crude insensitivity to Venice that Tanner imputes to him sorts oddly with his demonstrable visual acuteness. Witness his description of a "blank wall" neighboring the Bordereaus' palace: "Blank I call it, but it was figured over with the patches that please a painter, repaired breaches, crumblings of plaster, extrusions of brick that had turned pink with time; and a few thin trees, with the poles of certain rickety trellises, were visible over the top" (*Complete Tales* 6:281). His description of the palace itself displays an awareness that goes beyond the purely visual: "It was not particularly old, only two or three centuries; and it had an air not so much of decay as of quiet discouragement, as if it had rather missed its career" (280). This is hardly the voice of a callow American chauvinist who, as Tanner would have it, constantly betrays "a puerile, abusive contempt of Europe" (20). It is through his responses not to walls but to people—above all, to the Bordereaus—that the narrator's relation to Venice is called seriously into question. Although, as Miss Tita says, she and her aunt "'used to be'" American (287), they have long since blended in with the

Venetian fabric surrounding them. Juliana in particular, though for years secluded from that fabric, has grown to be its living embodiment, just as Theobald's model, Serafina, in "The Madonna of the Future" comes to personify Florence. Tanner notes James's tendency (13-14) to speak in his travel writings of Venice as a woman; and, indeed, James's references in *Italian Hours* to "the sad-eyed old witch of Venice" (72) call Juliana irresistibly to mind. According to the narrator's confederate, Mrs. Prest, both aunt and niece "have the reputation of witches" (280), and the narrator himself later concludes of Juliana that "[s]he was such a subtle old witch that one could never tell where one stood with her" (343).

Juliana proves to be so arrangeable in Venice that a symbiosis occurs between woman and city. The "sense of doom and decay" that in *Italian Hours* James sees as forming "a part of every impression [of Venice]" (65) belongs to the ancient lady by as fair a right as to the ancient city. If "the explanation of everything by the historic idea" provides the "great Venetian clue" (*Hours* 67), it provides an equally great clue to Juliana. "Dear old Venice," James says in the same sketch, "has lost her complexion, her figure, her reputation, her self-respect; and yet, with it all, has so puzzlingly not lost a shred of her distinction" (64). This could serve as a profile of Juliana, except that Aspern's ancient mistress still retains some self-respect along with her distinction. Although the narrator finds her grasping in her eagerness to exact an exorbitant rent from him, that same eagerness calls to mind the Venice that "has been accused of cultivating the occasion to grasp and to overreach" (*Hours* 17). However, Juliana, unlike the Florentine Serafina, is not in any simple sense a materialist. Where Venice, according to James, "has been accused further of loving if not too well at least too often" (*Hours* 17), Juliana has loved if not too often, then at least too well.

In *Italian Hours*, James protests that modern Venice gives him a "vexatious sense of the city of the Doges reduced to earning its living as a curiosity-shop" (11). The narrator of *The Aspern Papers* and his friend Mrs. Prest, astonished that Juliana Bordereau has found it "possible to keep so quiet as that in the latter half of the nineteenth century—the age of newspapers and telegrams and photographs and interviewers," speculate that the old lady has actually been protected in her obscurity by the surrounding "city of exhibition": "The only secret of her safety that we could perceive was that Venice contained so many curiosities that were greater than she" (279). It is precisely on the level of "curiosities" that the narrator approaches the Bordereaus themselves. Their reclusiveness strikes him as perverse: "I had never encountered such a violent *parti pris* of seclusion; it was more than keeping quiet—it was like hunted creatures feigning death" (303). What he neglects to mention is that he himself is at the front of the yelping pack. Far from shunning publicity, he takes as his "eccentric private errand" the securing for the public domain of the secrets of art:

"That element was in everything that Jeffrey Aspern had written and I was only bringing it to the light" (305). The word "only" is, at the very least, disingenuous. Such diligence takes on an especially sinister cast when set against James's own elegiac musings over Venice: "Nowhere else has the past been laid to rest with such tenderness, such a sadness of resignation and remembrance. Nowhere else is the present so alien, so discontinuous, so like a crowd in a cemetery without garlands for the graves" (*Hours* 32). Although he waves the banner of beauty and reverence, the narrator brings to the "unearthing" of the buried past a mentality belonging wholly to the present, and therefore hostile to the treasures he claims to adore. The garlands he bears to the Venetian cemetery are tinsel, though his spade is solid enough.

The narrator's idea of himself and his mission can nonetheless, on occasion, comically hit the mark. Talking with Miss Tita, he feels "particularly like the reporter of a newspaper who forces his way into a house of mourning" (335-6). His analogy captures, better than he knows, his true *persona*: the spirit of the journalistic-modern breaking and entering the crypt of the Venetian-historic. When Tita protests innocently against her aunt's belief that the publishing crowd would be willing to violate a tomb—"'She was not just, she was not generous!'"—the narrator has the brazenness to demur: "'Ah, don't say that, for we *are* a dreadful race'" (375). Typically, he takes care not to allow his candor to impede his work of tomb violation.

If Venice has become, in James's phrase, "the most beautiful of tombs," there is much to be said for treading lightly over its remains. That is precisely what the prying narrator refuses to do in regard to Juliana, who has lingered immured in her own personal past, feeding her leftover life with stale memories of passion and beauty. According to Maves, "Both to the narrator . . . and to Juliana Bordereau . . . Jeffery [*sic*] Aspern is more palpable and alive than the actual life around them" (88-89); but the equating of the narrator and Juliana is misleading. The ancient lady is at least preoccupied by a past that has been vibrantly proved upon her own pulses; the investigator is obsessed with a past that is not his own, that can only be flutteringly thumbed and ogled. Although his sleuthing may at first pique one's sympathy, the longer one reads, the more blurred becomes the line between sleuthing and downright snooping. Krook, noting that Juliana regards it "as a desecration of Aspern's memory and an intolerable violation of privacy to expose [Aspern's papers] to a stranger's eye," labels this a "haughty, uncompromising attitude." "[T]he frustration it induces in the narrator," she contends, "precipitates the central action of the story" (225). What Krook fails to recognise is that the sanctity of privacy and of the past supplies the central *value* of the story, while the action to which the narrator is "provoked" can fairly be called an ocular rape.

The subject of *The Aspern Papers* is not, as in *Death in Venice*, the lust for aesthetic possession but rather the yearning for intellectual proprietorship.

Nevertheless, motifs of looking, seeing, and showing pervade James's Venetian novella as thoroughly as they do Mann's. A climactic confrontation between the narrator and Miss Tita illustrates the point. Juliana has died, and the narrator is quizzing the bereft niece to discover the whereabouts of the famous papers:

"Do you mean that you have got them in there—and that I may see them?"

"I don't think you can see them," said Miss Tita, with an extraordinary expression of entreaty in her eyes, as if the dearest hope she had in the world now was that I would not take them from her. But how could she expect me to make such a sacrifice as that after all that had passed between us? What had I come back to Venice for but to see them, to take them? . . . "I have got them but I can't show them," she added. (370)

James's epithet for Venice in *Italian Hours*—"a battered peep-show"—is continually called to mind by such exchanges. The narrator's literary concupiscence drives him to an incessant probing and peering; it comes to be less the past than the view that holds his attention. Of Juliana, he confesses, "I think I had an idea that she read Aspern's letters over every night or at least pressed them to her withered lips. I would have given a good deal to have a glimpse of the latter spectacle" (299). "I used to watch—as long as I thought decent—the door that led to Miss Bordereau's part of the house," he notes several pages later, adding whimsically: "A person observing me might have supposed I was trying to cast a spell upon it or attempting some odd experiment in hypnotism" (305). An experiment in autohypnosis, he might more aptly say. His voyeurism pinions him entranced at his lookout post:

I sat in the garden looking up over the top of my book at the closed windows of my hostess. In these windows no sign of life ever appeared; it was as if, for fear of my catching a glimpse of them, the two ladies passed their days in the dark. But this only proved to me that they had something to conceal; which was what I wished to demonstrate. Their motionless shutters became as expressive as eyes consciously closed, and I took comfort in thinking that at all events though invisible themselves they saw me between the lashes. (306)

In Venice, the walls have eyes; and even when those eyes are shut, the most complicated flirtation games go on.

The entire novella verifies James's point that "Venetian objects" possess a "universal privilege . . . of being both the picture and the point of view." The actors engage in extravagant maneuvers as they jockey for vantage points:

"Tomorrow I shall come out again [says Juliana]. I want to be where I can see this clever gentleman."

"Shouldn't you perhaps see me better in your sitting-room?" I inquired.

"Don't you mean shouldn't you have a better chance at me?" she returned, fixing me a moment with her green shade.

"Ah, I haven't that anywhere! I look at you but I don't see you."

"You excite her dreadfully—and that is not good," said Miss Tita, giving me a reproachful, appealing look.

"I want to watch you—I want to watch you!" the old lady went on.

"Well then, let us spend as much of our time together as possible—I don't care where—and that will give you every facility."

"Oh, I've seen you enough for today. I'm satisfied". (348)

As Kenneth Graham remarks of another, similar passage, "A complete little ocular drama (of an almost surrealist kind) is played out throughout this scene" (71).

The eternal green eyeshade that blocks the narrator's view of Juliana accumulates a symbolic force all its own. Its first mention makes it instantly and eerily significant:

[I]t almost exceeded my courage (much as I had longed for the event) to be left alone with such a terrible relic as the aunt. She was too strange, too literally resurgent. Then came a check, with the perception that we were not really face to face, inasmuch as she had over her eyes a horrible green shade which for her, served almost as a mask. I believed for the instant that she had put it on expressly, so that from underneath she might scrutinise me without being scrutinised herself. At the same time it increased the presumption that there was a ghastly death's-head lurking behind it. The divine Juliana as a grinning skull—the vision hung there until it passed. (290-1)

In the ancient Juliana, the narrator confronts the hideously masked Venetian past—the sad-eyed old witch—as deathly revenant. That past proves both more inscrutable and (as *memento mori*) more frightening than his editorial gusto had led him to suppose. The "mask," a mocking reminder of bygone Carnival gaiety, serves Juliana not only as a cover for her own spying but also as a protective shield against the prying eyes of others. "'Does she never show you her eyes then? Have you never seen them?'" the narrator asks Miss Tita.

"You mean that she always wears something? She does it to preserve them" [Miss Tita replies].

"Because they are so fine?"

"Oh, to-day, to-day!" And Miss Tita shook her head, speaking low. "But they used to be magnificent!"

"Yes, indeed, we have Aspern's word for that." (351-2)

"Aspern's word for that"; unlike Aschenbach, who forsakes his mastery over words to yield to the seductive blur of an opaque foreign tongue, the narrator has as his peculiar vice a mania for verbal discourse in preference to immediate experience. His own ferret-eyes—eyes that seek relentlessly for words written on scraps of paper, eyes that he turns "all over the room, rummaging with them the closets, the chests of drawers, the tables" (352)—are far from magnificent.

"Magnificent" is, in fact, a word that James often uses in his travel sketches to describe classic Venetian grandeur. "Every one here is magnificent," he says of the Ducal Palace, "but the great Veronese is the most magnificent of all" (*Hours* 23). Or again, of the Academy: "It contains, in some of the most magnificent halls—where the ceilings have all the glory with which the imagination of Venice alone could over-arch a room—some of the noblest pictures in the world" (45). In *The Aspern Papers*, the contrast between Venetian magnificence and (to borrow a telling phrase from the same travel sketch) "the devouring American" (44) emerges dramatically when the narrator is pushing Juliana's chair back to her room. "Before we reached the door of her own apartment she commanded me to stop, and she took a long, last look up and down the noble sala. 'Oh, it's a magnificent house!' she murmured; after which I pushed her forward" (348). Here again, the "magnificence" of the old Venetian tradition (both the sala itself and Juliana's large appreciation of it) exposes the pushing meanness of the scholarly *parvenu*:

I scrutinised every article of furniture, every conceivable cover for a hoard, and noticed that there were half a dozen things with drawers, and in particular a tall old secretary, with brass ornaments of the style of the Empire—a receptacle somewhat rickety but still capable of keeping a great many secrets. . . . It was hard to remove my eyes from the dull mahogany front when I reflected that a simple panel divided me from the goal of my hopes. (349)

The room's intricacies make it a replica of the greater Venetian labyrinth without. To the narrator, however, it remains merely a challenge to his acumen at scholarly sleuthing. Panting to penetrate the occult mysteries of the furnishings, he is numb to the magnificence of the whole Venetian picture.

It is when he is about to carry out a scholarly raid on the provoking "simple panel" that

for the first, the last, the only time I beheld [Juliana's] extraordinary eyes. They glared at me, they made me horribly ashamed. I never shall forget her strange little bent white tottering figure, with its lifted head, her attitude, her expression; neither shall I forget the tone in which as I turned, looking at her, she hissed out passionately, furiously:
"Ah, you publishing scoundrel!" (362-3)

The tottering Venetian past, threatened with violation, unmasks itself in a desperate gesture of defiance. But if the "publishing scoundrel" never forgets the passionate, hissed rebuke, he never learns from it. Near the end of the story, faced with another painful human confrontation, he again takes refuge in contemplating an inanimate object:

"Well, you have made a great difference for me," said Miss Tita.

I looked at Jeffrey Aspern's face in the little picture [the portrait Juliana's father had painted of him], partly in order not to look at that of my interlocutress, which had begun to trouble me, even to frighten me a little—it was so self-conscious, so unnatural. I made no answer to this last declaration; I only privately consulted Jeffrey Aspern's delightful eyes with my own (they were so young and brilliant, and yet so wise, so full of vision); I asked him what on earth was the matter with Miss Tita. (372)

Here again, the irony is wryly comic. Nothing could be more typical of the narrator than his avoiding the "unnatural" expression in the eyes of a living woman who loves him, while seeking youth, brilliance, wisdom, and vision in the eyes of a man who exists only in painted effigy. The subject now shifts, with equally revealing effect, to Juliana's eyes. "'Yes, I saw something of that [Juliana's anger], that night,'" the narrator tells Tita. "'She was terrible. Then I saw her eyes. Lord, they were fine!'" His detached connoisseurship contrasts poignantly with Tita's haunted reminiscence: "'I see them—they stare at me in the dark!'" (373).

Eyes that stare and hearts that feel are intimately connected in James's story, but the narrator's own peering eyes are bigger than his heart. Although he assures the reader that he "adores the place," the heart he brings to Venice has room only for paper adorations, and the "opportunity" he perceives there is a bloodlessly literary one ("I foresaw that I should have a summer after my own literary heart, and the sense of holding my opportunity was much greater than the sense of losing it" [305]). Wayne C. Booth, while conceding (unlike Tanner) the narrator's sensitivity to the Venetian scene, is troubled by the apparent clash between the "poetic celebrant" of the city and the "comic schemer" for the papers (359). But the incongruity explains itself if one keeps in mind the literary nature of the whole Venetian project. The schemer remains comic even when he celebrates the city, precisely because his celebration never becomes more than mere cerebration; it never comes to life by being fully and warmly internalized.

The comedy is at its ripest in the narrator's dealings with Miss Tita. Like her aunt, Tita is, as Tanner suggests (24), closely identified with the city in which she lives; and her closeness to it is not a matter of surfaces. When the narrator assures her, "'We are of the same country and we have at least some of the same tastes, since, like you, I am intensely fond of Venice,'" she replies, "'I am not in the least fond of Venice. I should like to go far away!'" (315). Her revulsion, unlike his enthusiasm, is heartfelt instead of assumed; and it is she who later makes the equally heartfelt discovery of the city and its sumptuous promise. Ironically, she does so under the tutelage of the document-mad narrator himself. The experience turns out to be "an immense liberation," a "revelation" for the poor solitary:

We swept in the course of five minutes into the Grand Canal; whereupon she uttered a murmur of ecstasy as fresh as if she had been a tourist just arrived. She had forgotten how splendid the great waterway looked on a clear, hot summer evening, and how the sense of floating between marble palaces and reflected lights disposed the mind to sympathetic talk. We floated long and far, and though Miss Tita gave no high-pitched voice to her satisfaction I felt that she surrendered herself. She was more than pleased, she was transported; the whole thing was an immense liberation. The gondola moved with slow strokes, to give her time to enjoy it, and she listened to the plash of the oars, which grew louder and more musically liquid as we passed into narrow canals, as if it were a revelation of Venice. (330-1)

The narrator is capable of entering imaginatively into his companion's unguarded "transport," so that the reader, too, can vividly share it. He makes plain how Miss Tita's rediscovery of Venice and its charm takes her to the threshold of a return to the world and its unfamiliar pleasures. He can transmit a poignant sense of the woman's startled, pained state of mind: "I saw that she enjoyed [her return to society] even more than she told; she was agitated with the multitude of her impressions. She had forgotten what an attractive thing the world is, and it was coming over her that somehow she had for the best years of her life been cheated of it" (333). What he cannot do, unlike Tita, is surrender himself to his Venetian exposure. His response to Tita's dawning wonder and dismay is predictable: "[A]nd this gave me a chance to say to her, 'Did you mean a while ago that your aunt has a plan of keeping me on by admitting me occasionally to her presence?'" (333). The crisis of a woman's whole life is, to the narrator, merely a lucky loophole for self-insinuation.

A curious psychological crossover heightens the irony. While the reclusive Tita's vision begins to broaden after her re-exposure to Venice, to grasp with growing excitement the possibilities of life and love, the vision of the more worldly narrator shrinks, fixing more and more obsessively on Juliana's room and its seductive furnishings. Prowling in it just before being surprised by the old lady, he "had no definite purpose, no bad intention, but I felt myself held to the spot by an acute, though absurd, sense of opportunity" (361). His fixation looks all the more absurd by contrast with Miss Tita's own dawning sense of Venetian opportunity, cruelly as that is doomed to be wasted.

Roaming Venice, in flight from Tita, the narrator abruptly stumbles into his own tardy discovery of the city:

I was more than ever struck with that queer air of sociability, of cousinship and family life, which makes up half the expression of Venice. Without streets and vehicles, the uproar of wheels, the brutality of horses, and with its little winding ways where people crowd together, where voices sound as in the corridors of a house, where the human step circulates as if it skirted the angles of furniture and shoes never wear out, the place has the character of an immense collective apartment. . . And somehow the splendid common domicile, familiar, domestic and resonant, also resembles a theatre, with actors clicking over bridges and, in straggling processions, tripping along fondamentas. As you sit in your gondola the footways that in certain parts edge the canals assume to the eye the importance of a stage, meeting it at the same angle, and the Venetian figures, moving to and fro against the battered scenery of their little houses of comedy, strike you as members of an endless dramatic troupe. (379)

The narrator's sketch of the genial Venetian theatrical mode exposes the closet drama he himself has been performing for the shabby little charade it is. The emphasis on the domestic tenor of Venetian life comments damagingly on the narrator's position: it is, after all, domestic intimacy that he rejects in fleeing from the infatuated Tita. The despised but vital option the woman holds out he beholds mirrored and magnified in the city itself. But in fact he does not truly behold it; he appreciates the scene intellectually yet, as usual, fails to internalize it, to make it a meaningful feature of his emotional landscape.

This failure accompanies a fatal blindness in his perception of costs, those intensely Venetian matters. The narrator's comments on his ancient landlady's "aquisitive propensity" (326) rebound damningly against propensities of his own. In return for the exorbitant rent Juliana has required him to pay, he coolly determines to exact a *quid pro quo*: "I would pay her with a smiling face what she asked, but in that case I would give myself the compensation of extracting the papers from her for nothing" (294). As Tanner observes, "[T]he literal and metaphoric use of money" (21) figures prominently in the novella; and some of the narrator's embarrassing blunders have to do with the Venetian exchange rate. When he first delivers the "terrible three thousand francs" of rent to Miss Tita,

[i]t was in no jocular strain, yet it was with simplicity, that she inquired, weighing the money in her two palms: "Don't you think it's too much?" To which I replied that that would depend on the amount of pleasure I should get for it. Hereupon she turned away from me quickly . . . murmuring in a tone different from any she had used hitherto: "Oh, pleasure, pleasure—there's no pleasure in this house!" (303)

For the narrator, "pleasure" can be gauged according to the size of his expected editorial jack-pot. For Tita, instead, "pleasure" belongs to the currency of the human emotions, a medium of exchange that to the narrator remains bafflingly foreign.

Such discrepancies cluster with special vividness near the end of the story, in the narrator's negotiations with Tita over Aspern's portrait. While the narrator is estimating the worth to him of the little picture, Miss Tita is absorbed in her own, separate calculation: "'Well, you have made a great difference for me'" (372), she confides. Her offer of the papers implies a transaction remote from the narrator's imaginings: "'[I]f you were a relation it would be different . . . . If you were not a stranger. Then it would be the same for you as for me. Anything that is mine—would be yours, and you could do what you like'" (374). It is, of course, herself she is offering; and the only rejoinder that comes to the appalled narrator's mind is a counter offer in cold cash: "I put the picture in the pocket of my coat and said to Miss Tita, 'Yes, I'll sell it for you. I sha'n't get a thousand pounds by any means, but I shall get something good'" (374). He is not, in the usual sense, mercenary, but a merchant of Venice traffics in his heart.

To Tita's fond eyes, "something good" means nothing unless it means the object of her affection, whom she desperately wishes to acquire by making a gift of herself, with the papers thrown in as a "sweetener." This, however, is an offer the narrator cannot afford to accept: "That was the price—that was the price! And did she think I wanted it, poor deluded, infatuated, extravagant lady?" (376). The emphasis falls on the last of the four adjectives. As Tanner observes, it is his own economic judgment that is amiss: "He is refusing the one purchase which would have been 'worth the price'" (22). He misses the mark set by Hyacinth Robinson, who justifies his own Venetian extravagance on the grounds "that he had made a good bargain and become master of a precious equivalent. The equivalent was a rich experience" (*Princess* 338). Instead of being rich, the narrator's Venetian experience is threadbare, and it is also chronically unstable. Miss Tita herself, whose value had seemed nugatory, undergoes through a Venetian "optical trick" a sudden upward revaluation:

She stood in the middle of the room with a face of mildness bent upon me, and her look of forgiveness, of absolution made her angelic. It beautified her; she was younger; she was not a ridiculous old woman. This optical trick gave her a sort of phantasmagoric brightness, and while I was still the victim of it I heard a whisper somewhere in the depths of my conscience: "Why not, after all—why not?" It seemed to me I was ready to pay the price. (380-1)

Although the narrator's language retains its mercantile tinge ("ready to pay the price"), his tunnel vision shows signs, for once, of broadening into a more fully human way of seeing. But the depths of the narrator's conscience are all too quickly plumbed. In retrospect, he finds it easy to dismiss his fleeting new image of Tita as a mirage to which he has fallen victim.

If he has been hoodwinked, however, it is his own scholarly greed that is to blame. The woman's disclosure that she has burned the papers instantly breaks the spell: "The room seemed to go round me as she said this and a real darkness for a moment descended upon my eyes. When it passed Miss Tita was there still, but the transfiguration was over and she had changed back to a plain, dingy, elderly person" (381-2). The charm has been in the eye of the paper-obsessed beholder. Its vanishing does not, however, as he glibly supposes, restore him to true clarity of vision. Tita, meanwhile, has lost more than her fleeting glamor. "Here she did what I had not done when I quitted her—she paused long enough to give me one look. I have never forgotten it and I sometimes still suffer from it, though it was not resentful" (382).

It is the significant, valedictory Venetian gaze. The narrator's securing of Aspern's portrait, in exchange for which he later sends a large sum of money, helps to console him for his embarrassment but not for his most bitter loss: "[I]t hangs above my writing-table. When I look at it my chagrin at the loss of the letters becomes almost intolerable."[1] His rueful contemplation of his *bibelot* recalls, with crowning irony, the parting "one look" of the cheated woman.

Another meaningful exchange of looks has occurred a little earlier. The distracted narrator is contemplating Verocchio's renowned equestrian statue:

I was standing before the church of Saints John and Paul and looking up at the small square-jawed face of Bartolommeo Colleoni, the terrible *condottiere* who sits so sturdily astride of his huge bronze horse, on the high pedestal on which Venetian gratitude maintains him. The statue is incomparable, the finest of all mounted figures, unless that of Marcus Aurelius, who rides benignant before the Roman Capitol, be finer: but I was not thinking of that; I only found myself staring at the triumphant captain as if he had an oracle on his lips. The western light shines into all his grimness at that hour and makes it wonderfully personal. But he continued to look far over my head, at the red immersion of another day—he had seen so many go down into the lagoon through the centuries—and if he were thinking of battles and stratagems they were of a different quality from any I had to tell him of. He could not direct me what to do, gaze up at him as I might. (378)

According to Leon Edel, the narrator discovers in Colleoni an enlarged portrait of himself: "In the image of the true *condottiere* this would-be pirate recognises certain affinities, and fixes the scale of his own predatory impulses" (10). In fact, however, the main effect here is surely one of contrast. The stupendous bronze rider personifies the old Venetian spirit of passion and conquest, whose last vestige has departed with the haughty Juliana. The "battles and stratagems" of the overseer on horseback are of a different ilk indeed from those of the voyeur at the secretary. No wonder the terrible Colleoni, unshakably straddling his high horse, gazes far over the head of the modern literary ogler. There could be no more elegant or conclusive image of the magnificent Venetian past exposed to the trivial, dishonoring stare of the scribbling present.

Venice: Piazza S. Giovanni e Paolo, Colleoni Monument, by Andrea Verrocchio, c. 1483-88. Photograph reproduced courtesy of Fratelli Alinari.

12

L. P. Hartley's Islands of Identity

Although he criticized Thomas Mann for making Venice the scene of lurid melodrama, L. P. Hartley incorporates in his own fictional treatments of the city "distortions" closely resembling those he condemns in *Death in Venice*. Most notably in a small group of short stories—"Podolo," "*Per Far l'Amore*," "Two, or Three, for Dinner," "Mrs. Carteret Receives" (*Complete Short Stories*)—Hartley exploits energetically the Venetian milieu's affinity with the bizarre and the macabre, effects that appealed to him throughout his writing career. But it was Hartley's more serious concern with the psychological ramifications of solipsism that made Venice, city of mirrors, his natural habitat, both in his personal life and in his fiction. In two striking Venetian stories, separated by several decades, *Simonetta Perkins* (1925) and "The White Wand" (1954), Hartley succeeded in framing the theme of solipsism within the literary mode of the macabre or gothic. In their treatment of the Venetian setting, both narratives reflect Hartley's awareness of prior literary models; yet, like the best of Hartley's work, they bear the unmistakable stamp of his peculiar sensibility.

Simonetta Perkins, Hartley's brief first novel, obliquely recalls the contemporary writer he considered "our finest living exponent of the novelist's art," E. M. Forster (*E. M. Forster: The Critical Heritage* 336). But Peter Bien's statement that "Mr. Hartley shares Forster's view of the Continent, and of Italy in particular" (32) is hardly confirmed by Hartley's story. As can be seen from his review of Forster's collection *The Eternal Moment* (1928), Hartley's discipleship was hedged round with reservations:

Nowadays (one seems to conclude from [Forster's] pages) the "lovely brutality" of youth is at the mercy of the old, the hide-bound, the stupid, the respectable, and the philistine. More than once he has emphasized the contrast between youthful and ingenuous natures, full of animal grace and beauty, and the stern pedagogic persons, armed with ferrules and breathing the unenterprising maxims of middle-age, who crush the life out of them. The letter killeth, the spirit giveth life; with this few would disagree: but Mr. Forster seems to identify the spirit with a certain definite race of beings—amiable, animal natures akin to Pan; and at times he writes as though he were trying to organize a Society for the Prevention of Cruelty to Children of Nature. (*Critical Heritage* 349)

Simonetta Perkins demonstrates that the role of a Forsterian Child of Nature can be problematic, and that playing it in Venice can involve unpreventable cruelty. The novella makes an implicit sceptical comment on Forster's *A Room with a View*, and the scepticism is closely bound up with the shift of setting. Hartley incorporates sly hints at the buried connections between his Venetian story and Forster's Florentine one. "Her own bedroom opened on to an interior court," Hartley's young American protagonist, Lavinia Johnstone, reflects in her Venetian hotel: "[I]t must be pleasant to have a room with a view" (*Complete Short Stories* 28). Lavinia confides to her diary that her mother has read the American philosopher Emerson, "'because he was a connection of ours'" (21). There will, however, be nothing in any sense "Emersonian" about Lavinia's experiences. By implication, *Simonetta Perkins* corrects Forster's sunny Florentine optimism by exposing the heroine to the prevailing Venetian sensual miasma.

A summary will help to clarify the point. Lavinia, the youthful protagonist, is a wealthy Bostonian touring Venice in the company of her fussy, hypochondriacal mother. Possessed of the only puritan conscience left in America (44), Lavinia is, like Forster's Lucy Honeychurch, a hostage to Hebraism. Unlike Lucy, however, she is also a hostage to self-consciousness: "'I am forever making up my mind about myself'" (27), she notes in her earnestly self-scrutinizing diary. For Lavinia, breaking out of the straitjacket of self means risking the total, dismaying loss of her ego. That risk takes the form of an infatuation with a handsome young gondolier, Emilio.

Already, back in America, Lavinia has attracted several suitors, the most eligible being one Stephen Seleucis; she has rejected them all. The determined Stephen comes to Venice, tries Lavinia again, and again fails; though she wishes to deny it to herself, her passion for Emilio leaves no room for other likings. It is augmented by her difficulties in retaining the gondolier's services in the face of appeals by rival tourists. Distraught over her susceptibility to an emotion from which she had supposed herself exempt, Lavinia writes for advice to a female friend in Rome, pretending transparently that the predicament involves not herself but a certain "Simonetta Perkins." Nevertheless, once she is again able to monopolize Emilio's services, she has him conduct her on a tour of Venice by night. Afloat on the canals, she tells him that she loves him; she has come prepared with a wad of banknotes to make the requisite payment. Surprised but serviceable, the gondolier heads for a trysting place. At the eleventh hour, however, the last of the American puritans grows faint-hearted; she orders the gondolier to turn back to the hotel. The next day she leaves Venice.

Like Forster's Lucy, Hartley's Lavinia is caught between two poles of male attraction. The persistent Stephen Seleucis, though a four-square New Englander instead of a London aesthete, has enough of the pedantic snob in his makeup to qualify as a transatlantic bloodless-brother to Cecil Vyse. Stephen has on Lavinia, as Cecil has on Lucy, the effect of abstracting her from the physical world; he leaves her "feeling like a map . . . , all signs and no substance" (23). Emilio, the gondolier, displays a consummate, inherited "economy of movement" in handling his craft that makes the American's stiffness look foolishly gauche.

At every moment he was accessible to pleasure; at every moment, unconsciously, he could render pleasure back; it lived in his face, his movements, his whole air, where all the charms of childhood, youth and maturity mingled without losing their identity. (24)

Like Forster's George Emerson, Emilio is dynamic rather than static. The mode of transport that sustains him is, as opposed to George's railway, ancient and aquatic; but under his command it, too, becomes rapid. "'This man is a champion, my dear,'" remarks Mrs. Johnstone in a comically unconscious *double entendre*, "'[H]e knows how to put the pace on'" (7-8).

In *Simonetta Perkins*, however, the deities Eros and Pallas Athena remain unreconciled, and Hellenism, with its embrace of the physical, holds out no hope of a glorious integration of the self. The prime exponents of "Hellenism," a couple from Pittsburgh named Kolynopulo (the name reminds the parochial Lavinia of a "Greek toothpaste" [18]), stand for nothing better than a debased, cynical hedonism. It is Mrs. Kolynopulo who intimates to Lavinia that people may sometimes have "relations" (32) with gondoliers. Lavinia's lust for Emilio becomes identified in her mind as "the Kolynopulos' monster" (41). "Love felt and returned, love which our bodies exact and our hearts have transfigured, love which is the most real thing that we shall ever meet"—such love, which Florence nurtures in Lucy Honeychurch, Venice unmasks to the shrinking Lavinia as an incubus. Where Lucy's name alludes to Matthew Arnold's bywords in *Culture and Anarchy*, sweetness and light, Lavinia's recalls Shakespeare's Roman rape victim in *Titus Andronicus*.

Tormented by passion, Lavinia begins to perceive her Venetian surroundings in lurid terms:

She was conscious of a sort of drift going by her towards the sea, not a movement of the atmosphere, but an effluence of Venice. It was as though the beauty of the town had nourished itself too long and become its own poison; and at this hour the inflammation sighed itself away. (46)

As the imagery makes plain, we are not in Forster's Florence but in a far less healthy climate, the diseased, decadent atmosphere that envelops Mann's Gustave Aschenbach. The "inflammation" has begun to infect Lavinia herself; and it is, like Aschenbach's, an inflammation of the eye. If eyesight is a leading motif in Forster's Florence, in Hartley's Venice it becomes—as usual—an obsessive one. The author Lavinia is reading as the story opens speaks platitudinously of "the eye of desire" (5), but that expression, Lavinia soon learns, is far more than a platitude. Hartley's care with this strand in the novel emerges from his revisions to the original manuscript. A phrase like "'Not from me,' thought Lavinia, *eyeing* congratulation's twin subjects with ill-concealed distaste" (35) had first read "*regarding* congratulation's twin subjects" (ms. 28, my emphases). The sentence "From across the lagoon the great campanile had beckoned her eye" (ms. 43) is intensified in the final version to read "kept catching her eye" (55).

Venice does in fact "catch" Lavinia's eye, in the sinister sense of entrapping it; and the prime entrapper is Emilio. Lavinia spends her waking hours savoring the gondolier's visual appeal, even when he is physically absent:

Now that he was gone, oddly enough, she could see him much more clearly. The eye of her mind had its hesitations, but it was not intimidated so readily as her physical eye. The vestibule had lost its enchantment, the hotel had reclaimed it; but she would still recall the lustre of his presence, still remember how, as he stood before her, the building at her back, civilization's plaything, had faded from her consciousness, and the tremors and disappointments of the past days had receded with it. (35)

Here, as in *A Room with a View*, visual indulgence involves "the rout of a civilization." Lavinia, like Lucy, can accept passion only by demolishing civilized structures, above all the outwork of self-protective, respectable inhibition that she has painstakingly helped to erect around herself. In Forster's Florence, such a collapse can take place with impunity, because the milieu affords the protagonist a more relaxed and generous standard of civilization. But in Hartley's Venice, as in Mann's, no such alternative standard is available; and, in consequence, the sacrifice of the civilized to the visually seductive invites disaster.

A result of Lavinia's visual capture is her surrender of her old, apparently stable conception of herself. Her "new me" takes the shape of a monstrous Miss Hyde double. The "Simonetta Perkins" she invents to deceive her correspondent, Elizabeth Templeman, is no mere maidenly alias but a covert acknowledgment of a frightening identity change. The chief concern of this half-Italian half sister is, fittingly, to keep her Venetian idol perpetually under her eye. As Lavinia confides, "'[Simonetta] is not in love with [the gondolier], of course, but she very strongly feels she doesn't want to lose sight of him. Not to see him from time to time would be the death of her, she says'" (36). What she does not consider is the strong likelihood that to keep on seeing him may also be the death of her. Lavinia-Simonetta moves toward total self-alienation, entailing the perversion of her faculty of sight and her envelopment in darkness. "'I am intolerably lonely,'" she writes in her diary. "'I am in love with Emilio, I am infatuated by him: that explains me'" (47).

By allowing her obsession to define her whole identity, Lavinia inevitably subjects herself to a crisis of discontinuity. "'I am unrecognizable to myself, and to my friends. My past life has no claim on me, it doesn't stretch out a hand to me'" (47). If Forster's Florence is a "magic city" that has "the power . . . to evoke passions, good and bad, and to bring them speedily to a fulfillment" (65), Hartley's Venice has the power to work a blacker magic. It evokes a passion that defies rationality and that conduces to self-destruction. Miss Templeman, "proposing a solution based on reason," has "missed the mark altogether" (49); Lavinia is beyond the influence of reasoned discourse. Eros has flung Pallas Athena rudely from the temple.

His victory, however, is fleeting. Precisely because passion here takes a form so monstrous, it is bound in the end to be rejected by Lavinia's timorous puritan sensibility. Passion inwardly visualized is one thing; passion hotly enacted another. Once sexual consummation becomes more than hypothetical, the carnal Simonetta Perkins vanishes hurriedly from view.

Her assignation with the gondolier begins darkly: "The canal opened out, very black and very still. They passed under the shadow of a trawler" (54). After Emilio has grasped her desire and begun to head for a secluded spot, Lavinia's anxiety mounts, thrusting before her eyes a surrealist Venetian tableau of nausea and terror:

They turned into a little canal, turned again into a smaller one, almost a ditch. The V-shaped ripple of the gondola clucked and sucked at the walls of crumbling tenements. Ever and again the prow slapped the water with a clopping sound that, each time she heard it, stung Lavinia's nerves like a box on the ear. She was afraid to look back, but in her mind's eye she could see, repeated again and again, the arrested rocking movement of the gondolier. The alternation of stroke and recovery became dreadful to her, suggesting no more what was useful or romantic, but proclaiming a crude physical sufficiency, at once relentless and unwilling. It came to her overwhelmingly that physical energy was dangerous and cruel, just in so far as it was free; there flashed across her mind the straining bodies in Tiepolo and Tintoretto, one wielding an axe, another tugging at a rope, a third heaving the cross aloft, a fourth turning his sword upon the Innocents. And Emilio with his hands clasping the oar was such another; a minister at her martyrdom. (54)

As Lavinia glides along the canals of Venice toward her tryst, what she envisions is not Forster's "love which our bodies exact and our hearts have transfigured" but her own crucifixion and dismemberment. The gondolier's competent, rhythmic propulsion of his craft becomes for her the image of the naked act that will make her a martyr to male libido, like the Innocents put to the phallic sword. As opposed to the expansiveness attending the union of Forster's pair of lovers, what prevails here is a Venetian sense of claustrophobic constriction.

For Lavinia, the Venetian hall of mirrors has become a chamber of horrors. The artistic parallels that occur to her help to clinch the point. Moving from Forster's Florence to Hartley's Venice, one finds art history not repeating itself but reversing itself. Lucy Honeychurch progresses from the medieval, ascetic

Giotto to the robust, fleshly Della Robbia while achieving her personal
"renaissance." Lavinia Johnstone begins by admiring the early, sunny innocence
of Carpaccio. At the end, on her way to the cataract of a personal debacle, she
has shocking visions of the late, hectic canvases of Tintoretto and Tiepolo.

So where Lucy Honeychurch at last emerges, her self newly integrated, into
the spreading sunlight of her renaissance, Lavinia feels by the close of her
Venetian stay that she is sliding down a nightmarish black drain toward personal
disintegration:

A wall of darkness, thought-proof and rigid like a fire-curtain, rattled down upon her
consciousness.   She was cut off from herself; a kind of fizzing, a ghastly mental
effervescence, started in her head. It suddenly seemed to Lavinia that she was going down
a tunnel that grew smaller and smaller; something was after her. She ran, she crawled;
she flung herself on her face, she wriggled. . . .
        "*Gondoliere!*" she cried, "*Torniamo al hotel.*" (55)

"'I shall never forget him,'" she muses as her train reaches Brescia the next
morning. By recoiling, at the last minute, from her obsession, Lavinia Johnstone
survives her Venetian ordeal; she takes away a sumptuous mental pin-up on
which to feast her inward eye during her future of Bostonian chastity. Lavinia's
threatened, antiseptic identity has been preserved intact. It is only Simonetta
Perkins who has died in Venice.

In the much-later long story "The White Wand," Hartley returned with
greater boldness and complexity to the theme of the Venetian identity-crisis. The
result was a work of searching originality that has remained, regrettably, for the
most part unread. In his essay "Remembering Venice" Hartley argues that "there
is not . . . another city in the world where cartography and actuality bear so little
relation to one another" (*Novelist's Responsibility* 209). "The White Wand"
makes the discrepancies between mental maps and actualities the basis for a
disturbing Venetian tragedy of human isolation. The emphasis now falls not, as
in *Simonetta Perkins*, on the perils of carnality but on an alternative type of
Venetian entrapment: the lure of bodiless fantasy.

The protagonist, identified only by the initials C. F., returns to Venice after
the Second World War with the hope of reestablishing the bonds between
himself and others. As often in Hartley's fiction, isolation is linked to gaps of
communication, a concern revealed by the very structure of the novella.
Although the reclusive C. F. is the central narrative voice, his account is filtered
through a sympathetic but not uncritical auditor, Arthur. The frame serves more
than a purely formal purpose. C. F.'s whole narrative amounts to a dogged
attempt to communicate in the face of characteristic obstacles. His story is too
private to be easily imparted, and Arthur's manifest scepticism is a further
barrier.

As in other Venetian narratives, angles of vision govern action in "The White Wand." C. F. returns to Venice partly "'to see if the old spell still held'" (*Complete Short Stories* 267); but whether or not the spell holds depends on the Venice one's eyes behold. C. F. is offered a choice between two ways of beholding Venice: a vision that is literal and in some sense objective, and a vision that is more strictly "visionary." It is the second, visionary mode, whose talisman is the elusive white wand, that C. F. chooses. He thus accepts an "enchantment" that must perforce issue in barren disenchantment. The story restages in Venice the Keatsian clash between the Realm of Fact and the Realm of Fancy, two domains as hard to reconcile here as they are in *Lamia* or "La Belle Dame sans Merci." Like the woebegone knight-at-arms in the latter poem, C. F. proceeds through private vision to blank estrangement. The gondola he boards leaves him forlornly stranded "on the cold hill's side."

His tragic journey progresses through five phases, comparable to acts in a play. Act One concerns the reunion between C. F. and his former gondolier-manservant Antonio, a staunch, prosaic subject of the Realm of Fact. Antonio's hearty welcome of C. F. seems to dispel the air of unreality attending the war years and to establish as solidly factual the healing of wartime divisions: "'[T]alking to Antonio I felt that human solidarity was once more a fact'" (268). The facticity of human ties is something C. F. can no longer take for granted, as his nervousness about the meeting shows: "'My personal relationships were a tender area, as the doctors say. I had dreaded my meeting with Antonio, in case it turned sour on me, like food on an acid stomach'" (268).

Alimentary metaphors are so frequent in "The White Wand" that C. F.'s growing dyspepsia becomes the measure of his estrangement. Like Shakespeare's Malvolio, C. F. is sick of self-love, and tastes with a distempered appetite. His feast of friendship is followed by just the sort of souring he has feared. What causes the break is Antonio's tippling, which the gondolier attempts to disguise but which is publicized by the blunt, insulting factuality of a telltale black line drawn on a cognac bottle. During the quarrel that erupts, C. F. cancels the fact of personal fondness by producing an offensive myth: "'All Italians are thieves, especially gondoliers'" (273). Mortified, the normally "'darker than brick-red'" Antonio goes "'white as a sheet—the only time I have seen him without colour'" (273) and decamps. Predictably, C. F. becomes seriously ill with "'one of those gastric disorders that visitors to Venice sometimes get'" (275).

In "Remembering Venice," Hartley observes that "[t]he Venetian climate conduces to nervous irritability and a critical outlook" (211). C. F.'s malady, however, is as much the product of inner as of outer weather. His morale shattered by the battle with his old servant and confidant, he backtracks from the risks of relationship by withdrawing into his sickroom as into a fortress. Antonio, though now "'absent as a friend,'" is all the more loomingly "'present as an enemy'" (278).   The shut-in uses his illness as an alibi for remaining incommunicado, secluding himself within a cocoon of anonymity.

Act Two of "The White Wand" shows him breaking out of the cocoon, making up for the loss of Antonio's companionship by taking visual initiatives. Formerly, he explains, "'I won't say I never looked at Venice, but I looked at it with the eye of health and hurry—an eye that doesn't see much'" (277). Now, instead, he feels "'doubly a prisoner, a prisoner of myself and a prisoner of the flat; and when I got tired of the view of my own mind, I had the windows of my two rooms to look out of'" (278). The beauty of his dual vantage-posts is that they release him from his imprisoning cocoon, while sparing him the stress of human intercourse: "'From my bedroom windows I enjoyed a roof-scape. Domes and towers gave it grandeur and formal beauty, but what chiefly fascinated me was the roofs themselves. I came to know them as intimately as did the sparrows that hopped about on them: a sparrow on the house-tops, that's what I was myself'" (278).

C. F.'s Venetian bird's-eye view seems ideally fitted to his temper. It exalts him from cocoon to sparrow's perch, without risk of eye contact. "'There was something new every time one looked, some new arrangement of lines and surfaces. . . . This view had the slightly hypnotic effect on me that an abstract or a cubist picture might have. It took me out of myself, but not, as you will easily believe, towards anyone else'" (278-9). By calming himself with the anodyne of visual abstraction, he guards against further upsets like the quarrel with the far-from-abstract Antonio: "'It was a way of living by proxy, and it exactly suited me, in my limp convalescent state, to be a spectator of the spectators. I didn't try to write, I just sat looking'" (279).

Not even in Venice, however, can one subsist endlessly as a camera lens. It is his very persistence in visual lotos-eating—"'not taking in any special feature of what I saw but passively enjoying the sense of sight'"—that exposes C. F. to the scrutiny of an unseen pair of eyes; by a Venetian quirk of fate, the spectator of spectators unwittingly makes himself a spectacle. His Jamesian comparison of his own flat and the facing Palazzo Trevisan to "'two people looking at each other through half-closed eyes'" (280) succinctly hints at what is to come; the idea of an interchange at once double and partial sums up the curious love affair toward which he is bound. That affair is sparked by an optical confusion, the unknown observer in the palazzo misreading C. F.'s abstracted regard as amorous fascination: "'"It is many days now that I have seen you looking from your window and it seems to me that always your eyes have been fixed on me"'" (281), she naively writes. The unknown's syntax identifies her personal charm with the "spell" of Venice itself: "'"Do not leave Venice, do not leave me, without making a sign"'" (281).

Instead of making a sign, C. F. makes shift to screen himself from view. Nevertheless, he remains a prey to the hazards of this Venetian game of ocular hide-and-seek. One day, absentmindedly, he exposes himself at the accustomed window. At once, instinctively, he becomes "all eyes"; and so, as by a reflex action, does the portentous palace: "'Like eyes, the windows of the palace stared back at me'" (282). It is at this peak of visual tension that he glimpses in one of the windows the talismanic wand which gives the story its title. Although he "bolts" in a flurry back to the alternate window, he finds the view from this new vantage point insipid: "'The yellow campanile of Santa Eufemia on the Giudecca looked like a water-tower, just as functional as the chimney-stack beside it. And I saw a lot of other things that I didn't like, but they didn't vanish just because I didn't like them. They weren't so accommodating as she was'" (282). The prosaic Prospect of Fact, unlike the Prospect of Fancy, stubbornly declines to alter its lineaments to gratify the whims of C. F.'s eye.

Nonetheless, it is the Realm of Fact to which, in Act Three of his drama, C. F. reverts. "'Convalescence creates an appetite for life,'" he observes: "'I began to lose my morbid dread of being stared at'" (283). Rather than offer himself to the solitary pair of eyes in the palace, he is drawn to plunge into "'the chattering, clattering throng that drifts through the streets of Venice as sluggishly as the tide flows through its canals'" (283). Now, after years of reclusiveness, "'the need for friendship had come on me like a hunger'" (284). He embarks on an expedition into the city to forage for camaraderie.

For C. F., friendship has always fulfilled a special function, that of freeing him from his own dyspeptic ego. Chronically hard-put to live at peace within a hermetic self, he relies on others to secure release. "'Then, when I was with someone I was fond of, he or she was like a mirror to me: I don't only mean that they reflected me myself, which was agreeable, but the other reflections seemed to me true, unflawed and perfect also: I saw the world in a frame—their frame—and I could live in it and accept it'" (285). Unfortunately, the time for such consoling self-liberation has passed; C. F.'s Venetian promenade merely confirms his self-imprisonment. The three ancient cronies he tries to trace disappoint him by being either absent or dead; there are no Venetian mirrors to set in his waiting mental frame. His bid to break through the bars of his estrangement by renewing friendship succeeds only in making him seem "'to see "No Admittance" written on every door I passed. Closed doors, closed shutters, iron grilles, cats grimacing at me from behind the grilles: Venice on a wet day is barred like a fortress'" (290).

The sole meeting C. F. does manage to have is—discomfortingly—one with himself. Crossing the Piazza San Marco, he is mistaken for another man, a certain Engineer Tremontin. The engineer, when he materializes, turns out in grim earnest to be C. F.'s double. He provides a mirror but not the sort for which C. F. has been searching:

"I saw a man whose resemblance to me I at once recognized. And yet, I thought, he can't be really like me—he's an old man—that white hair, that whitening moustache!—while I'm a young one—and I remembered my age, which, like my friends in Venice, I had taken to concealing, even from myself. . . . Offence deepened into outrage; I looked with hatred at that Ancient of Days, my double. . . . I was aware of a process of disacquaintance going on in me". (286-7)

Gustave Aschenbach uses the magic of the Venetian "artist in cosmetic" to hide his advanced age from himself and others. C. F. has not needed rouge to flatter himself with rosy Venetian illusions. Now, however, his encounter with his ancient double drops him back into the Realm of Fact with an unflattering thump. C. F.'s quest for emotional nourishment has had only the result of whetting his hunger:

"But the expedition had created in me a hunger which I couldn't assuage. The idea of death haunted me as it sometimes does in Venice: the churches, the bells, the beauty, the overwhelming vitality of the people: all this insistence on what the senses can give one, on life: if one cannot accept it, what remains but its opposite, death? In Northern countries there are so many degrees of living: one can turn life down, like a gas-fire, and live by its dull glow: but Italy is a land of contrasts, not of half-tones. I felt that time was pressing and I had a legacy to give someone: myself." (290)

C. F.'s urge to make a bequest of his precious self is defeated not by his circumstances but by his whole cast of mind. His language raises doubts whether he hungers more keenly for life than for death; his idea of bestowing himself as a legacy belongs to the steady march of his "disacquaintance" from himself and his actual surroundings. He resumes his vigil at his customary window with a "'particular object in view'": making contact with the elusive stranger who, of all Venice, has at least "'felt the impulse to communicate'" (292). The communication he now seeks, however, is far different from that which he had been patrolling Venice to find.

In Act Four, C. F. takes the offensive, attempting to penetrate beyond cryptic Venetian surfaces to discover his anonymous correspondent's identity. Revealingly, he begins this operation by withdrawing his obsessive gaze from the Palazzo Trevisan's facade, only to turn it upon himself. "'I didn't lean out of the window any more: I didn't even look out: if an atom bomb had fallen into the canal I shouldn't have noticed. My sole occupation was trying to imagine who my correspondent could be'" (292-3). Having firmly shut himself off from the Venetian public scene, he proceeds to fabricate a mental image of his unknown lady. Pygmalion-wise, he then falls in love with the idol his mind has fashioned. Taking his hint from the locale, he models his ideal portrait along the generous lines of Renaissance Venetian painting: "'Her beauty grew on me with every hour. She was blonde, sumptuous, voluptuous, Venetian, a Veronese figure'" (293). With such an image to gladden his mind's eye, his outward senses might well be proof against distracting nuclear blasts.

But this development itself causes an explosive change in the terrain of C. F.'s inner life. His new devotion to "love" sweeps away the remaining filaments binding him to the common-sense Venetian world. His first overt act in pursuit of love is the preposterous one of laying siege to the Palazzo Trevisan, standing constant guard over its entrance. Although this may look like an invasion of the world outside his flat, in psychological terms it amounts to a retreat into still remoter reaches of fantasy. C. F. has come to suppose that his very identity is bound up with his obsession; foregoing that would mean "'requiring myself to deny my own existence'" (296). He shuffles through some pointless "exercises in realism" that have ultimately "no reality" for him—"'[M]y only reality was in some room in the Palazzo Trevisan which I had begun to think I should never see'" (296).

It is precisely now that C. F. stumbles into an unpremeditated, and devastating, "exercise in realism":

"I was sitting on my stone seat staring at the palace when Antonio came by. My eyes recognized him but for a moment my mind didn't—he had become an absolute stranger to my thoughts. Then, my whole being welcomed him, I scarcely remembered what had come between us, and for a moment, so potent was his presence in bringing back the past, I could hardly associate myself with the ghost I had turned into—it seemed a dream. He was striding along between the brightly-coloured nurse-maids and their charges, and I jumped up with hand outstretched, meaning to cross his path. But he looked right through me, and if I hadn't swerved I believe he would have walked right through me, as if I had been indeed a ghost." (296-7)

Antonio's "potent" presence does not merely bring back the past. It conjures up a whole forsaken pragmatic universe of comradeship, of Venetian color, warmth, and self-renewing life. C. F.'s outstretched, ungrasped hand is a poignant symbol of his loss of friendship, and beyond that of his unbridgeable distance from that concrete realm, with which he suddenly longs to converse. So far has C. F. now withdrawn from the matter-of-fact world's solidity that he has turned into the transparent ghost Antonio takes him for. Haunted by invisibilities, he has become an invisibility himself.

The encounter is C. F.'s divorce decree from the Venetian Realm of Fact, freeing him to be engulfed by the devouring mists of subjective Venetian Fancy. "'I jumped off the seat and crossed over to the palace with as much determination as if it had been a fortress I was going to take by storm'" (298). The ensuing assault on the Palazzo Trevisan is a strikingly original piece of seriocomic action. For C. F., it amounts to a defiant yet crazily self-defeating bid for visibility. He cannot begin to answer the standard questions put to him upon his entrance— "'Who was I, what did I want?'"—for the good reason that his identity and his purpose are exactly the things he himself needs to discover. His tirelessly repeated "'"Cerco una signorina! . . . I am looking for a young lady"'" puts into amusing relief the perplexing vagueness of his goal. Knocking on door after door and summoning signorina after signorina, he stages what he aptly terms an "identity parade." Paradoxically, it is his own identity that he hopes to validate. "'"But you would recognize her if you saw her?"' the man asked. Again I had to say no; and then I had the presence of mind to add, "But she would recognize me!"'" (299).

As the action reels on, the Palazzo Trevisan assumes the character of a fabulous maze—a replica of the greater, encompassing Venetian one—within whose recesses C. F. flounders. Eventually, a stratagem occurs to him: by determining the whereabouts of his own windows, he might infer the location of the unknown beloved's flat. So his blundering progress ends, fittingly, by confronting him with his own old, familiar perch: "'Looking through the four-arched window I could see my own . . . I had the fancy that I could see myself, looking out, looking at something I didn't know was there, something I had created without knowing it, as the burning-glass knows nothing of the fire it starts'" (300). C. F.'s syntax, multiplying monotony in a wilderness of mirrors, itself transmits a dizzying sense of infinite regress. The protagonist's own image flickers, shadowy and taunting, at the end of every corridor in the glassy Venetian labyrinth.

Any hope C. F. may still have of escaping his world of shadows is mocked by this eerie circularity; but he is too intent on tracking down the elusive object of his quest to probe the inner nature of the quest itself. Ringing the last remaining doorbell, he raises the curtain on the final act of his self-inflicted tragedy. Hearing that the signorina who lives there "receives no one," he senses "'that I had come to the end of my quest'" (301). As he shoulders his way into the lady's hermetic presence, his eyes confront a novel, entrancing picture:

"At that the pillars of reality seemed to dissolve, and framed in the doorway was not the maid keeping me out, or the wall of the passage behind her, but the green trees undulating upwards in golden light, a jungle in which forms had no time to harden into matter; and before the vision could be taken from me I pushed on into it, past the maid, through the door, down the passage whose terminal window faced my own, to where, on the left, another door stood open and the scent of flowers met me as I went through—met me and strengthened, and then I saw the flowers and the waving stems: they were banked up inside the open window, almost hiding it, keeping out the view, the view of me." (301)

This is not the Venetian "jungle" of which Gustave Aschenbach feverishly dreams, an orgiastic riot of carnal and forbidden lusts. It is a literary and wanly narcissistic construct. By making a leap through the looking glass into a mist of undulating forms and scents, C. F. bypasses fleshly reality while enthroning himself within his mystery lady's purview. He himself thereby gains a "vision" so private as to be ineffable: "'I can't—oh, well—externalize it'" (302). So inward a vision indeed defies description; to glimpse it at all, the subject must brush past maids in doorways and all the other stubborn, prosaic impedimenta cluttering the sensible, external world.

Though incommunicable itself, the vision magically fosters boundless communication:

"But in her room, there were no facts beside ourselves, everything was beginning, and it began afresh each time I saw her—for her as well as me, I know that, because we said to each other everything we'd been wanting to say all our lives. She was much younger than I was, but that didn't seem a fact, either. I don't speak Italian well, but do you know that I was never once at a loss for a word—and I said things that I couldn't ever have said in English. I expect that was part of the enchantment: in another language I was another person." (303)

Beyond the looking glass, awkward facts become negligible, whether the fact of age difference or the fact of language barriers. An interesting fact is that the whole idyll is financed with money saved from the salary of the estranged Antonio ("'I had Antonio's money, you see'" [303]). Fantasy has been purchased with *lire* borrowed from Fact—one more piquant Venetian "exchange." C. F., however, is too enthralled by the transforming power of his "love" to notice such details ("'in another language I was another person'"). The paradise he reaches through his love idyll is that utter plasticity of self for which he has always yearned:

"Everything else is a kind of stationariness that one shares with chairs and tables, the sense of being a fixture, imprisoned in oneself, never to alter, never to escape from the mould in which one has been cast. But then I had the freedom of a myriad existences, every day a change, a new growth, a new flower, like the plants in the window." (304)

Because she grants him release from a Hades of brute objects into a heaven of Protean subjectivity, C. F. is understandably grateful to his enchantress: "'[S]he was Venice's reward to me'" (304). The genuineness of the "reward," however, remains suspect. C. F.'s physical description of the mystery lady hardly inspires confidence:

"Myself I never cared much for . . . for amplitude, or even for warm colours. I like the Alps, you know, with the snow coming down to the pine-forests. And a sailing ship, when you can see the spars and the rigging. Not all sail set, that's too oncoming and voluminous for my taste. There's a kind of opulence that's rather vulgar, I think: well, she didn't have it. Her colouring was Northern, though her hair was very dark, nearly black. She had a Gothic fragility and fineness, like a saint from Burgundy or Chartres that had somehow strayed into Venice, though of course there is Gothic in Venice. . . . A greeny light filtered into her room, a forest light—just enough to throw a shadow . . . . The walls were nearly white, the furniture was white, the muslin on the dressing-table was white, the bedcover was white, and she . . . " he hesitated. "She was a little pale." (304-5)

Such a vessel, her spars and rigging showing, makes an unlikely model for the "sumptuous" and "voluptuous" Veronese portrait that C. F. has earlier been mentally adoring. Nor are matters mended by the news that the white object he glimpsed in the window was not "an enchanter's wand" but an emaciated limb—"'I think it may have been her arm. She was rather thin, you see'" (306). One can readily second Arthur's aside: "It was almost as if he had told me he had been in love with a skeleton" (306). There is, to be sure, gothic in Venice; but C. F.'s enchantress carries the mode to a chilling extreme.

C. F.'s bone-white beloved represents the opposite terminus of the journey that began with the "darker than brick-red" gondolier, Antonio. The color contrast (as C. F. observes, "'Italy is a land of contrasts, not of half-tones'") carries a conclusive symbolic force. The terra-cotta complexion of the gondolier connects him with the senses, with the solidity, warmth, and abundance of an earthly Venice; the blanched pallor of the lady associates her with a Venice in the clouds. "'"I am red, I have always been red, and when I am dead I shall still be red,"'" declares Antonio (273). The lady strikes one as having never been anything but white—or, for that matter, anything but dead. C. F.'s rhapsodic account of their joint sightseeing ("'And we went everywhere, you know, to—to the restaurants, and the churches, and the islands'" [305]) is abruptly halted by his avowal of the sad truth: "'It wasn't real, that part. You see, she was a cripple. She'd had an illness, and she was a cripple'" (305). Arthur's sudden doubt whether C. F. "had imagined the whole thing" is natural, but it poses no crux of interpretation. While the story of the love affair may be technically "true," in ontological terms it represents a delusive falsehood. The lovers' union is founded on the intercourse of private fantasies, devoid even of the physical concreteness belonging to the hackneyed tourist attractions C. F. catalogues. If C. F. regards his love as his passport to sublime Venetian realms of freedom, he is deceived. A psychological cripple himself, he has found in his shut-in gothic enchantress not the sumptuous genius of the city but the mirror image of his prison.

"White," Hartley declares in his novel *The Boat* (1949), "is the colour of eternity" (331). Reveling in the white bower, C. F. feels himself admitted into a Venetian holiday from time: "'The time-factor had ceased to exist for me; I felt I should stay in Venice all my life'" (306). But if for John Ruskin, Venice was "that beauty which seemed to have fixed for its throne the sands of the hour-glass as well as of the sea" (*Stones* 2:7), in Hartley's Venice the sands continue to run. The "eternal" lovers cannot fend off the bothersome fact of mortality; on the contrary, they personify it. The white lady's one reported name for C. F.— "Life-giver"—provokes instant scepticism. The truth is that C. F.'s own life flow is too meager to allow him to transfuse life into the veins of his bleached invalid; it is no wonder that he ends by dealing death to her. And the influence is reciprocal; his embrace of his skeletal Venetian love-object is, finally, an *amour* with the grave.

Typically, C. F. explains the demise of his idyll in self-vindicating terms. It is the doctor who has played the role of killjoy; C. F. deplores "'the irruption into our birch-grove of this alien figure, parting the branches, with the heat and dust and hurry of the streets still on him, holding his professional bag of tricks, wearing, until he saw us, his professional air of wary optimism'" (307). For C. F. the doctor is an assassin of love and life. He brings their parting "'in his bag, like a prescription,'" and the drug ghoulishly works: "'It took us unawares, like sudden death. Afterwards we were like ghosts, planning our reunion beyond the grave'" (307). But the sober truth, which C. F.'s rapturous account cannot mask, is that the two have been "like ghosts" all along. The enchantment C. F. has pursued, Venice's reward, has merely supplied him with a fellow fugitive from the streets of the actual Venice, from the "heat and dust and hurry" which, for all C. F.'s disdain, comprise the substance of life.

If such is Venice's reward, little wonder that C. F. should come "'to have a hatred for the place'" (309). Yet his acquired Rialtophobia merely masks his unacknowledged hatred of himself. His plea to Arthur betrays his guilt: "'It wasn't being with me that killed her—it was being without me. She died of a broken heart. . . . You agree with me, don't you?'" (310). The banal sentimentality of the speech betrays his besetting terror of looking fact in the eye. His experience of Venice has simply inflamed to the bursting point his old sore-spot: his inability either to accept solipsism or to reach out and encounter some authentic form of otherness, to form relationships that might do more than flash back at him his own wan mirror image.

C. F.'s failure, like Aschenbach's, is the failure of a writer. But if his return to Venice fixates C. F.'s creative imagination instead of liberating it, the blame is not solely the city's. Venice offers Hartley's protagonist a choice of paths: he can reach out toward solid, mundane realities, or he can stray fatally into an interior grove of enchantment. The Venice that C. F. comes to hate reflects the hatefulness of his own choice. Its sickening savor is not the token of a fetid and decaying organism but rather a symptom of the distempered appetite with which C. F. himself tastes. Hartley's Venice becomes deathly only when it is morbidly internalized.

In an extended essay on Nathaniel Hawthorne, Hartley defends against Henry James's criticism Hawthorne's practice of recording in his notebooks trivial details from everyday life:

[A]ll those *choses vues*, though trivial to a sophisticated mind, are extremely important in Hawthorne's case, because they reward the efforts—in some cases the *desperate* efforts—he made to get out of the prison of his mind and establish a contact with the humdrum life of the ordinary man (sacred symbol). They were valuable to him precisely because they were objective, and not subjective; they proved to him, and to his readers, that the world had an independent existence apart from his consciousness of it—which is a thing that James, with all his talent for digesting his impressions, could not do. James wouldn't have realized the importance of a mere external event, such as a dog chasing its own tail. (*Novelist's Responsibility* 83)

C. F.'s error, as a man and as a writer, lies in his refusal of the struggle to maintain contact with the "small beer," as Hartley calls it, of external reality. In fairness to C. F., one can grant that withdrawal into a labyrinth of Venetian mirrors is tempting in the face of a reality made hideous, as C. F. himself insists, by the anti-human meanness and violence of the twentieth century. Objective reality did not, for Hawthorne, include death camps or the prospect of nuclear annihilation.

Half-way through his narrative, C. F. pauses to ask himself,

"Where was I? Oh, yes, under the statue of Bartolomeo Colleoni, one of the two great equestrian statues of the world. Was there friendship in it? There was not. There was pride, and insolence, and success, and glory; the glory of war and conquest: every quality the statue had, except the quality of art, repudiated every quality I valued." (288)

The resemblance to the moment in *The Aspern Papers* when the narrator contemplates the very same monument cannot be a coincidence. Hartley, though at times critical of James, was not above taking a leaf out of that master's Venetian book. Yet the twinned passages are revealingly diverse in tendency. Where James's "scoundrel" is rebuked by Verocchio's colossus of now-vanished Venetian power and glory, C. F.'s fastidious gaze mourns the survival in Venice of those passions that have torn apart his world and defeated his lifelong quest for companionship. The moral victory does not go to the terrible *condottiere*. Nevertheless, the story leaves one suspecting that C. F., too, might have benefited from a stiffening dose of those rugged qualities—pride, insolence, success, glory—that Colleoni's Venetian patrons relished. The public life of the twentieth century may be appalling, but the obscure Venetian channel down which C. F. flees has nothing substantially better to offer.

13

Glass Menageries:
The Venice of Hecht and Malamud

In contemporary writing the familiar Venetian themes continue to recur with remarkable regularity, but they may undergo surprising variations. Two recent American works, Anthony Hecht's long poem "The Venetian Vespers" (1980) and the section "Glass Blower of Venice" from Malamud's *Pictures of Fidelman*, look consciously back to the treatment of Venetian motifs in earlier literature, more especially Mann's *Death in Venice*. Both Hecht's poem and Malamud's story focus on the Venetian clash between fact and fantasy; but they approach that clash in radically different ways. Where Hecht stays by and large within the tradition of "Venetian melancholy," Malamud, once again, inverts tradition, dissolving gloom in Rabelaisian laughter.

ANTHONY HECHT'S POLLUTED PALACE

In a recent interview, Anthony Hecht recalls:

"The Venetian Vespers" began without a story, merely with the city, and with a speaker I could not clearly identify at the beginning. But I knew I wanted to make some kind of correspondence or equation between the speaker and the setting. The city, for me, was full of grandeur and decay, the decay evidenced in that it was overtly parasitic, surviving off tourism . . . and it was the parasitic and defeated aspect of Venice I wanted to capture in my narrator. In this sense, the poem obviously owes much to Mann's *Death in Venice*, and involves at least some of the same clusters of images: the hearse-like sheen of the black gondolas, the curious sea-smells not altogether wholesome. It was these themes or images that led me, by way of *Hamlet*, curiously, to my speaker. (*Paris Review* 199-200)

The two epigraphs with which Hecht prefaces his poem call immediate attention to "the parasitic and defeated aspect of Venice." The first, from *Othello*, beginning with Iago's rhetorical question, "[W]here's that palace whereinto foul things / Sometimes intrude not?", introduces the paradoxical combination of "grandeur and decay" that Venice signifies to Hecht. The city, for him as for earlier writers, offers innumerable troubling contrasts between palatial splendor and the "foul things" that intrude on it:

> Venice has no curbs
> At which to curb a dog, so underfoot
> The ochre pastes and puddings of dogshit
> Keep us earthbound in half a dozen ways,
> Curbing the spirit's tendency to pride.
> The palaces decay. Venice is rich
> Chiefly in the deposits of her dogs.
> A wealth swept up and gathered with its makers.

(Vespers, pp. 44-45)

Like Hartley's C. F., Hecht's protagonist longs to soar beyond the bounds of mundane reality. He is more sharply aware than C. F., however, of the dangers and ironies attendant upon flights into fantasy. In the quoted passage, the deposits of the quotidian curb the ego's yearning for the ideal. Even the nonchalant offhandedness of Hecht's blank verse rhythms accords with the anti-transcendent thrust, as do the speaker's wry puns, like those on "wealth" and "deposits." With such verbal astringency, the swelling pomp of Venetian mercantilism is reduced to the pettiest of dimensions.

The second epigraph, from Ruskin's *The Stones of Venice*—"We cannot all have our gardens now, nor our pleasant fields to meditate in at eventide"—is similarly anti-idealist in its bearing, which the context in Ruskin's work illuminates. In the relevant passage, Ruskin is proposing conformity to natural paradigms as a criterion of excellence in architecture. Fine human structures serve to compensate us for the dreadful loss brought about by our choosing to live in cities, far from the beauty and spontaneity of forms occurring in nature. The function of such structures is

to replace these; to tell us about Nature; to possess us with memories of her quietness; to be solemn and full of tenderness, like her, and rich in portraitures of her; full of delicate imagery of the flowers we can no more gather, and of the living creatures now far away from us in their own solitude. (1: 411)

By contrast, the dreary architectural staples of Ruskin's London are "grim railings and dark casements."

In "The Venetian Vespers," it is precisely such eyesores that the urban surroundings of the narrator's New England childhood, like the "sagging blackness" of an "iron railing" (40), cheerlessly recall. His early years have been shadowed not only by such visual drabness but by an equally repellent family history: the disappearance of his father and the death of his Gertrude-like mother, herself the incestuous partner of his Claudius-like, fratricidal uncle. Little wonder, then, if he should have chosen to distance himself from the remembered ugliness of this melancholy North American Denmark. Yet why should he have chosen as a refuge what he himself calls "the world's most louche and artificial city," one that hardly affords gardens, or pleasant fields to meditate in? The answer lies in the seductive appeal that artifice *per se* exerts on him, owing to his un-Ruskinian revulsion from the natural. In his *Paris Review* interview Hecht speaks of the narrator's "pathological drive" (189). The pathology emerges plainly in the vehemence of the exiled aesthete's flight from nature to artifice.

Throughout "The Venetian Vespers," the narrator dwells on images of protection and shelter; it comes as no surprise when he describes his life as "monkish" (63). As a child, he sought refuge in a nest made of burlap potato sacks where, behind the counter of his uncle's grocery store, he could "lie and read or dream my dreams" (54). Once he grows up, he does not cease to feel orphaned or to long for the security of contrived womb-substitutes. Saint Mark's Church, evoked in a bravura descriptive passage, becomes in his eyes one vast, uterine nest:

> I enter the obscure aquarium dimness,
> The movie-palace dark, through which incline
> Smoky diagonals and radiant bars
> Of sunlight from the high southeastern crescents
> Of windowed drums above. Like slow blind fingers
> Finding their patient and unvarying way
> Across the braille of pavement, edging along
> The pavonine and lapidary walls,
> Inching through silence as the earth revolves
> To huge compulsions, as the turning spheres
> Drift in their milky pale galactic light
> Through endless quiet, gigantic vacancy,
> Unpitying, inhuman, terrible.
> In time the eye accommodates itself
> To the dull phosphorescence. Gradually
> Glories reveal themselves, grave mysteries
> Of the faith cast off their shadows, assume their forms
> Against a heaven of coined and sequined light,
> A splatter of gilt cobblestones, flung grains
> Or crumbs of brilliance, the vast open fields
> Of the sky turned intimate and friendly. (49-50)

For Hecht's orphaned narrator, "vacancy"—above all the vacancy of the "Unpitying, inhuman, terrible" natural universe—is a word charged with fearful associations. Local architecture offers him a shelter against the raw, indifferent light emanating from endless, empty space; the "coined and sequined light" of the church (sequins—*zecchini*—were Venetian coins) has been consolingly tempered by human expenditure, both of money and of decorative finesse. Within San Marco, consequently, he can enjoy the willing suspension of his customary unbelief. There, "Glories reveal themselves, grave mysteries / Of the faith cast off their shadows," and "the vast open fields of the sky" become intimate and friendly. By painful contrast, "Returning suddenly to the chalk-white sunlight / Of out-of-doors," he is brought face to face with the unfriendliness of profane, up-to-the-minute reality: "Those dissolute young with heavy-lidded gazes / Of cool, clear-eyed, stony depravity" (51). Even though he describes himself as "a twentieth-century infidel," he has ample reason to indulge his semi-weekly fetish of church visiting. Like C. F.'s green bower of love, it is his Venetian escape-route from the Realm of Fact.

For Hecht's life-weary aesthete, artifice in general becomes a passport to eternity:

> What is our happiest, most cherished dream
> Of paradise? Not harps and fugues and feathers
> But rather arrested action, an escape
> From time, from history, from evolution
> Into the blessed stasis of a painting. (62)

If the narrator cannot actually become a painting, he finds in Venetian stasis the next best refuge. "Lights. I have chosen Venice for its light, / Its lightness, buoyancy, its calm suspension / In time and water, its strange quietness" (62). Within the amniotic waters of the Lagoon, a quietist amnesia seems beguilingly within reach.

To such an anchorite sensibility, the Venetian bane of isolation comes as a blessing. In his purposeful shunning of human contact, the narrator recalls Hartley's C. F. at his most reclusive: "I take my loneliness as a vocation, / A policied exile from the human race, / A cultivated, earned misanthropy / After the fashion of the Miller of Dee" (51). What his "policied exile" above all gains for him is the pleasure of merely watching. That favorite Venetian pastime allows him to forego not only the companionship of others but the stress of communion with his own self and past. The poem's opening lines—"What's merciful is not knowing where you are, / What time it is, even your name or age, / But merely a clean coolness at the temple" (39)—are answered by others near the end: "In these late days / I find myself frequently at the window, / Its glass a cooling comfort to my temple" (64). The repeated word "temple" is charged with a special significance: the speaker's head is a sacred sanctuary into the privacy of which he withdraws, and from the safety of which he peers out at the world. He has assumed this stance in early childhood, following the trauma of his mother's death:

> I didn't go to school. I watched the rain
> From the bedroom window or from my burlap nest
> Behind the counter . . . .
> Perhaps that early vigilance at windows

Explains why I have now come to regard
Life as a spectator sport. But I find peace
In the arcaded dark of the piazza
When a thunderstorm comes up. (56-57)

His lifelong habit of spectatorship makes the Venetian piazza a logical terminus for him. Like Hartley's C. F., he is a confirmed gazer from secluded shelters, and he is able to clothe his gazing in philosophic respectability. Taking as his text the thunderstorm he has announced, he produces what amounts to a gospel of voyeurism:

To give one's whole attention to such a sight
Is a sort of blessedness. No room is left
For antecedence, inference, nuance.
One escapes from all the anguish of this world
Into the refuge of the present tense.
The past is mercifully dissolved, and in
Easy obedience to the gospel's word,
One takes no thought whatever of tomorrow,
The soul being drenched in fine particulars. (57)

For Hecht's narrator, Venice emphatically becomes what Mary McCarthy calls it: an eternal present. By seizing the Venetian day, he hopes to escape being seized himself by the day before or the day after. "I look and look, / As though I could be saved simply by looking," he adds in the poem's concluding lines, after a lush evocation of a Venetian sunset (65). Yet scepticism has by this point crept into his tone, a scepticism for which J. D. McClatchy sees ample reason: "And of course he cannot be saved: the grandeur is a delusion, and its excess a measure of his own inabilities" (155).

But why, after all, can the narrator not be saved? His Venetian "looking" is no humdrum sort of voyeurism; there *is* grandeur in the scene he scans. Hecht has endowed his protagonist with an impressive degree of visual sensitivity and verbal dexterity. The problem lies in a familiar Venetian conundrum: the inescapably subjective, equivocal nature of perception itself. The French word that the narrator applies to Venice—"louche"—takes on a special relevance here, not only in its common senses of "ambiguous," "shifty," or "shady" but also in its root senses of "cross-eyed" and "squinting." Instances of ocular misprision abound in the narrator's discourse. To mention just one, among the "derelict waste places" haunting the narrator's dreams like prototypes of hell, there is an abandoned boxcar that, in the fierce midsummer heat, ripples the air around it "[w]ith visible distortions" (40-41). He might well say of all such hallucinatory experiences, adapting Mephistopheles's phrase, "Why this is Venice, nor am I out of it."

In or out of Venice, he is chronically unable to draw a clear line between what he perceives of the world around him and what he projects onto it. This Venetian protagonist, like his earlier literary counterparts, is bedevilled by solipsism; the self he must inhabit is at once, and contradictorily, both a sanctuary from an unfriendly world and a prison cutting him off from potentially nourishing realities. The same can be said of the city he has made his refuge. He may enjoy contemplating life as a "spectator sport"; but he knows that what he beholds could be no more than a masque of illusions, the sport of his own juggling mind.

"Seeing is misbelieving, as may be seen / By the angled stems, like fractured tibias, / Misplaced by water's anamorphosis" (58)—so the narrator commences a lecture on the treachery of perception. "All lenses—the corneal tunic of the eye, / Fine scopes and glazier's filaments—mislead us / With insubstantial visions, like objects viewed / Through crizzled and quarrelled panes of Bull's Eye Glass" (58), he concludes. This loucheness of one's perceptions extends as well to matters of moral inference. As regards his own guilt-shadowed family history, he confesses that he "[n]o longer can distinguish between fact / As something outward, independent, given, / And the enfleshment of disembodied thought, / Some melanotic malevolence of my own" (59). ("Melanotic" refers here to the "darkening" of the pigmentation of his own corneal tissues.) Happiness, he insists with Swiftian cynicism, is "alas . . . composed / Of clouded, cataracted, darkened sight, / Merciful blindnesses and ignorance" (58). Elsewhere he protests: "The mind / Can scarcely cope with the world's sufferings, / Must blinker itself to much or else go mad" (51). Like Hartley's C. F., he is in retreat not only from his own personal anguish but from that of the whole violent, disordered world in which he lives. Yet his willingness to have his sight blinkered does not bring him happiness or keep his reason from tottering sickeningly on its throne.

For so extreme a sensibility, Venice represents a powerfully seductive, yet sinister, theater of action—or of inaction. The hermetic privacy of the narrator's mind furnishes him with a "movie palace," but one that is less consoling than the interior of Saint Mark's. Unlike the artist Fuseli's painted nightmare, which "was a great success," his own "[p]lays on the ceiling of my rented room / Or on the bone concavity of my skull / In the dark hours when I take away my lights" (47). Locked within his personal obsessions, he can gain only fitful recourse to "the refuge of the present tense"; his habit of taking life as a spectator sport leaves him the captive audience of his own defeats. Early in the poem, he intones a characteristic Venetian prayer:

San Pantaleone, heavenly buffoon,
Patron of dotards and of gondolas,
Forgive us the obsessional daydream
Of our redemption at work in black and white,

> The silent movie, the old *Commedia*,
> Which for the sake of the children in the house
> The projectionist has ventured to run backwards. (42-43)

He goes on to describe a fancied, bizarre reversal of time's process in which "[t]he Keystone Cops sprint from hysteria . . . Faultlessly backwards into calm patrol," and a high-diver emerges "from a sudden crater of water" to resume his station on the diving board (43). The whole tableau movingly evokes the narrator's yearning for a miraculous secular redemption:

> Something profoundly soiled, pointlessly hurt
> And beyond cure in us yearns for this costless
> Ablution, this impossible reprieve,
> Unpurchased at a scaffold, free, bequeathed
> As rain upon the just and the unjust,
> As in the fall of mercy, unconstrained,
> Upon the poor, infected place beneath. (43)

The rewording of Portia's "quality of mercy" speech purges the concept of mercy of its specifically Christian content. The reprieve of which the narrator dreams is "[u]npurchased at a scaffold," not mystically linked to Christ's Crucifixion. As his appending of the words "poor, infected" to Portia's homily suggests, what he envisions is a sort of universal, indiscriminate therapy for humanity's moral ills. Unhappily, as he knows too well, such a panacea is indeed "impossible"; there is no supreme doctor present in the house of the universe.

Least of all is one present in the movie house of Venice. The polluted city can offer no cleansing "ablution"; it cannot run the film of the narrator's soiled life backwards to the point of childhood spotlessness, nor can it freeze the frame into the stasis of a work of art. If anything, his immersion in the magnificent art-city makes him all the more witheringly aware of his failure to accomplish anything. "*Ho fatto un fiasco*, which is to say, / I've made a sort of bottle of my life" (62), he pronounces with punning self-scorn. (A *fiasco*, or worthless bottle, is what a master glass blower may make of the wasted glass when a fine vessel goes awry in the blowing.) The narrator cannot hope to arrest his drift toward the condition of a dotard in a gondola—or, worse, the condition of a piece of refuse amid the Venetian cloacal flux:

> We slip down by grades and degrees,
> Lapses of memory, the vacant eye
> And spittled lip, by soiled humiliations
> Of mind and body into the last ditch,
> Passing, en route to the *Incurabili*,
> The backwater way stations of the soul,
> Conveyed in the glossy hearse-and-coffin black

And soundless gondola by an overpriced
Apprentice Charon to the *Calle dei Morti*. (45-46)

Fantasies of a redemptive ascent to some original springboard are shattered by this scarily plausible evocation of the approach to the Venetian Hades: "One slides to it like a swoon, nearing the regions / Where the vast hosts of the dead mutely inhabit" (46).

By the end, the narrator has made plain the awful symbiosis between his inner corruption and the polluted city he calls home: "Viscid, contaminate, dynastic wastes / Flood through the dark canals, the underpasses, / Ducts and arterial sluices of my body . . . " (63). Venice lends itself exceptionally well to treatment by a poet of Hecht's peculiar gifts, because it is so fertile a ground for such lavishly morbid metaphysical conceits. The narrator's concluding image of himself as a Darwinian freak, at once host and parasite, is another example:

I wander these by-paths and little squares,
A singular Tyrannosauros Rex,
Sauntering towards extinction, an obsolete
Left-over from a weak *ancien regime*
About to be edged out by upstart germs. (64)

Such a moribund, aimless, and grotesque caricature of human obsolescence can qualify as the perfect literary citizen of Venice.

Yet "the lees of the Venetian underworld" (65), as the narrator calls them, do not tell the whole story. Hovering over the fetid canals there are still the clouds, which the narrator ends by contemplating:

Here is a sky determined to maintain
The reputation of Tiepolo,
A moving vision of a shapely mist,
Full of the splendor of the insubstantial . . . .
The tufted, opulent litters of the gods
They seem; or laundered bunting, well-dressed wigs,
Harvests of milk-white, Chinese peonies
That visibly rebuke our stinginess.
For all their ghostly presences, they take on
A colorful nobility at evening. (64-65)

Even while picturing Venice as the narrator's escape hatch into futile regression, Hecht's poem has dwelled much on Venetian realities: on human mortality and cloacal corruption. Here, at the end, it affords a glimpse of further, visionary Venetian possibilities: the abundance and variety of nature merging with the grandeur of art—the painter's and also, by extension, the poet's. Insubstantial though they may be, there are splendors to be seen above the fetid byways of

Hecht's Venice, and at times the orphaned, misanthropic protagonist leaves his bejewelled womb long enough to glimpse them.

BERNARD MALAMUD'S GLASS BLOWER

For Fidelman no buoy bells tolled, no church bells either; he kept no track of tide or time. On All Souls' Day, unable to resist, he rowed after a black-and-silver funeral barge and cortege of draped mourning gondolas moving like silent arrows across the water to San Michele, gloomy cypressed isle of the dead: the corpse of a young girl in white laid stiff in a casket covered with wreaths of hothouse flowers guarded by wooden angels. She waits, whatever she waited for, or sought, or hungered for, no longer. Ah, i poveri morti, though that depends on how you look at it. He had looked too long. (*Fidelman* 164-5)

The final, and culminating, section of Malamud's *Pictures of Fidelman*, "Glass Blower of Venice," shows Fidelman adrift in "Venice, floating city of green and golden canals": "Fidelman floated too, from stem to stern" (164). Exposed to the destabilizing witchery of the floating city, the ever-adaptable American painter has dutifully assumed the *persona* of Gustave Aschenbach. His consciousness undergoes the obligatory distortions. He wallows in the local aura of death, following the draped gondolas bound for the cemetery. In the best literary-obsessive fashion, he hunts for some elusive, visionary quest-object: "The ex-painter wandered wet-hatted, seeking in shop windows who knows what treat the tourists hadn't coveted and bought. Venice was full of goods he hungered for and detested. Yet he sought an object of art nobody would recognize but Fidelman" (165). The diagnosis of Fidelman's malaise is the classic Venetian one: "He had looked too long."

Like his Florentine misadventures, Fidelman's Venetian experience travesties through pungent reversal well-established literary precedents. Where Mann's master of decorous German prose, Aschenbach, plunges into uninhibited sensuality, unreality, and death, Malamud's feckless American dauber gains a secure hold on reality and a confident craftsmanship. His road to renewal is—as might have been expected—a plunge into uninhibited sensuality. It is life, not death, that Fidelman discovers in Venice.

Like Hartley's Venice in "The White Wand," Malamud's offers the artist dual options. On the one hand, he can locate in the city the daily bread of commonplace reality; on the other, he can treat the place as a magic springboard from which to soar into fantasy. Where C. F. chooses the second option, Fidelman blunders into the first. C. F.'s infatuation with a mysterious Venetian leads him to cross the bridge of sighs from Fact to Dream, but Fidelman's comparable infatuation leads him in the contrary direction. When the story begins, Fidelman is already making passages; he is, as Christof Wegelin puts it, "reduced to humble service as a kind of St. Christopher, carrying passengers piggy-back through the flooded squares of Venice. This useful function initiates his incorporation into the human community" (Salzberg 146). The tendency of Venice here is, for once, anti-isolationist.

Performing his useful function, Fidelman falls in love with a passenger who has shown a flattering responsiveness to his person. Afterward, still following the standard literary patterns, he scours the city obsessively, hoping to catch sight of her again. His quest is, like C. F.'s, motivated by a yearning to have his own waning identity objectively validated; looking through a shop window one evening, "he had the sudden sense he had glimpsed her, saw himself reflected in her large dark eyes. If he was truly conscious she was standing behind a counter, this slim-bodied, slant-eyed, long-nosed, handsome Venetian, staring at him as though contemplating the mark of fate in the face of a stranger" (167). Malamud develops this vein of epistemological burlesque with his usual *panache*. Fidelman's glimpse of the woman he calls "his dream girl" has all the elusiveness of a dream: "Fidelman never [on later occasions] saw his dream girl in the shop. He had doubts he ever had: trompe l'oeil, mirage, déjà vu, or something of the sort" (168). Venetian cognitive confusions are being re-run as farce.

Cheated of her physical reality, Fidelman absorbs the girl into an inner fantasy-pageant he constructs, somewhat like C. F., out of scraps of Venetian art and history:

The canals widened, golden light on green water, pure Canaletto all the way to the Rialto. A sense of sea enlivened the air, lagoon and Adriatic under high blue sky above the outer islands. Fantasticando: Eastern galleons, huge battletubs approaching with cannons booming, star and crescent billowing on red sails, from Byzantium of mosaic saints and dancing dolphins. Boom, tara, War! History, the Most Serene Venetian Republic, Othello singing Verdi as Desdemona tussles in the hay with Iago under a weeping-willow tree. Fidelman golden-robed Doge of Venice, though maybe better not since they garroted, stabbed, poisoned half the poor bastards. The Doge is dead, long live the dog that did him in! Boom, tara, yay! Fidelman III, Crusader on horse, hacking at Saladin and a thousand infidels! Fidelman in the Accademia! Ah Bellini, Giorgione, Tiziano, carissimi! The ex-painter wiped a wet eyelid, felt better and decided he hadn't given her up after all. She is still present, lives in the mind. (169)

This absurd romantic farrago, scrambling together undigested bits from Shakespeare, Verdi, and W. B. Yeats, eventually leads the Jewish-American artist to a surprising wish-fulfillment mission, that of quixotic ranger for the cause of Christ. The fantasy concludes aptly by echoing Childe Harold in Venice: "the beings of the mind are not of clay."

While lost in his dreams, however, Fidelman keeps "an eye cocked" for the earthly form of his ethereal idol. When at last he locates her, her solid circumstantiality soon begins to summon him back from his faery-lands forlorn: "They talked quickly, intensely, searching one another with six eyes. She spoke her name: Margherita Fassoli, that made it real, an immediate commitment. She was herself real at last, no longer wild-goose shade he chased in a maze of dead-end canals, under low arches, and in alleyways" (170). The name of the beloved, in "The White Wand" left cloudily indefinite, here provides the clue to the befuddling Venetian labyrinth.

The flesh-and-blood object of Fidelman's obsession turns out to have two flesh-and-blood children, with definite names, ages, and charms: "Riccardo and Rodolfo, eight and ten, little terrors"; she also has a too, too solid flesh-and-blood husband, Beppo. Best of all, she has a ravenous desire for Fidelman's body: "She gazed at him hungrily, eating with mouth, eyes." The ex-painter assures her that he longs to see her "'[p]assionately. But it's now or never, I'm frankly famished. Another day of dreaming and I'm a dead man. The ghost gives up. . . . I mean living on dreams. Sleeping with them. I can't any more though I've accomplished nothing'" (171). Carnal knowledge—for Hartley's Lavinia Johnstone the great menace to integrity of self—is for Fidelman the antidote to Venetian dreaming, the seal of objective reality.

Fidelman's next step away from dreams comes when he views his Venetian sylph's physique:

She was patient as he looked her over: heavier in the haunch and breasts than he had imagined; these were strong binding garments she wore. Her shapely legs were veined, splotched purple here and there. Slim at the waist but the stomach streaked with lesions of her pregnancies. She was forty if she was a day.
"Well, caro, are you disenchanted?"
"No more than usual," Fidelman confessed. (173)

It is a good Venetian bargain. Being routinely disenchanted is a price Fidelman gladly pays to gain release from enchantment; better to confront squarely the fact of Margherita's age and amplitude than to go on pursuing the slimmest of mirages. When they are in bed, he checks to see whether his beloved has not, by some Venetian conjuror's trick, been replaced by a changeling: "Her breasts were formless and he felt a roll of flesh above her hips. Fidelman snapped on the lamp. The same woman. He snapped it off" (173). This dreamer can live with disillusionment; by now, he prefers a surplus of substance to a deficit. For him, happiness is not, as it is for Hecht's narrator, "composed / Of clouded, cataracted, darkened sight, / Merciful blindnesses and ignorance."

Death in Venice is not the only Venetian intertext purposely evoked by Malamud's story. The name of Margherita's husband, Beppo Fassoli, recalls Byron's Beppo, the Venetian sea-going gentleman who strikes up a comradeship with his wife's lover, as Fassoli now proceeds to do with Fidelman. A glass blower who works on the island of Murano, Beppo reveals his essential character on his first appearance. Finding Fidelman at his house for supper, he "gave his guest a glass rose with six red petals. The radio was blaring Cavaradossi singing, 'L'arte nel suo mistero / Le diverse bellezze insiem confonde—' but

Beppo snapped it off impatiently" (174). Fassoli values beauty, but the text of the Puccini aria (Art in its mystery confuses diverse beauties with one another) is not to his liking. For him, only puerile art deals in mystifying confusions. Yet the glass blower's mind is "'full of facts and fantasy'"—a ripe Venetian blend. No chaser of funeral corteges, "'[h]e also likes to live life'" (176). When Fidelman nervously proposes to give his friend "a private exhibition" of his own work, but cautions, "'This isn't classic stuff, if you know what I mean. It's modernist and you mightn't care for it,'" Beppo replies "that he had attended the last five Biennali. 'My spirit is modern,' he said haughtily" (178).

The retrospective of his *oeuvre* that Fidelman stages for Beppo uproariously crushes his last, lingering artistic pretensions. The Venetian's tough-minded modern spirit easily punctures the chic avant-gardism of the American's canvases. Fidelman's caprice of basing a painting on "a series of crisscrossing abstract canals" collapses into bathos under the gaze of the dweller among canals that are not in the least abstract.

During the calamitous showing, Fidelman anxiously reflects, "You can pull up nails and let the past loose once too often" (180). Nonetheless, his opening of the Pandora's box of his past has one positive result. It finally liberates him (as the narrator of "The Venetian Vespers" can never be liberated) from his history of failure. It allows him to forget his fantasy of becoming a "name" and to work more seriously at finding out who he really is. Beppo aids him by mercifully applying a kitchen knife to the offending compositions. Fidelman struggles to protect them but suddenly has a change of heart. The glass blower justifies the proceeding with a shrewd piece of Venetian cost-analysis: "'Your painting will never pay back the part of your life you've given up for it'" (183). His outlook on life is eminently price-wise: "'In the end we pay for everything,'" he philosophizes (188).

The price that Fidelman pays for his Venetian redemption is the final loss of his inhibitions. The most important stage in his pilgrim's progress toward shamelessness comes last, in the form of a sensual love-relationship with the glass blower. It begins abruptly on a day when Beppo discovers Fidelman embracing his wife:

As they were in the midst of violent intercourse, Fidelman on top, Margherita more loving than ever, the bedroom door opened and he glimpsed a nude hairy body wearing a horn or carrying a weapon; before he could rise he felt Beppo land on him. Fidelman cried out, expecting death between the shoulders. Margherita, shoving herself up with a grunt, slipped out from under them and fled out of the room. (183)

Like Fidelman, the reader awaits the bloody denouement of a Venetian revenge-melodrama, the enraged cuckold venting his murderous wrath on the rival caught in the act; Venice is, after all, a city, as Howells notes, "forever associated with . . . unexpected dagger-thrusts" (*Venetian Life* 21). Once again, however, conventional wisdom is exploded by ribald eroticism: what Fidelman receives is not death between the shoulders but life elsewhere. So much for the cliché, mocked in politer fashion by Byron in *Beppo*, of the homicidally jealous Italian husband. Malamud's Beppo stabs steel blades into lifeless works of art, not into living flesh; the weapon with which he penetrates Fidelman is the shaft not of Thanatos but of Eros.

Fidelman, after recovering from the surprise attack, thrives:

> He stopped running.
> 　　Venice slowed down though it went on floating, its canals floating on Venice.
> 　　"Leonardo, Michelangelo," Fidelman murmured.
> 　　"If you can't invent art, invent life," Beppo advised him.
> 　　For good or ill Fidelman loved him; he could not help himself; he ought to have known. Beppo was handsome, hard-working, and loved to breathe; he smelled (and tasted) of oil and vinegar; he was, after all, a tender man and gentle lover. Fidelman had never in his life said "I love you" without reservation to anyone. He said it to Beppo. (184)

Where in *Death in Venice* a homoerotic compulsion leads the protagonist into a moral unravelling, the effect on Malamud's Aschenbach-surrogate is the reverse: the loose ends of Fidelman's life become at last bound together in stable feelings. Where Aschenbach can only mouth in secret his confession of love to Tadzio, who is in any case deaf to German words, Fidelman can communicate his feeling for Beppo without hindrance or embarrassment. For once, the island-city smiles on human intercourse. Fidelman soon comes to embrace not only the glass blower but his craft as a method of overcoming their physical isolation from each other "on separate islands" (185). "Beppo, who was teaching him the rites of love, also taught him to blow glass" (185).

Malamud misses no opportunity to link Venetian glass-blowing punningly with sexuality:

> Working with the hot molten glass excited Fidelman sexually. He felt creative, his heart in his pants. "With pipe, tongs, shears, you can make a form or change it into its opposite," Beppo said. "For instance, with a snip or two of the scissors, if it suits you, you can change the male organ into the female." The glass blower laughed heartily. Fidelman doubted he would be so minded; the thought evoked pain. Still it helped you understand the possibilities of life. (185)

Life's possibilities, which bloom so riotously in Malamud's revisionist Venice, are symbolically captured in the act of blowing glass, a medium whose essence is polymorphous plasticity. "Give the bubble a mouth and it became beaker, ewer, vase, amphora or burial urn, anything the mouth foretold, or heart desired, or blower could blow. If you knew how, you could blow anything" (186). What Fidelman gains is a protean licence utterly unlike the bodiless fluidity C. F.

enjoys with his spectral woman in white. The rhythms of the two men's erotic rapport permeate their work: "Every move they made was in essence sexual, a marvelous interaction because, among other things, it saved time and trouble: you worked and loved at once" (187). The purist who once took his stand on the fashionable separation between art and life now celebrates the marriage between craft and love.

That union is solemnized by the last object Fidelman fashions in Venice. "Before leaving Venice, Fidelman blew a slightly humpbacked green horse for Beppo, the color of his eyes. 'Up yours,' said the glass blower, grieving at the gray in Fidelman's hair. He sold the horse for a decent sum and gave Fidelman the lire" (192). The horse embodies Fidelman's feeling for Beppo, but the glass blower's unsentimental treatment of the gift reflects his own, firmer grasp of practicalities. In his Venetian eye—"true as a jeweller's lens," to apply Mary McCarthy's phrase—there is no conflict between honest personal affection and a sober regard for the cash needed to sustain precious, precarious life. In the Venetian novellas by James and Hartley, Verocchio's great bronze horseman stands as a reminder of the ferocious potency of the Venetian past. Fidelman's crooked green glass horse takes its own place as a more modest symbol of the potential to nurture life and fellowship still residing in the Venetian present. Starting out stranded in a Venice of sickening unreality, Fidelman, first with Margherita and then under Beppo's more expert tutelage, learns to realize that potential. In his later life, far from Venice, Fidelman's polymorphous Venetian wisdom travels with him: "In America he worked as a craftsman in glass and loved men and women" (192). For once in its fictive history, Venice marks not the termination of experience but its beginning.

PART III

ROME

Rome: Churches of Santa Maria Egiziaca and Santa Maria in Cosmedin. From *Attraverso l'Italia: Roma*, p. 140. Photographs by Gianni Bereango Gardin. Touring Club Italiano, 1986. Photograph reproduced courtesy of Touring Club Italiano.

O thou new comer who seek'st Rome in Rome
And find'st in Rome no thing thou canst call Roman;
Arches worn old and palaces made common,
Rome's name alone within these walls keeps home.

Behold how pride and ruin can befall
One who hath set the whole world 'neath her laws,
All-conquering, now conquered, because
She is Time's prey and Time consumeth all.

Rome that art Rome's one sole last monument,
Rome that alone has conquered Rome the town,
Tiber alone, transient and seaward bent,
Remains of Rome. O world, thou unconstant mime!
That which stands firm in thee Time batters down,
And that which fleeteth doth outrun swift time.
    Ezra Pound, "Rome" (from the French of Joachim Du Bellay)

Rome is still Rome. Its ruins and its squares
Stand sluiced in wet and all its asphalt gleaming.
The street fronts caged behind the slant of rain-bars
Sun is already melting where they teem:
Spray-haloed traffic taints your laurel leaves,
City of restitutions, city of thieves.
    Charles Tomlinson, "In the Borghese Gardens"

14

City of the Soul

"Oh Rome! my country! city of the soul! / The orphans of the heart must turn to thee . . . " (*Childe Harold* 4.78). Lord Byron's lines, though endlessly quoted, are not a platitude. In *Civilization and Its Discontents* (1930), Sigmund Freud, who was no Childe Harold, calls on the ancient city as an aid in charting the convolutions of the human psyche. To clarify his principle "that in mental life nothing which has once been formed can perish—that everything is somehow preserved and that in suitable circumstances . . . it can once more be brought to light" (16), he summons up the profusely layered Roman past.

Now let us, by a flight of imagination, suppose that Rome is not a human habitation but a psychical entity with a similarly long and copious past—an entity, that is to say, in which nothing that has once come into existence will have passed away and all the earlier phases of development continue to exist alongside the latest one. (17)

Freud's confidence in elaborating the analogy shows how closely he identified Rome with the intimate geography of human mental growth, which, as he conceived it, deposits stratum atop stratum while following its devious course.

Rome is a metaphor waiting to happen. This is one of the chief reasons for its appeal over the centuries to writers of all breeds, from Romantic poets to clinical psychologists. No other place has so compellingly joined the idea of limitless extent, both of time and space, with the idea of centrality. No other city has been so widely recognised as a microcosm: an epitome of life in its multifarious guises and disguises, a capital of human experience to which all roads of thought must lead. "Rome, in which all the ages are at home and jostle one another is, more than any other city, a world in miniature," says Arthur Symons (52). His words recall Hawthorne's epithet: "The city of all time, and of all the world!" (*Faun* 86).

Centrality is itself a function of the city's inclusiveness. Even the loftily self-possessed Goethe could be given pause by Roman magnitude and copiousness: "Wherever you turn your eyes, every kind of vista, near and distant, confronts you. . . . One would need a thousand styluses to write with. What can one do here with a single pen?" (120-1). Henry James, on an early visit, is similarly overwhelmed: "I feel here always the importunate *muchness* of the place—all the memories and materials and elements which one can't assimilate and do justice to" (*Letters* 1: 416). "The idea of putting Rome into a novel not only did not attract me it shocked me," protests Elizabeth Bowen—"*background*, for heaven's sake! The thing was a major character, out of scale with any fictitious cast" (51). Such a place presents to the writer's imagination a challenge at once exhilarating and intimidating.

S. Russell Forbes, author of the 1882 guide *Rambles in Rome*, advises the tourist that "[m]odern Rome . . . is a strange mixture of narrow streets, open squares, churches, fountains, ruins, new palaces, and dirt" (xvii). The fact of "strange mixture" strikes all visitors. Edmund Wilson, in Italy at the end of World War Two, found that "there were so many kinds of things in Rome, all mixed up yet with walls between them" (42); he was struck by "[t]he strange blend of informality and grandeur that is so much the quality of Rome" (62). Francis Marion Crawford claims in his hyperbole-strewn survey *Ave Roma Immortalis* (1898) that "there is no capital in all the world which has such contrasts to show within a mile of each other—one might almost say within a dozen steps" (110). An early twentieth-century observer notes: "Rome is a city of contrasts. In her streets at the same moment you have sunshine and shadow, palaces and ruins, disreputable odours and the fragrances of flowers, the automobiles of Roman Princes and the rolling oxen of the Campagna" (Potter 234). By 1957, the date of Guido Piovene's *Viaggio in Italia*, the oxen no longer dared intrude, but the general impression persisted:

Kitchen gardens and flower gardens; the palace and the street with its crowd and stalls, all neighboring and mixed together; the theologian and the ordinary preacher rubbing elbows; these are the images of Rome that most frequently recur. And today, one must add, ancient stones, cement stalls and buildings. One thing doesn't drive out another; everything coexists; the keynote is mixture. (653)

Juxtaposition has always been a prime ingredient of Rome's unique appeal. The group of the she-wolf suckling the human twins in the Capitoline Museum makes an uncannily apt insignia for this city of strange bedfellows, all the more because the mixture of periods (the wolf is classical, Romulus and Remus a Renaissance addition) turns the work into a sculptural collage. It is exactly this collage principle that Henry James, in his sketch "Very Modern Rome," singles out as the key to the city's unique fascination:

You think of the early antiquity and of the later, of the long period commemorated in the many—the too many volumes, of Gibbon and Merivale, of the dusky mediaeval interregnum, of the brilliant, blooming Renascence, of the hey-day of the Jesuits, of the cocked-hat civilization of the 17th and 18th centuries, of the proscriptions and revolutions of the 19th, of the wonderful present phase of the drama; and this jumble of the sternest antiquity and the most frivolous modernness, of pagan and Christian pontiffs, of soldiers and priests, of the extreme of profanity and the greatest pomp of ecclesiasticism, of the brutality of destruction and the ecstasy of creation, the superimposition of the later clerical arts and manners upon . . . the rugged heritage of the previous time, and of the fine fresh

Italian rule of today upon the whole promiscuous deposit—this huge historic compound has a potent and inexhaustible savor. (138)

Roman juxtaposition can, however, take unsavory forms. In literature, particularly, it has often bred melodramatic horror. Shelley's Beatrice Cenci, violated by her unspeakable father, bursts out: "Horrible things have been in this wide world, / Prodigious mixtures, and confusions strange / Of good and ill" (*Complete Poetical Works*, 3.1.51-53). Nathaniel Hawthorne's New England sensibility balked at prodigious Roman mixtures. The Romans, he laments in his notebook, "spit on the glorious pavement of St Peter's, and wherever else they like; they place mean-looking wooden confessionals beneath its sublime arches . . . . they put pasteboard statues of Saints beneath the dome of the Pantheon; in short they let the sublime and the ridiculous come close together, and are not in the least troubled by the proximity" (*French and Italian Notebooks* 88). Even less straight-laced foreign visitors have been "troubled by the proximity." Their dismay is wittily captured by Arthur Hugh Clough in "Resignation: To Faustus," a short poem evidently composed during Clough's stay in Rome in 1848:

> O land of Empire, art and love!
> What is it that you show me?
> A sky for Gods to tread above,
> A soil for pigs below me!
> O in all place and shape and kind
> Beyond all thought and thinking,
> The graceful with the gross combined,
> The stately with the stinking!
> Whilst words of mighty love to trace,
> Which thy great walls I see on,
> Thy porch I pace or take my place
> Within thee, great Pantheon,
> What sights untold of contrast bold
> My ranging eyes must be on! (lines 1-14, *The Poems*)

The ethereal and the fetid, the sacred and the profane, provide the literature of Rome with built-in, pervasive binary oppositions. Juxtaposition has roots buried in the darkness of the Roman past. Charles Dickens was perturbed to recognise "how many ruins of the old mythology: how many fragments of obsolete legend and observance: have been incorporated into the worship of Christian altars here; and how, in numberless respects, the false faith and the true are fused into a monstrous union" (*Pictures* 201). It is tempting for the moralizing northern visitor to impose ready-to-hand dichotomies like "false" and "true" on sprawling Roman profusion; only an unusually sophisticated observer can resist the temptation.

One such observer, Henry James, describes an hour spent at the Protestant Cemetery, "where the ancient and the modern world are insidiously contrasted. . . . It is a wonderful confusion of mortality and a grim enough admonition of our helpless promiscuity in the crucible of time" (*Hours* 94-95). James recognised in the mixed condition of Rome a pattern of the human condition itself. Twentieth-century observers, following James's lead, have more often relished than deplored Rome's helter-skelter temporal promiscuousness. "An impossible compounding of time," Eleanor Clark fondly calls the city, "in which no century has respect for any other and all hit you in a jumble at every turn" (17).

A prime example of such a "jumble" is the church of San Clemente. The extant, twelfth-century structure stands above the remains of a fourth-century basilica, which in turn partially replaced a still earlier church, possibly dating from the first century. Also visible are the remains of a Mithraic shrine that once occupied a space adjacent to the earliest Christian one. A recent poem by Charles Tomlinson, "In San Clemente," shows the imaginative use to which such distinctively Roman sites can lend themselves. The poet's descent down "steps that flow / Downwards through the sonorous dark beneath" becomes an unobtrusive but urgent search for cultural origins:

> Then, down once more, and past the humid cave
> Of Mithras' bull and shrine, until they lead
> To a wall of tufa and—beyond—the roar
> Of subterranean waters pouring by
> All of the centuries it takes to climb
> From Mithras to the myth-resisting play
> Of one clear jet chiming against this bowl
> In the fountained courtyard and the open day. (*Return* 4)

Rome boasts a multitude of such architectural palimpsests, which tease the literary consciousness out of thought—or into it. Describing the Via dei Fori Imperiali, a "propaganda and parade street" (90) built by Mussolini as a showcase for some of the principal ruins, Eleanor Clark notes that the monuments, from the Colosseum at one end to Trajan's Column at the other, have been put at risk by the alterations. Nevertheless, "[i]t would be futile anyway to wish they had not kept up with the times, however destructive, when Rome's deepest gift for the imagination is in its having always done just that" (93).

Richard Wilbur's poem "For the New Railway Station in Rome" (*Things of This World* 1956) might be read as a lyric elaboration of Clark's insight. In it, Wilbur chides antiquarians who insist on leaving ancient ruins undusted, the better to moralize over: "Those who said God is praised / By hurt pillars, who loved to see our brazen lust / Lie down in rubble, and our vaunting arches /

Conduce to dust" (49). This company—"Those pilgrims of defeat / Who brought their injured wills as to a soldier's home"—implicitly includes that most ostentatiously defeated of pilgrims, Childe Harold. They are confronted with "something new / To see in Rome": the train station, run by a triumphant architectural conceit onto a remnant of Roman masonry:

> See, from the travertine
> Face of the office block, the roof of the booking-hall
> Sails out into the air beside the ruined
> Servian Wall,
> Echoing in its light
> And cantilevered swoop of reinforced concrete
> The broken profile of these stones, defeating
> That defeat. (49)

Wilbur's Rome, unlike Byron's, is not "past Redemption's skill"; it is precisely the skill marshalled from age to age by the human constructive spirit that redeems ruin from nullity. The triumph is, finally, one of the fecundating imagination over the years' abrasion of rent walls, whose shards "sing out in stubborn joy":

> "What city is eternal
> But that which prints itself within the groping head
> Out of the blue unbroken reveries
> Of the building dead?

> "What is our praise or pride
> But to imagine excellence, and try to make it?
> What does it say over the door of Heaven
> But *homo fecit?*" (49-50)

The enjambment of modern concrete on ancient stone is cleverly echoed by the poem's conclusion, which mortises a living language to a "dead" one. The Latin words, which play on inscriptions like the one over the portico of the Pantheon—M. AGRIPPA. L. F. COS. TERTIUM. FECIT—close the poem on a note of sonorous assurance. "Homo faber" is alive and well, and living in the new Rome railway station.

The ending of "For the New Railway Station in Rome" admirably demonstrates how Roman juxtaposition, by infiltrating the verbal texture of a poem, can lend it novel force. Another, arrestingly different, example is a poem by Wilbur's compatriot Robert Lowell. Lowell's "Beyond the Alps" (1959)[1] bristles with ironies that look all the more acerb when placed next to Wilbur's cisalpine optimism. The brand of optimism that Lowell is most directly challenging, however, dates from an earlier century. "Beyond the Alps" implicitly questions romantic hindsights like those Shelley included in a letter of 1819 to Thomas Love Peacock, *apropos* of Pompeii:

O, but for that series of wretched wars which terminated in the Roman conquest of the world; but for the Christian religion, which put the finishing stroke on the antient system; but for those changes that conducted Athens to its ruin,—to what an eminence might not humanity have arrived! (*Complete Works* 10: 26)

Lowell is no more receptive than Shelley to the bullying of Roman imperialism and the blandishments of Roman Catholicism. In "Beyond the Alps" he glances sardonically at "the skirt-mad Mussolini" and at Pius XII's promulgating of "the dogma of Mary's bodily assumption." But Lowell refuses to concede that the Roman swerving of history from pristine Greek ideals was a mere quirk of fate. From its opening lines, his poem casts doubt upon vaulting humanity's power to "arrive at an eminence": "Reading how even the Swiss had thrown the sponge / in once again, and Everest was still / unscaled, I watched our Paris pullman lunge, / mooning across the fallow Alpine snow" (lines 1-4, *Life Studies*).

Lowell's train is lunging toward a terminus far removed from Wilbur's triumphant Rome station. The Roman juxtapositions through which his poem proceeds do not reassure. His somber ironies lay bare the futility of ancient Catholic superstitions in the face of modern upheaval and genocide: "Pilgrims still kissed Saint Peter's brazen sandal. / The Duce's lynched, bare, booted skull still spoke. / God herded his people to the *coup de grace*" (23-25). In another vivid collocation, Pius is glimpsed using an electric shaver while listening to the rapturous shouts of the throng without; enjoying the benisons of modern technology, he still spearheads the legions of primitive obscurantism: "His electric razor purred, / his pet canary chirped on his right hand. / The lights of science couldn't hold a candle / to Mary risen, gorgeous as a jungle bird!" (18-21).

From his berth on the train, the poet sees "each backward wasted Alp, a Parthenon, / fire-branded socket of the cyclops' eye" (47-48). Humankind, led by its Odysseus-artificers and its conquering Caesars, has swept down the ringing grooves of change, but only by heedlessly wasting any one-eyed child of nature unlucky enough to be standing on the tracks. Lowell's emphasis falls not, like Wilbur's, on the proud continuum of man's creative spirit but on the tragic coupling of the creative and the ruthlessly destructive, reaching back to the origins of Western civilization:

There are no tickets to that altitude,
once held by Hellas when the Goddess stood,
prince, pope, philosopher and golden bough,
pure mind and murder at the scything prow—
Minerva the mis-carriage of the brain. (49-53)

Of Olympus, too, it could be said "homo fecit"; but whether the making was good or ill remains for Lowell a tormenting riddle. The "eminence"—"that altitude"—to which Shelley supposed a purely Hellenic humanity might have scaled is for Lowell as equivocal as it is unreachable. Aspiring Greece evolves into insolent Rome. Man's unreason and rapacity pervert from the start the "march of mind": Augustus engenders Mussolini. Lowell drives home the paradox in his climactic, shocking conceit, the "scything prow" that mutilates as it advances; the Western vanguard of progress has become a grim reaper. The image of physical and linguistic bonding that concludes Wilbur's poem, the image of deadly sundering that closes Lowell's—here, at their most eloquent, are two profoundly opposed ways of visualizing the thrust of Western history. Yet they are both equally "Roman." As metaphor, the Eternal City retains its power both to focus and to polarize the poetic imagination.

The idea of the "Eternal City" is of course a myth, a piece of poetic licence; but the licence has been earned. The evidence of Rome's staggering longevity confronts the visitor at every turn. The title of Crawford's study *Ave Roma Immortalis* itself endorses the cherished myth; and at the book's conclusion Crawford assures his reader that "a man can no more say a last farewell to Rome than he can take leave of eternity. The years move on, but she waits; the cities fall, but she stands; the old races of men lie dead in the track wherein mankind wanders always between two darknesses; yet Rome lives, and her changes are not from life to death, as ours are, but from one life to another" (563).

Paradoxically, however, the Eternal City is the place of all places that thrusts most importunately before the literary mind the stealthy clock-hand creeping of time. "Whose arch or pillar meets me in the face," asks Byron, "Titus or Trajan's?"

> No—'tis that of Time:
> Triumph, arch, pillar, all he doth displace
> Scoffing; and apostolic statues climb
> To crush the imperial urn, whose ashes slept sublime. (*Childe Harold* 4.110)

The ticking of the clock is the most common of sounds in Roman fictions. "Opulent as to time," declares Elizabeth Bowen, "the city is scornful of any lack of it; *that* is the one form of poverty Rome treats badly" (11-12). Characters in Roman narratives, rich or poor, are often victims of this intangible form of poverty. Karen Stone, the aging actress-heroine of Tennessee Williams's novel *The Roman Spring of Mrs. Stone* (1950), finds that her monetary wealth does not ward off the affliction:

She stood very still and listened, so intently that she could hear the clock in the next room ticking. And sleep was drifting. Sleep was drifting over the ancient city. If she looked out of the windows, or wandered out upon the terrace, she could see that even the sky was drifting. Everything was drifting. Was there anything else but this enormous drifting of time and existence? (144-5)

The protagonist of Max Davidson's novel *Suddenly in Rome* (1988), Mark Barham, is determined to redeem time by reviving a passionate love-affair that had terminated eight years earlier. He is haunted by his beloved's verdict that it is "too late"; and the name of the man he jealously believes to have succeeded him in her affections, Tardelli, is a mocking reminder of belatedness. Again and again, matters of timing assume a crucial importance within the Eternal setting. A bizarre example is Muriel Spark's novel *The Public Image* (1970), in which the heroine's malicious husband schedules his suicide to occur at the most embarrassing possible moment: the exact hour of a party in the couple's Rome flat, to which he has privately invited a horde of dissolute zanies.

Besides being a source of anxiety, however, time's dominance may also endow Roman characters with a sobering privilege of perspective. "Plod your way / O'er steps of broken thrones and temples, Ye! / Whose agonies are evils of a day," Byron adjures the reader—"A world is at our feet as fragile as our clay" (*Childe Harold* 4.78). In Virginia Woolf's *The Waves* (1931), Bernard, from his Roman vantage point, finds that his previous London life has magically dwindled: "Now I sit on a stone seat in these gardens surveying the eternal city, and the little man who was shaving in London five days ago looks already like a heap of old clothes. London has also crumbled. London consists of fallen factories and a few gasometers" (158). Rome, being eternal, makes even the most venerable among other places look laughably ephemeral.

Narratives that unfold within the "eternal" frame tend to be profoundly conditioned by the whole idea of temporality. Over and over, Roman stories feature formidable age differences between sexual partners. Ronald Beard, in Anthony Burgess's recent novel *Beard's Roman Women* (1976), is merely a descendant of a long line of male characters who must straddle the gap in age between themselves and the younger women whom they pursue or marry. Such gaps occur between Count Guido and his teenaged wife Pompilia in Browning's *The Ring and the Book* (1868); between Gilbert Osmond and Isabel Archer in James's *The Portrait of a Lady* (1881); between the unlovely Sam Scrope and his lovely fiancée Adina in James's story "Adina" (1874, *The Tales*, Vol. 2); between the celebrated author Miles Fanning, and his young admirer Pamela Tarn in Aldous Huxley's novella "After the Fireworks" (*Brief Candles* 1930); between Miriam's betrothed, who haunts her like a ghastly shadow, and Miriam herself in *The Marble Faun*. Typically, such age discrepancies give personal focus to a more general preoccupation with matters of time or timing.

Occasionally the pattern is reversed, as in *The Roman Spring of Mrs. Stone*, whose aging leading lady becomes fascinated by a youthful, conniving Roman gigolo, or in "Mrs. General Talboys" (1861, *Complete Short Stories*), Anthony Trollope's jocose tale of the British colony in Rome, which recounts the wooing of a fatuous but respectable English matron by a much younger Irishman. ("'She's old enough to be his mother,' said Mrs. Mackinnon. 'What does that matter to an Irishman?' said Mackinnon" [105]).

The distance in age between George Eliot's Dorothea and Dorothea's husband, Casaubon, has much to do with the more serious emotional distance dividing them. During the Roman episodes of *Middlemarch*, details of temporality work subtly to define that distance. In response to Dorothea's impetuous request to know how soon he will let her aid him with his research, Casaubon says, "with irritation reined in by propriety," "'you may rely upon me for knowing the times and the seasons'" (233). Casaubon's defensiveness matches his sterile, mechanically linear ordering of time, which helps to make him a foil for his youthful cousin, Will Ladislaw. Will's perception of time is, by contrast, holistic; he finds that "the very miscellaneousness of Rome . . . made the mind flexible with constant comparison, and saved you from seeing the world's ages as a set of box-like partitions without vital connection. . . . Rome had given him quite a new sense of history as a whole; the fragments stimulated his imagination and made him constructive" (244). Meanwhile, her time in Rome is giving Dorothea "quite a new sense" of her own personal history: "[H]er view of Mr. Casaubon and her wifely relation, now that she was married to him, was gradually changing with the secret motion of a watch-hand from what it had been in her maiden dream" (226). When the narrator mischievously asks about Mr. Casaubon, "[D]id his chronology fail him?" (227), the reader knows the answer.

Time is not all that flows in Rome. "Rome is the city of fountains," observes the nineteenth-century American sculptor William Wetmore Story. "Wherever one goes he hears the pleasant sound of lapsing water. In every square it plies its columns in the sunshine, toppling over with the weight of myriad pearls and diamonds, and plashing back into the carven basin" (479-80). To Eleanor Clark, the play of the Roman fountains mirrors the ceaseless fluidity of life in the Eternal City: "For the Anglo-Saxon mind, ruled by conscience and the romantic, rigid in its privacies, everything here is shocking—an endless revelation and immersion; this is the vocabulary of our sleep; and the key image is always water" (34). Shocking or not, the flow can furnish a recourse against the rigidity lurking in the stony Roman surroundings themselves. Dickens's Amy Dorrit, crushed by her sense of Roman stasis, finds in the fountains her only channel of escape from the thralldom of immemorial fixity: "[T]here they took up their abode, in a city where everything seemed to be trying to stand still for ever on the ruins of something else—except the water, which, following eternal laws, tumbled and rolled from its glorious multitude of fountains" (*Little Dorrit* 512).

"Water lives, stone not," comments Elizabeth Bowen *apropos* of Maderna's fountains in Saint Peter's Square (116). Visitors to Rome used to become stone fanciers—Goethe "could not resist the temptation to fill [his] pockets with tablets of granite, porphyry and marble which lay around in thousands" (127)—but the material, and the word, tend to have chilling associations. To the reader versed in the Roman lexicon, a mere title like *The Roman Spring of Mrs. Stone* portends the sinister reawakening the narrative unfolds. To evoke the sternly confining character of Castel Sant' Angelo, Crawford notes that "in the vast thickness of the surrounding foundations there is but stone, again stone, and more stone" (496). "I will take you where you may persuade / The stones you tread on to deliver you," snarls old Cenci at his young wife Lucrezia in Shelley's *The Cenci* (1819) (*Complete Poetical Works* 2.1.163-4). The omnipresence of stone contributes to the impression of Roman fixity, which Amy Dorrit is by no means unique in dreading.

Not all visitors have found stone incompatible with ideas of life, warmth, and movement. According to Olave Muriel Potter, the author of a lavishly produced 1923 guidebook, *The Colour of Rome*, "The Roman sun gilds and warms these old, old stones [of the Palatine]; they are full of the majesty of the Beginning of Things. . . . [T]hey are invested with the virility of the first Roman who conceived the possibility of Rome" (46-47). The American poet James Wright, in "The Vestal in the Forum," finds the face of an eroded, rose-enwrapped female statue "[c]learer to me than most living faces" (*Above the River* 329). In her very decay, the stone girl becomes for the poet an image of humanity:

> A dissolving
> Stone, she seems to change from stone to something
> Frail, to someone I can know, someone
> I can almost name. (329)

Connected with the notion of life in the stones of Rome is the metaphor of their eloquence, repeated by commentators almost *ad nauseam*. "Every stone has its story," says Augustus Hare of the Forum (142). "'There are sermons in stones,'" muses Hawthorne's Hilda, dusting off the inevitable Shakespearean figure for local application, "'and especially in the stones of Rome'" (*Faun* 151). But the text of the sermons preached by Roman stones is most often one of loss and life-denial. Byron's famous personification—"The Niobe of nations! there she stands, / Childless and crownless, in her voiceless woe" (*Childe Harold* 4.79)—reveals its full force only when viewed within the broader context of

Roman literary iconography. Niobe is the ultimate Roman emblem: a petrified fountain.

Niobe is also, of course, the emblem of bereaved motherhood, which makes her all the more at home in the city that has been called "The mother city of the western world" (Morton 416). Over the world's orphans of the heart, the bereaved Niobe of nations has long exerted a potent attraction. It seems only natural, therefore, that characters in Roman fictions tend to be either literal or virtual orphans. Both Madame de Staël's Corinne and Corinne's Scottish lover, Nelvil, are parentless and suffer from being so. George Eliot's Dorothea Brooke has been for some years an orphan at the time of her Roman honeymoon. Isabel Archer, when she arrives in Rome, has lost both her real father and her father-protector, Mr. Touchett. Hawthorne's Hilda, in *The Marble Faun*, comes to long for her dead mother during her Roman sojourn; Miriam has apparently no living parents, and Donatello is the last of his line. Pietro and Violante in *The Ring and the Book* are Pompilia's ostensible, not real, mother and father; and even they are out of reach when she needs their support. "Rome must be one of the biggest refugee camps in Europe," observes Davidson's Mark Barham. "Almost everyone who wasn't born a Roman has the air of having run away from somewhere else" (*Suddenly in Rome* 143). But if such literary orphans seek in Rome itself the kindly parental nurturing they have missed, their yearnings are seldom assuaged by their ancient foster-mother.

The metaphor of the bereaved Niobe succinctly captures the spirit of a place that has been counting up its losses since time immemorial. "I've seen the Tiber hurrying along, as swift and dirty as history!" exclaims the young Henry James after his arrival (*Letters* 1: 160); and James is only one among innumerable writers to marvel at the volume of water—and dirt—that has passed under the Roman bridges. Rome is, of all cities, the most haunted by the past, and literary treatments of it are equally haunted. "Rome is as the desert, where we steer / Stumbling o'er recollections," as Byron observes (*Childe Harold* 4.81). William Dean Howells, revisiting Rome as a septuagenarian forty years after his first visit there, stumbles in fancy over the recollection of his earlier, youthful Roman self: "I could not tell my proud young double that we were one . . . ; he would never have believed it of my gray hairs and sunken figure" (*Roman Holidays* 123). A legion of Roman characters find cause to say, with Orsino in *The Cenci*, "Oh, I fear / That what is past will never let me rest!" (5.1. 93-94). A curious instance is that of Annabel Christopher, heroine of Spark's *The Public Image*, who is kept from ever resting by a series of posthumous letters from the Machiavellian pen of her husband Frederick.

A more powerful instance is that of Dickens's William Dorrit. The scene of Dorrit's collapse and death, among the most striking in all Dickens, has its resonance enormously enhanced by the Roman surroundings amid which it takes place. The abruptly enriched, fatuously self-deluding ex-prisoner has up to this point succeeded in blotting out every vestige of his unmentionable Marshalsea past; but in Rome, great storehouse of vestiges, he "stumbles over recollections" with a vengeance. His breakdown at Mrs. Merdle's formal dinner, in which he regresses convulsively into the past, suddenly shrinks his palatial Roman opulence down to the beggarly dimensions of a prison cell.

The Roman compulsion to look backward can tax the patience even of those visitors who normally regard the past with affection. The young James finds that he has conceived in Rome "a tenfold deeper loathing than ever of the hideous heritage of the past," and that he has "felt for a moment as if [he] should like to devote [his] life to laying rail-roads and erecting blocks of stores on the most classic and romantic sites" (*Letters* 1: 182). In *Italian Hours*, describing the Protestant Cemetery, James confesses to a sense of annihilating pressure: "[T]he weight of a tremendous past presses down upon the flowery sod, and the sleeper's mortality feels the contact of all the mortality with which the brilliant air is tainted" (199). The cemetery makes a fitting resting place for Daisy Miller, that ephemeral American butterfly crushed under the stony weight of Roman precedent and Roman mortality.

"Here," Stendhal grumbles on his arrival, "all is decadence, all is memory, all is death. The active life is in London and Paris" (45). A chorus of nineteenth-century voices mourns the "deadness" of the Eternal City. Shelley conducts his obsequies in a fashion typically unflattering to the living occupants: "Rome is a city, as it were, of the dead, or rather of those who cannot die, and who survive the puny generations which inhabit and pass over the spot which they have made sacred to eternity" (*Complete Works* 10: 14). Samuel Rogers produces a lugubrious Roman meditation:

> [Death's] form and fashion here
> To me, I do confess, reflect a gloom,
> A sadness round; yet one I would not lose;
> Being in unison with all things else
> In this, this land of shadows, where we live
> More in past time than present, where the ground,
> League beyond league, like one great cemetery,
> Is covered o'er with mouldering monuments;
> And, let the living wander where they will,
> They cannot leave the footsteps of the dead. (146-7)

Even a contemporary poet like James Wright still finds the footsteps of the Roman dead difficult to leave. In his prose poem "Two Moments in Rome," he observes mordantly that "[t]he dead loiter indecently here in the fresh sunlight, bound and determined to get revenge on somebody if it's the last thing they ever do" (*Above the River* 306).

By the end of the nineteenth century, however, such an attitude had already begun to seem passé. The reason lies partly in the changed status of Rome itself. Having at last become the capital of a newly unified Italy, the modern city was not so readily relegated to the historical dust-bin. "She is still an ancient city," Olave Potter observes in 1923, "but young life is stirring in her veins" (5). Some years earlier, Edith Wharton, as William Vance notes, "clearly articulated the revision [of attitudes toward Rome] that had to take place" (2: 101). Wharton complains strenuously that "in Rome for centuries it has been the fashion to look only on a city which has almost disappeared, and to close the eyes to one which is still alive and actual" (*Italian Backgrounds* 181). Refusing to indulge in nostalgia for the picturesque squalor of the Older Rome, Wharton's compatriot Howells proclaims himself "a Newer-Roman to the core" (*Roman Holidays* 79).

An alive, actual city must by definition be receptive to change, and Rome's receptiveness is self-evident. "One . . . cannot fail to be impressed by the strange changes through which this wonderful city has passed," the sculptor Story observes (167). In "Very Modern Rome" James speaks of "those transformations which constitute the specialty, as it were, of Rome" (139). H. V. Morton cites his favorite Roman square, Piazza Navona, as a signal example of this "specialty":

I do not know of a more striking illustration of the process which has continued throughout Roman history of the transformation of the old into the new. The piazza [which was built on the site of Domitian's stadium] still looks like a Roman racecourse. When a taxi rushes from a side street and encircles the piazza, it is repeating on the same ground the course of ancient chariots, and even the *spina* of the stadium is represented today by the three groups of statuesque fountains in the centre. (285)

Dizzying transformations have a strange way of overtaking fictional characters, too, during their Roman sojourns. Bernard, in *The Waves*, becomes convinced that he is inwardly undergoing such a Roman refashioning: "'Here am I shedding one of my life-skins, and all they will say is, "Bernard is spending ten days in Rome""'" (161). If it takes but ten Roman days to shake the world of Bernard's sensibility, a greater or even lesser amount of time spent in Rome shakes the worlds of a gallery of other fictional characters. The presiding genius of the Roman literary imagination is the Ovid of the *Metamorphoses*. The title of the English edition of Hawthorne's *The Marble Faun*—"Transformation"—is the more authentically Roman one.

"At last—for the first time—I live!" Thus the young Henry James exults after his first, intoxicating Roman stroll:

It beats everything: it leaves the Rome of your fancy—your education—nowhere. It makes Venice—Florence—Oxford—London—seem like little cities of paste-board. I went reeling and moaning thro' the streets, in a fever of enjoyment. (*Letters* 1: 160)

James's "Roman fever" has an aura of erotic release; and this side of the city's transforming power, too, has not gone undetected. "Rome is famous for its strange sexual effects on foreigners," observes Eleanor Clark (204), and such a work as Williams's *The Roman Spring of Mrs. Stone* reads like a gloss on her insight.

But Roman transformation, as Williams's macabre story demonstrates, is more often death-dealing than life-giving. The concept of "renaissance" has shallower roots in Rome than in Florence; the characteristic Roman vein is gothic rather than redemptive. In Venice, too, transformation, especially of an erotic sort, can be deathly, as Gustave Aschenbach's fate bears witness. In Rome, however, parables of change tend to involve further complexities; in such a milieu, the fictionalizing imagination cannot escape history. "The story of Rome is a tale of murder and sudden death, varied, changing, never repeated in the same way; there is blood on every threshold; a tragedy lies buried in every church and chapel," confides Crawford (299). Invented Roman stories, like the historical annals, are typically secret, sinister and bloody. Reminiscences of Roman history sometimes trouble the reflections of fictional characters, as they do those of Hawthorne's American sculptor, Kenyon:

And what localities for new crime existed in those guilty sites, where the crime of departed ages used to be at home, and had its long, hereditary haunt! What street in Rome, what ancient ruin, what one place where man had standing-room, what fallen stone was there, unstained with one or another kind of guilt! To Kenyon's morbid view, there appeared to be a contagious element, rising foglike from the ancient depravity of Rome, and brooding over the dead and half-rotten city, as nowhere else on earth. It prolonged the tendency to crime, and developed an instantaneous growth of it, whenever an opportunity was found. (*Faun* 412)

Over a century later, Anthony Burgess's Ronald Beard applies himself just as extravagantly to conjuring up ancient stains: "He considered that he detested Rome, meaning its bloody history, its cowardly citizens, its godless bishops who were also godless popes, its boastful baroque, its insipid cuisine, its sour wine. A venal city and a cruel city and a city of robbers" (9). As often happens in Roman narratives, perception is in this instance luridly tinged by personal recollection: "Here his wife Leonora had had her first liver collapse and had loosed black blood over the hotel bedroom" (9).

"A word will tell what it has been—the heart of the world," says Crawford. What he means by "heart" turns out to be disturbingly literal: "Blood, blood, and more blood,—that was the history of old Rome,—the blood of brothers, the blood of foes, the blood of martyrs without end" (541). Blood is a substance that flows through Roman fictional annals as copiously as water from Roman fountains. A signal instance is *The Cenci*, whose villain, the Count, adjures the wine he is drinking: "Be thou the resolution of quick youth / Within my veins, and manhood's purpose stern, / And age's firm, cold, subtle villainy; / As if thou wert indeed my children's blood / Which I did thirst to drink!" (1.3.173-7). "He has trampled me / Under his feet, and made the blood stream down / My pallid cheeks," says the wretched Beatrice of her terrible father (2.1.64-66). Later, raped by him, she cries out, "My God! / The beautiful blue heaven is flecked with blood!" (3.1.12-13). James Wright, in his prose poem "Poppies in Trajan's Market," marvels that "[f]or once among the centuries, it is not human blood, this scattering of a wild thing among the stones of a splendid human place" (*Above the River* 275). "And today, for once, in Rome," Wright notes, "a whole week has gone by, and I have not heard of a single recent murder" (275).

The formula of the "Roman murder story" fits any number of Roman plots. "If the secrets of old Rome could be known and told, they would fill the world with books," confides Crawford, whose own efforts at Roman secret-telling fill a sizable shelf. "Every stone has tasted blood, every house has had its tragedy, every shrub and tree, and blade of grass and wild flower has sucked life from death, and blossoms on a grave" (139). Secrecy and ancient stones have an occult, gothic affinity for one another. For Eleanor Clark, Rome is "a place secret, sensuous, oblique, a poem and to be known as a poem" (23).

But if Rome is a poem, then it may naturally foster misreading. Misinterpretations abound in Roman fictions, and they are often spurred by willful deception; one misreads because one has been misled. In the imagined worlds of Rome, misty-eyed innocence again and again encounters open-eyed conspiracy and is undone by it. Such scheming ranges from the crudely physical, like the assassination of Pompilia and her parents by Count Guido and his bravos in *The Ring and the Book*, to the subtly manipulative, like Gilbert Osmond's and Serena Merle's hoodwinking of Isabel Archer in *The Portrait of a Lady*. Often, as in James's novel, conspiratorial plotting derives from events buried in the opaque past. In Davidson's *Suddenly in Rome*, the protagonist, after murdering his supposed rival Tardelli, plumes himself on having committed "a perfect crime: no eye-witnesses and a motive so rooted in ancient history it would take a team of archaeologists to unearth" (126). Yet buried Roman secrets have a way of getting unearthed, even without benefit of archaeologists. In Davidson's story the repressed material returns, and the protagonist's complacency is shattered.

This motif of recovery—of "unearthing" what has been long buried—recurs persistently in Roman narratives. Actual archaeological "finds" occur in *The Marble Faun* and in two of James's short stories: "Adina" (*Tales* Vol. 2) where the object is a priceless imperial topaz, and "The Last of the Valerii" (1874, *Tales* Vol. 2), where it is a magnificent Juno. In the latter tale, the unearthed statue comes close to wrecking a Jamesian transatlantic marriage; the moral of such a narrative is "let sleeping gods lie." Less literal manifestations of this "recovery" *topos*, in which the buried secrets of the past resurface, also abound. In Wharton's story "Roman Fever" (1934), the disclosure of an ancient love-tryst at the Colosseum puts two whole lives into a stunning new perspective.

> Rome has fallen, ye see it lying
> > Heaped in undistinguished ruin:
> Nature is alone undying.
> > (Shelley, "Fragment: Rome and Nature," *Poetical Works* 588)

That Rome is full of ruins is news to no one; but the commonplace assumes literary relevance as a metaphor for the more poignant commonplace of mortality. It was Byron who most boldly showed how poetic changes can be rung upon literal historic remains. The famous passage from *Childe Harold* about the Colosseum—"A ruin—yet what ruin!"—lies behind the many appearances of the ancient amphitheater in later poetry and fiction. Byron begins his evocation (4.143) with contrasted "takes" of the structure, the first a radiant long-shot, the second a close-up that exposes the rude evidence of decay. What comes next, the familiar advice to visit the monument by moonlight ("When the light shines serene but doth not glare, / Then in this magic circle raise the dead" [4.144]) conforms to a standard romantic assumption: night is the time when the animating poetic fancy, like a Faustian necromancer summoning the shades of the departed, is best able to transmute prosaic fact into spirit. Byron's own poetic invention soars spectacularly as the passage proceeds. Physical detail—"And the low night-breeze waves along the air / The garland-forest, which the grey walls wear / Like laurels on the bald first Caesar's head"(4.144)—serves as a piquant reminder of how mortality mocks the most triumphant human greatness. The cynical close—"these three mortal things are still / On their foundations, and unalter'd all; / Rome and her Ruin past Redemption's skill, / The World, the same wide den—of thieves, or what ye will"(4.145)—disperses moonlit revery with an alliterative jolt. But by this point, the cliché of "ruin" has absorbed new life from the shifting and unsettling moral perspectives within which it has been framed.

The moralizing of ruin is a poetic trope that novelists, too, have exploited. Dickens describes how "Little Dorrit would often ride out in a hired carriage that was left them, and alight alone and wander among the ruins of old Rome":

The ruins of the vast old Amphitheatre, of the old Temples, of the old commemorative Arches, of the old trodden highways, of the old tombs, besides being what they were, to her, were ruins of the old Marshalsea—ruins of her own old life—ruins of the faces and forms that of old peopled it—ruins of its loves, hopes, cares, and joys. Two ruined spheres of action and suffering were before the solitary girl often sitting on some broken fragment; and in the lonely places, under the blue sky, she saw them both together. (612)

The graduated shift from public past to personal reminiscence (old amphitheatre, old temples, old arches, old Marshalsea, own old life, faces and forms that of old peopled it) typifies Dickens's ability, as potent in its own way as Byron's, to transmute the daily bread of external setting into the inward substance of feeling.

In *The Waves* Bernard, who has himself begun to internalize Roman topography, seems to hear "a fatal sound of ruining worlds and waters falling to destruction" (162). In Roman narratives the motif of "ruin" is closely associated with its linguistic root, the idea of falling. The whole theme of "decline and fall" is of course, thanks above all to Gibbon, proverbially linked with Rome. Roman myth and fiction are criss-crossed by abysses, and Roman characters are chronically subject to falls, both literal and figurative. Marcus Curtius, who appeased the gods by riding fully armed into a chasm that had opened in the middle of the Forum, set a precedent for many a later Roman protagonist.

With the idea of "falling," the mode of tragedy is inescapably associated. Rome's own incorrigible habit of declining and falling makes it the home ground of the tragic. It is, in Crawford's words, "always great, always sad, always tragic, as no other city in the world can ever be" (249). To Dorothea Brooke, honeymooning forlornly amid Rome's heaped ruin, the city seems to dwarf her personal unhappiness by reflecting it back at her in a stupendous enlarging mirror. Confronted with "the city of visible history, where the past of a whole hemisphere seems moving in funeral procession with strange ancestral images and trophies gathered from afar" (224), the "little histories which made up [Dorothea's] experience" (230) dwindle into triviality.

Over and over in Roman fictions, innocence awakens, sadder if wiser, from its exposure to worldly experience; the distinguishing mistake of the Roman protagonist is biting the apple. A recurrent metaphor is that of appetite. "I gazed and gazed as if I would have drunk it all in at my eyes," records Anna Jameson of her ecstatic first view of Rome from atop the Spanish Steps (140). James's American sculptor, Roderick Hudson, entitles his early masterpiece "Thirst." The subject infallibly locates the young New Englander on the primrose way to the Eternal City. That road will lead him to fatal "falls" on the physical and moral levels alike.

In Roman fiction and poetry, tension often exists between the hunger or thirst for experience and the contrary pull of the past and of memory. Burgess in *Beard's Roman Women* dwells on the frustrations that attend the aging hero's efforts to keep on foraging for experience. Ronald Beard goes against the Roman grain by attempting to elude his personal past in the Eternal City through a liaison with a youthful Roman photographer, Paola. Meanwhile, ironically, he is composing a screenplay about Byron and the Shelleys, a shoddy tribute to the Anglo-Italian literary past. His own past literally haunts him in the bizarre form of recurrent phone calls purportedly from his deceased wife, Leonora, employing (he assumes) old tape recordings of her voice. Emotionally as well, Beard's past remains naggingly alive. Contact with Paola's youthful body alerts him to the danger of "physical nostalgia." "Dangerous to revive that past which contained a young and comely Leonora; he wanted to live in the future" (42). By the novel's conclusion, undaunted by a series of farcical reverses and the grimmer threat of an allegedly terminal illness, Beard is back in Rome. The sentence that opens the final paragraph certifies that Beard has not lost his healthy Roman appetite for experience: "Beard had a hell of a thirst on him" (155).

The Roman cup from which Ronald Beard, Roderick Hudson, and their counterparts hope to slake their thirst is no Grail. Nevertheless, drinking deep of Rome amounts to a secular initiation. Though the draught so often has a bitter smack, the city continues to draw to itself its troops of would-be initiates. "We ask in vain," says Crawford, "wherein lies the magic of the city that has fed on terror and grown old in carnage, the charm that draws men to her, the power that holds, the magic that enthralls men soul and body, as Lady Venus cast her spell upon Tannhauser in her mountain of old" (299). Rome is the supreme siren city. Even Hawthorne, about to leave, exasperated by the grim weight of the past and footsore from the detested cobblestones of the pavements, finds himself waylaid by a "strange affection" for the place:

It is very singular, the sad embrace with which Rome takes possession of the soul. Though we intend to return in a few months, and for a longer residence than this has been, yet we felt the city pulling at our heart strings far more than London did, where we shall probably never spend much time again. It may be because the intellect finds a home there, more than in any other spot in the world, and wins the heart to stay with it, in spite of a great many things strewn all about to disgust us. (*French and Italian Notebooks* 232-3)

Hawthorne's reflections signal a return along the *Via Romana* to our own starting point. Rome, whatever its things strewn about to disgust us, remains the unrivalled City of the Soul. Its rewards and impositions are as bewilderingly mingled as those of the human psyche itself—as terrifying, and as inviting. For all its associations with crime and tragedy, with confusion, deception and decay, with running blood and with frozen stone, the city has offered, to Byron and his successors, a matchless emblem of the vitality and complexity of the collective human spirit.

Rome: Church of Saint Praxed, Monument to Cardinal Alano, Bishop of Sabina (1474): Sarcophagus. Photograph reproduced courtesy of Fratelli Alinari.

15

Juxtaposition: Browning and Clough

Robert Browning and Arthur Hugh Clough, two poets as dissimilar as contemporaries could well be, were alike in one important respect: both responded with powerful originality to the idea of Rome. The city has a central position in a number of Browning's poems, among them "The Bishop Orders His Tomb at Saint Praxed's Church" (1845, *The Poems* Vol. 1), one of the most compelling of his shorter monologues, and *The Ring and the Book*, his most ambitious work. Clough's direct experience of Rome permeates his epistolary novel in verse *Amours de Voyage* (1858, *The Poems*), a performance whose imaginative use of setting deserves to be more widely recognised. Not surprisingly, the two poets' ways of treating the Roman milieu are markedly distinct in their emphasis. Browning's "reading" of the city is predominantly historical, Clough's personal and contemporary. Nevertheless, both writers show an impressive boldness in seizing upon well-thumbed Roman motifs and making them peculiarly their own. The obsession with the loom of the past and the menace of its petrifying shadow, the immersion in the densely material Roman medium, and the dubious battle to resist its downward tug—these elements assume new life in the Roman poems of both men. And the controlling term that binds those other terms together is a supremely Roman one: juxtaposition.

BROWNING'S POETRY OF ROMAN EXPERIENCE

Architectural juxtaposition presides in the ancient Roman church of Santa Prassede. It is a curious fact, however, that critics have shown scant interest in juxtaposing the actual Saint Praxed's with the drama Robert Browning set there. According to Jacob Korg, the poem "could have been written by a poet who had never been to Rome, and its connection with the actual church of Santa Prassede is altogether dispensable" (60). Several inaccuracies of detail in "The Bishop Orders His Tomb" do indeed suggest either that Browning's recall of the church was not perfect or that he exercised poetic licence in modifying some features of it—as he of course was quite entitled to do. But they hardly prove that Saint Praxed's was for Browning, as Korg claims, "an arbitrary choice." Browning's freedom in treating the building does not establish his ignorance of it, nor does his failure to mention one or another specific architectural feature rule out that feature's possible relevance.

The church as a whole has more relevance than may at first appear. It is, according to Peter Gunn, "particularly associated with these earliest days, when the Christian faithful heroically faced the brutality of their persecutors, and by their perseverance in the face of death secured the eventual triumph of their faith" (Gunn and Beny 30). "Perseverance in the face of death" is undeniably a trait of Browning's Bishop; but what triumphs in him is not the devotion of the early martyrs. His is not the faith that moves mountains but the greed that empties stone quarries. His monologue hinges on an implied, ironic contrast between Renaissance Roman decadence and the uncorrupted first Christian centuries, of which Saint Praxed's itself is a surviving testament.

One Renaissance titular of the church, Saint Charles Borromeo, "said Mass each day in the Chapel of the Flagellation, standing by the column of oriental jasper at which Christ is said to have been scourged, and he spent entire nights in prayer in the crypt" (Gunn and Beny 33). Such behavior, however, made Borromeo an exception to the rule that Browning's Bishop exemplifies. The fictional Bishop's dealings with jasper do not recall the Flagellation, and his nights have plainly not been passed in a crypt. The Roman Renaissance may have paid lip service to standards that were Augustinian and self-denying, but it was powerfully drawn in directions that were pagan and worldly. Browning's Bishop shares these pagan leanings. He is a throwback, not to the early Christian martyrs but to their profane tormentors. In his habit of gazing backwards, the Bishop recalls Browning's Andrea del Sarto; but in this Roman setting the past casts a still more portentous shadow. "What's done is done," the Bishop mutters (line 6); yet his own earlier life—his uncanonical union with his tall, pale mistress, the brood of "nephews" it produced, the rivalry, at once sexual and clerical, with his detested predecessor Gandolf—is manifestly not "done." The whole "life before I lived this life" (93) continually seeps through to the present, infecting "this life too" and clouding the future.

"Swift as a weaver's shuttle fleet our years; / Man goeth to the grave, and where is he?" (51-52). So the Bishop piously meditates; yet but one line earlier, imagining his own tomb topped off by a great blue lump of lapis lazuli, he exults that "Gandolf shall not choose but see and burst!" The juxtaposition is a pregnant one. It is the Bishop's Roman foible that, poised on eternity's brink, he can image the future only as the densely material extension of his familiar past and present. "And then how I shall lie through centuries, / And hear the blessed mutter of the mass, / And see God made and eaten all day long" (80-82). In one audacious bound he reverses the holy sacrament wherein the bread and wine are transmuted into the body and blood of Christ. His unswerving materialist vision resubstantiates a spiritual concept into a crudely physical "show."

The Bishop's Roman obduracy about time feeds his passion for that most obdurately Roman of substances, stone. Stone, for him, is the measure of all things. Not the sort of measure, however, suggested by the verses from the Apocalypse illuminated in the Saint Praxed's mosaics: "And he carried me off in a trance to a great mountain, high up, and there showed me the holy city Jerusalem. . . . The light that shone over it was bright as any precious stone, as the jasper when it is most like crystal" (Gunn 33). What precious stone measures for the Bishop is, instead, a clinging, unlawful *earthly* attachment: "Nay, boys, ye love me—all of jasper, then! / 'Tis jasper ye stand pledged to, lest I grieve / My bath must needs be left behind, alas!" (68-70). Even the mistresses he conjures up to bribe the "nephews" run true to form; they are collectable chiefly for their "great smooth marbly limbs" (75). Unlike his fellow titular, Borromeo, the Bishop aspires not to beatification but to petrifaction:

> For as I lie here, hours of the dead night,
> Dying in state and by such slow degrees,
> I fold my arms as if they clasped a crook,
> And stretch my feet forth straight as stone can point,
> And let the bedclothes, for a mortcloth, drop
> Into great laps and folds of sculptor's-work. (85-90)

The Roman clock ticks the expiring Bishop, by slow degrees, toward his coveted aesthetic "eternity."

With its presumed permanence, stone serves the Bishop as his best approximation of "Heaven." Yet because it is in actual fact corruptible, stone can approximate for him the less desirable alternative, as well: "Stone— / Gritstone, a-crumble! Clammy squares which sweat / As if the corpse they keep were oozing through" (115-7). The substance acquires overtones of conspiracy and cloaked malfeasance, invoking the Roman motif of "unearthing": "Go dig / The white-grape vineyard where the oil-press stood," he tells his sons,

> Drop water gently till the surface sink,
> And if ye find . . . Ah God, I know not, I! . . .
> Bedded in store of rotten fig-leaves soft,
> And corded up in a tight olive-frail,
> Some lump, ah God, of *lapis lazuli*. . . .(38-42)

The "lump" symbolizes the whole buried mass of his past indiscretions, such as his involvement in "that conflagration of my church" (34). His trespasses have been bedded in the rotten fig-leaves of euphemism and evasion.

The wrapping of precious stone in rotten leaves sums up the incongruities that compose the Bishop's character. Such juxtapositions emerge, above all, in the fantastic tomb his dying words commission. Heaping one decorative detail upon another, his fantasy swells into the prodigious material embodiment of his split sensibility. The profligate cleric possesses, if not cloven hooves, a cloven mind, and the fissure runs along predictable Roman lines. It emerges in the naked disjunction between the moral maxims he mouths and the sensual impulses by which he has lived. It culminates in the bronze bas-relief he complacently sketches:

> Those Pans and Nymphs ye wot of, and perchance
> Some tripod, thyrsus, with a vase or so,
> The Saviour at his sermon on the mount,
> Saint Praxed in a glory, and one Pan
> Ready to twitch the Nymph's last garment off,
> And Moses with the tables . . . . (57-62)

Prurient pagan *dishabille* sorts oddly with the decalogue and the precepts of Jesus; but such clashes do not perturb the Bishop. A thoroughgoing apostle of the Roman Renaissance eclectic mode, he makes inclusiveness his sole object. Moral consistency is not *comme il faut*.

Ultimately, the Bishop's fantasized monument is but a further, futile projection of his entire life history. That life history has evinced not pagan joy but a schizoid incoherence and a stony, joyless stasis. The gloating unction with which the Bishop closes is belied by his verbs, which are, like so many of Andrea del Sarto's, in the past tense:

> And leave me in my church, the church for peace,
> That I may watch at leisure if he leers—
> Old Gandolf, at me, from his onion-stone,
> As still he *envied* me, so fair she *was*. (122-5, emphasis added)

The Bishop's hatred and lust are as unalterably fixed as the all-too-Roman stone memorial he vainly projects. They are his true, and enduring, monument.

> *Occidit*, and he killed them here in Rome,
> *In Urbe*, the Eternal City, Sirs. (*Ring* 8.1671-2)

The words of the learned procurator Dominus Hyacinthus de Archangelis are for once to the purpose. The work that Browning liked to call his "murder poem" has, like so many Roman narratives, the shedding of blood as its pivotal event. That event itself occurs in Rome, but more generally the action shuttles back and forth between Rome and the Tuscan city of Arezzo. This divided focus forms only one among the numerous sets of contraries by which the work progresses. As Richard Altick and James Loucks observe, "[T]he total thematic movement of the poem . . . embraces a series of religious antitheses or polarities: law *vs.* Gospel, letter *vs.* spirit, old *vs.* new dispensation, old *vs.* new Adam, fall *vs.* salvation" (197).   Many of these polarities are summed up in the key juxtaposition of the Aretine murderer, Guido, with his Roman victim, Pompilia.

"My blood / Comes from as far a source [as yours]," Guido challenges the Tuscan aristocrats who make a last-minute visit to his cell: "ought it to end / This way, by leakage through their scaffold-planks / Into Rome's sink where her red refuse runs?" (11.15-18). Guido has been, to quote William Buckler, "an alien Tuscan trying to adapt to mysterious Roman ways" (105). Yet the ways of blood-stained Rome are not altogether mysterious to Guido the red-handed. Despite his plea that his Aretine blood is too dear for Roman sewers, he has rated the blood of others cheaply enough. Indeed, the medium wherein Guido lives is blood, that intensely Roman element; "hot bull's blood," he brags, is the sustenance "fit for men like me" (11.2409). Pompilia, who abhors such sustenance, can only exult at being released by a divorce Roman style from her bloodthirsty mate. The shedding of her own blood mystically wipes the slate of her life clean, releasing her from a world that men like Guido defile:

> Himself this way at least pronounced divorce,
> Blotted the marriage-bond: this blood of mine
> Flies forth exultingly at any door,
> Washes the parchment white, and thanks the blow. (7.1716-8)

A murder story is commonly a mystery. In *The Ring and the Book*, the killer's identity is plain; it is his moral inwardness that needs to be detected. What confuses the issue is the ethical mixedness of the Roman scene of the crime. Even in Giuseppe Caponsacchi's ecclesiastical sphere, priestly submission needs to be rounded out by a mastery of the pagan classics. A superior, advising the young priest on how to prepare himself for Rome, "the eventual harbour" of a successful career, tells him:

> Now go do duty: brisk, break Priscian's head
> By reading the day's office—there's no help.
> You've Ovid in your poke to plaster that;
> Amen's at the end of all: then sup with me! (6.389-92)

Such counsel would doubtless please the Bishop of Saint Praxed's, in whose mind "office" and "Ovid" have become interchangeable. Yet Ovid—as author of the *Metamorphoses* rather than the *Ars Amatoris*—makes no bad guide even for a more honestly devout priest, like Caponsacchi. "If the world of the poem is one of illusion, it is equally one of change," observe Altick and Loucks. "Man's existence . . . is marked by ceaseless instability of forms and appearances" (102).

It is Rome, the endlessly mutable, that provides the great theater for the operation of change, a force with which all the major characters must contend.

Already as a child, Pompilia is identified by a playmate as Daphne undergoing Berninian metamorphosis: "'—And there are you, Pompilia, such green leaves / Flourishing out of your five finger-ends, / And all the rest of you so brown and rough: / Why is it you are turned a sort of tree?'" (7.193-6). For Pompilia, such instability has governed the whole course of her life:

> I touch a fairy thing that fades and fades.
> —Even to my babe! I thought, when he was born,
> Something began for once that would not end,
> Nor change into a laugh at me, but stay
> For evermore, eternally quite mine. (7.201-5)

Even a daughter of the Eternal City, she discovers, can possess nothing that deserves truly to be called everlasting.

Pompilia's husband, Guido, unlike the worldly Bishop of Saint Praxed's, is capable of imagining a "life beyond this life." Yet he is no nearer salvation than the Bishop, for his vision of the next world is ferociously unChristian:

> Only, be sure, no punishment, no pain
> Childish, preposterous, impossible,
> But some such fate as Ovid could foresee,—
> *Byblis in fluvium*, let the weak soul end
> In water, *sed Lycaon in lupum*, but
> The strong become a wolf for evermore!
> Change that Pompilia to a puny stream
> Fit to reflect the daisies on its bank!
> Let me turn wolf, be whole, and sate, for once,—
> Wallow in what is now a wolfishness
> Coerced too much by the humanity
> That's half of me as well! (11.2046-57)

Guido, too, has Ovid in his poke. Despising Christian notions of heaven and hell, he ransacks the master of metamorphosis for fantasies of suitable pagan reincarnation. At bottom, however, Guido's nature, like the Bishop's, repudiates change, a fact of which he boasts:

> Cardinal, take away your crucifix!
> Abate, leave my lips alone, they bite!
> 'Tis vain you try to change, what should not change,
> And cannot. I have bared, you bathe my heart—
> It grows the stonier for your saving dew!
> You steep the substance, you would lubricate,
> In waters that but touch to petrify! (11.2219-25)

Guido, again like the Bishop, can be "transformed" only into the changeless, stony effigy of himself. He looks forward to retaining in the afterlife "something changeless at the heart of me / To know me by, some nucleus that's myself"; meanwhile, in this world, "All that was, is; and must for ever be. / Nor is it in me to unhate my hates" (11.2392-3, 2397-8). Pompilia, by contrast, is constitutionally open to change. Her discovery of her pregnancy is an epiphanic moment dramatizing the *expectancy* that defines her entire nature:

> Up I sprang alive,
> Light in me, light without me, everywhere
> Change! . . .
> My heart sang, "I too am to go away,
> I too have something I must care about,
> Carry away with me to Rome, to Rome! (7.1223-5, 1237-9)

Like the child she carries in her womb, the Rome she carries in her head signifies fruitfulness. For her, Rome is a city of promise and gestation, not of inert, monochromatic stone. In her modest sphere, she aims her life at the trans-Ovidian "gloriously-decisive change, / The immeasurable metamorphosis / Of human clay to divine gold" in which the far-seeing Pope Innocent places his trust (10.1614-6).

Like other Roman narratives, *The Ring and the Book* hinges on the tension between the temporal and the eternal. Pompilia on her deathbed, breathlessly cognizant of both dimensions, counts the minutes separating her from Eternity. The proverb "swift as a weaver's shuttle fleet our years" (51), for the Bishop of Saint Praxed's a mere maxim to be mouthed, is for her the simple truth. Circumstances have afflicted the girl with that worst form of Roman penury, a dearth of available time. Nevertheless, she is determined to invest wisely the slender capital she possesses. She regrets that, having "a whole day to live out" (7.84), she is incapable of writing down her thoughts for her son to read in later years. "In a life like mine," she touchingly observes, "[a] fortnight filled with bliss is long and much" (7.1681-2).

Guido, too, has been harried by time's winged Roman chariot, but in a different guise. "Brief, one day I felt / The tick of time inside me" (5.342-3)—so he explains his quirk of marrying in middle age. His "creed's one article" is "'Get pleasure, 'scape pain,—give your preference / To the immediate good, for time is brief, / And death ends good and ill and everything'" (11.768-70). Such hedonism, listening obsessively to "the tick of time inside," ignores other, supernal clocks. It shuns Pompilia's achieved consciousness of "God's instant men call years" (7.1841). The tick-tock of Guido's inward clock spells destruction rather than creation; and when he decides on the ruse of surprising his fugitive wife at the Comparini's house in Rome, its latent horror is made manifest:

> At once,
> Silence: then, scratching like a death-watch tick,
> Slowly within my brain was syllabled,
> "One more concession, one decisive way
> And but one, to determine thee the truth." (5.1612-6)

Pompilia comes to perceive this present world, epitomized by Rome, as a slippery stepping-stone to the next. For Guido, this world is the be-all and end-all; and it is grimly appropriate that the Pope should "demand / That his poor sole remaining piece of time / Be plucked from out his clutch" (10.197-9). And Guido does end up "clutching" at time. "'Tis I preach while the hourglass runs and runs,'" he confides wryly during his deathwatch (11.1518).

Giuseppe Caponsacchi, whose role in this Roman story exposes him to jolting changes, undergoes a seismic shift in his own orientation vis-à-vis time. On the brink of his decision to rescue Pompilia from her hell with Guido in Arezzo, he finds himself turning from the flinty stasis of scholastic theology to the kinetic truth of human need:

> So, I went home. Dawn broke, noon broadened, I—
> I sat stone-still, let time run over me.
> The sun slanted into my room, had reached
> The west. I opened book,—Aquinas blazed
> With one black name only on the white page.
> I looked up, saw the sunset: vespers rang:
> "She counts the minutes till I keep my word
> And come say all is ready." (6.1022-9)

Pompilia's own sense of time's urgency awakens the young priest from his stony passiveness. "And thus," he goes on, "Through each familiar hindrance of the day / Did I make steadily for its hour and end— / Felt time's old barrier-growth of right and fit / Give way through all its twines, and let me go" (6.1124-8). On the night appointed for their escape to Rome, Pompilia comes into view "when the ecstatic minute must bring birth" (6.1128)—even Caponsacchi's metaphor reflects the pregnant, ardent girl's redemptive influence.

The young priest's smooth urbanity is, through a paradoxical Roman juxtaposition, ravished by the innocence of Guido's child-wife. In the marriage between Guido and Pompilia, the characteristic Roman extremes of innocence and experience are again juxtaposed, but to grimmer effect. The question Guido's bride imagines her "friends" posing—"'Why, you Pompilia in the cavern thus, / How comes that arm of yours about a wolf?'" (7.124-5)—sums up the horror of the mismating chillingly, all the more because Pompilia herself is persistently identified as a lamb. As for Guido, his very existence mocks the Roman emblem of the wolf as mystic nurturer. He scoffs at the triumph of the lamb ethos—the Christianizing of Roman paganism—as a mere passing suppression of the living Pan by the forces arrayed against life. He justifies his own deceit by pointing to the hypocrisy that Christianity has imposed on all the world around him:

> I, like the rest, wrote "poison" on my bread;
> But broke and ate:—said "those that use the sword
> Shall perish by the same;" then stabbed my foe.
> I stand on solid earth, not empty air. (11.2003-6)

For Guido, that devout materialist, the air is indeed "empty"; whereas Pompilia, rejoicing over her pregnancy, spontaneously envisages the air as a densely life-sustaining medium: "A broad yellow sun-beam was let fall / From heaven to earth,—a sudden drawbridge lay, / Along which marched a myriad merry motes" (7.1225-7). Pompilia, responding with all the force of her nature to earthly ties, gains thereby the freedom to march up a luminous drawbridge to heaven. It is her capacity to do so that stamps her as redeemed.

So, too, does her capacity to cleanse herself of the soilure of her own past, a capacity that Guido lacks. Not only is Guido "Unable to repent one particle / O' the past" (11.944-5), he is also fixated upon the ancient, fabulous roots of his family tree:

> I boast myself Etruscan, Aretine,
> One sprung,—your frigid Virgil's fieriest word,—
> From fauns and nymphs, trunks and the heart of oak,
> With,—for a visible divinity,—
> The portent of a Jove Aegiochus
> Descried 'mid clouds, lightning and thunder, couched
> On topmost crag of your Capitoline. (11.1919-25)

His Etruscan antecedents hand him down his mantle of "a primitive religionist" (11.1917). For Browning, who was no D. H. Lawrence, such a clutching of the dim Etruscan past bespeaks a willed regression to barbarity.

Pompilia's relation to the past bespeaks, by contrast, her essential civility. History, that great Roman element, comes obliquely to have on her an ennobling influence; by making peace with her own small portion of it, she is empowered to transcend it. Giving an account of her life to Caponsacchi, she tells the priest that her marriage to Guido has in effect despoiled her memory, "Burning not only present life but past, / Which you might think was safe beyond his reach" (6.780-1). Early in her monologue, thinking of her son Gaetano's future knowledge of her history, she mourns that history's obliteration: "But then how far away, how hard to find / Will anything about me have become, / Even if the boy bethink himself and ask!" (7.88-90). Yet she goes on to reflect, "On second thoughts, I hope he will regard / The history of me as what someone dreamed, / And get to disbelieve it at the last" (7.108-10); and this new willingness to relinquish the past, to accept Roman changes, marks a crucial moment in her spiritual progress. "It comes, most like, that I am just absolved, / Purged of the past, the foul in me, washed fair" (7.351-2), she muses; and adds, "To me at least was never evening yet / But seemed far beautifuller than its day, / For past is past" (7.357-9). Having come to terms with her history, she can at last contemplate it dispassionately: "Begin the task, I see how needful now, / Of understanding somewhat of my past,— / Know life a little, I should leave so soon" (7.1664-6). The selfless devotion of one man, Caponsacchi, has given her "foretaste too / Of better life beginning where this ends" (11.1679-80). Through knowing the priest, she learns to give a Christian sense to the Socratic precept "Know thyself."

Pompilia's scanning of her past for its redemptive power has a parallel in the larger reclamation that Browning himself accomplishes through the act of narrating his Roman murder story. By wedding imagination to historical truth, the poet performs a rite of resurrection:

> Yet, something dead may get to live again,
> Something with too much life or not enough,
> Which, either way imperfect, ended once:
> An end whereat man's impulse intervenes,
> Makes new beginning, starts the dead alive,
> Completes the incomplete, and saves the thing. (1.729-34)

The entire poem, therefore, while it originates in the "criminal record" and deals extensively in Roman "ruin," finally takes a sacramental turn. Early on, the poet describes his narrative's "round from Rome to Rome" as "the tragic piece"; Rome itself he calls "the ghastly goal" (1.526, 1.523, 1.518). Yet the tormented Rome over which Innocent presides is more than just ghastly, and the "goal" toward which the whole work tends is the City of God, for which the Eternal City serves as a way station. It is, most dramatically, in the experience of Caponsacchi that the poem's shift in dominant direction from tragic "falling" to creative "rising" is enacted. That shift makes itself felt in the very diction and structure of Caponsacchi's monologue; as W. David Shaw demonstrates, "With his conversion to Pompilia's cause, his very rhetoric undergoes 'conversion'" (279).

Caponsacchi's inward pilgrimage begins when, frustrated by his effete life in Guido's narrow, Etruscan Arezzo, he considers "turning Christian" and seeking the grander horizons of Rome: "This your Arezzo is a limited world," he tells his patron; "There's a strange Pope,—'tis said, a priest who thinks. / Rome is the port, you say: to Rome I go" (6.477-9). Only now, contemplating the downward tendency of his career so far, does he realize "into what abysm the soul may slip" (6.488). Rome, so often the locus of "falling," becomes for the priest the final goal of his upward surge. Exalted by the "Spring" of Pompilia's trust in him, he envisions himself "soaring" in a swift translation to the heavens:

> In rushed new things, the old were rapt away;
> Alike abolished—the imprisonment
> Of the outside air, the inside weight o' the world
> That pulled me down. Death meant, to spurn the ground,
> Soar to the sky,—die well and you do that. (6.948-52)

Next morning, he seems to hear his own church, the superb Pieve of Arezzo, rebuking him for his all-too-human ecstasy:

> "But am not I the Bride, the mystic love
> O' the Lamb, who took thy plighted troth, my priest,
> To fold thy warm heart on my heart of stone
> And freeze thee nor unfasten any more?
> This is a fleshly woman,—let the free
> Bestow their life-blood, thou art pulseless now!" (6.977-82)

But as the precedent of the Bishop of Saint Praxed's suggests, the gateway to heaven is not built of stone—not even of consecrated stone. In his ascent, even a priest cannot leave the life-blood of human affection behind. Pompilia may, like the Bishop's quondam mistress, be tall and pale, and her eyes may even talk; but they do not glitter for Caponsacchi's soul—they save it. What she says of Caponsacchi in her dying words he might as easily say of her: "Through such souls alone / God stooping shows sufficient of His light / For us i' the dark to rise by. And I rise" (7.1843-5). She herself, rising, has taken Caponsacchi with her; she "completes the incomplete, and saves the thing." The priest's flight with her to Rome has itself been "converted" from profane, galloping getaway to sacred ascension. Meanwhile, it is Guido, the deep-rooted ancient Etruscan, whose soul has slipped irrevocably down into a bottomless Roman abyss.

"AND WHAT IS JUXTAPOSITION?": CLOUGH'S ROMAN *AMOURS*

> *Is it an idol I bow to, or is it a god that I worship?*
> *Do I sink back on the old, or do I soar from the mean? (Amours de Voyage 1.281-2, The Poems).*

Claude, the protagonist of Clough's *Amours de Voyage*, confronts Roman questions similar to those faced by the principal figures of *The Ring and the Book*. He must choose between idolatry and true worship, between sinking and soaring, between a fixation on the past and liberation from it. Like Browning's Caponsacchi, Clough's young Englishman on tour is urbane, intellectual, and ascetic; but he undergoes a Roman moral odyssey that is more circuitous and less conclusive. He, too, must come to grips with the problem of human attachments, but within a context where personal relationship is not defined by Christian belief. His pilgrimage to Rome opens a door not to self-redemption but, at most, to fragmentary self-discovery.

Discovery, for Claude, begins in disillusionment: "Rome disappoints me much,—St. Peter's, perhaps, in especial" (1.13), he writes, soon after his arrival, to his correspondent Eustace. A chronic defeatist, he is at first overwhelmed by the weight of the age-old Roman mountain of heaped-up failures:

> Somehow a tyrannous sense of a superincumbent oppression
> Still, wherever I go, accompanies ever, and makes me
> Feel like a tree (shall I say?) buried under a ruin of brick-work.
> Rome, believe me, my friend, is like its own Monte Testaceo,
> Merely a marvellous mass of broken and castaway wine-pots.
> Ye gods! what do I want with this rubbish of ages departed,
> Things that Nature abhors, the experiments that she has failed in? (1.36-42)

Although he does not yet suspect it, Rome is to be the scene of Claude's own hesitant experiment with life. At first, however, he sees the city merely as time's dustheap, inimical to his enlightened Victorian belief in "progress," both personal and historical. What most disturbs him about the Roman heap is its indiscriminateness, which strikes an exposed nerve: his latent dread of the random, "factitious," non-providential nature of life. As Robindra Kumar Biswas observes, Claude's mind is "trapped in and isolated by its awareness of miscellaneousness and indeterminacy" (311).

It is precisely the promiscuousness of Roman juxtaposition that causes the young traveller, initially, to recoil:

> All the foolish destructions, and all the sillier savings,
> All the incongruous things of past incompatible ages,
> Seem to be treasured up here to make fools of present and future.
> Would to Heaven the old Goths had made a cleaner sweep of it!
> Would to Heaven some new ones would come and destroy these churches!
> (1.21-25)

Juxtaposition is not only the central concern of *Amours de Voyage* but its controlling structural principle. Clough's placement of one letter next to another produces both comedy and insight; thus, Claude's exploratory Roman musings are thrust up against Georgina Trevellyn's dimity tourist banalities—"Here we all are at Rome, and delighted of course with St. Peter's, / And very pleasantly lodged in the famous Piazza di Spagna" (1.54-55). The two young English tourists are, one quickly grasps, visiting two altogether different Romes.

Claude's Rome, at least, is charged with a grandeur that eludes genteel commonplaces, but such grandeur is something Claude himself comes only gradually to perceive. The lines that open Canto II intimate the stirring in him of a shift toward a more charitable view of the Roman scene: "*Is it illusion? or does there a spirit from perfecter ages, / Here, even yet, amid loss, change, and corruption abide?*" The reversal of Claude's attitude begins backhandedly: "Rome is better than London, because it is other than London" (1.27). For the young Englishman, the ancient city paradoxically represents an escape from the past, and especially from fixed concepts of one's self:

> All the *assujettissement* of having been what one has been,
> What one thinks one is, or thinks that others suppose one. (1.30-31)

It is a place, then, that frees one from the Prufrockian compulsion to prepare a face to meet the faces that one meets. During the weeks he passes there, Rome will call upon Claude to try on several unaccustomed faces. He becomes, in turn, the investigator of antiquity and his own cultural roots; the attentive but awkward lover; the semi-engaged witness of political upheaval. His Roman itineraries lead him from diligent sight-seeing to self-exploration.

Most immediately, the city thrusts him up against the Trevellyns, a family belonging to a class with which he does not normally rub his well-connected shoulders: "Middle-class people these, bankers very likely, not wholly / Pure of the taint of the shop" (1.125-6). Although his acquaintance with the family is, as he reflects, "only juxtaposition," he soon finds, to his surprise,

> That for the first time in life I am living and moving with freedom.
> I, who never could talk to the people I meet with my uncle,—
> I, who have always failed,—I, trust me, can suit the Trevellyns. (1.216-8)

With some alarm, he observes himself succumbing to the Roman compulsion to mix: "Fusing with this thing and that, entering into all sorts of relations" (1.229).

Such Roman mixing, predictably, aggravates the chronic mixedness of Claude's own feelings. His epistolary style, roundabout and studied at best, becomes even more so. In Letter XII of Canto I, he rationalizes his growing intimacy with the mercantile Trevellyns by spinning out a convoluted metaphor of descent and ascent: "Lo, with the rope on my loins I descend through the fissure; I sink, yet / Inly secure in the strength of invisible arms up above me" (1.242-3). He concludes confident that, even should he tumble into entanglements,

> ere the end I
> Yet shall plant firm foot on the broad lofty spaces I quit, shall
> Feel underneath me again the great massy strengths of abstraction. (1.249-51)

Despite his tone of assurance, the "great massy strengths" Claude counts on lack emotional substance. His metaphorical stone is no more trustworthy a prop than the Bishop of Saint Praxed's literal jasper and basalt.

Abstraction turns out, in fact, to be just what the peremptory voice of the Roman milieu will *not* permit Claude to take refuge in. Instead, it compels him to confront a more immediate problem: how to "reconcile Ancient and Modern" (1.200)—the historical and the contemporary—in his own personal life. The contemporary presents itself in two guises: the political struggle to protect the new-born Roman Republic against its French attackers, and Claude's dawning interest in Mary Trevellyn. The epilogue to Canto II hints that Claude has begun to make antiquarian pursuits serve as a shield against involvement in current events—"Seeking from clamour of arms in the Past and the Arts to be hidden, / Vainly 'mid Arts and the Past seeking one life to forget" (1.341-2). Claude is, in effect, being offered two types of Roman "engagement," the martial and the marital, which through Clough's use of suggestion become subtly interfused in the reader's mind. (Some suppressed lines from Canto II make the point more boldly; in them, Claude declares himself tempted to "Enter the great bridal bed of the combat and conflict of men" [*Poems* 627].)

The outbreak of fighting surprises the aloof Claude into patriotic involvement: "I, who nor meddle nor make in politics . . . Could in my soul of souls, this day, with the Gaul at the gates, shed / One true tear for thee, thou poor little Roman republic!" (2.16, 2.21-22). The sentiment seems inspired more by his reading of Caesar than by real passion for republican principles, and a tear is all he is prepared to shed. Still, when the citizens defy prudence and man their barricades, his allegiance to the eternal Rome wavers in the face of the sudden, suspect charm of the temporal one: "Alas! 'tis ephemeral folly, / Vain and ephemeral folly, of course, compared with pictures, / Statues, and antique gems!" (2.54-56), he deprecatingly assures his correspondent, Eustace—and himself.

As Canto II proceeds, Claude, who does "not like being moved," becomes, in several senses, mentally "mobilized." In Letter V he recounts how, guidebook in hand, he goes to breakfast in a cafe, "thinking mostly of Murray, / And, for to-day is their day, of the Campidoglio Marbles" (2.98-99). Military developments, however, make short work of his plans; instead of spending his day contemplating a marble repose, he finds himself witnessing a parade of flickering kinetic images:

Smoke, from the cannon, white,—but that is at intervals only,— . . .
And we believe we discern some lines of men descending
Down through the vineyard-slopes, and catch a bayonet gleaming. (2.117, 2.119-20)

A letter that would normally have been an account of a dutiful antiquarian's Roman round turns into a sheaf of hour-by-hour dispatches from the Front:

"Twelve o'clock, on the Pincian Hill. . . . Half-past one, or two. The report of small arms frequent" (2.113, 2.130). Similarly, in Letter VII an intended tour of monuments turns into a nervous patrol, this time with more disturbing results. "So, I have seen a man killed! An experience that, among others!" (2.162), Claude begins with assumed offhandedness; but what follows makes it apparent that this Roman "experience" has hit home.

Exposure to scenes of public violence causes a fundamental shift in Claude's temporal orientation, detaching his thoughts from the settled Roman past and training them on the turbulent Roman present. "[R]eturning home from St. Peter's; Murray, as usual, / Under my arm" (2.167-8), Claude observes the murder of a turncoat priest. Once again, we see the monumental-meditative mode give way to the kinetic. "Gradually, thinking still of St. Peter's, I became conscious / Of a sensation of movement opposing me" (2.170-1). Switching his discourse pointedly from the past into the present tense, Claude focuses cinematically on the "bare swords" of the outraged crowd:

> They descend; they are smiting,
> Hewing, chopping—At what? In the air once more upstretched! And
> Is it blood that's on them? Yes, certainly blood! Of whom, then? (2.183-5)

The bloodless connoisseur of placid basilicas stumbles upon the Roman reality of bloodshed, and his very syntax becomes breathless under the shock. From an unscholarly angle, he glimpses a sight not included in his eternal guidebook: "Passing away from the place with Murray under my arm, and / Stooping, I saw through the legs of the people the legs of a body" (2.196-7). He concludes his report to Eustace by describing his arrival, at last, at "the great Coliseum, / Which at the full of the moon, is an object worthy a visit" (2.215-6). Amusingly, though Claude professes to detest Byron, the stress of Roman experience drives him to Byronic commonplaces.

Beyond the battle for Rome itself, then, a battle between Rome the Immortal and Rome the immediate and fleeting is raging in Claude's mind. The exact relevance of that inner conflict to Claude's moral coming-of-age is, however, open to interpretation. According to Biswas,

[U]nderlying this undetermined Rome of present political violence, there is another Rome felt as an organic presence— Rome as the Eternal City, the seat of civilization, the embodiment of achievement and culture, where the tides of history have been stilled into the poised and mythic tranquillity of art. The evidences of this Rome are everywhere and they bring memories of wholeness and of meaningful continuities which mock the perspiring, inchoate, distracted, and dislocated present. (312)

To read Clough's irony in this antiquarian sense is surely to leap to an unwarranted conclusion. It is, after all, precisely the perspiring Roman present that, by forcing Claude's gaze away from bygone Roman grandeur, causes him to become for once *less* distracted and dislocated. He begins to relinquish his habit of measuring "inchoate" patriotism against the cool, monumental standards of aesthetic tranquillity. He suddenly finds it possible to speak of the Roman populace with unaccustomed warmth:

> Ah, 'tis an excellent race,—and even in old degradation
> Under a rule that enforces to flattery, lying, and cheating,
> E'en under Pope and Priest, a nice and natural people.
> Oh, could they but be allowed this chance of redemption! (2. 243-6)

The epithet with which Clough had wryly inscribed one of his own letters from besieged Republican Rome—"A. H. C. Le citoyen malgré lui" (*Correspondence* 1:264)— exactly captures the role that Claude now surprises himself by assuming.

An equally startling accompaniment to all this is Claude's growing fondness for the mercantile Trevellyns. In his courtship of the modest but perceptive Mary Trevellyn, Claude is a lover even more awkwardly *malgré lui*. Here, where he needs to be more than just a vigilant observer, he shrinks from the field of battle:

> I do not like being moved: for the will is excited; and action
> Is a most dangerous thing; I tremble for something factitious,
> Some malpractice of heart and illegitimate process. (2.270-2)

He has not yet absorbed the truth contained in that hoariest of Roman proverbs, *tempus fugit*:

> Ah, let me look, let me watch, let me wait, unhurried, unprompted!
> Bid me not venture on aught that could alter or end what is present!
> Say not, Time flies, and Occasion, that never returns, is departing! (2.274-6)

In his idealistic, visionary attitude toward love, there is a damning touch of the leisured voyeur: a malpractice of eye and head.

Mary Trevellyn's departure from Rome finally melts Claude's romantic inertia ("She goes,—therefore I go; she moves,—I move, not to lose her" [2.289]). Inwardly, however, he still temporizes. The introduction to Canto III suggests that the static perfection of art and antiquity retains its powerful grasp upon Claude, offering him a self-contained refuge from the stress of emotional entanglement:

> *yet to the Vatican walls,*
> *Yet may we go, and recline, while a whole mighty world seems above us*
> *Gathered and fixed for all time into one roofing supreme.* (3.2-4)

"He talked of the Vatican marbles," Mary perplexedly explains Claude's decision not to accompany the Trevellyns on their further travels. The metaphor she applies to Claude's behavior—"She that should love him must look for small love in return,—like the ivy / On the stone wall, must expect but a rigid and niggard support" (3.37-38)—hits off all too truthfully the affinity that exists between the stones of Rome and her ungiving suitor. Frightened by his growing, unplanned attachment, Claude clings to Roman stone as a defence against the threat of erotic invasion.

"Ah, good Heaven, but I would I were out far away from the pother!" (3.78), Claude is driven to exclaim. He is speaking of Roman politics, but his words might apply equally to the "pother" of sexual skirmishing. He engages in a rhetorically ingenious attempt at self-persuasion, designed to demolish marriage as a tenable life-choice:

> Juxtaposition, in fine; and what is juxtaposition?
> Look you, we travel along in the railway-carriage, or steamer,
> And, *pour passer le temps*, till the tedious journey be ended,
> Lay aside paper or book, to talk with the girl that is next one;
> And, *pour passer le temps*, with the terminus all but in prospect,
> Talk of eternal ties and marriages made in heaven. (3.107-12)

What Claude rejects here is the idea that life's haphazard collisions should regulate one's personal destiny. What he insists on, instead, is "a perfect and absolute something" ideally suited to one's individual nature. At bottom, it is a great Roman principle that he is rejecting: the tolerance of *mélange*, the welcoming of those motley experiences that time tosses in one's path with blind liberality. Ultimately, he is slamming the door on all possibility of personal fulfillment within this time-bound, Roman carnival of a world.

As might have been expected, Claude's revolt against crass temporality issues in an acute fit of Roman time-sickness:

> *HANG* this thinking, at last! what good is it? oh, and what evil!
> Oh, what mischief and pain! like a clock in a sick man's chamber,
> Ticking and ticking, and still through each covert of slumber pursuing. (3.207-9)

The ticking of the Roman clock seems, at the eleventh hour, to have penetrated Claude's consciousness. He at last opts for the human and topical as against the classical and storied:

> Tibur I have not seen, nor the lakes that of old I had dreamt of;
> Tibur I shall not see, nor Anio's waters, nor deep en-
> Folded in Sabine recesses the valley and villa of Horace;
> Tibur I shall not see;—but something better I shall see. (3.287-90).

Following the Trevellyns' touristic traces, he now becomes involved— inevitably
—in a race against time. Accordingly, he launches into yet another round of up-
to-the-minute "dispatches from the front." "Five days now departed," he reports
from Florence, "but they can travel but slowly" (4.13). He resolves to pursue
them: "Why, what else should I do? Stay here and look at the pictures, /
Statues, and churches? Alack, I am sick of the statues and pictures!" (4.15-16).
A chastened Nero, he suddenly repents his "fiddle-faddling" while the Roman
flame of passion was burning.

But with Claude, repentance is no guarantee of action. Finding the
Trevellyns not readily traceable, he consoles himself with eloquent self-
condemnation. His metaphors hit the mark only too damagingly:

> I, who believed not in her, because I would fain believe nothing,
> Have to believe as I may, with a wilful, unmeaning acceptance.
> I, who refused to enfasten the roots of my floating existence
> In the rich earth, cling now to the hard, naked rock that is left me. (5.64-67)

Claude has learned the worth of the earthy Roman promiscuousness celebrated
by Clough in "Resignation: To Faustus": "The stem that bears the ethereal flower
. . . / From mixtures fetid foul and sour / Draws juices that those petals fill" (47,
49-50). And yet, ironically, the very accuracy of his self-disparagement becomes
itself a paralyzing pretext for surrender: "I am a coward, and know it. / Courage
in me could be only factitious, unnatural, useless" (5.84-85).

Viewed within the wider Roman panorama of ruin, Claude's personal
retreat from the field appears to be merely a minor disaster. The collapse of his
romantic hopes is overshadowed even in his own eyes by the concurrent fall of
the Roman Republic:

> Rome is fallen, I hear, the gallant Medici taken,
> Noble Manara slain, and Garibaldi has lost il Moro;—
> Rome is fallen; and fallen, or falling, heroical Venice.
> I, meanwhile, for the loss of a single small chit of a girl, sit
> Moping and mourning here,—for her, and myself much smaller. (5.113-7)

But Claude, swinging from one extreme to another, is here putting juxtaposition
to uses that are both self-minimizing and self-serving. He finds a pallid
consolation in the thought that his mental images of the great Roman monuments
have remained fresh, even if his image of that "single small chit," Mary
Trevellyn, is fading:

> After all, do I know that I really cared so about her?
> Do whatever I will, I cannot call up her image;
> For when I close my eyes, I see, very likely, St. Peter's,
> Or the Pantheon facade, or Michel Angelo's figures. . .

> But that face, those eyes,—ah no, never anything like them. (5.156-9,161)

His epitaph on his great love affair relegates it to the dustbin of mere "history," making it a fit subject for his endless previsions and revisions: "It is a curious history, this; and yet I foresaw it" (5.171).

Claude's epitaph on Rome itself reverts sadly to his very first, dismissive impressions: "Rome will not suit me, Eustace; the priests and soldiers possess it" (5.186). Forgetting the vital, temporal Rome that once seduced him into engagement on several fronts, he dwells reductively upon a Rome that is "eternal" only in its unending round of trivialities:

> No, happen whatever may happen,
> Time, I suppose, will subsist; the earth will revolve on its axis;
> People will travel; the stranger will wander as now in the city;
> Rome will be here, and the Pope the *custode* of Vatican marbles. (5.190-3)

Public events have, admittedly, gone far toward justifying Claude's final tone of disillusionment. Yet cynicism is at all times the most convenient *pis aller* for Claude; it takes little to deflect him from the rough course of hand-to-hand combat with life. Having exhausted love and politics, he now shrugs off even Roman sight seeing.

Since "Rome will not do . . . for many very good reasons," Claude settles on a new historical trajectory: "Eastward, then, I suppose, with the coming of winter, to Egypt" (5.204-5). Amid the stony remains of an older civilization even than Rome's, the spontaneous life of his emotions may well be forever mummified. Having failed in his Roman attempt to "soar from the mean," he is now preparing to sink back halfheartedly on the old.

For Clough's protagonist, as for Browning's Pompilia and Caponsacchi, Rome poses the critical test of character. Despite the profound differences between them, the two poets frame that test in broadly similar terms. To pass, one must risk "falling" into the Roman realm of experience; only then can one hope to "soar" through energetic involvement in the living moment and in human relatedness. To fail means to lapse into stony imprisonment within the walls of the ego and the unliving past. Nathaniel Hawthorne, as we shall now see, confronts the actors in his Roman drama with similar alternatives, but the questions they must resolve are even more painfully vexed with tragic ambiguities.

16

Pearls and Carbuncles:
The Marble Faun

When we have once known Rome, and left her where she lies, like a long decaying corpse, retaining a trace of the noble shape it was, but with accumulated dust and a fungous growth overspreading all its more admirable features;—left her in utter weariness, no doubt, of her narrow, crooked, intricate streets, so uncomfortably paved with little squares of lava that to tread over them is a penitential pilgrimage, so indescribably ugly, moreover, so cold, so alley-like, into which the sun never falls, and where a chill wind forces its deadly breath into our lungs; . . . left her, sick at heart of Italian trickery, which has uprooted whatever faith in man's integrity had endured till now, and sick at stomach of sour bread, sour wine, rancid butter, and bad cookery, needlessly bestowed on evil meats; . . . left her, in short, hating her with all our might, and adding our individual curse to the Infinite Anathema which her old crimes have unmistakably brought down;—when we have left Rome in such mood as this, we are astonished by the discovery, by-and-by, that our heart-strings have mysteriously attached themselves to the Eternal City, and are drawing us thitherward again, as if it were more familiar, more intimately our home, than even the spot where we were born! (Nathaniel Hawthorne, *The Marble Faun* 325-6)

Few critics have claimed that Hawthorne's *The Marble Faun* is a masterpiece, or even that it is an assured artistic success. Yet in its use of setting the novel deserves to be ranked among its author's most original achievements. What Browning and Clough accomplished in verse, Hawthorne was among the first to accomplish in prose fiction: he shows how Rome, as an enveloping presence, can be brought to bear dramatically on the lives of individual characters. But, for reasons of personal temperament and national background, Hawthorne was emotionally disoriented by Rome in a way that made the artistic distancing managed by Clough and Browning difficult for him. In fact, Rome was the place of all places most liable to exacerbate the dividedness that is Hawthorne's besetting sin—and virtue—as a writer. As much as anything Hawthorne ever wrote, *The Marble Faun* justifies L. P. Hartley's likening of him to Mr. Facing-Both-Ways in *Pilgrim's Progress* (*Novelist's Responsibility* 139). The novel verges on the schizophrenic in its treatment of its major themes: guilt and innocence, art, sexuality, and above all, history.

For Hawthorne, the roads leading to Rome are at once arduous and enticing. The single sentence quoted (in abbreviated form) to begin this chapter, fiercely distended by the effort to bundle together the contradictions of Roman experience, could serve as a microcosm of the entire novel. Like Clough and Browning, Hawthorne was sensitive to Roman juxtaposition, but he evokes it with a feverishness all his own:

We know not how to characterize, in any accordant and compatible terms, the Rome that lies before us; its sunless alleys, and streets of palaces; its churches, lined with the gorgeous marbles that were originally polished for the adornment of pagan temples; its thousands of evil smells, mixed up with the fragrance of rich incense, diffused from as many censers; its little life, deriving feeble nutriment from what has long been dead. Everywhere, some fragment of ruin, suggesting the magnificence of a former epoch; everywhere, moreover, a Cross—and nastiness at the foot of it. As the sum of all, there are recollections that kindle the soul, and a gloom and languor that depress it beyond any depth of melancholic sentiment that can be elsewhere known. (110-1)

As the hyperbole suggests, "accordant and compatible terms" have little to do with the vision of Rome that Hawthorne transmits; the contradictions are built into the stony scene.

Rome, for Hawthorne, is at once a freakish sport among human settlements and the epitome of human life, a living paradox of universality in oddity. "[T]hat state of feeling which is experienced oftenest at Rome" he describes as

a vague sense of ponderous remembrances; a perception of such weight and density in a by-gone life, of which this spot was the centre, that the present moment is pressed down or crowded out, and our individual affairs and interests are but half as real, here, as elsewhere. (6)

And yet, strangely, "[v]iewed through this medium, our narrative . . . may seem not widely different from the texture of all our lives" (6). The city possesses a singular power to impress on the characters their subjection to the common lot: mortality. The American sculptor, Kenyon, comes in a time of dejection to realize

what a dreary city is Rome, and what a terrible weight is there imposed on human life, when any gloom within the heart corresponds to the spell of ruin, that has been thrown over the site of ancient empire. He wandered, as it were, and stumbled over the fallen columns, and among the tombs, and groped his way into the sepulchral darkness of the catacombs, and found no path emerging from them. (409-10)

For Hawthorne's people, the fatal spell of Rome derives from the correspondences it ceaselessly offers between inner and outer landscapes. It is a place where the inward and personal gets soberingly translated into the outward and historical, where the touring expatriate reads in the ruins "the myriads of dead hopes that lie crushed into the soil of Rome" (411). The crushing of hope was, of course, by this point in Hawthorne's career anything but a new subject for him. The New England surroundings of his earlier novels exact their own stern tolls; even the nascent Boston of *The Scarlet Letter* cannot dispense with a burial ground and a prison. But these New World settings, whatever the losses sustained among them, do not externalize human corruption and failure with the remorseless symbolic clangor of Hawthorne's Rome. On the characters of *The House of the Seven Gables* the Salem past lies heavy; but its weight cannot match the constant, terrible pressure exerted by this ruin strewn Roman tableau. Sin and death may, for Hawthorne, be in all lands the inescapable hallmarks of the human condition; but in Rome they beckon the stroller from every niche and street corner.

This coalescence of inward and outward culminates sensationally in the Capuchin Cemetery, where the merging of the personal and the public, the human and the architectural, becomes appalling:

The arrangement of the unearthed skeletons is what makes the special interest of the cemetery. The arched and vaulted walls of the burial recesses are supported by massive pillars and pilasters, made of thigh-bones and skulls; the whole material of the structure appears to be of a similar kind; and the knobs and embossed ornaments of this strange architecture are represented by the joints of the spine, and, the more delicate tracery, by the smaller bones of the human frame. (193)

Despite the tone of guide book matter-of-factness, the human capacity for artistic creation—something Hawthorne always viewed with nervous ambivalence—acquires here peculiarly horrific associations. In these quintessentially Roman surroundings, ornament serves only to accent the unlovely fact of mortality; as the narrator observes, "[T]he soul sinks forlorn and wretched, under all this burthen of dusty death" (194).

If Rome is for Hawthorne the wedding place of art and death, the conjunction is no accident. Contrasting, as narrator, the "picturesque" squalor of Roman dwellings with "the newly painted pine-boxes in which . . . [Americans] live and thrive," he concludes: "[T]here is reason to suspect that a people are waning to decay and ruin the moment that their life becomes fascinating either in the poet's imagination or the painter's eye" (296). There is a stubborn linkage in Hawthorne's New England mind of art and sexuality with ruin. It is no coincidence that Hester Prynne, that "fallen woman," is plainly identified as the chief artist-figure of her tiny community. Early in *The Marble Faun*, the narrator tentatively ascribes Miriam's morbid melancholy to "the stimulating and exhaustive influences of imaginative art, exercised by a delicate young woman, in the nervous and unwholesome atmosphere of Rome" (36). Over and over, the artistic and the picturesque are linked with blood, dirt, pollution, and decrepitude. Guilt by such association colors the entire city; to Kenyon's excitable fancy, "'[A]ll the blood that the Romans shed, whether on battlefields, or in the

Coliseum, or on the cross . . . formed a mighty subterranean lake of gore, right beneath our feet'" (163). And yet artists, breathing what Hawthorne persists in calling the city's "enchanted air," can feel themselves "free citizens" of "this Land of Art" (132). Since Kenyon and the two female principals are in fact artists, the consequences of such freedom are exposed searchingly to question in the delineation of the novel's central characters.

In *Adonais*, Shelley, prompted by Rome, wrote the lines: "Life, like a dome of many-coloured glass, / Stains the white radiance of Eternity" (lines 462-3, *Complete Poetical Works*). The young American copyist, Hilda, would willingly sweep aside the staining chromatic filter. When her friend Kenyon exclaims "'[G]ive me—to live and die in—the pure, white light of Heaven!'", she heartily concurs: "'I love the white light, too!'" (366). She is specifically disclaiming the technicolor garb of Roman Catholicism, by which she has been fleetingly attracted. In her longing for eternity's white radiance, however, Hilda seems disquietingly eager to bypass the tinted reality of Rome, if not indeed the great, staining dome of life itself.

Hilda is one of the "young and pure" who "may have heard much of the evil of the world, and seem to know it, but only as an impalpable theory" (204). Yet unlike even so immaculate a figure as Browning's Pompilia, she shows little capacity for ever confronting the fact of evil with unblinking eyes. "'I am a poor, lonely girl,'" she confides to her guilty and even lonelier friend Miriam, "'whom God has set here in an evil world, and given her only a white robe, and bid her wear it back to Him, as white as when she put it on'" (154). It seems a harsh condition for the Almighty to have imposed on a daily walker amid the blood and filth of Hawthorne's Rome. Indeed, after Hilda has suffered for months from her knowledge of Miriam and Donatello's crime, a perceptive young Italian artist paints a portrait of her that he entitles "Innocence, Dying of a Blood-stain": "It represented Hilda as gazing, with sad and earnest horrour, at a blood-spot which she seemed just then to have discovered on her white robe" (330). Nevertheless, it is unimaginable that Hilda's robe could become indelibly stained; her innocence is guaranteed from the start to be soilure-resistant.

Hilda's dwelling, located in a tower "at a height above the ordinary level of men's views and aspirations" (52), abstracts her symbolically from the terrestrial level of the dusty and bruising Roman pavements. She lives in her eyrie "free to descend into the corrupted atmosphere of the city beneath" (54), but such a freedom to descend is not a freedom to fall. Tending the "never-dying lamp" that has burned for centuries within the shrine of the Virgin in her tower, Hilda assumes the curious role of a Christianized Roman vestal. Her placement sets her apart not only from pagan tradition but also from Roman Catholic designs. For as long as the flame is tended, the tower will stay out of the hands of the Church, and moreover the "sole human form" to be found at

Hilda's altitude is the crypto-Protestant one of Saint Paul perched atop the column of Antoninus (53).

Eventually, however, the knowledge of her friend's guilt shakes the moral pedestal atop which Hilda herself is perched. When such a loved one falls, the consequences are catastrophically Roman: "[T]he effect is almost as if the sky fell with him, bringing down in chaotic *ruin* the *columns* that upheld our faith" (328, my emphasis). Or—in terms of an alternate Roman metaphor—Hilda's inner world becomes a fountain hideously polluted: "Poor sufferer for another's sin! Poor well-spring of a virgin's heart, into which a murdered corpse had casually fallen" (330). But the most disturbing Roman threat to Hilda's unearthly height is Kenyon's request that she acknowledge, *apropos* of Miriam and Donatello's crime, "'what a mixture of good there may be in things evil'" (276). "'If there be any such dreadful mixture of good and evil as you affirm (and which appears to me almost more shocking than pure evil,) then the good is turned to poison, not the evil to wholesomeness,'" she heatedly replies (384). To the puritan, all things mixed are impure.

Predictably, Hilda begins to pine for the cleanly, unmixed simplicities of her New England home:

Her pictorial imagination brought up vivid scenes of her native village, with its great, old elm-trees; and the neat, comfortable houses, scattered along the wide grassy margin of its street, and the white meeting-house, and her mother's very door, and the stream of gold-brown water, which her taste for colour had kept flowing, all this while, through her remembrance. Oh, dreary streets, palaces, churches, and imperial sepulchres of hot and dusty Rome, with the muddy Tiber eddying through the midst, instead of the gold-brown rivulet! How she pined under this crumbly magnificence, as if it were piled all upon her human heart! How she yearned for that native homeliness, those familiar sights, those faces which she had known always, those days that never brought any strange event, that life of sober week-days, and a solemn Sabbath at the close! (342)

The tick tock alternation of sobriety with solemnity for which Hilda yearns banishes carnival along with crime. Such eventlessness excludes the turbulence not only of the Tiber but of history itself. Even the narrator seems here to grow homesick along with Hilda for the ahistorical regularity and "naturalness" that make the New England village Rome's antitype: no dark marauders can prowl the grassy streets of a place to which no roads lead, and there is no need to fear pitfalls in a site still innocent of excavation. Hilda has been from the beginning a white-frame heroine displaced among corroded stones. In the end, when she is seen "coming down from her old tower, to be herself enshrined and worshipped as a household Saint, in the light of her husband's fireside" (461), she has undergone the only sort of transformation imaginable for her: a fortunate fall into a cosy American parlor.

It is Miriam Schaefer, not the immaculate Hilda, who is the novel's true heroine. Miriam is neither cosy nor domestic; her origins are not American, and she is not a saint. Temperamentally she stands at the opposite end of the spectrum: "Her nature had a great deal of colour, and, in accordance with it, so likewise had her pictures" (21). It is she, in fact, who exposes the colorless Hilda to the vividly encrimsoning "stain" of her adoptive city. She does so, however, against her will; she shrinks from confiding even to Kenyon the secret of her past life. "'It is no precious pearl, as I just now told him; but my dark-red carbuncle—red as blood—is too rich a gem to put into a stranger's casket'" (130). If the imagery connects Miriam firmly with Rome and its "subterranean lake of gore," so does the cloud of mystery, conspiracy and sexuality that envelops her from the start. When Kenyon insists to her that the "'white, shining purity of Hilda's nature is a thing apart'" from "'whatever mass of evil may have fallen'" into Miriam's life (287), he is asserting his beloved's essential foreignness not only to Miriam but to Rome itself.

In a revealing moment, Hilda answers Miriam's reference to Beatrice Cenci's sin of parricide with the astonishing admission, "'Ah! . . . I really had quite forgotten Beatrice's history'" (66). What frightens Hilda most about Miriam is that her friend threatens to make history unforgettable for her. And indeed, the act of violence that Miriam and Donatello jointly commit and that Hilda inadvertently observes impresses itself upon Hilda's consciousness like an historical inscription: "Poor Hilda had looked into the courtyard, and saw the whole quick passage of a deed, which took but that little time to grave itself in the eternal adamant" (171).

Hilda's espial of that deed, as Miriam soon recognises, causes "a great chasm" to open itself between the two of them: "[S]ince the chasm could never be bridged over, they must tread the whole round of Eternity to meet on the other side" (207). What makes the chasm unbridgeable is the very nature of Miriam's being; involuntarily, Miriam thrusts upon her friend the Roman reality of change: "'Then, will you not touch my hand? Am I not the same as yesterday?'" Miriam asks; "'Alas! No, Miriam!'" Hilda forlornly replies (207). Her deadly glimpse has brought Hilda face to face with a fact that her whole mentality rejects, the generational linking of human deeds to form historical continuities: "'Ah, now I understand how the sins of generations past have created an atmosphere of sin for those that follow!'" (212). Miriam's temporal experience "stains the white radiance of eternity" with a vengeance: "'Your deed, Miriam, has darkened the whole sky!'" (212).

The two women never do, in fact, "meet on the other side." The closest thing to a token of reconciliation between them is the object described in the novel's closing lines, Miriam's bridal gift to Hilda. "It was a bracelet, evidently of great cost, being composed of seven ancient Etruscan gems, dug out of seven sepulchres, and each one of them the signet of some princely personage, who had lived an immemorial time ago" (462). But even the bracelet stands as a talismanic reminder to Hilda of the realities upon which she is turning her back: the reality of history, the reality of pagan princeliness, the reality above all—quietly underscored by the repeated numeral—of the City of the Seven Hills. It is a Parthian shot launched by Miriam from "the other side of a fathomless abyss" (461), from beyond a continental divide separating Miriam's old, old world from the new one to which Hilda is about to retreat.

An earlier old-world fictional heroine, Corinne, was identified in Madame de Staël's famous novel as "the image of our beautiful Italy" (*Corinne* 28). Hawthorne's Miriam, who can claim literary descent from Corinne, might be called the image of Rome incarnate—and incarnadined. As Jane Lundblad has demonstrated, there are numerous parallels between the two heroines (157-8). A quality that both possess by right of lineage is the Roman, anti-puritanical one of mixedness. Just as the furnishings of Corinne's rooms are a "happy *mélange* of all that was most agreeable in the three nations, French, English and Italian" (*Corinne* 42), so Corinne herself is a "happy *mélange*" of nationalities. Miriam's ancestry is a still more exotic mixture of English, Jewish, and "princely" southern Italian blood (429-30). Where Corinne, however, is "one of those beautiful Greek women who charm and subjugate the world" (395), Miriam's composite nature resists classification. Her roots are in the Judaeo-Christian world as well as in the pagan world of Magna Graecia; she seems to encompass uneasily within herself, like a pair of quarrelsome twins, both of Arnold's principles of Hebraism and Hellenism. Little wonder, then, that she appears "as unlike herself, in different moods, as if a melancholy maiden and a glad one were both bound within the girdle about her waist, and kept in magic thraldom by the brooch that clasped it" (83).

The grim subjects Miriam chooses to paint—"Jael driving the nail through the temples of Sisera," and Judith with the head of Holofernes (43)—recall, like her name, the Hebraic rather than the pagan side of her ancestry; yet violence between the factions and the sexes abounds in Roman annals as well. Her immersion in historical facticity harmonises with her equally Roman, stony fatalism before the march of events: "'As these busts in the block of marble,'" she reflects when viewing Kenyon's sculptures, "'so does our individual fate exist in the limestone of Time. We fancy that we carve it out; but its ultimate shape is prior to all our action'" (116). If she harbors an anti-sculptural impulse to "'[fling] off this great burthen of stony memories, which the ages have deemed it a piety to heap upon [the world's] back'" (119), that is because her life has made her all too well acquainted with such Roman impositions.

In an early scene of *The Marble Faun*, Miriam, together with Hilda, Kenyon, and Donatello, descends into a catacomb (that of Saint Calixtus) that seems the concrete objectification of the sepulchral, fragmentary, promiscuous Roman past. "They went joyously down into that vast tomb, and wandered by torch-light through a sort of dream, in which reminiscences of church-aisles and grimy cellars—and chiefly the latter—seemed to be broken into fragments and hopelessly intermingled" (24). It is strikingly appropriate that Miriam should encounter in such an ancient crypt the shadowy figure who haunts her from some recess of her own personal past. This "mysterious, dusky, death-scented apparition" (36) is not only a walking *memento mori*; he is also a *memento historiae*. His profession, that of an artist's model, makes him all the more Roman. Later, seeing this "strange creature" attempting to rinse his hands in the Fountain of Trevi, Kenyon observes: "'He cannot be an Italian; at least, not a Roman. . . . I never knew one of them to care about ablution. See him, now! It is as if he were trying to wash off the time-stains and earthly soil of a thousand years!'" (147). But the sculptor is mistaken; it is precisely the millennial film of grime on his hands that makes the model the living image of Rome and its sullying history. When, near the end of the novel, it is divulged that Miriam's familiar is the sinister marchese she had been expected to marry, one is hardly surprised to learn that the match would have been "a family arrangement, between two persons of disproportioned ages" (430). The girl has been betrothed to Antiquity itself.

If the model embodies for Miriam the life-crushing burden of the past, his own life seems equally burdened. "'I was as anxious as yourself to break the tie between us—to bury the past in a fathomless grave'" (94), he assures her. What he represents is, to apply Byron's verdict on Rome itself, past redemption's skill. "In this man's memory, there was something that made it awful for him to think of prayer" (95). It is the unredeemable purport of their memories (left indefinite by Hawthorne) that binds the model and Miriam indissolubly together. As they walk back from the Borghese Garden, they discuss "some strange and dreadful *history* of their former life, belonging equally to this dark man and to the fair and youthful woman, whom he persecuted" (97, my emphasis). It is he who has spotted the "white gown" that Miriam, unlike Hilda, cannot hope to restore in its pristine cleanliness to the giver. When he insinuates that her "white hand had once a crimson stain," she retorts bitterly, "'It had no stain . . . until you grasped it in your own!'" (97).

Stained by the touch of the past, both in its inward form of memory and in its objectified form of the model, Miriam has difficulty containing her anguish within a socially acceptable demeanor. When at last she vents her pent-up feelings in a way that recalls Milton's Satan, beginning "to gesticulate extravagantly, gnashing her teeth, flinging her arms wildly abroad, stamping with her foot . . . concentrating the elements of a long insanity into that instant," she stages her display, fittingly, in the most time-honored Roman locale of suffering and unbridled violence—"under the dusky arches of the Coliseum" (157).

But Miriam's close identification with Roman topography and legend extends further. In the soul of Miriam's prototype, Corinne, there are "abysses of sadness" she can guard against only by shielding herself from love (89).

Miriam perceives a similar abyss in herself, but one that has a more pointed local relevance. She connects it with the Roman chasm into which the legendary hero Curtius rode his horse:

"The chasm was merely one of the orifices of that pit of blackness that lies beneath us, everywhere. The firmest substance of human happiness is but a thin crust spread over it, with just reality enough to bear up the illusive stage-scenery amid which we tread. It needs no earthquake to open the chasm. A footstep, a little heavier than ordinary, will serve; and we must step very daintily, not to break through the crust, at any moment. By-and-by, we inevitably sink! It was a foolish piece of heroism in Curtius to precipitate himself there, in advance; for all Rome, you see, has been swallowed up in that gulf, in spite of him. The Palace of the Caesars has gone down thither, with a hollow, rumbling sound of its fragments! All the temples have tumbled into it; and thousands of statues have been thrown after! All the armies and the triumphs have marched into the great chasm, with their martial music playing, as they stepped over the brink. All the heroes, the statesmen, and the poets!" (161-2)

The shadows that darken the girl's awareness are far more than morbid personal preoccupations. Unlike the serenely ahistorical Hilda, Miriam can never escape Rome because she is doomed to carry it about with her. She is a walking compendium of decline and fall, and she speaks in the somber accents of mortality itself.

The voice of Miriam's lover, Donatello, speaks with a different accent. Although he is initially associated with Praxiteles' ancient Faun in the Capitoline Museum, his native place is the timeless Etruscan countryside, and Roman thoughts sit on him lightly if at all. He is unburdened by Christian thoughts, as well. If "there is not an atom of martyr's stuff in all that softened marble" of the Faun (9), there is not an iota of such stuff in the young Italian's still softer flesh. Like the Faun, Donatello himself is paganism personified, "a poet's reminiscence of a period when man's affinity with Nature was more strict, and his fellowship with every living thing more intimate and dear" (11). Such a being, in whose composition "the animal nature . . . is a most essential part" (9), will be loath to follow a Curtius into his flesh-engulfing abyss. The mingling in Donatello's nature of animal impulse (betokened by his reputed furry ears) and human intelligence implies no uneasy "*mélange*" but rather a finer synthesis. "What an honest strain of wildness would it indicate! And into what regions of rich mystery would it extend Donatello's sympathies, to be thus linked (and by no monstrous chain) with what we call the inferiour tribes of being, whose simplicity, mingled with his human intelligence, might partly restore what man has lost of the divine!" (71).

Like Hilda, but without her puritanism, Donatello is at first innocent of the burden of memory that overwhelms Miriam and her dusky familiar. What more, he is not cursed by the corresponding burden of foresight. What says of the sculpted Faun applies to the living one: "'I suppose the conscience, no remorse, no burthen on the heart, no troublesome recollections of any sort; no dark future neither!'" (14). Hilda cannot guess at Donatello's age because "'[h]e has nothing to do with time, but has a look of eternal youth in his face'"; when asked directly by Miriam how old he is, he ingenuously replies, "'Signorina, I do not know'" (15). Miriam, who has everything to do with time, exclaims, "'Not to know his own age! It is equivalent to being immortal on earth. If I could only forget mine!'" (15). For the inveterate Roman, amnesia is bliss.

Hilda, however, has been "looking . . . too long" at the ancient Faun, "'and now, instead of a beautiful statue, immortally young, I see only a corroded and discoloured stone. This change is very apt to occur in statues'" (17). Apt to occur, one might add, in living Fauns as well. As Hilda's words unconsciously hint, Donatello is destined to undergo a change that will leave him, too, corroded and discolored. A little later, showing Donatello a series of gloomy sketches in her studio, Miriam asks him rhetorically, "'[W]hat should a boy like you—a Faun, too—know about the joys and sorrows, the intertwining light and shadow, of human life?'" (46). *The Marble Faun* recounts how the boy ceases to be a Faun, and to be marble, through his immersion in the destructive—yet also, finally, creative—element of intermixture. He becomes humanized, at the cost of becoming Romanized.

Donatello's ancestral line, the narrator reports, "was supposed to have had its origin, in the sylvan life of Etruria, while Italy was yet guiltless of Rome" (232). The concluding phrase is a revealing one. Anticipating D. H. Lawrence's revisionist history in *Etruscan Places* (1927-28), Hawthorne identifies the founding of Rome as a pagan "fall" from Etruscan innocence. Like Browning's Count Guido, but without Guido's savagery, Donatello is a Tuscan who fatefully exposes himself to the Roman medium. At first, his Arcadian origins distance him not only from the great, anti-Arcadian city but also from the character, Miriam, who most richly represents it and whom he perversely insists on adoring. "'There are not two creatures more unlike, in this wide world, than you and I!'" Miriam admonishes him (79). The ensuing narrative traces the "likening" of the two creatures, along with the correspondent narrowing of their world.

First, in the agreeably pastoral grounds of the Villa Borghese, Donatello is able for one rare moment to draw Miriam out of her stony, confining Roman reality into his atemporal Arden: "'My reality! What is it?'" she asks. "'Is the past so indestructible?—the future so immitigable? Is the dark dream, in which I walk, of such solid, stony substance, that there can be no escape out of its dungeon?'" (82). The plunge into irresponsible mirthfulness that she subsequently allows herself with Donatello grants her "'a glimpse far backward into Arcadian life, or, farther still, into the Golden Age, before mankind was burthened with sin and sorrow, and before pleasure had been darkened with those shadows that bring it into high relief, and make it Happiness'" (84). But just as Hilda's revered masterpieces lose their luster from being too long eyed through the corroding medium of the Roman air, so Miriam's Arcadian visions fade as if "some profane eye had looked at them too closely."

Just an instant before, it was Arcadia, and the Golden Age. The spell being broken, it was now only that old tract of pleasure-ground, close by the people's gate of Rome; a tract where the crimes and calamities of ages, the many battles, blood recklessly poured out, and deaths of myriads, have corrupted all the soil, creating an influence that makes the air deadly to human lungs. (90)

The reappearance of the ancient model spells the end of the holiday from history, the return to Roman chronology. "'Your hour is past,'" Miriam darkly warns Donatello; "'his hour has come!'" (90).

Roman chronology dominates the novel's climactic episode, the model's assassination. The abrupt violence of this turn of events has troubled some critics; Robert Emmet Long, for example, objects that "[t]he melodramatic murder for which Miriam is responsible cheapens Hawthorne's theme of man's fall from grace" (46). But there is more here than melodrama. The scene gains a powerful symbolic resonance from its place within the whole enclosing Roman context; the murder itself eerily recalls ancient Roman models. As Hyatt Waggoner argues, "All Rome, all history, made the crime inevitable" (165); the assassins, however, give historical determinism a self-conscious nudge. Joining Miriam at the Tarpeian Rock, Donatello struggles "to make himself conscious of the historic associations of the scene" (170). The historical neophyte accordingly seeks instruction from his well-schooled companion. To his question, "'Who are they . . . who have been flung over here, in days gone by?'" Miriam knowledgeably replies "'Men whose lives were the bane of their fellow-creatures. Men who poisoned the air, which is the common breath of all, for their own selfish purposes. There was short work with such men, in old Roman times'" (170). Suggestively, at this point a figure steps forth from "a deep, empty niche, that had probably once contained a statue" (170); the model emerges from classic immobility into living chronicle, only to be made short work of.

After Donatello has flung the interloper over the precipice, he answers Miriam's guilty query—"'What have you done!'"—with a ringing Roman *sententia*: "'I did what ought to be done to a traitor!'" (172). He has been a prompt student. Their victim, a shadowy reminder of mortality even in life, now becomes a mere "heap of mortality" lying upon "the small, square stones." "'You have killed him, Donatello! He is quite dead!'" Miriam announces, and adds the most Roman of coroner's verdicts: "'Stone dead!'" (173).

In her eyes, the act of violence, in which she shares full complicity, binds her and Donatello together in a mystic marriage compact. "'The deed knots us together for time and eternity, like the coil of a serpent!'" (174). Miriam's simile, however, is double-edged. The pair may have "tied the knot," but it is a suffocating one; such a marriage is infernally mixed. The serpent image most obviously recalls the biblical account of the Temptation, with Miriam as Eve and Donatello as a Roman-style Adam ("The woman tempted me, and I did shove"). But Miriam's serpent evokes a local analogy, as well: the famous Vatican group of the Laocoön, which Kenyon later sees as "a type of the long, fierce struggle of Man, involved in the knotted entanglements of Errour and Evil, those two snakes, which if no Divine help intervene will be sure to strangle him and his children, in the end" (391). The group possesses the special Roman penchant for distending the temporal into an image of the eternal. "Thus, in the Laocoön, the horrour of a moment grew to be the Fate of interminable ages" (391). In a similar fashion, Donatello and Miriam's split-second deed of violence seals, like the stony serpent, their interminable destinies. "Their deed—the crime which Donatello wrought, and Miriam accepted on the instant—had wreathed itself, as she said, like a serpent, in inextricable links about both their souls, and drew them into one, by its terrible contractile power" (174). The word "contractile" assumes here sardonically punning overtones. The "contract" between the man and the woman will indeed "contract" the compass of their lives within its cruel grip.

By putting an end to the model's life, they have made him eternal in their psyches. The union that is, as Donatello says, "'[c]emented with his blood'" (175) implicates a shadowy third who will be always beside them. Their attempt to "'[f]orget it,'" as Miriam advises—"They flung the past behind them, as she counselled" (176)—is at once redundant and futile. The murder has itself amounted to "flinging" the personified Roman past over a cliff; yet paradoxically, by so doing, they have merely enrolled themselves in the long, soiled annals of Roman history. "They trode through the streets of Rome, as if they, too, were among the majestic and guilty shadows, that, from ages long gone by, have haunted the blood-stained city" (176). "'Who knows,'" Miriam asks, "'but we may meet the high and ever-sad fraternity of Caesar's murderers, and exchange a salutation?'" Thus, by entering the grim pageant of Roman history, "Miriam and her lover were not an insulated pair, but members of an innumerable confraternity of guilty ones, all shuddering at each other" (177). It seems a high price to pay for admission to the Roman hall of fame.

Ultimately, the pair's attempt to "throw over" the past succeeds only in making the past all the more appallingly resurgent. Miriam is eventually obliged to admit, "'My mind is not active any longer. . . . It deals with one thought, and no more. One recollection paralyzes it'" (280). Not even their love escapes the paralytic grip; to Miriam's question, "'And surely you did love me?'", Donatello replies, "gloomily and absently," "'I did'" (198)—the historical past tense has conquered. For the young Tuscan, too, recollection has become damnation. To Miriam's demand, "'Leave me, therefore, and forget me!'" he counters: "'Forget you, Miriam! . . . If I could remember you, and behold you, apart from that frightful visage which stares at me over your shoulder—that were a consolation, at least, if not a joy'" (200). His undying love affair has become a triangle, with a death's head at one corner. Even though when Miriam departs he "stretch[es] himself at full length on the stone bench, and [draws] his hat over his eyes, as the idle and lighthearted youths of dreamy Italy are accustomed to do," his apparent ease masks an agony suffered on the stony Roman bench of desolation: "In this dismal mood, bewildered with the novelty of sin and grief, he had little left of that singular resemblance, on account of which, and for their sport, his three friends had fantastically recognized him as the veritable Faun of Praxiteles" (201). Disjoined at last from his marble twin, the Faun has lost repose without gaining animation. He remains morally petrified.

Eventually, the downward movement of the narrative, climaxing in the Tarpeian plunge ("O, what a fall was there, my countrymen! Then I, and you, and all of us fell down"), is succeeded by a compensating upward swing, whose visible emblem is Donatello's ancestral tower at Monte Beni. The new direction is announced by Miriam's voice, running the gamut from despair to exaltation as it issues from a hidden recess of Donatello's dwelling. "But, when the emotion was at its profoundest depth, the voice rose out of it, yet so gradually that a gloom seemed to pervade it, far upward from the abyss, and not entirely to fall away as it ascended into a higher and purer region" (269). The symbolic suggestion is translated, some pages later, into didactically literal terms by the singer herself, when she hints "'that she, most wretched, who beguiled [Donatello] into evil, might guide him to a higher innocence than that from which he fell'" (283).

Such an ascent to a "higher innocence," problematic at best, seems all the more so because it obliges Donatello to make his peace not only with Miriam but with the city that witnessed their fall. This last, arduous reconciliation entails a prolonged meander away from the city. Even in pre-Tarpeian days, Miriam had already suspected Rome of having a baleful influence on her rustic friend: "'My poor Donatello, you are ill! . . . This melancholy and sickly Rome is stealing away the rich, joyous life that belongs to you'" (149). Once the fatal act has been committed, "that simple and joyous creature was gone forever" (172); the Faun has dropped into a Roman abyss. Or Rome, one could say, has once and for all "fallen" into him. After this, Miriam's panicky urge to save Donatello by rusticating him—"'But we must get him away from this old, dreamy, and dreary Rome, where nobody but himself ever thought of being gay'" (181)—is simply irrelevant. The "creature" has been obliterated by the sculptural visage that the dead model now presents: an "image of wax—or clay-cold reality" (182).

Even when Donatello does accept exile in his Tuscan retreat, the local *contadini* gravely observe that "the young Count was sadly changed, since he went to Rome" (238). What Rome, immemorial center of contrivance and convention, has transformed above all is the spontaneous kinship with the natural world that was his Etruscan birthright:

He could not live their healthy life of animal spirits, in their sympathy with Nature, and brotherhood with all that breathed around them. Nature, in beast, fowl, and tree, and earth, flood, and sky, is what it was of old; but sin, care and self-consciousness have set the human portion of the world askew; and thus the simplest character is ever the surest to go astray. (239-40)

Sin, care, and self-consciousness: there could be no more infallible symptoms of the Roman sickness, which only death itself can remedy.

"'We all of us, as we grow older . . . lose somewhat of our proximity to Nature," Kenyon reassures his Tuscan friend. "'It is the price we pay for experience.'" "'A heavy price, then!'" Donatello replies, "rising from the ground" (250). "Experience" is itself a synonym for the Roman malaise; but by the very act of rising, Donatello unconsciously affirms the promise that accompanies his affliction. As the narrator comments soon after, "a soul had been inspired into the young Count's simplicity, since their intercourse in Rome":

Every human life, if it ascends to truth or delves down to reality, must undergo a similar change; but sometimes, perhaps, the instruction comes without the sorrow, and oftener, the sorrow teaches no lesson that abides with us. In Donatello's case, it was pitiful, and almost ludicrous, to observe the confused struggle that he made; how completely he was taken by surprise; how ill-prepared he stood, on this old battle-field of the world, to fight with such an inevitable foe as mortal Calamity, and Sin for its stronger ally. (262)

According to Hawthorne's curious, quasi-Platonic eschatology, "truth" is an entity that exists in the heavens above, where presumably such pure beings as Hilda can soar up to possess it. "Reality," by contrast, is another sort of commodity that can be found only in the trenches, or below them; to grasp it requires digging enough to soil anybody's white robe. Donatello has had to come to grips with his own reality on a fiercely harrowing Roman battlefield. The bitterness of his response to Kenyon's inquiry whether he will return to Rome is therefore understandable: "'Never! I hate Rome . . . and have good cause'" (264).

Yet despite his deep-seated loathing of the ancient city, Donatello shows little enthusiasm for the brave new world that Kenyon hopefully holds out to him: "'You should go with me to my native country. . . . In that fortunate land, each generation has only its own sins and sorrows to bear. Here, it seems as if all the weary and dreary Past were piled upon the back of the Present.'" "'The sky itself is an old roof now,'" Donatello answers movingly, "'and, no doubt, the sins of mankind have made it gloomier than it used to be'" (302). He has irreversibly entered the grand and terrible amphitheater of history. Even by switching, in mid narrative, from "the Faun" to "the Count" as Donatello's customary title, Hawthorne signals that fact, removing the young man from the world of mythology to the world of public responsibilities. Whatever the price he must pay, Donatello must ultimately choose to return to the Roman field. Only by taking that route can he complete the purgatorial upward journey the narrator sketches for him: "In the black depths, the Faun had found a soul, and was struggling with it towards the light of Heaven" (268).

The outcome of Donatello's Dantesque progress from Hades to heavenly light remains doubtful. In the Boston version of the "Conclusion" (or "Postscript"), the last mention of him leaves him locked in the Roman depths: "'The Castle of Saint Angelo,' said Kenyon sadly, turning his face towards that sepulchral fortress, 'is no longer a prison; but there are others which have dungeons as deep, and in one of them, I fear, lies our poor Faun'" (cxxvi).[1] Nonetheless, the concluding Carnival sequence reaffirms Rome as the central, though always ambiguous, stage for meaningful human action. Kenyon's glimpse of his friend garbed as a penitent puzzles him: "'How strange! . . . What can bring him to Rome, where his recollections must be so painful, and his presence not without peril?'" (393). But it is altogether logical that Donatello should return to the scene of his crime, for it has also been the scene of his moral initiation. Miriam herself plausibly explains the circular logic of this "fortunate fall":

"Is he not beautiful?" said Miriam, watching the sculptor's eye as it dwelt admiringly on Donatello. "So changed, yet still, in a deeper sense, so much the same! He has travelled in a circle, as all things heavenly and earthly do, and now comes back to his original self, with an inestimable treasure of improvement won from an experience of pain." (434)

A disappointing weakness of *The Marble Faun* is that the Roman transformation Miriam so confidently describes is never dramatized by the narrative; it is at best theoretically asserted. Still, the idea itself confirms Rome's place within the design of the novel as the supreme site of creative human suffering and recognition. Such an arena is not meant for the Hildas of this world, who can dwell contentedly only by their husband's fireside, with eyes upturned to the City of God. It remains, however, the great City of Man, and the roads leading away from it circle unerringly back to it. Those who take permanent leave, like Hilda and Kenyon, mark themselves as refugees from the serious Carnival of human history.

A Large Capacity for Ruin:
Roderick Hudson and
The Portrait of a Lady

Largely because of its Roman setting, Henry James's first full-fledged novel, *Roderick Hudson*, has sometimes been treated as a mere offshoot of *The Marble Faun*. Alwyn Berland warns sensibly against such a view: "A reader fresh from looking at both of the novels . . . will be struck at once by a radical and characteristic difference of representational strategy and of tone" (67). It is precisely in the treatment of the Roman milieu that the difference of tone Berland detects emerges most strikingly. While James's approach to Rome has its ambivalences, it does not waver in Hawthorne's schizoid fashion between enthusiasm and dismay. The urbane Jamesian sense of balance, even in this initial phase, prevails.

What James in his Preface calls Roderick's "large capacity for ruin" (*Art of the Novel* 13) earmarks the young sculptor as the perfect candidate for Roman misadventure. Making his first appearance "clad from head to foot in a white linen suit," he is patently a *tabula rasa* awaiting inscription at the hands of life. The suit has already "quite lost its vivifying and redeeming crispness" (*Roderick Hudson* 37); unlike Hawthorne's stainless Hilda, Roderick is not to be soilure-proof. One of his early works, admired by Rowland Mallet, his future patron, bespeaks his lust for worldly experience. It is a bronze statuette representing "a naked youth drinking from a gourd," and its title is "Thirst"—in Greek script (33). "'He's youth, you know; he's innocence, he's health, he's strength, he's curiosity,'" Roderick explains. "'. . . The cup is knowledge, pleasure, experience'" (39). The contents of the chalice are unmistakably Roman; the Eternal City is to be Roderick's fatal watering-place.

The idyllic terrain of Northampton, Massachusetts—"Here were kindness, comfort, safety, the warning voice of duty, the perfect absence of temptation" (65)—is unsatisfactory to Roderick precisely because of the bland attractions catalogued. No lover of moral level ground, he is in search of precipices over which to lean. His desultory legal studies offer him no precarious horizons; his mother, he complains, "'would fain see me all my life tethered to the law, like a browsing goat to a stake'" (49). When Rowland proposes to untether Roderick by conducting him to Rome—"'I simply offer you an opportunity,'" as he ingenuously declares (44)—he provides the young artist with a chance to escape "the law," in several senses at once. It is not long before Roderick smashes his bust of Mr. Barnaby Striker, the solemn attorney to whom he is apprenticed. The act is, as Mrs. Hudson perceives, an ominously "lawless" one.

A domestic dispute arises over what Roderick's opportunity will mean. "'Transplanted to Rome,'" Rowland optimistically contends, "'I fancy he will put forth some wonderful flowers. I should like vastly to see the change'" (53). But Mrs. Hudson, good puritan that she is, dreads Roman changes. As Roderick confides, "'Rome is an evil word in my mother's vocabulary, to be said in a whisper, as you'd say "damnation"'" (49). Whether Roderick, in accepting Roman transplantation, is heading for flames or flowers is the question that the ensuing action will determine.

Once transplanted, Roderick soon concludes that "'[f]or a man of my temperament Rome is the only possible place'" (129); he repeatedly assures Rowland "that he meant to live and die within the shadow of St Peter's" (129). What Roderick finds in Rome, according to the narrator, is

what he had been looking for from the first—the complete contradiction of Northampton. And indeed Rome is the natural home of those spirits . . . with a deep relish for the artificial element of life and the infinite superpositions of history. It is the immemorial city of convention. (79)

It may seem paradoxical that the young nonconformist should find the immemorial city of convention to his liking; but the conventions he encounters in Rome are those best suited to liberating his peculiar brand of individuality. Roderick has "intuitively, as an artist, what one may call the historic consciousness" (78). He is consequently at home in Rome as his precursor Hilda is not, and vulnerable, as she is not, to Rome's risky allure.

Compelled by Rome to make the crucial Arnoldian choice, Roderick chooses unblinkingly: "'I mean never to make anything ugly. The Greeks never made anything ugly, and I am a Hellenist; I am not a Hebraist!'" (94). His decision already places him at a moral remove from his fiancée, Mary Garland, whose native town—West Nazareth—declares by its very name her American and Hebraistic origins. When she at length joins Roderick in Rome, she is predictably disconcerted to find that "'[h]ere it is such a mixture; one doesn't know what to choose, what to believe'" (305). She spends a morning on the Palatine among "that sunny desolation of crumbling overtangled fragments, half excavated and half identified, known as the Palace of the Caesars" (238). "Nothing in Rome is more interesting than this confused and crumbling garden," the narrator observes, "where you stumble at every step on the disinterred bones of the past" (238). But the impressionable Mary is more unsettled than interested by the skeletal "remains"; "it was coming over [Mary] after all that Rome was a ponderously sad place" (238).

Mary's escort on this outing, Rowland Mallet, has inherited from his own puritan ancestors a distrust of indiscriminate moral mixedness. Yet even he is readier than Mary to embrace Roman intricacies and Roman juxtaposition:

"Is this what you call life?" she asked.
"What do you mean by 'this'?"
"Saint Peter's—all this splendour, all Rome—pictures, ruins, statues, beggars, monks."
"It is not all of it, but it is a large part of it. All these things are impregnated with life; they are the results of an old and complex civilization."
"An old and complex civilization: I am afraid I don't like that." (238)

It naturally follows that Mary has difficulty liking the novel's Roman leading lady, Christina Light. "Directness seemed to fail," James observes in his Preface, "unless Mary should be, so to speak, 'plain', Christina being essentially so 'coloured'" (*Art of the Novel* 18). The antithesis self-consciously, perhaps parodically, recalls the contrast between Hawthorne's pallid Hilda and encrimsoned Miriam. Christina, like Miriam, turns out to be of "mixed" parentage, and she is mixed in other ways as well. Her friend Madame Grandoni sees her as "'a mixture of good and bad, of ambition and indifference'" (*Roderick Hudson* 124); and in a moment of theatrical self-disparagement Christina calls herself "'a miserable medley of vanity and folly'" (182). As the narrator observes, "[I]n poor Christina's strangely commingled nature there was circle within circle and depth beneath depth" (300), a psychological makeup that replicates the "infinite superpositions of history" (79) so profusely manifest in Rome itself.

Christina is in fact, as one critic sums her up, the very "genius" of Rome (Auchard 21). The girl's vibrancy of personality is closely allied with that of the place to which she belongs. Her seductive charm calls to mind the sobriquet that, in *Italian Hours*, James fondly applies to the city: "the Witch of the Seven Hills" (224). His use of such an epithet, like the similar one ("sad-eyed old witch") he bestows upon Venice, carries no burden of moral disapprobation, and categorical moral judgments are certainly out of place with regard to Christina herself. "Perhaps," Kenneth Graham suggests, "one should see Christina as a catalyst, rather than as being simply baneful or beneficent":

In that way, her function would be like the various descriptions of Rome and Italy with which she is so deliberately associated. . . . Christina, with all her contradictions, and with her hair in its classic coil and her "step and carriage of a tired princess," is very much a Roman Muse. She simultaneously brings out both sides of Roderick's nature, the self-destructive and the creative. And like the city itself, she acts as a zone of power and influence within which certain of the elemental conflicts of living are enacted with new clarity and force. (37)

Graham's argument needs to be taken a step further. What makes both Christina and Rome hazardous to Roderick is that the two "sides" of the young man's nature, the creative and the self-destructive, are not in truth opposed but tragically interlinked. It is the boundlessness of his creative ambition that renders it life-threatening.

Rowland harbors a nagging suspicion that Christina "was unsafe; that she was a complex, wilful, passionate creature who might easily engulf a too confiding spirit in the eddies of her capricious temper. And yet he strongly felt her charm; the eddies had a strange fascination!" (*Roderick Hudson* 137). Roderick, for his part, responds to the girl's fascination, as he responds to Rome's, with headlong abandon. For him, Christina is the contrary of the *tabula rasa* he himself has only lately been; she presents to him a *tabula inscripta* of Roman experience. "'And then, bless you, she has seen so much of the world! Her talk is full of the strangest allusions!'" (138).

Christina's allusions emanate, young though she is, from a Roman source: fathomless antiquity. "'I am not young; I have never been young!'" she says of herself. "'My mother took care of that. I was a little wrinkled old woman at ten'" (194). Like Rome's, Christina's past derives as much from legend as from fact: "She had a fictitious history in which she believed much more fondly than in her real one, and an infinite capacity for extemporized reminiscence adapted to the mood of the hour" (193). It is dramatically right that Rowland should learn of her personal "history" in the Trastevere district: "There are few monuments here, but no part of Rome seemed more historic, in the sense of being weighted with a ponderous past, blighted with the melancholy of things that had had their day" (191).

Like Rome's, Christina's blighted history is to be one of decline and fall. Her imperial vision of her own destiny will be nullified by the agents of conspiracy and convention. What makes her all the more vulnerable is her Roman proneness to vicissitude and change. "'She is never the same'" (138), Roderick observes admiringly. Rowland, thinking of Christina, asks himself, "'How many more metamorphoses am I to be treated to before we have done?'" (255); and later he has cause to reflect on "all that was tragic and fatal in her latest transformation" (330). Mary, by contrast, mistrusts the transforming tendency of her multifarious Roman impressions, even though she displays a genuine capacity to absorb them and grow by them. She is far from flattered when Rowland calls her "'a capital subject for development,'" and she resists his injunction to "'Give yourself the best company, trust yourself, let yourself go!'"; "'But what you say,' she said at last, 'means *change*!'" (228).

The luckless Roderick is only too ready to "let himself go"; his susceptibility to change matches Christina's. It takes all of Rowland's ample patience "to wait for Roderick to complete the circle of his metamorphoses" (191), a circle that unfortunately eventuates in a downward spiral. As happens so often in Roman fictions, the protagonist's openness to local influences disrupts his inner chronology. Roderick's Roman sojourn, even while expanding his sense of time, destabilizes it. He embarks on "a tissue of lugubrious speculations as to the possible mischances of one's genius. 'What if the watch should run down,' he asked, 'and you should lose the key? What if you should wake up some morning and find it stopped—inexorably, appallingly stopped?'" (163). His fears are warranted. Before long, Rowland finds himself describing his protégé to Christina as "'a very old clock indeed. He's moody, desultory, idle, irregular, fantastic'" (198). He cannot help concluding that Christina herself is responsible for having "beguiled [Roderick] into letting the time slip" (221).

Rowland's suspicion merely confirms the occult link between girl and city. Rome, James had written his father in 1873, "is a wonderful place for stealing away your time, and giving you it may be much and it may be little in return" (*Letters* 1: 327). While Roderick at the outset of his career seems likely to gain much from both Rome and Christina (our first glimpse of him in the city coincides pointedly with his first, dazzling glimpse of the girl), as time passes his returns from both dwindle. By ironic contrast, the diligent little American artist, Sam Singleton, reminds Roderick "'of a watch that never runs down. If one listens hard one hears [him] always—tic-tic, tic-tic'" (323). Even though Singleton considers Rome the only conceivable dwelling place, he lacks Roderick's wholehearted, foolhardy responsiveness to the city's siren charm. His steady cultivation of his own small, "equable" talent, which makes him Roderick's foil, shows that an artist's life even in the shadow of Saint Peter's can retain its steady, modestly productive pulse.

"'You have gone up like a rocket in your profession they tell me,'" Christina remarks to Roderick during their tense interview in the Colosseum. "'[A]re you going to come down like the stick?'" (183). Roderick's brilliant Roman candle does, before long, sputter and plummet; indeed, he risks a fatal fall even on this occasion by staging a daredevil climb in order to impress the girl. In *Roderick Hudson*, as in *The Marble Faun*, the fascination of Rome conceals abysses; but here it is the hero's wayward temperament that makes the abysses inescapable.

Alarmed by the boundless rage with which Roderick greets the news of Christina's engagement to Prince Casamassima, Rowland admonishes the infatuated young sculptor: "'You are standing on the edge of a gulf. If you suffer this accident to put you out, you take your plunge'" (210). His remonstrances, however, fall on deaf ears. For Roderick, Rome has become synonymous with "opportunity" in ways Rowland could not have hoped to foresee. It is the appointed site for his quixotic attempt to take the prize of self-realization by storm. "'You are blind, you are deaf, you are under a spell. To break it you must leave Rome,'" Rowland expostulates after Mary's arrival on the scene. "'Leave Rome!'" Roderick retorts. "'Rome was never so dear to me'" (244).   When the sculptor at last does agree to quit the city, he swears that he is "'bidding farewell to beauty, to honour, to life!'" (311).

Consequently, although (like the murder in *The Marble Faun*) Roderick's death by a fall in the Alps has been criticized as melodramatic, the event is but the metaphoric culmination of his erratic Roman trajectory.   The "stony Alpine void" that destroys Roderick's life simply objectifies the moral *"descensus Averni"* that begins with his arrival in Rome.   Rowland discovers the hapless sculptor "tumbled upon the stones," destroyed through having "fallen from a great height" (348).   One more unwary Roman adventurer has ended up "stone dead."

Roderick's Roman tragedy takes its toll on another, pathetic victim: his mother, who blames all her son's misfortunes on his residence in "'this wicked, infectious, heathenish place'" (265).   Ironically, the endlessly weeping Mrs. Hudson becomes in the end identified with Byron's hackneyed symbol for the city she deplores: "'Oh, Mr. Mallet, aren't you satisfied?' cried Mrs. Hudson, in the tone in which Niobe may have addressed the avenging archers after she had seen her eldest born fall" (306-7).   But if the unfortunate lady is a Niobe, she is a serio-comic rather than a tragic one.   Her exchanges with her son reveal her stunned bafflement over his Roman fascination:

Mrs. Hudson surreptitiously wrung her hands. "Listen to him, please!" she cried. "Not leave Rome, when we have stayed here later than any respectable family ever did before! It's this dreadful place that has made us so unhappy. Roderick's so fearfully relaxed!"

"It's very true that I'm relaxed!" said Roderick serenely. "If I had not come to Rome I shouldn't have risen, and if I had not risen I shouldn't have fallen."

"Fallen—fallen!" murmured Mrs. Hudson. "Just hear him!" (292)

Despite the sorrow that shadows Roderick's career, the tone of such an exchange is one of humorous caricature.   It is plain that Mrs. Hudson's abhorrence of "this dreadful place" is naively provincial.   It is equally plain that Roderick's fatalism derives from his cavalier refusal to shoulder any responsibility for his own destiny.   The impression of Rome that the novel finally leaves is itself a medley; it is a place where risks and opportunities are perplexingly, often comically, juxtaposed.   In *The Portrait of a Lady* Roman complexities attain an altogether new, somber depth.   James's sense of the possibilities of character has expanded, and so has his feeling for the possibilities of his august setting.

Isabel would become a Rome-lover; that was a foregone conclusion. (*Portrait* 283)[1]

She had always been fond of history, and here was history in the stones of the street and the atoms of the sunshine. . . . The sense of the terrible human past was heavy to her, but that of something altogether contemporary would suddenly give it wings that it could wave in the blue. Her consciousness was so mixed that she scarcely knew where the different parts of it would lead her, and she went about in a repressed ecstasy of contemplation, seeing often in the things she looked at a great deal more than was there, and yet not seeing many of the items enumerated in her Murray. Rome, as Ralph said, confessed to the psychological moment. (*Portrait* 287)

The youthful heroine of *The Portrait of a Lady*, Isabel Archer, progresses from being fond of history to being part of it. Historical process becomes inextricably bound up with the destiny she must affront. Hence, it seems inevitable that the majestically winding roads of James's great novel should lead her to Rome. Isabel's early feeling for her gaunt old Albany home—"'I like places in which things have happened,'" she says, "'even if they're sad things'" (28)—foreshadows her residence in the ancient Roman palace that will be the scene of the saddest thing of all, her marital union with Gilbert Osmond. Yet this same Isabel harbors an apparently conflicting "desire to leave the past behind her and . . . to begin afresh" (32). It is this forward-looking side of Isabel's nature that explains her comradeship with Henrietta Stackpole, who, as Ralph Touchett marvels, "'does smell of the Future—it almost knocks one down!'" (94). When Ralph's father teases Isabel, "'I forget whether you're on the side of the old or on the side of the new. I've heard you take such opposite views,'" the girl grandly but honestly replies, "'I'm on the side of both'" (73). Rome, the supremely mixed city, where the "altogether contemporary" rubs shoulders with the altogether ancient, will draw powerfully upon both her loyalties.

Isabel's inner dividedness is never resolved, but during her time in the Eternal City it is matured. Her American innocence gives her "a fixed determination to regard the world as a place of brightness, of free expansion, or irresistible action" (51). Her destiny will take her to the purgatorial Roman world of darkness, concentration, and unavoidable suffering. To "become a true Rome-lover" means to qualify not as a sightseer but as a seer, to enter bravely into "the terrible human past." Here, as in *The Marble Faun*, to become a citizen of Rome means to become irrevocably implicated in the human condition.

Isabel is finely qualified to encounter such a Roman destiny because she is eminently open to change. (Most of the other characters resist it; Richard Poirier speaks aptly of "the relative 'fixity' or deadness of these others" [236].) Isabel's thirst for experience renders her, like Roderick Hudson, amenable to the modifying force of travel, but she takes along with her a weightier cargo of self-awareness than the young creator of "Thirst." "'I don't wish to touch the cup of experience,'" she confides to Ralph, "'It's a poisoned drink. I only want to see for myself'" (150). "Seeing for herself" is an objective that Isabel does finally attain; but in Rome she will learn that seeing and touching (and being touched) cannot be so readily segregated. During her stay at Gardencourt, Ralph warns Isabel that to see the ghost in his venerable English house, "'[y]ou must have suffered first, have suffered greatly, have gained some miserable knowledge. In that way your eyes are opened to it'" (48). Fifty chapters later, after returning to Gardencourt to be by her cousin's deathbed, she does "see" the ghost—Ralph's own spirit, bidding her adieu. What has opened her eyes is the miserable knowledge she has gained in the interim, and her preceptor has been Rome.

Italy, Isabel reflects on the threshold of that country, "stretched before her as a land of promise, a land in which a love of the beautiful might be comforted by endless knowledge" (223). The knowledge that she is destined to obtain in Rome will be a knowledge of ugliness, more than of beauty; yet, on a profounder level, her expectations are realized. Her unaffected recognition of the grandeur of Saint Peter's sets a pattern for her whole experience of the Roman dimension: "She had not been one of the superior tourists who are 'disappointed' in Saint Peter's and find it smaller than its fame; the first time she passed beneath the huge leathern curtain . . . her conception of greatness rose and dizzily rose. After this it never lacked space to soar" (294-5). Isabel's impression of the church bears a suggestive resemblance to James's record of his own: "The place struck me from the first," James reports, "as the hugest thing conceivable—real exaltation of one's idea of space" (*Hours* 150); "The soul infinitely expands there, if one will, but all on its quite human level. It marvels at the reach of our dream and the immensity of our resources" (151). It is the expansive, humanizing magic worked by Rome on Isabel's imagination that sets in perspective her other, equally Roman experience of stifling enclosure.

Affecting her sense of time as well as space, the influence of Rome operates so as to magnify Isabel's reach and resources. "From the Roman past to Isabel Archer's future was a long stride, but her imagination had taken it in a single flight and now hovered in slow circles over the nearer and richer field" (*Portrait* 288). Yet it is the past that, as she sits "among the shining antique marbles" (302) of the Capitoline Museum, saturates her consciousness; "the deep stillness of the past, so vivid yet, though it is nothing but a void full of names, seems to throw a solemn spell" upon her impressions (303). "Isabel sat there a long time, under the charm of [the sculptures'] motionless grace, wondering to what, of their experience, their absent eyes were open, and how, to our ears, their alien lips would sound" (303). Under the spell of the past, and through her own bitter experience, Isabel will undergo a far-reaching transformation. Henrietta's words to her, late in the novel—"'You *have* changed'" (489)—apply in a wider sense than Henrietta herself intends.

Serena Merle, a controlling architect of Isabel's change, introduces herself as having "'lived much in Florence'" (174). Behind a Florentine facade, however, Madame Merle bears the hallmarks of Rome. Stray clues to her true affinities quickly emerge: "Madame Merle had thick, fair hair, arranged somehow 'classically' and as if she were a Bust, Isabel judged—a Juno or a Niobe" (175). Isabel's musings associate her new acquaintance with maternal figures drawn from the Roman pantheon, yet these betoken, significantly, a maternity frozen into marble paralysis. According to Isabel's aunt, Mrs. Touchett, Madame Merle possesses an occult breadth of knowledge—"'She knows absolutely everything on earth there is to know'" (194). She thus serves Isabel as a Roman touchstone of sagacity garnered from wide and esoteric experience. Instead of liberating the girl, however, her guidance will lead Isabel into moral catacombs.

A true Roman *prima donna*, Serena Merle combines mystery with history. Like Christina Light, she traces her personal history back to an earlier epoch: "'I speak as if I were a hundred years old, you say? Well, I am, if you please; I was born before the French Revolution. Ah, my dear, *je viens de loin*; I belong to the old, old world'" (196). She confesses to Isabel that, like some ancient relic, she has "'been shockingly chipped and cracked'" (192). Isabel herself senses "that Madame Merle's ties always somehow had histories, and such an impression was part of the interest created by this inordinate woman" (245). Her own progress to knowledge will involve her in reluctant delving into her friend's "histories" and will lead to her dismaying recognition of the way she herself has become an actor in that obscure chronicle.

Roman knowledge conducts Isabel circuitously to a peculiarly damaging "fall." That catastrophe issues from her own self-deception, but also from the Roman conspiracy that is practiced upon her. Madame Merle herself confides to her co-conspirator, Gilbert Osmond, that she is "'frightened at the abyss into which I shall have cast her'" (286). Ralph Touchett, with his finer intuition, more precisely describes the "drop" awaiting Isabel in her contemplated marriage:

"You seemed to me to be soaring far up in the blue—to be sailing in the bright light, over the heads of men. Suddenly someone tosses up a faded rosebud—a missile that should never have reached you—and straight you drop to the ground. It hurts me . . . as if I had fallen myself!" (344)

Like Roderick Hudson, Isabel "goes up like a rocket." She "comes down like a stick," however, only because others have covertly taken aim at her.

Gilbert Osmond does not just (as Ralph's metaphor suggests) "bring down" Isabel by hurling at her the faded rosebud of his gallantry; essentially, he *is* the Roman abyss into which she falls. Although Madame Merle first describes him to Isabel as having "'no past, no future'" (197), the description is guilefully misleading. Osmond's censored Roman past turns out to be of momentous importance, above all as it bears on the future Isabel will share with him. The visage Osmond presents to Isabel in Florence is a studied fabrication; the one he uncovers in Rome, the insolent reality. As Poirier observes, Osmond's "scorning the city of Rome to live in Florence" bears out "the consummate irony of *The Portrait of a Lady*," namely, "the degree to which Osmond is a mock version of the transcendentalist" (219). Pinnacled in solitary intellectual splendor atop a Florentine hill, living in "a sorted, sifted, arranged world" (262), Osmond does indeed seem, in Emersonian fashion, to transcend all that is mundane. Marriage to him, however, brings Isabel no Florentine rebirth but a removal to Rome and a living burial under a stony mass of convention. Early in their acquaintance, Osmond hints that he has not always lived in Florence but has spent "'many years in Rome'" (266). For him, as for his confederate, Madame Merle, it is the more ancient and corroded city that provides the more fitting frame.

His sister, the Countess Gemini, lists for Isabel Osmond's "favourite subjects": "'One's Machiavelli; the other's Vittoria Colonna; the next is Metastasio'" (259). In Osmond's makeup, political expediency, aristocratic pretension, and stiffly conventionalized art merge to produce a curiously repellent Roman mixture. He does not scruple to give the uncritical Isabel a glimpse of his overweening presumption: "'There were two or three people in the world I envied—the Emperor of Russia, for instance, and the Sultan of Turkey! There were even moments when I envied the Pope of Rome—for the consideration he enjoys'" (265). During their married life Osmond will exact from Isabel herself papal "consideration." He is capable, alternatively, of posing as a Caesar; according to Countess Gemini, once again, "'he has always appeared to believe that he's descended from the gods'" (272).

Even Osmond's literal lineage is tinged with Roman pretension, of a spuriously literary sort; his mother had enjoyed the sobriquet of "the American Corinne" (281). To Isabel, he laments his family's "decline and fall": "'But we're dreadfully fallen, I think, and perhaps you'll pick us up'" (356). He philosophizes upon the decline of Rome's own fortunes with bland condescension:

"You'll like it," he went on at last. "They've spoiled it, but you'll rave about it."

"Ought I to dislike it because, poor old dear—the Niobe of Nations, you know—it has been spoiled?" she asked.

"No, I think not. It has been spoiled so often," he smiled. (284)

The American girl's anxiousness to patronize Rome by producing the accepted Byronic cliché ("'poor old dear—the Niobe of Nations, you know'") amusingly betrays her lack of cultural self-assurance. By contrast, Osmond's implicit claim to ownership of the classic Roman values that "they" are spoiling seems not amusing but disquieting. Once back on "that wonderful ground," Osmond composes "a little sonnet to which he prefixed the title of 'Rome Revisited'" (305). The title of "this piece of correct and ingenious verse" sums up the faded tinge of *déjà vu* imbuing its author's response to Rome, and Osmond's use of the most hackneyed of poetic forms underscores his essential lack of originality. His fashionable dictum that "'one ought to make one's life a work of art'" (307-8) only reveals his habit of locking up spontaneous impulse within the little rooms of "correct and ingenious" artifice.

Osmond promises Isabel, "'[Y]ou'll discover what a worship I have for propriety'" (312); and that promise, at least, is not broken. What such worship will involve, in their married life, is Osmond's making their marriage the centerpiece of a self-glorifying Roman pageant. To do this is vulgarly to expropriate, in the name of private connoisseurship, the grand Roman cultural inheritance. "'No, I'm not conventional: I'm convention itself'" (312), Osmond pontificates. While Rome may be what James calls it in *Roderick Hudson*, "the immemorial city of convention" (79), it is other things as well. If Osmond's Rome stifles feeling, Rome in a broader sense contains resources by which feeling can be nurtured; and Isabel's destiny will bring her into contact with these.

Indulging in a pre-nuptial rhapsody, Osmond sketches to his fiancée the prospects for their married life:

"My dear girl, I can't tell you how life seems to stretch there before us—what a long summer afternoon awaits us. It's the latter half of an Italian day—with a golden haze, and the shadows just lengthening, and that divine delicacy in the light, the air, the landscape, which I have loved all my life and which you love today. . . . It's all soft and mellow—it has the Italian colouring." (351-2)

Like Osmond's Roman sonnet, this pictorial set-piece sounds too premeditated to be the overflow of real feeling (though it convinces the impressionable Isabel); it reduces the whole Italian peninsula to a static, substanceless "composition." "'I can't get over the sense that Osmond is somehow—well, small'" (345), Ralph protests to Isabel. She defends Osmond by citing his supposed indifference to his own importance: "'I call that large—it's the largest thing I know'" (346). The cruelly precise Roman measure of Osmond's inner dimensions will later be supplied by the spacious scene within which their marriage unfolds. Ironically, it is amid the superb magnitude of Rome that Isabel's own large aspirations will be cut down to size by Osmond's petty overlordship.

Isabel's marriage is, in fact, a singularly refined specimen of a familiar mode: the Roman murder story. Osmond and Merle conspire to do to Isabel's spirit what Guido and his bravos do to Pompilia's body, or what Miriam and Donatello do to the model's. Isabel, too, must risk her life by suffering a plunge into a Roman abyss.

Instead of leading to the high places of happiness, from which the world would seem to lie below one, so that one could look down with a sense of exaltation and advantage, and judge and choose and pity, [Isabel's marriage] led rather downward and earthward, into realms of restriction and depression where the sound of other lives, easier and freer, was heard as from above, and where it served to deepen the feeling of failure. (424-5)

Osmond, too, acts out, before Isabel's eyes, his own Roman fall: "He was going down—down; the vision of such a fall made her almost giddy: that was the only pain" (482). In *The Portrait of a Lady*, James brilliantly refashions the mode of Roman gothic, endowing it with a new, more searching inwardness. The dark intrigue that victimizes the freedom-seeking Isabel does not endanger her physical well-being, but it plunges her into an imprisoning vault of sterile convention and dusty private history.

Isabel's first impression of Osmond in Florence suggests (in the wording of the New York Edition) "histories within histories" (232): "It spoke of the kind of personal issue that touched her most nearly; of the choice between objects, subjects, contacts . . . of a thin and those of a rich association; of a lonely, studious life in a lovely land; of an old sorrow that sometimes ached today" (232). Her preconception turns out, of course, to be lamentably romanticized. Her husband's "histories within histories," upon closer contact, expose Isabel to the corrosion of time in ways she is as yet unprepared to foresee. Resurfacing in Rome some months after her marriage, she appears to be as yet spiritually undamaged: "[T]he years had touched her only to enrich her; the flower of her youth had not faded, it only hung more quietly on its stem" (367). Already, however, she seems a hostage to the denser social and historical medium within which she now moves. "Now, at all events, framed in the gilded doorway, she struck our young man [Ned Rosier] as the picture of a gracious lady" (367). This "portrait" of Isabel, fixed at a standstill within the elegant bric-a-brac of her Roman house, is drastically at odds with the pre-Roman sense one has of her vaguely defined, mobile promise.

The house that Osmond has chosen, "a pile which bore a stern old Roman name, which smelt of historic deeds, of crime and craft and violence" (364), itself has disturbing gothic associations. (As Cristina Giorcelli observes, the name, Palazzo Roccanera, "suggests a medieval dungeon or fortress" [92].) Increasingly the palace becomes identified as the material embodiment of Osmond's stifling mentality:

It was the house of darkness, the house of dumbness, the house of suffocation. Osmond's beautiful mind gave it neither light nor air; Osmond's beautiful mind indeed seemed to peep down from a small high window and mock at her. (429)

Despite Isabel's fondness for history, the smell of historic deeds is too rarefied to nourish her life. The "big cold Empire clock" (371) perched on her chimney piece bespeaks her surrender to the Roman sway of the temporal, enforced upon her by the pontificating Caesar she has chosen to serve.

From this subjection, however, Isabel painfully climbs toward the knowledge that has always been her goal, and a vital source of that knowledge is her growing intimacy with Rome itself. Ralph, on a visit, notices her "eagerness . . . to explore the neighbourhood of Rome, to enter into relation with certain of the mustiest relics of its old society"; he is troubled to detect "a kind of violence in some of her impulses, of crudity in some of her experiments" (393). Yet it is through such strenuous initiatives that Isabel will become, as she must, a "true Rome-lover." Her shocking discoveries of human baseness are possible for her to assimilate only in so far as she can place them within a broader Roman perspective—a perspective that Roderick Hudson, for all his "historic consciousness," never acquires. What James says in *Italian Hours* of the restorative influence of Saint Peter's calls Isabel irresistibly to mind:

When you are weary . . . of the unremunerative aspects of human nature on Corso and Pincio . . . of ruin and dirt and decay, of priests and beggars and takers of advantage, of the myriad tokens of a halting civilisation, the image of the great temple depresses the balance of your doubts, seems to rise above even the highest tide of vulgarity and make you still believe in the heroic will and the heroic act. (152)

If Isabel retains her belief in "the heroic will and the heroic act," the credit belongs largely to the Roman images she contemplates. Her endurance is fed not only by the great monuments but also by the natural surroundings of the Campagna, where she walks with Pansy Osmond, and more generally by a subtly restorative spirit of place. In *Italian Hours*, again, James attempts to define that elusive spirit:

Rome, which in some moods, especially to new-comers, seems a place of almost sinister gloom, has an occasional art, as one knows her better, of brushing away care by the grand gesture with which some splendid impatient mourning matron—just the Niobe of Nations, surviving, emerging and looking about her again—might pull off and cast aside an oppression of muffling crape. This admirable power still temperamentally to react and take notice lurks in all her darkness and dirt and decay. (192)

In *The Portrait of a Lady*, this vibrant antigothic Roman spirit competes with the murky gloom of the Palazzo Roccanera. Isabel's success in communing with it helps to sustain her own "admirable power still temperamentally to react and take notice."

The things of which she is obliged to take notice are brutally disagreeable. Her dawning recognition of the schemes her husband and her friend have contrived endangers her trust in human relationships, and in her own capacity to direct her life rewardingly. Amid this looming personal storm, she finds new meaning in the austere, impersonal grandeur of her surroundings:

She had long before this taken old Rome into her confidence, for in a world of ruins the ruin of her happiness seemed a less unnatural catastrophe. She rested her weariness upon things that had crumbled for centuries and yet still were upright; she dropped her secret sadness into the silence of lonely places, where its very modern quality detached itself and grew objective, so that as she sat in a sun-warmed angle on a winter's day, or stood in a mouldy church to which no one came, she could almost smile at it and think of its smallness. Small it was, in the large Roman record, and her haunting sense of the continuity of the human lot easily carried her from the less to the greater. She had become deeply, tenderly acquainted with Rome: it interfused and moderated her passion. But she had grown to think of it chiefly as the place where people had suffered. This was what came to her in the starved churches, where the marble columns, transferred from pagan ruins, seemed to offer her a companionship in endurance and the musty incense to be a compound of long-unanswered prayers. There was no gentler nor less consistent heretic than Isabel; the firmest of worshippers, gazing at dark altar-pictures or clustered candles, could not have felt more intimately the suggestiveness of these objects nor have been more liable at such moments to a spiritual visitation. (517-8)

What Rome cannot do for George Eliot's miserably honeymooning Dorothea Brooke, it does for Isabel. Where Dorothea is a mere passerby in the Eternal City, Isabel is in the process of making it her permanent home. Dorothea views the place through the lenses of a provincial, Protestant sensibility, and recoils in confusion; Isabel views it with eyes that are becoming wisely non-sectarian, and takes it to her heart. Embracing the age-old sadness of Rome, she accepts the long continuum of human suffering, finding in it an antidote to the peculiarly modern, hermetic privacy of her domestic unhappiness.

Thus, the Roman panorama reconciles Isabel to ruin by enabling her to objectify her private suffering, by endowing her with the local privilege of perspective. In a symbolic pose, she sits "on a stone that had once had a use and gaze[s] through the veil of her personal sadness at the splendid sadness of the scene" (518-9)—propped on her stone of desolation, she is beginning to understand her own, circumscribed reality as a mere antechamber to the greater reality without. Isabel's scrutiny of Rome brings her a broad perception of the pervasiveness of human tragedy that is not discouraging but liberating.

At the same time, her expanded sense of history lends substance and assurance to Isabel's understanding of her own extraordinary situation and of the other people implicated in it. In Rome, human malignity becomes for her no longer an interesting hypothesis but an incontrovertible fact. After her shattering conversation with Madame Merle in Chapter 49, "[s]he asked herself, with an almost childlike horror of the supposition, whether to this intimate friend of several years the great historical epithet of *wicked* were to be applied" (519). But as she uncovers the details of the plot that has victimized her, a more mature compassion supersedes judgment. She receives Countess Gemini's disclosure of Pansy Osmond's parentage as if it were "some fine sinister passage of public history" (544), and though she afterwards bursts into tears, she is moved more intensely by Madame Merle's presumed suffering than by her own. Her time in Rome has thus taught her to frame her own predicament within the greater historical palimpsest embodied by the place; to choose a finer Roman spirit of comprehension over the cruder Roman tradition of vengefulness. Her Roman "fall" is followed by an arduous re-ascent. (To call it "fortunate" would be glib;

James has transmitted too particularized a sense of Isabel's anguish for it to be readily subsumed within any neat redemptive scheme.)

Isabel grows in Rome through the painful process of becoming a better reader of personal history, both her own and other people's. During her married life there, her past parades by her, in the persons of those who have loved her—Ralph, Lord Warburton, Caspar Goodwood, Henrietta. While confronting the solicitations of the past embodied in this form, she must also deal with new, urgent concerns of her Roman present, like the obstructed love affair between her stepdaughter Pansy and that amiable young *bibelot*-fancier, Ned Rosier. When Warburton himself becomes a suitor for Pansy's hand, with the possible ulterior motive of nurturing his intimacy with Isabel, the claims of past and present begin to intersect, creating a bewildering, multi-levelled Roman imbroglio.

The sickening page of history inscribed by her husband and Madame Merle, when she learns to read it, completes the Romanizing of Isabel's consciousness. Her sudden, revelatory glimpse of a private colloquy between the two gives her an inkling of the past they have shared—of the abyss next to which she has ignorantly been walking. But if Isabel is enlightened by the past, she is also cruelly punished by it. It is, in fact, in the cleavage between their attitudes toward the past that she and Osmond are most tellingly at variance.

He was fond of the old, the consecrated, the transmitted; so was she, but she pretended to do what she chose with it. He had an immense esteem for tradition; he had told her once that the best thing in the world was to have it, but that if one was so unfortunate as not to have it one must immediately proceed to make it. (431)

Isabel's response to tradition is reverent but creative; Osmond's response to it (like his response to Isabel herself) is disingenuous and exploitative.

Osmond's patronizing of that "traditionless" pilgrim, Caspar Goodwood, is one instance of his readiness to use his factitious Roman roots for self-congratulatory ends. "'I'm very fond of Rome, you know . . . ,'" Osmond tells his guest, "'but there's nothing I like better than to meet people who haven't that superstition. The modern world's after all very fine. . . . We've liked you because—because you've reconciled us a little to the future'" (505). Ironically, what Osmond hands down to Isabel from his hidden Roman past makes her own future nearly impossible for her to accept. His posture when Isabel comes, late in the novel, to tell him of her wish to go to Ralph's deathbed (he is copying the drawing of an antique coin) captures the meanly secondhand quality of his feeling for Roman tradition. While voicing his doubts about the gravity of Ralph's illness, Osmond examines his drawing through a magnifying glass—an action that precisely captures his habit of inflating the magnitude of his own concerns while minimizing the importance of other people's. His myopically "magnifying" vision is the reverse of the power of seeing in perspective that Isabel absorbs from her exposure to Rome.

Once their affair—"'their little carnival'" as the Countess sarcastically labels it (548)—has ended, Merle and Osmond remain, like Hawthorne's Miriam and Donatello, irrevocably leagued. "'The whole past was between them'" (545), the Countess explains to Isabel. It is upon Isabel that that "whole past" has been visited. Little wonder that when, defying Osmond, she travels to the dying Ralph's bedside, her time sense is (like Roderick Hudson's) destabilized: "The past and the future came and went at their will, but she saw them only in fitful images, which rose and fell by a logic of their own" (560). Journeying away from Rome, she seems to herself to be leading a posthumous existence; she has become "so detached from hope and regret, that she recall[s] to herself one of those Etruscan figures couched upon the receptacle of their ashes" (561). To Ralph's assurance, "'There are many things in life. You're very young,'" she responds simply, "'I feel very old'" (578). Antiquity, for dwellers among ruins, can be contagious.

Upon returning to England, Isabel can view Rome only with dread: "[N]ow that she was at a distance, beyond its spell, she thought with a kind of spiritual shudder of Rome. There was a penetrating chill in the image, and she drew back into the deepest shade of Gardencourt" (581). Viewed from the Touchetts' leafy British Eden, Rome looks to Isabel appallingly barren. To the devoted Caspar Goodwood, the city seems a grotesquely distorting "stage," whereon Isabel must perforce lose touch with her true self: "'It's too late to play a part,'" he expostulates with her. "'[D]idn't you leave all that behind you in Rome?'" (588). His evocation of the Roman "atmosphere" sounds a conventional note of superstitious awe: "'It's too monstrous of you to think of sinking back into that misery, of going to open your mouth to that poisoned air'" (589).

Although Isabel responds to Goodwood's passionate kiss, she comes a moment later to her final, clarifying knowledge. "She had not known where to turn; but she knew now. There was a very straight path" (591). Straight paths, Isabel now perceives, lead infallibly to Rome, the capital of crookedness. The final confrontation between Isabel and Goodwood juxtaposes the American sense of possibility against the Roman knowledge, so dearly bought by Isabel, of confinement:

"If you'll only trust me, how little you will be disappointed! The world's all before us—and the world's very big. I know something about that."

Isabel gave a long murmur, like a creature in pain; it was as if he were pressing something that hurt her. "The world's very small," she said at random. (590)

As Isabel tells Henrietta, returning to Osmond "'won't be the scene of a moment; it will be a scene of the rest of my life'" (565). Her meaning is not entirely simple. The scene of her life will in one sense be the odious closet-drama of her marriage, but it will also be the immensely greater spectacle of the Eternal City.

Isabel is by now, indeed, as indissolubly wedded to the city as she is to her husband. That metaphorical marriage, at least, has been made in heaven.

Isabel's decision to return has been a source of contention among critics. To some, it represents a lofty affirmation of commitment; to others, a defeatist submitting to sterile convention. Isabel's stoicism in accepting a pinched and flinty estimate of her life-possibilities is bound to strike many modern readers as itself narrow. In fact, however, her decision issues from her whole scarring, yet stirring, Roman experience. To turn her back on the place would mean to deny the hard-earned knowledge it has conferred upon her. As Dorothy Van Ghent says, "Isabel, still seeking that freedom which is growth, goes back to Osmond's claustral house, for it is there, in the ruin where Pansy has been left, that she has placed roots, found a crevice in which to grow straightly and freshly, found a fertilizing, civilizing relationship between consciousness and circumstances" (228). While this perhaps suggests a sunnier view of Isabel's lot than circumstances warrant, Van Ghent is surely right to stress Rome's importance for Isabel as a source of civilizing values. By contrast, Madame Merle's ignominious flight from Rome to the United States signals her defeat at the hands of life. The fabled "land of opportunity" can offer only the chilliest of refuges for an unfrocked Roman opportunist.

Hawthorne's Donatello returns to Rome as a penitent; revisiting the scene of his crime means for him revisiting his birthplace as a moral being. Isabel, for whom returning means revisiting the scene of other people's crimes, treads a different path. It is one closer to that travelled by George Eliot's Romola, who, growing beyond repugnance, reenters Florence to lay claim to her true identity. But unlike Romola, who achieves self-awareness through her self-identification with the larger polity, Isabel can locate her authentic self only in relation to individual agents, through the ethical complexities of her dealings with them.

Alwyn Berland has maintained "that Isabel, like James, is to place civilization primarily within the compass of the arts—as Culture—and outside the arena of what is commonly called history—outside the social, political, economic, institutional life of men" (105). I have argued that "what is commonly called history" does enter into and shape Isabel's consciousness, through her sensitivity to her Roman surroundings and her growing aptitude for absorbing their import into her own private experience. Nevertheless, for Isabel historical awareness operates on an essentially personal level; it does not manifest itself in her thinking about her place within the larger society to which she belongs. One reason, perhaps, is that her sprawling Roman world, unlike Romola's compact Florentine one, does not foster a sense of coherent community; self-definition can proceed here exclusively on private and individual terms.

Nevertheless, the Rome of Browning, Clough, and even Hawthorne draws more abundantly than James's on the public dimension of the city to highlight the individuality of the various actors. In *Amours de Voyage*, as we have seen, the love interest is meaningfully juxtaposed with the political struggle to save the Roman Republic. In *The Ring and the Book*, the individual lives gain resonance from being played out against a background of Roman public proceedings—the official inquest, the Pope's deliberations, Guido's incipient execution. Hawthorne, too, transmits some relevant sense of the larger life of the city, as in the culminating scenes of Carnival, where an ancient festivity draws together the destinies of the novel's wayward modern principals. In the next chapter, we will see how a recent work, Malamud's "Behold the Key," places an American visitor to Rome in precise social perspective against a forcefully realized picture of the city's frantic, post-war collective life.

In *The Portrait of a Lady*, James does not connect his protagonist with such a concretely evoked public scene. James's Rome could be called, by contrast, rarefied or aestheticized—it is represented largely by its famous monuments, such as Saint Peter's—yet it makes, for all that, its own powerful statement about the tragedy implicit in the individual's striving for full self-realization. On her own special terms, Isabel Archer achieves an impressive destiny. She returns to the Eternal City equipped to play out the scene of the rest of her life with a complex awareness that is, in the noblest sense, Roman.

18

Brief Roman Candles:
Wharton, Huxley, and Malamud

"I was just thinking . . . what different things Rome stands for to each generation of travelers. To our grandmothers, Roman fever; to our mothers, sentimental dangers—how we used to be guarded!—to our daughters, no more dangers than the middle of Main Street. They don't know it—but how much they're missing!"

(Edith Wharton, *Collected Short Stories* 2: 837)

As Edith Wharton's American matron Alida Slade observes, the sentimental commonplaces about Rome current in the nineteenth century have become unfashionable in the twentieth. Yet writers like Aldous Huxley, Bernard Malamud, and Wharton herself share with such nineteenth-century predecessors as Hawthorne and James a fondness for the motif of the Roman fall from innocence into knowledge. These more recent figures favor ironic and comic modes in their treatment of such Roman material; in their fiction, those who fall tend to sprawl. Yet the tragedy inherent in the idea of falling has not vanished; it continues to be heard as a haunting undertone.

EDITH WHARTON, "ROMAN FEVER"

Roman falls, as both Wharton and Huxley demonstrate, can occur to seasoned middle age as easily as to blithe inexperience. In Wharton's well-known story "Roman Fever," two American matrons, Grace Ansley and Alida Slade, learn that truth in a curiously painful fashion. The return of these two genteel and well-to-do widows to the Rome of their youth has a typically Roman outcome: the startling recovery, and reappraisal, of the vanished past.

The story's opening paragraph strikes a deceptively serene keynote:

From the table at which they had been lunching two American ladies of ripe but well-cared-for middle age moved across the lofty terrace of the Roman restaurant and, leaning on its parapet, looked first at each other, and then down on the outspread glories of the Palatine and the Forum, with the same expression of vague but benevolent approval. (2: 833)

Both women, as Mrs. Slade explains to the head waiter, are "'old lovers of Rome'" (834). Their sedateness distinguishes them from their smartly modern daughters, who have flown to Tarquinia for tea with some young Italian aviators.

By contrast with such buoyant up-to-dateness, both women find, as they sit contemplating the ruins, that "there was a relief in laying down their somewhat futile activities in the presence of the vast Memento Mori which faced them" (837). Their thoughts hang suspended between this immense, sobering reminder of time past and the clamorous Roman heralds of time passing: "Suddenly the air was full of that deep clangor of bells which periodically covers Rome with a roof of silver. Mrs. Slade glanced at her wristwatch. 'Five o'clock already,' she said, as though surprised" (837). The surroundings harmonise perfectly with the spasm of reminiscence that the story enacts.

Reminiscence is, in fact, a mode that the women's casual conversation has already broached. "'When we first met here we were younger than our girls are now. You remember?'" asks Mrs. Slade. "'Oh, yes, I remember,'" Mrs. Ansley murmurs in reply (834). But memory remains as yet occluded. "So these two ladies visualized each other," Wharton comments drily, "each through the wrong end of her little telescope" (836). The movement of Wharton's Roman narrative turns the telescopes around, bringing into focus dismayingly unexpected images of the past.

According to William L. Vance, the "basic action" of "Roman Fever" "could have occurred anywhere"; "[t]he Roman setting exists in the story primarily because it was so important a part of the social history of Mrs. Wharton's period" (*America's Rome* 2:318). But such a view not only ignores the relevance of the story's title; it seriously underestimates the force of Wharton's Rome as a psychological metaphor. It is, above all, the mute testimony of the Roman scene—"the great accumulated wreckage of passion and splendor" (*Collected Short Stories* 2:838) which the women contemplate—that prompts revelation, bringing to light the skeletons buried in the secret passages of their past lives. As Mrs. Slade observes of the panorama, "'[I]t all brings back the past a little too acutely'" (838). For Grace Ansley as well, "too many memories rose from the lengthening shadows of those august ruins" (838).

It is Alida Slade who takes the initiative in raising the memories, at first invoking what seems a mere rumor of a long-forgotten Byronic sight-seeing ritual: "'You don't remember going to visit some ruins or other one evening, just after dark, and catching a bad chill? You were supposed to have gone to see the moon rise'" (840). "'It was all so long ago,'" Mrs. Ansley evasively protests; but the recollection, once stirred, lays bare the foundations of both women's emotional histories.

Like other Roman narratives, this one hinges on the issue of "knowledge." Mrs. Slade tells Mrs. Ansley that she can no longer bear "'your not knowing that I've always known why you went'" to the ruins (840). She reveals her knowledge of the letter—ostensibly written by Delphin Slade, the man she later married—summoning Grace to a love tryst at the Colosseum. She goes on to disclose, shockingly, that "'I know what was in that letter because I wrote it'" (841). Her knowledge even includes a penetrating awareness of Grace's hidden romantic feelings: "'I knew you were in love with Delphin—and I was afraid; afraid of you, of your quiet ways, your sweetness'" (841). These startling revelations provoke in Mrs. Ansley a small Roman "collapse." "Her bag, her knitting and gloves, slid in a panic-stricken heap to the ground. She looked at Mrs. Slade as though she were looking at a ghost" (840). It is, in fact, the ghost of an old passion, long repressed, that has returned to squeak and gibber on the quiet Roman terrace.

The one significant fact which Mrs. Slade has *not* known—and which she now painfully learns—is that Delphin did appear on that long-past evening at the appointed rendezvous. As Alida comes to realize, Mrs. Ansley has remained for all these years convinced that the idea for the meeting originated with Delphin. The other woman, she suddenly understands, has "been living on that letter. How she must have loved him, to treasure the mere memory of its ashes!" (842). But this mutual unearthing of past passion and loss divides the two women, rather than uniting them: "Mrs. Slade . . . was conscious of a strange sense of isolation, of being cut off from the warm current of human communion" (842).

When at the end of the story she turns her gaze toward "the dusky secret mass of the Colosseum" (843), her choice of vista is appropriate. The ruin has determined the course of both women's lives, but more than that it has come to stand for the looming violence of the past, the menace of human history, and its cunning corridors. By the end, the two respectable American matrons have unearthed a corpse as unsightly as any to be found buried in Serena Merle's garden. Mrs. Slade gloats unpleasantly over her quarter century of enjoyment of the "prize," Delphin: "'After all, I had everything; I had him for twenty-five years'" (843). Mrs. Ansley trumps her by flaunting her possession of a less evident prize, the fruit of her illicit tryst with Delphin: "'I had Barbara,' she said, and began to move ahead of Mrs. Slade toward the stairway." Genteel American surfaces have fallen away, to disclose bitter, inveterate Roman grudges. In the land of ruin, dissimulation has an alarming habit of withering into stony truth.

ALDOUS HUXLEY: "AFTER THE FIREWORKS"

In April of 1925, Aldous Huxley was cheerfully looking forward to leaving Florence for Rome. "After a third-rate provincial town, colonized by English sodomites and middle-aged Lesbians, which is, after all, what Florence is, a genuine metropolis will be lively. Not to mention the fact that it is incomparably the most lovely place in the world" (*Letters* 246). While Huxley's feeling for Florence eventually grew warmer, his liking for Rome did not cool. Yet characteristically, when Huxley used it as a setting, "the most lovely place in the world" became the occasion for unlovely ironies.

In his novella "After the Fireworks," from the collection *Brief Candles*, the irony derives from the protagonist's special susceptibility to the passage of time, that signally Roman dimension.   The gap of years separating the aging, celebrated author Miles Fanning and his young admirer Pamela Tarn causes time to be the central issue in their relationship—in part, because Fanning insists on making it an issue.   A question Fanning asks Pamela soon after they meet—"'And do you realise what the time is?'" (134-5)—unconsciously betrays his besetting preoccupation. In fact, however, the question might more fittingly have been put to Fanning himself, whose problems with temporality clearly have not started with Pamela.

The story's opening words, directed to Fanning by his censorious friend Judd—"'Late as usual. Late'" (114)—already hint at the losing battle the writer has been waging against time's peremptory demands. It is, however, his meeting with Pamela that jars him awake to the mortal, and mortifying, combat in which he has been engaged. "It was as though he had suddenly lifted his head out of the sand and seen time bleeding away—like the stabbed bull at the end of a bull-fight, swaying on his legs and soundlessly spouting the red blood from his nostrils—bleeding, bleeding away stanchlessly into the darkness" (127). Essentially, Fanning's rash love-involvement with a girl many years his junior represents his last-ditch attempt to stanch the frightening flow.

To the world, Fanning normally manages to present the facade of a prodigy exempt from the wasting effects of the years. His old (indeed, by implication, extinct) friend Dodo del Grillo considers him "'positively indecent. Like Dorian Gray'" (136). Pamela herself records in her diary that Fanning is "'very good-looking and you don't think of him as being either old or young, but just as being there'" (153). So Fanning, too, likes to think of himself; but his Roman misadventure thrusts him into a Dorian Gray-like confrontation with the truth.

Fanning's urbanely cynical outlook accords with his Roman wealth of experience and worldly wisdom. Comically, however, his cynicism fails him in his erotic midlife crisis. His interest in the ingenue Pamela embarrassingly arouses his equally Roman penchant for experimentation. "Moreover, he was an experimentalist, he genuinely wanted to see what would happen" (158)—but erotic curiosity has results that even the adept investigator cannot predict.

A follower of the hedonist golden rule *carpe diem*, Fanning has no patience with dusty antiquarianism. Pamela notes in her diary his approval of her breezy judgment on the Roman Forum as "'a rubbish heap . . . he . . . said he always preferred live dogs to dead lions and thinks it's awful the way the Fascists are pulling down nice ordinary houses and making holes to find more of these beastly pillars and things'" (179). His sentiments are in keeping with the quality Huxley himself approvingly termed Italian "presentism," the robust refusal to let the life of the moment be a hostage to the revered past. Nevertheless, Fanning's variety of presentism amounts, by his own admission, to one more stratagem of escape: "'I flee from time by living as far as possible only in and for the present'" (199).

"'Consult the oracles of passion,'" Fanning urges receptive readers like Pamela in his novel *The Return of Eurydice*. "'A god speaks in them, or else a devil'" (155). Fanning is a sincere apostle of his literary code of erotic experience as its own end, but he possesses the self-knowledge to describe himself as "'an old satyr. . . . A superannuated faun'" (141). His voluptuary presentism, he realizes, can lead him to serve a devil as easily as a god. It cannot safeguard him against the ravages of time or the importunities of memory. Fanning remains, off the record, consumingly taken up by the past; even his favorite oaths ("'Sblood!'" "'Hell and Death!'" [187]) are archaisms. When he is moved to kiss Pamela, he cannot avoid conflating her in his mind with "that Jenny Something-or-Other he had danced the polka with at Uncle Fred's one Christmas, how many centuries ago!—and yet only yesterday, only this instant" (177).

True to Roman form, the January-and-May affair between Fanning and his young reader proves a mere passing vicissitude. Precisely because she is so impressionable an admirer, the aptly named Pamela Tarn represents a dangerous pool for an aging Narcissus to plunge into. What he can offer her, at best, is a perspective like the one they both view from Monte Cavo: "'What a panorama of space and time!' he said. 'So many miles, such an expanse of centuries! You can still walk on the paved road that led to the temple here'" (175). Unfortunately, such a Roman road is not likely to be the one most natural for Pamela, at her fresh stage of life, to tread.

Following in the footsteps of other literary pilgrims, Pamela has come to Rome seeking her own identity. This she believes, in her innocence, to be mapped out for her on the pages of Fanning's novel *The Return of Eurydice*, in the figure of Joan, "who had emerged from the wintry dark underworld of an unawakened life with her husband . . . into the warmth and brilliance of that transfiguring passion . . . for the adorable Walter whom she had always imagined must be so like Miles Fanning himself" (126-7). While the appeal to Pamela of such an erotic renewal-myth is understandable, the girl plainly has no idea of what a passion for a real-life Walter might involve. She must learn "the ultimate lesson," as George Woodcock calls it, "of the folly of romantic expectations" (167).

Fanning dishonestly rationalizes his exploitation of his young admirer's innocence by appointing himself director of her "education," an enterprise to which he gives his own peculiar Roman twist. Rather than exposing Pamela to "'a lot of beastly old Roman odds and ends'" (161), he steers her in the direction of the Villa Giulia's splendid Etruscan collections. Foremost among these stands the great Apollo of Veii, for Fanning "'the most beautiful statue in the world'" (165) because it symbolizes a joyous consciousness that antedates "'the great split that broke life into spirit and matter, heroics and diabolics, virtue and sin and all the other accursed antitheses'" (168). His enthusiasm for this emblem of pre-Christian unity of being betrays, however, his own inner dividedness. Fanning's vivid memory of the statue's unearthing itself mentally distances him from his young companion: "'It's a question of age,'" he tells her, "'or the experience of a particular time that's not your time'" (167).

Pamela can share neither Fanning's memory of the event nor his philosophic commitment to the Apollo principle. She can hardly be blamed if his lecture inspires her not with a like ardor but with a powerful urge to yawn. Such Apollonian notions, however finely formulated, make no vital engagement with her own slender store of accumulated experience. Ultimately, Fanning furthers Pamela's "education" more through example than through precept, endowing her at least with the negative knowledge of what to avoid in future.

The attraction between the two is, while it lasts, intense. Nevertheless, they are chronically—and above all chronologically—at odds. Fanning's admonition in the wise, paternal letter Pamela never receives—"'For you and I are foreigners to one another, foreigners in time. Which is a greater foreignness than the foreignness of space and language'" (196)—proves unhappily true. Small details subtly highlight the generational "foreignness," such as the disparity between Pamela's journal record of an evening with her contemporary, Guy Browne ("'Danced till 2.15'" [183]) and her entry about dancing with Fanning ("'[H]e dances really very well, but we stopped before midnight, because he said the noise of the jazz would drive him crazy'" [185]).

In Huxley's fiction, passion goeth before a fall; the conclusion of this particular Roman misalliance is foregone. Pamela, determined as she is to take an emotional Roman plunge, can be excused for failing to predict it. But the seasoned Fanning is himself perversely naive in assuming that he can dally without risk. "When the time came, he would revoke the licence, step back again into the daily world" (188). In their discussion of the fireworks display that gives the novella its title, the two demonstrate their complementary varieties of myopia:

Her heart beat very fast, exultantly. "I mean, why shouldn't it be fireworks all the time?"

"Because it just isn't, that's all. Unhappily." It was time to step back again; but he didn't step back.

"Well, then, it's a case of damn the intervals and enjoy . . . Oh!" She started. That prodigious bang had sent a large red moon sailing almost slowly into the sky. It burst into a shower of meteors that whistled as they fell, expiringly.

Fanning imitated their plaintive noise. "Sad, sad," he commented. "Even the fireworks can be sad."

She turned on him fiercely. "Only because you want them to be sad. Yes, you want them to be. Why do you want them to be sad?" (189)

The dispute between the energy of explosive libido and the hesitancy of dampening prudence is cleverly dramatized by the dialogue. It is settled, by the course of events, in Pamela's favor.

Huxley points up the irony of these developments by means of a series of adroitly managed time-juxtapositions. "'By the time you receive this letter'" (195), Fanning opens his intended apology for backing off; but Fanning's message is never received. Pamela's untimely appearance topples her sage correspondent into a Roman abyss—"He felt as though his heart had fallen into an awful gulf of emptiness" (199)—and the letter is dead. By succumbing to the plunge of passion, Fanning guarantees for himself just the sad aftermath his disclaimer had been designed to forestall. His erotic antics, which he carries to excess in the wryly named cells of the Passionist Fathers at Monte Cavo, lead up to the anticlimax of physical exhaustion:

But at midnight they had found themselves, almost suddenly, on earth again, shiveringly cold under the moon. Cold, cold to the quick, Fanning had picked himself up. They stumbled homewards through the woods, in silence. It was in a kind of trance of chilled and sickened exhaustion that he had at last dropped down on his bed in the convent cell. (208)

Huxley's narrative chronology sharpens the irony of Fanning's breakdown through another deflating use of juxtaposition. The account "cuts" startlingly from the morning after the affair is consummated, when Fanning destroys his "farewell" letter, to the scene in the Tuscan health spa of Montecatini:

The architectural background was like something out of Alma Tadema. But the figures that moved across the sunlit atrium, that lingered beneath the colonnades and in the coloured shadow of the awnings, the figures were Hogarthian and Rowlandsonian, were the ferocious satires of Daumier and Rouveyre. Huge jellied females overflowed the chairs on which they sat. Sagging and with the gait of gorged bears, old men went slowly shambling down the porticoes. (204)

The delusory triumph of pagan sensuality is followed, without warning, by a travesty of the pomp and splendor of a Roman bath. Fanning's regimen of purgative drinking—"'This morning at eight to the pump-room, where M. has to drink eight glasses of different kinds of water before breakfast'" (209)—bleakly recalls his reckless quaffing of sexual pleasure. In the story's closing pages Huxley makes similarly deft use of juxtaposition. Shuttling back and forth in time, he relies on Pamela's diary entries to counterpoint past against present, continually thrusting uncomfortable discordances before the reader's eyes.

The "Roman" qualities in Fanning that originally made him attractive to Pamela—his knowingness, his worldly sophistication—turn out to be the very ones that set draconic limits to the emotional depth of their love affair. As Pamela resentfully records, he rules out *a priori* any except a bodily communion between them. "'But he said . . . when two minds are of different ages it's hard for them to understand each other when they speak, but bodies can understand each other, because they don't talk, thank God'" (221). While hymning to Pamela the praises of a sensual "eternity," he allows the force of time to create an unbridgeable abyss of silence between them. He employs his sexual expertise to keep Pamela submerged in an erotic netherworld—"'and he was so *divinely* sweet and gentle that it was like gradually sinking, sinking and being drowned'" (221). Meanwhile, he exerts his superior force of personality to dampen her warmth of feeling: "From the first he had refused to come up to her emotional level. From the first he had taken it for granted—and his taking it for granted was in itself an act of moral compulsion—that she should descend to his" (216). It is an up-to-date variation on that Roman standby, the *descensus Averni.*

Still, if Pamela has lost her innocence by the end of Huxley's novella, she has gained a new, pragmatic readiness to come to terms with reality. Now she can see in perspective what she had earlier only glimpsed: the true, synthetic nature of her infatuation with Fanning. "Looking back now, from the further shore of his illness, Pamela felt astonished that she could have gone on obstinately imagining, in spite of these loop-holes on reality, that she loved him. 'Because I didn't,' she said to herself, clear-sighted, weeks too late. 'I didn't'" (222). Time, her great enemy during the affair, has at least blessed her with the Roman gift of hindsight: "From this distance of time she could see all that had happened in perspective, as it were, and as a whole" (216). Because her passion for the eminent author has itself been at bottom a literary construct, she can, once that passion has vanished, turn the page—move beyond her belief in her own "fictional" self-image. "She remembered how she had tried to imagine that she was like her namesake of [Fanning's novel] *Pastures New*—the fatal woman whose cool detachment gives her such power over her lovers. But the facts had proved too stubborn; it was simply impossible for her to pretend that this handsome fancy-picture was her portrait" (218). While she ripples through the telltale pages of her diary, "[t]he days [flick] past under her thumb." The detail neatly captures Pamela's increased mastery over time, and over the experience that comes with it. If she can no longer picture herself as a "fatal woman," she has at least made a modest advance in her control over her own fate. As the story ends, she embarks on a letter to Guy Browne, who (true to his name) is undistinguished but whose age and temperament may make him a more suitable lover.

As for Fanning, his part in this sexual tragicomedy endows familiar Roman motifs with novel ironies. Equipped with worldly knowledge, but chronically self-infatuated, the noted writer fails to escape the abyss of involvement with his charming, adoring protégée, even though he himself foresees the grief it will bring to both. What is more, his very sophistication and cynicism cause his prophecies of disaster to become self-fulfilling. He turns into exactly the thing he had most hoped to avoid becoming: time's laughingstock. Meanwhile, Pamela, though a slighter and less cultivated seeker of Roman knowledge than James's Isabel Archer, gains, in her own measure, a mature cognizance of intractable realities. If her "education," in Fanning's cerebral terms, has not been a success, she has emerged from her baptism by fireworks with an enlarged awareness and with her determination to affront her own modest destiny intact.

BERNARD MALAMUD'S ROMAN LOCKS AND KEYS

But first the maid led them onto a broad terrace to show them the view of the city. The sight excited Carl—the variety of architecture from ancient to modern times, where history had been and still, in its own aftermath, sensuously flowed, a sea of roofs, towers, domes; and in the background, golden-domed St. Peter's. This marvelous city, Carl thought. (*The Magic Barrel* 67-68)

Like other American fictional visitors, Carl Schneider, a graduate student in Italian at Columbia, comes to Rome inclined to take a lofty, idealized historical view of the Eternal City. But as Bernard Malamud's story "Behold the Key" makes clear, the "sensuous flow of history" that Carl is pleased to associate with the place has remarkably little to do with the pace of the lives actually being lived there after the end of the Second World War. The story of which Carl is the protagonist vigorously explores the potential for farce inherent in this cultural time lag.

In making the decision to go to Rome, Schneider is already influenced by an anxiety about time. "He was twenty-eight—his years weighed on him—and [Norma, his wife] was thirty, and when else could they go if not now?" (57-58). He is confident that, once there, "they could get settled satisfactorily in a short time" (58). After a month of unsuccessful house hunting, however, he becomes "nervous over the way time was flying" (60); he is "disappointed in finding himself so dissatisfied in this city of his dreams." His fantasies quickly become tarnished by Roman realities—"Rome, a city of perpetual surprise, had surprised unhappily" (57). Despite his background as a student of the culture, he vents his displeasure on the local populace. "When he was not blaming himself he was blaming the Italians. They were aloof, evasive, indifferent to his plight. He couldn't communicate with them in their own language, whatever it was" (61). Carl's fictional Roman frustrations are by no means unique; they evoke the experiences of a whole new generation of American students and writers abroad. They strikingly match those reported by John Cheever, himself the author of several compelling Roman stories: "'We have been here a little over a week now, but with the exception of my first days in the infantry I have never felt time to be so distorted. . . . I look at four and five apartments a day, and Mary visits schools. . . . The whole expedition from the moment we boarded the boat has meant a complete reconstruction of my machinery" (*Home Before Dark* 109).

But it is not only foreign visitors who suffer time dislocations in Rome. Against Carl Schneider's reconstruction of his own machinery, Malamud sets the *endemic*, stultifying combat with time in which the native Romans turn out to be engrossed. Exhibit A of this predicament is Bevilacqua, the harried free-lance house agent whom Carl engages to work for him. Frustratingly, the agent first promises to arrive at the Schneiders' hotel "at thirteen sharp" (Malamud's consistent reference to Continental train-time cleverly underscores the "foreignness" of Bevilacqua's time sense) but does not show up until ten to two. He is, in fact, moonlighting over his dinner hour; he confides to Carl that "he hoped to expand his time later" (63). Bevilacqua, Carl comes to learn, is engaged in a perpetual losing battle against time's inelasticity.

That essential fact about the little Roman's life quickly emerges. On their way to the first address they inspect, "[t]wice he asked Carl the time, and when Carl told him, his lips moved soundlessly" (64). After the first two leads fall through, he urges Carl, "'I have an exceptional place in mind for you now, but we've got to hurry'" (66). Asking for an American cigarette only to be told that Carl does not smoke, "Bevilacqua shrugged and walked faster" (67); acceleration is his anodyne against daily disappointment. But this frantic time obsession is by no means a personal quirk of the agent's; it reveals itself as pervasive throughout the Eternal City. Aldo De Vecchis, the recalcitrant ex-tenant of the apartment Schneider finally fastens upon, asks Carl promptly at their first meeting, "'Where may we speak? My time is short'" (77). When they begin to discuss business, he assures Carl courteously, "'I won't waste your time'" (77). During this post-war phase of scarcity, the item most severely rationed is time; there is too meager a stock of sand in the Roman hourglass.

The panic haste suffusing the city is in fact the symptom of a deadly ratrace, a savage competition for slender resources. Rome, far from offering the picturesque, old-world haven of which Carl had dreamed, has become a surrealist version of the urban fast-track he has fled.

Traffic was heavy, a stream of gnats—Vespas, Fiats, Renaults—roared at them from both directions, nobody slowing down to let them pass. They plowed across dangerously. At the bus stop the crowd rushed for the doors when the bus swerved to the curb. It moved away with its rear door open, four people hanging on the step. . . . I can do as well in Times Square, Carl thought. (71)

Romans need, if anything, to out-hustle even Manhattanites in order to inch ahead on the daily treadmill. Bevilacqua moodily informs Carl, "'In eight years of hard work I advanced myself only from thirty-thousand lire to fifty-five thousand a month" (70)—the exact figure that the "needy" American student is prepared to spend on rent alone. He briefs the still half-sceptical Schneider about the local situation:

"For every piece of bread, we have twenty open mouths. You Americans are the lucky ones."
    "Yes, in that way."
    "In what way no?"
    "We have no piazzas."
    Bevilacqua shrugged one shoulder. (71)

While showing the American the apartment on that day's agenda, Bevilacqua puts his damp briefcase on his knees: "He opened the straps, took out a chunk of bread, and chewed thoughtfully" (73). The hustler eats his daily bread anxiously even when out of sight of the nineteen other open mouths. The idea of a hand-to-mouth existence could not be more graphically evoked.

The downward Roman path from innocence to disillusionment takes Carl skidding into a drastic readjustment, and it is his sense of time that, above all, gets readjusted. The central episode is the absurd Roman apartment intrigue involving the Contessa who owns the apartment upon which Carl has pinned his hopes, as well as De Vecchis, the ex-tenant who has been the Contessa's lover and who refuses to open the apartment. This adventure begins with a phone call from Bevilacqua at 7:30 in the morning, completing the demolition of Carl's ordinary time frame. By this point, however, the American has begun to adapt himself to the vagaries of the Roman meridian. When Bevilacqua offers, "'I will come to your hotel precisely at thirteen and a quarter,'" Carl answers indulgently, "'Give yourself time. Make it fourteen'" (69). Later, negotiating with the Contessa, he strives, with a touch of Roman fatalism, to impose the necessities of his timetable upon the amenities of hers:

"Say the word and I'll bring you the rent in an hour."
    "Come back in two weeks, young man, after I finish my honeymoon."
    "In two weeks I may be dead," Carl said.
    The Contessa laughed. (81)

Under the pressure of circumstance his New-World moral scruples, too, begin to crumble. At first, when De Vecchis tries to extort money from him in return for the key to the apartment, he responds sanctimoniously: "'No, thanks. I won't be party to a bribe'" (78). Soon, however, in order to extract the Contessa's address from the *portiere*, Carl finds himself dangling a modest bribe: "'If you tell me her address I will give you one thousand lire.' Carl felt his tongue thicken" (79). Getting wholeheartedly into the local spirit, he proceeds to offer the Contessa a higher rent to obtain immediate entry, eliciting from her a haughty reply: "'Listen,' said the Contessa, 'I come from an honorable family.

Don't try to bribe me'" (80). At last, he decides "to go to the portiere and offer him ten thousand lire if he would have a new key made, however they did it—door up or door down" (82).

When he arrives, he finds the door open. Malamud's epic description of the mysterious apartment's disarray brings the story to a colorful Roman conclusion:

With a gasp they all entered. From room to room they wandered like dead men. The place was a ruin. The furniture had been smashed with a dull axe. The slashed sofa revealed its inner springs. Rugs were cut up, crockery broken, books wildly torn and scattered. The white walls had been splashed with red wine, except one in the living room which was decorated with dirty words in six languages, printed in orange lipstick. (82)

Instead of the palatial comfort Carl had dreamed of enjoying on settling into the apartment, the reality he beholds is a microcosm of Roman ruin, his own tawdry little Palatine.   And another ruin, as well, is thrust before his reluctant eyes: the collapse of decent human relationships in this literally and figuratively "unaccommodating" Roman world.

De Vecchis, in his pea green suit, appeared in the doorway. "Ecco la chiave!" He held it triumphantly aloft.
     "Assassin!" shouted Bevilacqua. "Turd! May your bones grow hair and rot."
     "He lives for my death," he cried to Carl, "I for his. This is our condition."
     "You lie," said Carl. "I love this country."
     De Vecchis flung the key at them and ran. Bevilacqua, the light of hatred in his eyes, ducked, and the key hit Carl on the forehead, leaving a mark he could not rub out. (82-83)

The cost of Roman living, to the naive, is once again a scarring by the indelible mark of experience. Malamud's young American student has been presented, to his chagrin, with the key to the Eternal City.

"Last Mohican," another story included in *The Magic Barrel* (1958) became, in slightly altered form, the opening episode of *Pictures of Fidelman*. Like "Behold the Key," "Last Mohican" concerns an American's discovery of Rome and of himself; but the scope now broadens to include the protagonist's relation to his racial and cultural past, and his personal responsibility for the tragic facts of modern history. As presented in "Last Mohican," the city proves less unaccommodating to the American visitor; while it again thrusts upon him a knowledge of cruelty and privation, it ends by beckoning him to fellowship.

Arthur Fidelman, "self-confessed failure as a painter," now attempting "to prepare a critical study of Giotto" (11), arrives in Italy with the opening chapter in a new pigskin briefcase. He is wearing new shoes, a new tweed suit, a new shirt, and new underwear. Evidently unbothered by the contradiction, he hopes to turn over a new leaf in the age-old city. Like other visitors, however, he is immediately staggered by the antiquity of what he beholds:

after twenty minutes still absorbed in his first sight of the Eternal City, he was conscious of a certain exaltation that devolved on him after he had discovered directly across the many-vehicled piazza stood the remains of the Baths of Diocletian.   Fidelman remembered having read that Michelangelo had helped in converting the baths into a church and convent, the latter ultimately changed into the museum that presently was there. "Imagine," he muttered. "Imagine all that history." (11-12)

His own ability to "imagine all that history" does not at this point reach beyond a casual tourist's, and, since he plans to spend barely two weeks in Rome, he is allowing himself scant opportunity to extend it. While the schedule he arranges for himself "made the most of his working hours" (18), it hardly enables him to grasp the "elusive spirit" he soon comes (like Henry James) to perceive in the city. He spends mornings in libraries, naps for an hour after lunch, and hurries off in the afternoon to inspect art works in churches and museums.   "He was anxious to get to Florence, and the same time a little unhappy at all he would not have time to take in in Rome" (18). Only while wandering the streets after dark does he find leisure to engage in misty, quasi-Jamesian musings: "It was an inspiring business, he, Arthur Fidelman, after all, born a Bronx boy, walking around in all this history. History was mysterious, the remembrance of things unknown, in a way burdensome, in a way a sensuous experience. It uplifted and depressed, why he did not know except that it excited his thoughts more than he thought good for him" (18-19).

Already, however, Fidelman has encountered the shadowy figure who will take him on a more concretely serious tour of history, and who will excite his thoughts in a way that is certainly good for him. The professional refugee and beggar, Shimon Susskind, who has accosted him outside the railway station, appears to be a time-waster *par excellence*. Yet his devious dealings with Fidelman have a positive secret object: to oblige Fidelman to keep faith with himself, his deepest impulses, and his racial heritage. Susskind represents the Eternal Jew, quaintly but meaningfully juxtaposed with the Eternal City.

Before Fidelman takes notice of Susskind, the refugee's steady gaze gives him "the sensation of suddenly seeing himself as he was, to the pinpoint, outside and in" (12), a feeling that is prophetic, since his dealings with Susskind will leave him with a new power of self-recognition. Fidelman's first image of Susskind is replete with symbolic reverberations: "a stranger—give a skeleton a couple of pounds—loitering near a bronze statue on a stone pedestal of the heavy-dugged Etruscan wolf suckling the infant Romulus and Remus" (12). As a surviver of the Holocaust, Susskind has a right to be twinned with the eternally suffering, eternally surviving city. His appearance, above all "his experienced nose . . . weighted at the tip" (13), makes Susskind the Jew Roman to the core. His greeting, "'Shalom,'" which Fidelman hesitantly returns, "uttering the word—so far as he recalled—for the first time in his life" (13), is at once an invitation to share in Hebraic culture and a welcome to the immemorial city in which Fidelman has arrived. It is the twentieth-century translation of "Ave." Fidelman, in typical fashion, sees it as a mere irrelevancy.

Susskind, the ultimate Jewish refugee, has forsaken even Israel: "'I'm always running'" (14). He adds that he has also fled from "'Germany, Hungary, Poland. . . . Where not?'" (14). "'Ah, that's so long ago,'" comments Fidelman, the aspiring student of Giotto and connoisseur of history. When Susskind offers his services—"'You wish a guide in Rome?'" (15)—he is giving Fidelman the chance to have just the sort of preceptor that he needs, but the American scholar is searching for expertise of a more cut-and-dried sort.

What he must learn to see, by dint of a series of trying experiences, is that Susskind represents his key to the city. Pursuing his research, Fidelman begins to develop visionary tendencies: "Once, after a couple of days in the Vatican Museum, he saw flights of angels—gold, blue, white—intermingled in the sky. 'My God, I got to stop using my eyes so much'" (19), he says to himself. But his hallucinations are more to be trusted than his scholarly gleanings. In fact, he needs to use his eyes not less but more, and to use them on Susskind. When, late one night, his door opens "and instead of an angel, in [comes] Susskind in his shirt and baggy knickers," it is at once obvious that the refugee is a celestial messenger in disguise. Fidelman, however, is not yet prepared to accept a Roman *schnorrer* as an angel. Instead, he regards Susskind as an intruder and vehemently disclaims responsibility for him:

"Am I responsible for you then, Susskind?"
    "Who else?" Susskind loudly replied.
    "Lower your voice, please, people are sleeping around here," said Fidelman, beginning to perspire. "Why should I be?"
    "You know what responsibility means?"
    "I think so."
    "Then you are responsible. Because you are a man. Because you are a Jew, aren't you?"
    "Yes, goddamn it, but I'm not the only one in the whole wide world. Without prejudice, I refuse the obligation. I am a single individual and can't take on everybody's personal burden. I have the weight of my own to contend with." (22-23)

After this evening, the tables are turned; Fidelman becomes himself a refugee from the eternal Susskind. "Is there no escape from him? thought Fidelman, severely vexed. Is this why I came to Rome?" (24). There is, he learns, to be no escape from Susskind; and the refugee does turn out to be a more valid reason for coming to Rome than Fidelman's Giotto monograph.

Under Susskind's torpedo influence, the "research" that Fidelman has meticulously planned gets decisively scuttled. Or rather, it undergoes a metamorphosis into an unscheduled quest that is more to the point than any academic research. When one evening he discovers that the briefcase containing his extant Giotto chapter is missing, he immediately suspects the refugee. That night he dreams of Susskind in a fashion that discloses his feelings both about his own Jewishness and about the city:

He dreamed of pursuing the refugee in the Jewish catacombs under the ancient Appian Way, threatening him a blow on the presumptuous head with a seven-flamed candelabrum he clutched in his hand; while Susskind, clever ghost, who knew the ins and outs of all the crypts and alleys, eluded him at every turn. Then Fidelman's candles all blew out, leaving him sightless and alone in the cemeterial dark; but when the student arose in the morning and wearily drew up the noisy blinds, the yellow Italian, somewhat shrunken, sun winked him cheerfully in both bleary eyes. (28-29)

The nightmare sums up Fidelman's unconscious quest for the ghost of elusive knowledge amid the burial places of both Roman and Jewish history, here tellingly united. The scholar's Jewishness—the menorah that he brandishes as a weapon—provides him as yet with no trustworthy illumination; but Susskind, his quarry, becomes in effect his guide into a fruitful darkness, from which he awakes into the reassuring sunlight of workaday Roman reality.

Frustrated, Fidelman decides to postpone going to Florence. But the delay is not simply the hindrance he deems it; Rome and Susskind have not yet finished their work with him. From a Giotto-scholar Fidelman now turns into a Susskind-hunter. "He searched for him in neighborhoods where he had seen him before, and though Fidelman spent hours looking, literally days, Susskind never appeared" (29). "Time went without work, without accomplishment" (30); Fidelman regards the whole venture as an "appalling waste." When at last he succeeds in running Susskind to earth, the refugee inquires, with bland impertinence, "'Rome holds you?'" (37). "'Rome,'" Fidelman falters in reply, "'—the air.'" The "hold" that Rome is acquiring over him, though it seems to the American a stranglehold, is in reality a nurturing embrace. Here, as again later in Florence and Venice, Fidelman is a hero who needs to lose his presumed way in order to stumble onto his true one, and Susskind's role is to provoke him into creative stumbling. Rome and Susskind together set a Roman pitfall—for once, a benign one. They conspire to produce in Fidelman the complete reconstruction of his machinery that unmans and humanizes him.

Redemption is brought nearer even by Fidelman's fanatical struggles to reconstitute his purloined chapter. It is only through such disorienting anxiety that his rescue from secondhand compilation can occur. Meanwhile, his dogged search for Susskind is giving him a knowledge of Rome that it was never his purpose to seek. Haunting far-flung quarters of the city to scan its countless inhabitants, "he sought in their faces the missing Susskind. Where in all of modern and ancient Rome was he?" (31). Now, "instead of visiting museums he frequented movie houses, sitting in the cheapest seats and regretting the cost. . . . He had got to know the face of Rome and spoke Italian fairly fluently but his heart was burdened, and in his blood raged a murderous hatred of the bandy-legged refugee" (32). In the suffering and rage that accompany his growing intimacy with the modern city, Fidelman is arduously changing from tourist and scholar to Roman citizen.

During his wanderings in the great storehouse of history, he trips momentously over his own racial heritage. "One Friday night, as the first star glowed over the Tiber, Fidelman, walking aimlessly along the left river-bank, came upon a synagogue and wandered in among a crowd of Sephardim with Italianate faces" (32). The synagogue, unlike those in his native Bronx, boasts a marble floor. The whole Jewish scene is, indeed, a preeminently Roman mixture; with fine indiscriminateness, it combines the local and the exotic. So Rome, city of teeming legacies, confronts the American stranger with what he has long denied: the relevance to him of his own legacy as a Jew. Inquiring about the refugee, he describes him evasively to the beadle as "'[n]ot exactly'" a relative. In return, the beadle discloses his own horribly immediate relation to the history of Jewish suffering: "'My own son—killed in the Ardeatine Caves.' Tears stood forth in his eyes" (33).

Pursuing Susskind through the intricacies of the Ghetto, Fidelman wanders among the impoverished heirs of poverty, "oppressed by history although, he joked to himself, it added years to his life" (34). His ramblings extend his life in a sense that is more than a joke. He learns from a local boy that the refugee sometimes works in the Jewish section of the Campo Verano, the Rome cemetery, praying for the dead. The "trail" sends Fidelman, too, exploring "among the graves, reading legends on tombstones, many topped with small brass candelabra, whilst withered yellow chrysanthemums lay on the stone tablets of other graves" (35). This new twist on the Roman gothic mode looks beyond merely macabre effects, for it compels Fidelman to confront salient facts of recent history. He reads the inscription on a marble slab lying next to an empty grave site: "'My beloved father / Betrayed by the damned Fascists / Murdered at Auschwitz by the barbarous Nazis / O Crimine Orribile'" (35). Such "findings," could the researcher but recognise the fact, are far more important than the whereabouts of his chapter, confiscated by the maddening Susskind.

His subsequent dealings with the refugee complete the Roman phase of his education in life priorities. He obtains a sighting of Susskind after poring over Giotto's Navicella mosaic in the porch of Saint Peter's:

He hazarded a note or two in shaky handwriting, then left the church and was walking down the sweeping flight of stairs, when he beheld at the bottom—his heart misgave him,

was he still seeing pictures, a sneaky apostle added to the overloaded boatful?—ecco,
Susskind! (36)

Ecco, Susskind; *ecce homo*—the moment suddenly invests the Jewish scapegrace
with the aura of a holy icon: "Susskind looked, it must be said, unchanged, not
a pound more of meat or muscle, the face though aged, ageless" (37).
Susskind's aged, ageless face is thoroughly at home in Saint Peter's Square; it
is the timeless, time-worn visage of Rome itself.

Susskind's house turns out to have its own sacramental aura. It is "a pitch-
black freezing cave" (39), the sort of refuge that might have belonged to a
hunted early Roman Christian—or modern Roman Jew. Its contents, Fidelman
discovers, include "half a flask of red wine, part of a package of spaghetti, and
a hard panino. Also an unexpected little fish bowl with a bony goldfish
swimming around in Arctic seas" (39-40). Bread, wine, and fish, traditional
Christian symbols of communion and salvation, seem curious things to find in
the lair of the Wandering Jew. But Susskind has pointed the obtuse, self-
absorbed Fidelman toward a saving sense of human community. Roman
discovery produces here a result exactly contrary to the division it creates in
Wharton's "Roman Fever." Even in "Last Mohican," however, it takes a
supernatural visitant to convince a self-obsessed American of the need for
inclusive fellowship. Though he has led his fortunate victim to an
acknowledgment of Jewish connections, what Susskind stands for transcends the
sectarian.

In Fidelman's dreams, Susskind is finally transformed into the ultimate
Roman guide: "[Fidelman] was spending the day in a cemetery all crowded with
tombstones, when up out of an empty grave rose this long-nosed brown shade,
Virgilio Susskind, beckoning" (40). In the best spirit of Roman medley, the
Jewish refugee undergoes a Christ-like resurrection as the foremost of pagan
poets. The synagogue Fidelman has visited in the Ghetto merges with a Roman
temple: "Fidelman, willy-nilly, followed, and the ghost, as it vanished, led him
up steps going through the ghetto and into a marble synagogue" (40). A painting
improbably adorns the synagogue's sunlit vault: "The fresco therein revealed this
saint in fading blue, the sky flowing from his head, handing an old knight in a
thin red robe his gold cloak. Nearby stood a humble horse and two stone hills"
(40). It is Giotto's "Saint Francis Gives His Clothing to the Poor Knight"
mysteriously transferred from its customary wall in Assisi. Fidelman's dream
displacement of it is meaningful. His ecumenical dreamwork has helped him to
assimilate the spirit of Giotto's Christian masterpiece to his own religious
heritage; and when he awakens he applies his insight to his personal
circumstances. His living perception of Giotto's art, not laboriously culled from
archives but proved upon his pulses, permits him to affirm a solidarity with
Susskind at last, as a fellow sufferer and fellow Jew. Taking Saint Francis as
his Gentile model, he runs to offer the refugee his blue gabardine suit.

But he has still to learn one further lesson in forbearance. On his arrival at Susskind's house, he is confounded to see the man "standing at the table, lighting the candle with a flaming sheet of paper. To Fidelman the paper looked the underside of a type-written page. Despite himself the student recalled in letters of fire his entire chapter" (41). He grasps that the refugee has taken it upon himself to "illuminate" his Giotto manuscript in tongues of Pentecostal fire. Earlier, when asked by Fidelman whether he had studied the painter, Susskind replies, "'Who doesn't know Giotto?'" (15). Only now does Fidelman learn the answer to that rhetorical question:

"You bastard, you burned my chapter!"
    "Have mercy," cried Susskind. "I did you a favor."
    "I'll do you one and cut your throat."
    "The words were there but the spirit was missing." (41)

It is Fidelman who has not "known" Giotto. But his pursuit of Susskind through the vastness of Rome has given him an at least momentary insight into the painter's spirit, and other Roman insights to boot. At the end of the story, amidst the whole Christian, Jewish, and pagan farrago of centuries-old experience, Fidelman is transfixed by a sudden moment of grace:

The ghetto Jews, framed in amazement in their medieval windows, stared at the wild pursuit. But in the middle of it, Fidelman, stout and short of breath, moved by all he had lately learned, had a triumphant insight.
    "Susskind, come back" he shouted, half sobbing. "The suit is yours. All is forgiven."
    He came to a dead halt but the refugee ran on. When last seen he was still running. (42)

The Eternal City remains what it has eternally been. The Eternal Jew continues to do what he has always done: flee. Between them, they have endowed Malamud's American pilgrim with the Roman knowledge to stop running from himself and his human responsibilities. As Jackson Benson pertinently asks, "[W]here else would a Jew go to find his soul?" (23). In Rome, the world's least exclusive city, there is always room for one more bewildered orphan of the heart.

19

Story's End

There are always endings, but there are not always conclusions.

Robert Coover, *Pinocchio in Venice* (45)

In a plot observing with perfect fidelity the paradigms elaborated in the preceding chapters, the protagonist would first go to Rome and fall from innocence. He or she would then proceed to Florence to be regenerated, only to drift on to Venice, become enveloped in befuddling dreams, and expire.

Needless to say, no work of fiction so mechanically predictable would, if published, be read through to its watery end. The paradigms I have outlined are approximations; they are regularly and joyously violated by the literary works that incorporate them. It is precisely in variation, contradiction, and sheer waywardness that the life of those works resides; in their insistence on defeating expectation, or on satisfying it in unexpected ways. The identity of each city, the uniqueness of its hallmarks have been grist for a thousand diverse authorial mills. James's Florence is a Jamesian city, Lawrence's a Lawrencean one. David R. Weimer puts the case succinctly: "There are as many cities as there are imaginations" (6). Still, an acquaintance with the patterns passed down from one imagination to another prepares the reader to come to terms with this diversity. By familiarizing oneself with the literary tradition a locale has accumulated over time, one can more perceptively gauge what individual talents have made of it.

These storied cities are special cases of the general tendency of setting to function as metaphor. It is the word "special" that I would stress. Few other cities on our globe have produced so dense and so lasting a galaxy of symbolic significances as these three. That is not, of course, to say that other cities have no symbolic dimension in the literary works that feature them. London and Paris, to mention two obvious examples, have for centuries held a potent emblematic value, for native and non-native writers alike. What they stand for tends, however, to be relatively generalized. In Fielding, Thackeray, and Dickens, London is *the* city, as opposed to the provinces, just as Paris is *the* city in Balzac or Proust.

Several American cities have, during their relatively brief lives, become "storied" in ways that endow them with distinctive literary profiles. In James's fiction, the Boston of *The Europeans* and *The Bostonians* plays a role recognisably different from the New York of *Washington Square*. In the work of a contemporary novelist like Saul Bellow, there is a comparable distinction between New York and Chicago as settings. The constricting, febrile Manhattan of *The Victim* and *Seize the Day* makes a clear contrast with the more fluid, expansive Chicago milieu of *The Adventures of Augie March*. But perhaps a closer parallel to the case of our three Italian cities is the way Russian writers have treated their two great complementary capitals: Moscow and Petersburg/Leningrad. In nineteenth-century Russian fiction above all, the first of those two cities tends to represent the informal and the unplanned, the second, instead, the official and (as Dostoevsky terms it) the "premeditated" (*Notes From Underground* 5).

But despite such parallels, our triad of cities—Florence, Venice, and Rome—cannot be matched in the sharpness with which their profiles are etched in the literature they serve. The reasons for their special status are not entirely mysterious. The cities' geographical closeness to one another (already in the nineteenth century, the distances could be covered in hours rather than days) has tended to highlight their differences, because of the ease with which comparisons can be made. In turn, the wealth of literature about the three cities has schooled the expectations of foreign newcomers. The longer each place has proved its power to quicken the writer's imagination, the more commandingly does it focus the perceptions of the first-time literary beholder.

Whether Florence, Venice, and Rome still hold their quickening power in the 1990's is another, as yet unanswerable, question. The cities themselves are alive and (more or less) well, but literary sub-genres follow their own, more restricted life cycles. The number of stories to tell about even a storied city may not be infinite. There is an obvious danger that a paradigm, exploited for centuries, may give up its animating ghost.

Novels, stories, and poems set in all three cities still bravely emerge year after year; some of these display an impressive degree of originality in treating well-thumbed motifs. For their authors, the late twentieth-century vogue of literary self-consciousness has been something of a godsend. A work like Bernard Malamud's *Pictures of Fidelman* has a complex appeal, as at once a fictional narrative in its own right and an implied critique of the way its settings have been treated by such earlier models as James, Mann, and Hawthorne. Instead of seeming derivative, Malamud's novel cunningly exploits the wealth of prior works ready to do service as intertexts.

Venice in particular, possibly because of its long association with the idea of self-consciousness or "mirroring," has proved a fertile ground for contemporary experiment. In the Venetian episode of her novel *The Bird of Night*, Susan Hill uses the locale to explore the vagaries of the poetic imagination as it encounters and creatively deforms reality. More recently, in *Stone Virgin* Barry Unsworth has staged a self-conscious Venetian extravaganza, ingeniously illuminating the kaleidoscopic distortions to which the producers and restorers of art are subject. How much promise there is in such experiment remains an open question. One fears that once so specialized a mode of writing begins to cannibalize itself, it is nearing extinction.

A case in point is the American writer Robert Coover's *Pinocchio in Venice* (1991), a novel that comments metafictively on Venice as a literary metaphor. A post-modernist reworking of Carlo Collodi's classic children's fantasy *Pinocchio* (1881-83), Coover's novel also ostentatiously parodies Mann's *Death in Venice*. In it, the aged Pinocchio, a.k.a. Professor Pinenut, a Nobel Prize-winning idealist philosopher, returns on a sudden impulse to Venice, "the original wet dream" (175). There, he loses all he possesses, including his dignity, and meets—of course—his death. Along the way, he is duly subjected to catastrophic Venetian distortions: his eyesight fails, he obsessively pursues a bubblegum-chewing American co-ed (the Blue Fairy coyly disguised), he becomes the dupe of mercenary rogues, he suffers "the collapse of his precious ontology" (281). Like Aschenbach, he plummets fatally from high-mindedness; for the ex-puppet, that lapse involves the loss of his human flesh and a painful reversion to his original wood. Both in his fame and in his inward decay, Pinenut stands for Venice itself ("Like this crumbling old city . . . he too, perversely, lingers on" [178]).

Situated in a Venice where the ancient institution of Carnival has been reinvented, Coover's narrative is a studied exercise in the "carnivalesque" mode. The book alludes insistently to the triteness, at this date, of the whole Venetian *mise-en-scène*. The Winged Lion of Saint Mark, speaking for his city, derisively calls himself "'[a] fucking joke, too old to merit another telling'" (296). Presumably, this does not represent Coover's own judgment; the point of his Venetian joke lies precisely in the inventiveness with which he revives well-worn conventions. Yet one cannot help wondering how much real vitality even such inventiveness can lend to Coover's philosophical harlequinade. His toying with the stock Venetian motifs, though at times amusingly innovative, seems all too often a desperate search for novelty amid the clichéd and polluted canals. As an augury of what lies ahead for the literature of Italian cities, his novel is not altogether reassuring.

Nevertheless, the fact remains that Florence, Venice, and Rome have not yet relinquished their grip upon the literary imagination, and for good reason. We live today in a contradictory intellectual climate. We have grown too sophisticated to believe in universal truths, yet our scepticism does not stop us from indulging in rampant generalization. Setting, in much contemporary literature, reflects that generalizing bent. The prevailing wind has for some time been blowing in an anti-mimetic quarter. The objective of much modern writing is not to reflect but to bypass or transcend recognisable locality. The placeless places of Samuel Beckett's novels and dramas epitomize this contemporary drive to elude the boundaries of defined milieu; they brilliantly, sometimes profoundly, demonstrate the suggestive power of the unlocalized. They are doubtless a limiting case, but they are not a unique one. Even when recent fiction or drama makes use of settings that are more concretely specified, these, too, tend to be relatively abstract.

A consequence has been the widespread underestimation, in twentieth-century criticism, of the value of identifiable setting. That tendency may also, in part, depend on the increasingly uniform physiognomies of the cities in which we live. The triumph of the "international style" in urban design has probably reinforced the interchangeable nature of literary locales. The Manhattanizing of cityscapes in the developed (or even "underdeveloped") world promotes a like Manhattanizing of fiction. For the most part, what anonymous cityscapes contribute to the works set in them is, not surprisingly, a feeling of anonymity. As David Weimer has observed:

Now all the great, uniform cities—particularly the American ones, which have remained by and large impervious to individuation—would seem to have lost whatever power they once had to arouse awe or dread, or to address anyone in a distinctive idiom. They simply are *there*—measureless, prodigious, blank. (145)

In the quarter century since Weimer's *The City as Metaphor* (1966) appeared, the cities of which he speaks have unhappily regained much of their power to arouse dread but relatively little of their power to stir the imagination.

Amid a world of disheartening urban replication, the three storied Italian cities of which I have written continue to blazon forth their uniqueness. In some respects, the differences between them, too, have diminished. Florence and especially Rome have spawned vast, impersonal tracts of suburban development. Although Venice has only the sea to sprawl into, the adjacent mainland has become the site of massive industrial development. All three cities are plagued by pollution, which menaces the very existence of their monuments, not to mention the lives of their inhabitants. A latter-day Aschenbach would still have good cause to fear the Venetian lagoon; the current threat takes the form, however, not of cholera but of chemicals. All three fabled cities are increasingly beset, as well, by hordes of invaders—not spear-wielding Goths but camera-clutching tourists. These, while they swell local coffers, tend to distort the normal pulse of each city's life and, paradoxically, to obscure that very uniqueness that causes it to be religiously visited.

For the reason outsiders still flock to Florence, Venice, and Rome is that all three cities conserve that most unlikely of anachronisms in our latter age: urban individuality. In the literary works I have discussed, individuality of place speaks in a variety of tongues to an array of individual imaginations, and is honored by them. Over time, those imaginations have created a coherent set of conventions for fictionalizing each of the three sites. The result, from one generation to another, has been a fecund recurrence, not a trite repetitiveness.

Our own increasingly monocolor world sets no theoretical limits to literary experiment, yet it may mechanically impose subliminal bounds upon the imagination's outreach. Whether or not our three storied cities retain their power to inspire new and compelling stories, those they have already inspired document the persistent relevance of defined place to fictional meaning. It is in the unfading local color of these three unique scenes that our writers' eyes have discerned the magical colors of artistic truth.

Notes

CHAPTER 3

1. For an illuminating analysis of prosodic effects in "The Statue and the Bust" see Lawrence Poston, "Counter and Coin: Form as Meaning in 'The Statue and the Bust,'" *Victorian Poetry* 21.4 (Winter 1983): 379-91.

CHAPTER 5

1. See Melchiori for a discussion of James's indebtedness to Browning in the story. See also the present author's "Henry James's 'Half-man': The Legacy of Browning in 'The Madonna of the Future,'" *Browning Institute Studies* 2 (1974): 25-42, composed without knowledge of Melchiori's prior article in Italian.

CHAPTER 7

1. In general, however, Lawrence's ideas about Florence's gender seem to have been somewhat fluid. In a letter to his mother-in-law written (in German) when he was still revising the typescript of *Aaron's Rod*, he describes the view of Florence from Fiesole: "It's so lovely, when one can see far, far, and on the plain the city so alone, so feminine (*weiblich*)" (*Letters* 4: 83-84).

2. The dream sequence has been variously interpreted. See particularly the extended discussion in Paul G. Baker, 134-8.

CHAPTER 10

1. For a useful analysis of Mann's treatment of Platonic ideas and the evolution of that treatment, see T. J. Reed, 156 *et seq*.

CHAPTER 11

1. The ending as revised for the New York Edition implies the idea more blatantly: "When I look at it I can scarcely bear my loss. I mean of the precious papers." As Tanner comments, "The inserted hesitation . . . says everything" (24).

CHAPTER 14

1. "Beyond the Alps" was first included in the volume *Life Studies* (1959). An expanded version of the poem, containing a section that alludes to the poet Ovid's life in exile, appeared in Lowell's later book *For the Union Dead* (1964).

CHAPTER 16

1. The English edition gives a briefer form of Kenyon's reply: "'In prison,' said Kenyon sadly" (467). Fredson Bowers considers this version more consonant with the possibility, hinted at elsewhere, of Donatello's eventual release and rehabilitation. See his discussion in the Centenary Edition, Textual Introduction, cxxi-cxxix.

CHAPTER 17

1. Unless otherwise noted, quotations from *The Portrait of a Lady* are taken from the original (1881) edition of the novel.

Works Cited

Acton, Harold. *Memoirs of an Aesthete*. London: Methuen, 1948.

Addison, Joseph. "A Letter from Italy to the Right Honourable Charles Lord Halifax, in the Year 1701." *The Works of the Honourable Joseph Addison*. Vol. 1. London: George Bell, 1877.

Altick, Richard, and James Loucks. *Browning's Roman Murder Story: A Reading of "The Ring and the Book."* Chicago and London: U of Chicago P, 1968.

Arnold, Matthew. *Culture and Anarchy*. 1869. Cambridge: Cambridge UP, 1966.

Auchard, John. *Silence in Henry James*. University Park and London: Pennsylvania State UP, 1986.

Baker, Paul G. *A Reassessment of D.H. Lawrence's "Aaron's Rod."* Ann Arbor: UMI Research P, 1983.

Bakker, J., et al., eds. *Essays on English and American Literature and a Sheaf of Poems*. Amsterdam: Editions Rodopi, 1987.

Bassani, Giorgio. *Le parole preparate*. Torino: Einaudi, 1966. (My translations)

Benson, Jackson. "An Introduction: Bernard Malamud and the Haunting of America." *The Fiction of Bernard Malamud*. Ed. Richard Astro and Jackson Benson. Corvallis: Oregon State UP, 1977.

Berland, Alwyn. *Culture and Conduct in the Novels of Henry James*. Cambridge: Cambridge UP, 1981.

Berryman, John. *Henry's Fate*. New York: Farrar, Straus and Giroux, 1977.

Bien, Peter. *L.P. Hartley*. University Park: Pennsylvania State UP, 1963.

Biswas, Robindra Kumar. *Arthur Hugh Clough: Towards a Reconsideration*. London: Oxford UP, 1972.

Bonaparte, Felicia. *The Triptych and the Cross: The Central Myths of George Eliot's Poetic Imagination*. Brighton: Harvester P, 1979.

Booth, Wayne C. *The Rhetoric of Fiction*. 1961. 2nd ed. Chicago and London: U of Chicago P, 1983.

Bowen, Elizabeth. *A Time in Rome*. London: Longmans, 1960.

Browning, Elizabeth Barrett. *Aurora Leigh*. 1857. Vols. 4 and 5 of *The Complete Works of Elizabeth Barrett Browning*. 1900. New York: AMS P, 1973.

_____. *Casa Guidi Windows*. 1851. Vol. 3 of *The Complete Works of Elizabeth Barrett Browning*. 1900. New York: AMS P, 1973.

Browning, Robert. *The Letters of Robert Browning and Elizabeth Barrett Browning.* 2 vols. New York and London: Harper and Brothers, 1899.

————. *Luria.* 1846. Vol. 4 of *The Complete Works of Robert Browning.* Athens: Ohio UP, 1973.

————. *The Poems.* Ed. John Pettigrew. 2 vols. New Haven and London: Yale UP, 1981.

————. *The Ring and the Book.* Ed. Richard D. Altick. 1868. Harmondsworth: Penguin, 1971.

Buckler, William Earl. *Poetry and Truth in Robert Browning's "The Ring and the Book."* New York: New York UP, 1985.

Burckhardt, Jacob. *The Civilization of the Renaissance in Italy.* 1860. London: Phaidon, 1960.

Burgess, Anthony. *Beard's Roman Women.* New York: McGraw-Hill, 1976.

Byron, George Gordon, Lord. *Poetical Works.* London: Oxford UP, 1970.

Calvino, Italo. *Invisible Cities.* London: Picador, 1974.

Cecchi, Emilio. *"Fiorentinità" e altri saggi.* Firenze: Sansoni, 1985. (My translation)

Chambers, Jessie. *D.H. Lawrence: A Personal Record.* 1935. Cambridge: Cambridge UP, 1980.

Cheever, Susan. *Home Before Dark.* Boston: Houghton Mifflin, 1984.

Churchill, Kenneth. *Italy and English Literature 1764-1930.* Totawa: Barnes and Noble, 1980.

Clark, Eleanor. *Rome and a Villa.* N.p.: Atheneum, 1950.

Clough, Arthur Hugh. *The Correspondence of A.H. Clough.* Ed. Frederick L. Mulhauser. 2 vols. Oxford: Clarendon, 1957.

————. *The Poems of Arthur Hugh Clough.* Oxford: Oxford UP, 1974.

Collins, Wilkie. *The Haunted Hotel: A Mystery of Modern Venice.* 1879. London: Chatto and Windus, n.d.

Collodi, Carlo. *The Adventures of Pinocchio: The Story of a Puppet.* Berkeley: U of California P, 1986.

Coover, Robert. *Pinocchio in Venice.* New York: Linden, 1991.

Crawford, Francis Marion. *Ave Roma Immortalis.* 1898. New York: Macmillan, 1902.

cummings, e.e. *E.E. Cummings: A Miscellany Revised.* New York: October House, 1965.

Daleski, H.M. *The Forked Flame.* Evanston: Northwestern UP, 1965.

Davidson, Max. *Suddenly in Rome.* 1988. London: Grafton, 1989.

DeLaura, David. "The Context of Browning's Painter Poems." *PMLA* 95 (1980): 367-88

de Staël, Madame. *Corinne ou l'Italie.* 1807. Paris: Librairie Garnier Frères, n.d. (My translations)

Dickens, Charles. *Little Dorrit.* 1857. London: Oxford UP, 1953.

_____. *Pictures from Italy*. 1846. London: Andre Deutsch, 1973.

_____. Working notes for *Little Dorrit*. Ed. Harry Stone. *Dickens' Working Notes for His Novels*. Chicago and London: U of Chicago P, 1987.

Dostoevsky, Fyodor. *Notes from Underground*. 1863. Trans. Michael R. Katz. New York and London: Norton, 1989.

Douglas, Norman. *Alone*. London: Chapman and Hall, 1921.

Durrell, Lawrence. *Spirit of Place*. London: Faber and Faber, 1969.

Edwards, Caterina. *The Lion's Mouth*. Edmonton: NeWest P, 1982.

Eliot, George. *Essays of George Eliot*. Ed. Thomas Pinney. London: Routledge and Kegan Paul, 1963.

_____. *The George Eliot Letters*. Ed. Gordon Haight. Vol. 3. New Haven: Yale UP, 1954.

_____. *Middlemarch*. 1871-72. Harmondsworth: Penguin, 1965.

_____. *The Mill on the Floss*. 1860. Harmondsworth: Penguin, 1979.

_____. *Romola*. 1863. Harmondsworth: Penguin, 1980.

_____. *A Writer's Notebook, 1854-1879, and Uncollected Writings*. Charlottesville: UP of Virginia, 1981.

Eliot, T. S. "The Love Song of J. Alfred Prufrock." *The Complete Poems and Plays of T.S. Eliot*. London: Faber, 1969.

Engel, Monroe. *The Maturity of Dickens*. Cambridge: Harvard UP, 1959.

Erickson, Lee. *Robert Browning: His Poetry and His Audiences*. Ithaca and London: Cornell UP, 1984.

Eustace, John Chatwode. *A Classical Tour through Italy*. Leghorn: Claucus Masi, 1817.

Fleishman, Avrom. *The English Historical Novel*. Baltimore and London: Johns Hopkins UP, 1971.

Forbes, S. Russell. *Rambles in Rome*. London, Edinburgh, and New York: Thomas Nelson, 1882.

Forster, E.M. *The Longest Journey*. 1907. London: Edward Arnold, 1984.

_____. *The Lucy Novels: Early Sketches for "A Room with a View."* London: Edward Arnold, 1977.

_____. *A Room with a View*. 1908. London: Edward Arnold, 1977.

_____. *Selected Letters of E.M. Forster*. Ed. Mary Lago and P. N. Furbank. Vol. 1. London: Collins, 1983.

_____. *Where Angels Fear to Tread*. 1905. London: Edward Arnold, 1975.

Freud, Sigmund. *Civilization and Its Discontents*. 1930. New York and London: Norton, 1961.

Gelley, Alexander. "Setting and a Sense of World in the Novel." *Yale Review* 62 (1973): 186-201

Giorcelli, Cristina. *Henry James e l'Italia*. Roma: Edizioni di Storia e Letteratura, 1968. (My translation)

Gissing, George. *The Emancipated*. 1890. London: Hogarth, 1985.

Goethe, Johann Wolfgang. *Italian Journey*. 1816-17. Trans. W. H. Auden and Elizabeth Mayer. New York: Pantheon, 1962.

Graham, Kenneth. *Henry James: The Drama of Fulfilment*. Oxford: Clarendon, 1975.

Gunn, Peter, and Roloff Beny. *The Churches of Rome*. New York: Simon and Schuster, 1981.

Hare, Augustus. *Walks in Rome*. (11th ed. rev.) London: Smith, Elder and Co., 1883.

Hartley, L.P. *The Boat*. London: Putnam, 1949.

————. *The Complete Short Stories of L.P. Hartley*. London: Hamish Hamilton, 1973.

————. *Eustace and Hilda*. 1952. London: Faber, 1965.

————. *The Novelist's Responsibility*. London: Hamish Hamilton, 1967.

————. Rev. of E.M. Forster, *Aspects of the Novel*. *The Saturday Review* 17 Dec. 1927, 858-9. Rpt. in *E.M. Forster: The Critical Heritage* Ed. Philip Gardner. London and Boston: Routledge and Kegan Paul, 1973.

————. Rev. of E.M. Forster, *The Eternal Moment*. *The Saturday Review* 28 April 1928, 530-2. Rpt. in *E.M. Forster: The Critical Heritage* Ed. Philip Gardner. London and Boston: Routledge and Kegan Paul, 1973.

————. Rev. of Thomas Mann, *Death in Venice*. *The Saturday Review* 10 Nov. 1928.

————. Ms. of *Simonetta Perkins*. 1925. John Rylands Library, Manchester.

Hatfield, Henry. *Thomas Mann*. Norfolk, Conn.: New Directions, 1951.

Hawthorne, Nathaniel. *The French and Italian Notebooks*. 1872. Columbus: Ohio State UP, 1980.

————. *The House of the Seven Gables*. Columbus: Ohio State UP, 1962.

————. *The Marble Faun*. 1860. Columbus: Ohio State UP, 1968.

————. *The Scarlet Letter*. Columbus: Ohio State UP, 1965.

Hecht, Anthony. Interview. *The Paris Review* 108 (1988): 160-205.

————. *The Venetian Vespers*. New York: Atheneum, 1980.

Hill, Susan. *The Bird of Night*. 1972. Harmondsworth: Penguin, 1976.

————. *The Lighting of the Lamps*. London: Hamish Hamilton, 1987.

Honan, Park. *Browning's Characters: A Study in Poetic Technique*. New Haven: Yale UP, 1961.

Howells, William Dean. *A Foregone Conclusion*. 1875. Boston and New York: Houghton Mifflin, 1902.

————. *Indian Summer*. 1886. Bloomington: Indiana UP, 1971.

————. *The Lady of the Aroostook*. 1879. Boston: Houghton Mifflin, 1921.

————. *Roman Holidays and Others*. New York and London: Harper and Brothers, 1908.

————. *Tuscan Cities*. 1894. Leipzig: Heinemann and Balestier, 1900.

————. *Venetian Life*. 1866. Boston: Houghton Mifflin, 1907.

Huxley, Aldous. *Brief Candles*. 1930. Frogmore, St. Albans: Granada, 1977.

_____. *Letters*. London: Chatto and Windus, 1969.

_____. *On the Margin*. 1923. London: Chatto and Windus, 1928.

Jack, Ian. *Browning's Major Poetry*. Oxford: Clarendon, 1973.

James, Henry. *The Art of the Novel*. New York: Scribner's, 1934.

_____. *The Aspern Papers*. 1888. Vol. 6 of *The Complete Tales of Henry James*. Ed. with Introduction by Leon Edel. Philadelphia and New York: Lippincott, 1963.

_____. *Daisy Miller*. 1878. Vol. 4 of *The Complete Tales of Henry James*. Ed. with Introduction by Leon Edel. Philadelphia and New York: Lippincott, 1962.

_____. *Henry James Letters*. Ed. Leon Edel. Vol. 1. London and Basingstoke: Macmillan, 1974.

_____. *Italian Hours*. 1909. London: Century, Hutchinson, 1986.

_____. "The Madonna of the Future." 1873. Vol. 2 of *The Tales of Henry James*. Ed. Maqbool Aziz. Oxford: Clarendon, 1978.

_____. *Partial Portraits*. 1888. London: Macmillan, 1919.

_____. *The Portrait of a Lady*. 1881. Harmondsworth: Penguin, 1963.

_____. *The Portrait of a Lady*. Boston: Houghton Mifflin, 1963. (New York Edition)

_____. *The Princess Casamassima*. 1886. Harmondsworth: Penguin, 1986.

_____. *Roderick Hudson*. 1875. Harmondsworth: Penguin, 1969.

_____. "Very Modern Rome." 1878(?). *Harvard Library Bulletin* 8: 125-40.

_____. *The Wings of the Dove*. 2 vols. 1902. 1909. Fairfield, N.J.: Augustus M. Kelley, 1976.

Jameson, Anna. *Diary of an Ennuyée*. London: Henry Colburn, 1826.

Keate, George. *Ancient and Modern Rome*. 1755. London: R. and J. Dodsley, 1760.

King, Roma A., Jr. *The Bow and the Lyre: The Art of Robert Browning*. 1957. Ann Arbor: U of Michigan, 1964.

Korg, Jacob. *Browning and Italy*. Athens, Ohio, and London: Ohio UP, 1983.

Krook, Dorothea. "The Aspern Papers: A Counter-Introduction." Ed. J. Bakker, *et al. Essays on English and American Literature and a Sheaf of Poems*. Amsterdam: Editions Rodopi, 1987.

LaCapra, Dominick. *History, Politics and the Novel*. Ithaca and London: Cornell UP, 1987.

Lawrence, D. H. *Aaron's Rod*. 1922. Cambridge: Cambridge UP, 1988.

_____. *Etruscan Places*. New York: Viking, 1961.

_____. *Lady Chatterley's Lover*. 1928. Harmondsworth: Penguin, 1961.

_____. *The Letters of D.H. Lawrence*. Vol. 2 (1913-16). Ed. George Zytaruk and James Boulton. Cambridge: Cambridge UP, 1981.

_____. *The Letters of D.H. Lawrence.* Vol. 4 (1921-24). Ed. Warren Roberts *et al.,* Cambridge: Cambridge UP, 1987.

_____. *Movements in European History.* 1921. Oxford: Oxford UP, 1981.

_____. *Phoenix: The Posthumous Papers of D. H. Lawrence.* London: Heinemann, 1936.

_____. *Sea and Sardinia.* 1921. London: Heinemann, 1956.

_____. "Sun." 1926,

1928. *The Princess and Other Stories.* Harmondsworth: Penguin, 1971.

Leavis, F. R. *The Great Tradition.* 1948. Harmondsworth: Penguin, 1962.

Lively, Penelope. *Perfect Happiness.* 1983. Harmondsworth: Penguin, 1985.

Long, Robert Emmet. *The Great Succession: Henry James and the Legacy of Hawthorne.* Pittsburgh: U of Pittsburgh P, 1979.

Lowell, Robert. *Life Studies.* New York: Farrar, Straus and Giroux, 1959.

_____. *For the Union Dead.* New York: Farrar, Straus and Giroux, 1964.

Lucas, E.V. *A Wanderer in Florence.* 10th ed. rev. New York: Macmillan, 1927.

Lundblad, Jane. *Nathaniel Hawthorne and European Literary Tradition.* 1947. New York: Russell and Russell, 1965.

Lutwack, Leonard. *The Role of Place in Literature.* Syracuse: Syracuse UP, 1984.

Malamud, Bernard. *The Magic Barrel.* New York: Farrar, Straus and Cudahy, 1958.

_____. *Pictures of Fidelman.* 1969. Markham, Ontario: Pocket Books, 1975.

Mann, Thomas. *Death in Venice.* 1911. Trans. H. T. Lowe-Porter. New York: Vintage, 1958.

_____. *The Letters of Thomas Mann.* Ed. Richard and Clara Winston. Harmondsworth: Penguin, 1975.

Maves, Carl. *Sensuous Pessimism: Italy in the Work of Henry James.* Foreword by Ian Watt. Bloomington and London: Indiana UP, 1973.

McCarthy, Mary. *The Stones of Florence.* 1959. New York and London: Harcourt, 1963.

_____. *Venice Observed.* San Diego, New York and London: Harcourt, 1963.

McClatchy, J. D. "Anatomies of Melancholy." *Grand Street* 6.1 (1986): 141-59.

Melchiori, Giorgio. "Browning e Henry James." *Friendship's Garland: Essays Presented to Mario Praz on His Seventieth Birthday.* Ed. Vittorio Gabrieli. Vol. 2. Rome: Edizioni di Storia e Letteratura, 1966. (My translations)

Meyers, Jeffrey. *Painting and the Novel.* Manchester: Manchester UP, 1975.

Morgan, Lady Sydney. *Italy.* London: Henry Colburn, 1824.

Morris, Jan (James). *Venice.* 2nd rev. ed. London: Faber, 1983.

Morton, H.V. *A Traveller in Rome.* London: Methuen, 1957.

Newton, K.M. *George Eliot: Romantic Humanist.* London: Macmillan, 1981.

Nuttall, A.D. *A New Mimesis.* London: Methuen, 1983.

Offenbach, Jacques. *The Tales of Hoffmann (Les Contes d'Hoffmann).* Libretto by Jules Barbier and Michel Carré. New York: G. Schirmer, 1959.

Oliphant, Margaret. *The Makers of Florence: Dante, Giotto, Savonarola, and Their City.* 1876. London: Macmillan, 1980.

Pater, Walter. *The Renaissance.* 1873. London and New York: Macmillan, 1893.

Piovene, Guido. *Viaggio in Italia.* 1957. Verona: Mondadori, 1966. (My translations)

Poirier, Richard. *The Comic Sense of Henry James.* London: Chatto and Windus, 1960.

Poston, Lawrence, III. "Setting and Theme in *Romola.*" *Nineteenth Century Fiction* 20 (1966): 355-66.

Potter, Olave Muriel. *The Colour of Rome.* London: Chatto and Windus, 1923.

Pound, Ezra. *Personae: The Collected Shorter Poems of Ezra Pound.* New York: New Directions, 1926.

Proust, Marcel. *Remembrance of Things Past.* 3 vols. 1913-27. London: Penguin, 1983.

Reed, T.J. *Thomas Mann: The Uses of Tradition.* London: Oxford UP, 1974.

Rogers, Samuel. *Italy: A Poem.* London: T. Cadell *et al.,* 1830.

Rosenthal, A.M., and Arthur Gelb, eds. *The Sophisticated Traveler.* Harmondsworth: Penguin, 1985.

Ruskin, John. *Mornings in Florence.* 1875-77. London: George Allen, 1906.

————. *Ruskin in Italy.* Ed. Harold I. Shapiro. London: Oxford UP, 1972.

————. *The Stones of Venice.* 3 vols. 1851-53. London: George Allen, 1903.

Ryals, Clyde de L. *Becoming Browning: The Poems and Plays of Robert Browning, 1833-1846.* Columbus: Ohio State UP, 1983.

Sagar, Keith. *The Art of D. H. Lawrence.* London: Cambridge UP, 1966.

Salzberg, Joel, ed. *Critical Essays on Bernard Malamud.* Boston: G. K. Hall, 1987.

Sand, George. *Leone Leoni.* 1834. Trans. George Burnham Ives. 1900. Chicago: Academy, 1978.

Sassoon, Siegfried. *Collected Poems 1908-1956.* London: Faber and Faber, 1961.

Schwarzbach, F.S. *Dickens and the City.* London: Athlone, 1979.

Shaw, W. David. *The Dialectical Temper: The Rhetorical Art of Robert Browning.* Ithaca: Cornell UP, 1968.

Shelley, Percy Bysshe. *The Complete Poetical Works of Percy Bysshe Shelley.* London: Oxford UP, 1943.

_____. *Letters 1818 to 1822*. Ed. Roger Ingpen. Vol. 10 of *The Complete Works of Shelley*. London: Ernest Benn; New York: Gordian Press, 1965.

Shuttleworth, Sally. *George Eliot and Nineteenth-Century Science*. Cambridge: Cambridge UP, 1984.

Sitwell, Osbert. *Great Morning!* 1947. Westport: Greenwood, 1972.

Slinn, E. Warwick. *Browning and the Fictions of Identity*. London and Basingstoke: Macmillan, 1982.

Smith, F. Hopkinson. *Gondola Days*. Boston and New York: Houghton Mifflin, 1897.

Spark, Muriel. *The Public Image*. Harmondsworth: Penguin, 1970.

Spencer, Elizabeth. *The Light in the Piazza*. 1960. Markham: Penguin Books Canada, 1986.

Stendhal (Henri Beyle). *Rome, Naples et Florence en 1817*. 1817 1826. Paris: Editions Julliard, 1964. (My translations)

Story, William Wetmore. *Roba di Roma*. 1862. Boston: Houghton Mifflin, 1887.

Symons, Arthur. *Cities of Italy*. London: J. M. Dent, 1907.

Tanner, Tony. "Proust, Ruskin, James and *le Desir de Venise*." *Journal of American Studies* 21 (1987): 15-29.

Tomlinson, Charles. *The Return*. Oxford and New York: Oxford UP, 1987.

Trollope, Anthony. *The Complete Short Stories*. Vol. 2. Fort Worth: Texas Christian UP, 1979.

Tucker, Herbert F., Jr. *Browning's Beginnings: The Art of Disclosure*. Minneapolis: U of Minnesota P, 1980.

Unsworth, Barry. *Stone Virgin*. 1985. Harmondsworth: Penguin, 1986.

Van Ghent, Dorothy. *The English Novel: Form and Function*. New York: Holt, 1953.

Vance, William L. *America's Rome*. 2 vols. New Haven and London: Yale UP, 1989.

Waggoner, Hyatt. *"The Marble Faun."* *Hawthorne: A Collection of Critical Essays*. Ed. A.N. Kaul. Englewood Cliffs: Prentice Hall, 1966.

Wegelin, Christof. "The American Schlemiel Abroad: Malamud's Italian Stories and the End of American Innocence." *Critical Essays on Bernard Malamud*. Ed. Joel Salzberg. Boston: G.K. Hall, 1987.

Weimer, David R. *The City as Metaphor*. New York: Random House, 1966.

Welty, Eudora. *The Eye of the Story*. New York: Random House, 1978.

Wharton, Edith. *The Glimpses of the Moon*. Toronto: McLeod, 1922.

_____. *Italian Backgrounds*. New York: Scribner's, 1905.

_____. "Roman Fever." 1934. *The Collected Short Stories of Edith Wharton*. Vol. 2. New York: Scribner's, 1968.

Wilbur, Richard. *Things of This World*. New York: Harcourt, 1956.

Wilde, Alan. *Art and Order: A Study of E.M. Forster.* New York: New York UP, 1964.

Williams, Tennessee. *The Roman Spring of Mrs. Stone.* New York: New Directions, 1950.

Wilson, Edmund. *Europe without Baedeker.* New York: Farrar, Straus and Giroux, 1966.

Woodcock, George. *Dawn and the Darkest Hour.* London: Faber, 1972.

Woolf, Virginia. *The Waves.* 1931. Harmondsworth: Penguin, 1964.

Wright, James. *Above the River: The Complete Poems.* N.p.: Farrar, Straus and Giroux and UP of New England, 1990.

Index

About the Author

MICHAEL L. ROSS is Associate Professor of English at McMaster University, Hamilton, Ontario, Canada. His academic specialty is nineteenth- and twentieth-century British literature, and Robert Browning, D. H. Lawrence, and George Orwell appear frequently as subjects of his published literary criticism.